DISCARDED

MARCO GIROLAMO VIDA
✦ ✦ ✦
CHRISTIAD

TRANSLATED BY

JAMES GARDNER

THE I TATTI RENAISSANCE LIBRARY
HARVARD UNIVERSITY PRESS
CAMBRIDGE, MASSACHUSETTS
LONDON, ENGLAND
2009

Series design by Dean Bornstein

Library of Congress Cataloging-in-Publication Data

Vida, Marco Girolamo, ca. 1485–1566.
[Christiados libri sex. English & Latin]
Christiad / Marco Girolamo Vida ; translated by James Gardner.
p.   cm. — (The I Tatti Renaissance library)
First published in 1535 in Latin under title: Christiados libri sex.
Includes bibliographical references and index.
ISBN 978-0-674-03408-2 (cloth : alk. paper)
1. Christian poetry, Latin (Medieval and modern) —
Translations into English.   I. Gardner, James.   II. Title.
PA 8585.V6A66   2009
871′.04 — dc22   2008054853

Contents

꽃

Introduction

꙰꙰꙰

Even if no other claim could be made for Marco Girolamo Vida's *Christiad*, the fact that it had a profound influence on two of the foremost literary masterpieces of the Renaissance and the Baroque, Torquato Tasso's *Gerusalemme Liberata* and John Milton's *Paradise Lost*, would be sufficient to compel the attention of posterity. But the *Christiad*, an epic poem in six books, fully deserves to be read in its own right. More than an historical curio, it is a fluent and effective narrative that moves along with novelistic and at times even cinematic force. Its characters can spring to life at any moment, and its numbers flow in the best and smoothest tradition of Vergilian Latin.

Not for nothing was the *Christiad* one of the most successful literary works, certainly among those in Latin, of the sixteenth century. Between its first publication in 1535 and Vida's death in 1566, the poem had appeared in twenty different editions, and twenty more would be published by the beginning of the seventeenth century. In the eighteenth and nineteenth centuries alone, the *Christiad* was translated eighteen times into Italian, twice into English, French and German, and once each into Spanish, Armenian, Croatian and Portuguese.[1]

It is also worth recalling the testimony of two of the greatest poets of the English language. In "The Passion," an early poem, Milton invokes Girolamo Vida and his birthplace thus: "Loud o're the rest Cremona's Trump doth sound." Several generations later, when Pope's "Essay on Criticism" turns to consider the Renaissance, the one man whom the poet mentions, after the painter Raphael, is the author of the *Christiad*:

Immortal Vida! on whose honored brow
The poet's bays and critic's ivy grow;
Cremona now shall ever boast thy name
As next in place to Mantua, next in fame! (705–8)

Fairly little is known of the life of Marco Girolamo Vida, and
that was the way the poet wished it. Five years after the comple-
tion of the *Christiad*, Bartolomeo Botta sought to write a life of
Vida and, to that end, made inquires of him. But the poet demurred: "Please do not seek from me any information regarding
my life or my affairs. . . . For I surely have not undertaken so difficult and challenging a task through any hope of personal glory or
immortality."[2] What we know of Vida is that he was born in the
Lombard city of Cremona, on the border with Emilia Romagna,
at some point between 1480 and 1485 and that he died in Alba in
1566. His was baptized Marcantonio and, though he was born into
straitened circumstances, his parents were of the minor nobility. In
due course Vida was sent to Mantua where he frequented the brilliant court of Isabella d'Este Gonzaga. It was there that he made
his first attempts at poetry and presumably encountered the
court's foremost poet, Battista Spagnuoli, called Mantuanus.
Though this poet is perhaps better known today for his astound-
ing productivity (more than 55,000 lines survive) and his popularity with Renaissance schoolmasters than for any genuine poetic
gifts, he is important to Vida on account of his attempts to turn
the New Testament into Latin hexametric verse, especially in his
Parthenice Mariana, a work that portrays the life of the Virgin.

After 1500 Vida returned briefly to Cremona, where he entered
the Order of Canons Regular of St. John Lateran and took the
name of Marco Girolamo. But before long he traveled to Rome,
early in the pontificate of Julius II. While there, Vida began to
study law, theology and philosophy. But he did not neglect poetry
and even began to write an epic of Julius's military exploits, the

Julias, of which nothing has survived. Over the next decade Vida remained in Rome and wrote a series of eclogues and hymns, as well as his *On the Art of Poetry* (*De arte poetica*, published 1527) which was to achieve immense fame throughout Europe in the seventeenth and eighteenth centuries and exerted considerable influence on the neo-classical literary theories of Nicolas Boileau-Despréaux and Alexander Pope, among others. Vida's fame was further enhanced among his contemporaries by two shorter poems, *On the Silkworm* (*De bombyce*, published 1527), a didactic poem, modeled on Vergil's *Georgics*, but dedicated to sericulture rather than agriculture, and *The Game of Chess* (*De ludo scaccorum*, published 1527), a mock-poem in the style of Vergil, involving the ancient Roman gods. These poems too became immensely popular in the early modern period. He also found time to write several prose works, of which the best known was *Dialogues on the Dignity of the Commonwealth* (*De rei publicae dignitate dialogi*), first published in 1556.

According to Mario A. Di Cesare, it was the warm reception of his earlier poems that induced Leo X to commission the *Christiad* and to support it financially, even providing the poet with a sinecure, the priory of San Stefano in Frascati. On the pontiff's death, his successor Clement VII continued to act as Vida's patron. "The work-in-progress aroused considerable expectations," Di Cesare writes. "Vida's friends — including Giberti, Castiglione, Sadoleto, Tebaldeo, and Paolo Giovio — came to his priory at Frascati to hear him read portions of it. When it was finally published in 1535 in a handsome small quarto, it was recognized, according to the literary canons of the period, as the achievement of the true *Vergilius Christianus*."[3] Clement was so pleased with the result that, in 1533, before the epic was published, he awarded Vida the bishopric of Alba, a position the poet would keep to the end of his life.

The resurrected Latin epic, of which the *Christiad* represents the paramount example, was for the Renaissance something like what the Great American Novel was for our compatriots a generation or two back. One of the first full-blown attempts at epic, near the dawn of the rebirth of letters, was Petrarch's *Africa*, which even in his own day was considered a work of questionable success. A major difference, however, between the Great American Novel and the Great Neo-Latin Epic is that, whereas any number of weighty aspirants to the former have rolled off our national presses, the number of full-length attempts at epic in Latin in the Vergilian manner was relatively small. Far commoner were epyllions or "brief epics," narratives of several hundred to a few thousand lines.

In one sense, the pre-eminent ambition of the Renaissance was conservative, in that it defined itself as the revival of an earlier stage of Western culture. In this vein, Vida's *Christiad*, like the neo-Latin poetry of his contemporaries, strove so fully to imitate the letter, the form and the spirit of antiquity that, subject matter aside, it could pass for an ancient composition. Vida aspires to write as an Augustan poet, if not Vergil himself, would have written if he had been a Christian. Indeed, it is almost as if Vida were rewriting Scripture itself, translating it out of what was felt to be the crude and demotic idiom of Saint Jerome's Vulgate into the more "elevated" language of Vergilian Latin.

At the same time, however, it is evident that the translation of Scripture into epic and into hexameters was and would have seemed to many of Vida's contemporaries to be a modernization, in the strictest sense of the word, a bringing up to date. This was for much the same reason that, although the architecture of Bramante, Vida's contemporary, was based on ancient principles, it seemed more "modern" than Gothic architecture, even if the formal principles of the latter were, in a strictly chronological sense, newer.

Perhaps in part the charm that the *Christiad* possessed for Vida's contemporaries was comparable to the appeal that our own contemporaries find in the many cinematic re-enactments of the

Gospels that have arisen over the past century. Whereas the Scriptures appeared to sixteenth century readers, no less than to us, as an ancient and thus somewhat alien expression of Christ's passion, the *Christiad* rendered that story in a manner that, at least to Latin readers, would have seemed strikingly, thrillingly contemporary. And though, by our lights, Latin is a "dead" language, to learned readers in the Renaissance it was at once timeless and essentially modern, freed from the medieval dross that had accumulated around the sundry vernaculars.

Vida was hardly the first poet to retell the stories of the Old and New Testaments in classical Latin. According to Craig Kallendorf, the emulation of Vergil in a Christian context was one of the fixtures of the Renaissance poetic imagination, at least as concerned the Neo-Latin poets. Kallendorf cites Landino's attempt at a *theologia poetica*, a synthesis of ancient prosodic and formal traditions and Christian theology, and he sees the *Christiad* as the embodiment of it. "Form and content become one, as *theologia poetica* finally becomes *theologia nostra*, our Christian theology."[4]

A number of Christian poets of late antiquity and the early Middle Ages, like Dracontius in his *De laudibus Dei* and Sedulius in his *Carmen Pascale*, had, for better or worse, already attempted such a synthesis. These authors, as the notes to this edition disclose, were well known to Vida. More importantly, some of the earlier Neo-Latin poets, starting in the Quattrocento, had devoted considerably more attention to the Judaeo-Christian tradition, as well as to the lives of the saints, than to pagan mythology. Even the scenes that Vida sets in Hell, through which he was to exert so powerful an influence on Tasso and Milton, were foreshadowed with striking frequency, not only in the *Odyssey*, the *Aeneid* and Claudian's *De Raptu Proserpinae*, but also in such Quattrocento poems as Maffeo Vegio's account of Saint Anthony,[5] Leonardo Dati's *Carmen ad Nicolaum V in Thurcum Mahamet*,[6] and Giacomo Bon's *De vita et gestis Christi*, in which this native of Serbia undertook, like Vida, to relate Christ's passion in Latin verse. Meanwhile, other poems like Mantuanus's *Parthenice Mariana*, already referred to, and Jacopo Sannazaro's *De partu Virginis*, had related the story of Christ's nativity, much as Vida does in the third book of the *Christiad*.

But compared with these biblical antecedents, it is the *Christiad* of Girolamo Vida alone that, both in scale and in its sustained competence, reads like a finished work of epic poetry. Poets like Vegio and Sannazaro may have been his equals in the quality of their verse, but their ambitions, as least as regards the poems in question, were far smaller. As for men like Bon and Mantuanus, the general conception of their poems and the specific quality of their verse are inferior to Vida's. In the *Christiad*, several of the characters do indeed rise to life after a fashion and, on numerous occasions, the poet attains to a rich and stirring eloquence.

Structurally, as well, the *Christiad* is marked by an admirable lucidity. Obedient to classical practice and to the well-known Horatian injunction, the poem opens *in medias res*, after a brief invocation of the Holy Ghost. We are in the last days of Christ's earthly ministry, and he is just about to enter Jerusalem. In this first book he is introduced to us and performs several miracles. In the doom-laden second book, he foretells his imminent betrayal and capture, and this is brought to pass. In the third and fourth books, Joseph and John respectively hasten to plead for leniency before Pontius and in the process, they inform him, and the reader, of the story of Christ's life. The fifth book is devoted to Christ's passion and execution, while the sixth and final book describes the aftermath and the resurrection. In all of this there are none of the episodic digressions that characterize the narrative verse of sixteenth-century Italians like Tasso and Ariosto, or even of Vergil in the *Georgics*. Vida always has the plan of the poem before his mind.

Vida remains in conflict, however, as to how he should depict his characters. He is not in this respect a consummate artist like Vergil and Tolstoy: even against their will and personal inclinations, perhaps, they follow the directives of their art wherever these might lead and, in the process, they endow their creations with a natural and organic complexity. Vida at times is willing and able to bring forth shades of character in two of the central characters, Jesus and his mother Mary. In the case of Jesus, the complexity and paradox of Vida's treatment follow the narrative of the Gospels. The hero, as Christ is often called, is by turns irascible, inscrutable, generous and impulsive. At the same time, however, as in the Gospels themselves, he is not entirely fleshed out. That is to say that there is no point in the narrative when we feel that the character of Christ rings false. And yet the poet reveals it to us in abrupt sequences, without much concern for transition, though we do feel some imperfect continuity between them.

Mary as well is endowed with something of human complexity. We encounter her first in Book III, in which Joseph — also a somewhat complex creation — recounts to Pilate the story of Jesus' birth. In that book, Mary possesses, in addition to holiness, the self-absorbed obstinacy of the adolescent that she then was. When in Book V we first encounter her in real time, so to speak, she runs wildly through the streets of Jerusalem seeking her dying son. In the frantic energy with which she is depicted, we can see a plausible continuity with the headstrong and emotional adolescent she had once been.

For the most part, however, Vida's characters tend toward a kind of totemic simplification, far more typical of Silver Latin poets like Lucan, Statius and Silius than of Vergil or Homer. John the Evangelist, who relates the deeds of Christ to Pontius in Book Four, is the type of an angelic youth, somewhat dull in his spiritual elevation, his earnest self-effacement and his devotion to his master. This can become inadvertently comical, as at the beginning of Book IV: "Everyone turned and marveled at the young man standing there in silence, as though lifeless or weighed down by sleep, and they energetically shook him awake." Peter as well is presented as an earnest, if somewhat irascible old man, often craven in the event. Vida attempts to endow Judas, in his remorse, with some complexity, but this consists in a formulaic inversion of his previous behavior and does not provide depth so much as indicate it.

An analogy suggests itself between the characters of Vida's epic and the stock figures in the paintings of Vida's contemporaries. Even artists as great as Titian and Raphael, in their depictions of New Testament subjects, tend toward what seem to us stereotypical conceptions of pious emotion. Now there is a well-known Horatian saw, *ut pictura poesis*: as in painting, so in poetry. But it would seem that there are things more easily tolerated in the former than in the latter. The magisterial chromatic and compositional sophistication of these great painters brought charm and power to their stereotypical depictions of scriptural subjects. The same cannot be said for the characters of Vida.

There is yet another sense, important to the success of this poem, in which *ut pictura poesis* can be taken too far. The climactic moment of the poem, of course, is the crucifixion itself, an event that was obviously central in Western art, especially among Vida's contemporaries. But in Italy, at least, the frequent pictorial depiction of Christ's passion was rarely if ever gruesome. Neither its point not its effect was to communicate a sense of the gory horror of the actual event. Rather artists sought to ennoble and beautify the figure of Christ, in such a way that the event was, remarkably, purged of its gruesomeness. What was indeed being done to Christ seemed almost a pretext for the display of physical perfection and an aestheticized sense of the world.

Far different is the manner in which Vida proceeds. It is perhaps a paradox that the words of Vida—precisely because they commend themselves directly to the mind rather than to the eye—possess a far greater experiential immediacy than the paintings of his contemporaries. In this respect, Vida comes far closer to the effect of German artists like Matthias Grünewald in his Isenheim altarpiece, except that Vida is never expressionistic, but rather—at least by the standards of his age—something of a realist. It is difficult not to flinch when one reads, in Book V of the *Christiad*:

Hic digitis vellit concretam sanguine barbam;
ille oculos in sidereos spuit improbus ore
immundo et pulchrum deformat puluere corpus. (5.388–390)

One man plucked his beard, stiff with blood, while another spat from his filthy mouth into Jesus' celestial eyes and sullied his noble body with dirt.

Or elsewhere in the same book:

Iamque trabem infandam scandens pendensque per auras
horruit atque deum ueluti se oblitus, acerbi
pertimuit dirum leti genus; aestuat intus,
atque animum in curas labefactum dividit acres,
tristia multa agitans animo, totosque per artus
pallentes mixto fluit ater sanguine sudor. (5.494–9)

Now he had mounted the unspeakable timber and, as he hung suspended, he shuddered. He seemed to forget that he was divine and, dreading this frightful and bitter kind of death, he was in turmoil within. His wavering heart was rent with sharp cares, as sweat, mixed with blood and filth, covered his entire body, now grown pale.

Stylistically, one of the more striking qualities of the *Christiad* is that—pursuant to Vida's own directives in his *Art of Poetry*—there is little ostentatious display of learning, other than the obvious fact that he is composing very proper Latin hexameters. An apparent exception, the catalogue of Hebrew tribes from Book II, is modeled on the *Iliad*, but its lengthy enumeration of Hebrew names is surely pertinent to the subject of the poem. There is, however, hardly any invocation or acknowledgement of pagan traditions, few of the classical allusions that abound in the writings of other neo-Latin poets like Poliziano, Sannazaro and Pontano, not to mention the mythological machinery that marks Vida's shorter poem, *The Game of Chess*, or such vernacular epics as Camoes' *Os Lusiados* and Milton's *Paradise Lost*.

Beyond Vida's few formulaic paganisms, if you will—his referring to heaven as Olympus, for instance, or to angels as divinities—he rarely if ever avows the existence of classical culture. This is in keeping with the point made earlier, that he seems almost to be translating the Vulgate into Vergil, without importing much that was not in either the Vulgate itself or in the apocryphal literature that surrounded it. In this regard, he is very different from Milton, whose relation to the classical pagan traditions was far more complicated. There is no moment in the *Christiad* comparable to those priamels in *Paradise Lost* in which, as in Book One, Milton compares the assembly of fallen angels to various armies from ancient and medieval times (1.573–587), or in Book Four, where he compares Eden to

> that fair field
> Of Enna, where Proserpin gathering flowers,
> Herself a fairer flower, by gloomy Dis
> Was gathered, which cost Ceres all that pain
> To seek her through the world. (4.268–272)

At the most elementary level of language, of the pure stuff and matter of the *Christiad*, Vida's model was, of course, Vergil's *Aeneid*. This was, and remains, obvious to anyone acquainted with Latin poetry. In fact, Vida drew not only from the great Roman poet's epic, but from his *Eclogues* and his *Georgics* as well. Several decades before the publication of the *Christiad*, Vida had declared his sympathies for the Mantuan poet in his *Art of Poetry*, where he declared Vergil to be

> vocem, animumque deo similis. . . .
> Unus hic ingenio praestanti gentis Achivae
> divinos vates longe superavit et arte,
> aureus, immortale sonans. Stupet ipsa pavetque,
> quamvis ingentem miretur Graecia Homerum.

> In voice and spirit like a god. . . . Through his eminent wit and his art, he alone, resplendent and possessed of undying eloquence, far surpassed the divine poets of Greece. Greece itself was astonished and afraid, however much it marveled at great Homer. (1.168–173)

With indefatigable diligence, Richard T. Bruère has tracked down nearly 200 passages in the *Christiad* that are inspired by Vergil, usually, but not exclusively, by the *Aeneid*.[7] Vida's devotion to Vergil should come as little surprise in a culture in which, one hundred years earlier, the Lombard poet Maffeo Vegio had undertaken to write a Thirteenth Book for the *Aeneid*, which was thought to be incomplete; in a culture in which, one hundred years after Vida, the Scotch Latinist Alexander Ross would compose his own *Christiad* as a Vergilian cento, that is, a compilation of lines lifted bodily, with little or no modification, from Vergil.[8]

As Hazel Stewart Alberson has written, "Vida follows Dante in upholding Vergil as a great master and a great author, but he is more liberal in his apprenticeship and following. Where Dante has avowed his debt to Vergil and yet created according to his own grand design, Vida has analyzed the greatness of the master, has attempted to see him in a more nearly true perspective, and to set his finding into a formula in his *Art of Poetry*. He has gone a step farther and given an excellent demonstration of the relation of theory and practice in his *Christiad*, an epic of Christ."[9]

Two pairings that she offers from the *Aeneid* and the *Christiad* respectively will serve for nearly two hundred.[10] Compare these descriptions of night:

> Tempus erat, quo prima quies mortalibus aegris
> Incipit et dono divom gratissima serpit. (*Aeneid* 2.268–9)

> It was the time when the rest first begins, insinuating itself among weary mortals, a most welcome gift of the gods.

with:

> Tempus erat per membra quies quum grata soporem
> irrigat ac positis affert oblivia curis. (*Christiad* 2.22–3)

> It was that time of night when care is set aside and welcome rest brings sleep and oblivion to weary bodies.

Or compare:

> Dant signum; fulsere ignes et conscius aether . . . (*Aeneid* 4.167)

> [They] gave the signal and the stars and the complicit air burned brightly.

with:

> Emicuere ignes; diffulsit conscius aether. (*Christiad* 5.969.)

> The fires of heaven flashed and the aether in complicity grew dark.

One area in which Vida has followed Vergil most assiduously is his similes, several of which Vergil himself derived from Homer. Some books of the *Christiad* have very few similes, while others have three to a page. Concerning Vida's use of them, Julius Caesar Scaliger, the great Renaissance scholar and critic, says: "Vida displayed the choicest inventiveness when it came to his similes. . . . In them there are indeed charm, strength, brilliance, and tact. Still, I shouldn't wish, with the poet, to compare Jesus to the river Po [Scaliger is referring to *Christiad* 1.25–31], enhanced by the confluence of tributaries. Concerning his following this is accurate; concerning Christ, it is impious."[11] Whatever the propriety of Scaliger's comments concerning the simile in question, he is certainly correct in objecting to what is, on occasion, a bizarre inappositeness in Vida's similes. In Book III, for example, the poet compares the old Priest Simeon, in his excitement at beholding the infant Jesus, to a barking dog:

Ergo ubi adesse deum praesensit numine plenus,
qualis ubi gressum per agros comitatus herilem
forte canis leporem vi longe sensit odora,
continuo intenditque aures atque aera captat
naribus, et coeptum rumpens iter avius errat
atque oculis incerta ferae vestigia lustrans,
nunc hos, nunc illos cursus fert atque recursus
incertus; longe latratibus arua resultant. (3.694–701)

Thus filled with divine presence, he had a presentiment that a god was near, as when a hound that accompanies his master through the fields and with his keen nose senses far off the presence of a hare. Immediately he pricks up his ears and sniffs the air, and as he shoots from the intended path, his eyes survey the uncertain tracks of the hare, now darting this way and now that, and, baffled, fills the fields with barking.

In Book IV, Vida incongruously compares Christ's numerous followers to the sutlers (and implicitly, perhaps, to the prostitutes) who linger about a mercenary encampment:

Haud secus ac bellum si cui rex maximus urbi
indixit, iamque arma ciet iamque agmina cogit,
cladem orae exitiumque ferens populisque ruinas,
non tantum iurata manus lectaeque cohortes
incedunt, sed praeterea quos dirus habendi
duxit amor, varia cupidos ditescere praeda,
agglomerant multi atque iniussi castra sequuntur. (4.847–53)

It was as if some great king had declared war on a city, brandishing arms and marshalling troops to bring slaughter and
death to the land and ruin to the people: not only do the
sworn troops and selected cohorts join in, but also men attracted by a love of gain, hoping to enrich themselves on the
spoils of war, follow the camp unbidden.

At the same time, however, Vida can occasionally hit upon a
truly wonderful and superbly contemporary allusion, as when, in
Book II, he compares the effect of Nicodemus's words before the
Sanhedrin to the firing of a cannonball:

Qualiter aere cavo, dum sulfura pascitur atra,
inclusus magis atque magis furit acrior ignis
moliturque fugam, nec se capit intus anhelans,
nulla sed angustis foribus via, nec potis extra
rumpere, materiam donec comprenderit omnem;
tum piceo disclusa uolat glans ferrea fumo.
Fit crepitus: credas rupto ruere aethere coelum.
Iamque illa et turres procul ecce stravit et arces;
corpora et arma iacent late et uia facta per hostes. (2.205–213)

As when poisonous sulfur consumes itself within the chamber of a bronze cannon, the confined fire rages with ever
greater force. Hissing and seeking to break out, it can no
longer contain itself, yet it has no avenue of escape through

the narrow channels of the bore, no means of freeing itself, until all the matter is consumed. Then amid pitchy smoke, the iron bullet discharges and takes wing with a thunderous sound. You would think that the sky had split open and the heavens were falling! And behold, the cannonball has laid waste to distant towers and fortifications, bodies and arms lie scattered everywhere, and a path has been cut through the enemy camp!

Richard Bruere has suggested that this fine simile is reminiscent of *Aeneid* 7.462–6, concerning a cauldron:

> magno ueluti cum flamma sonore
> uirgea suggeritur costis undantis aëni
> exsultantque aestu latices, furit intus aquai
> fumidus atque alte spumis exuberat amnis,
> nec iam se capit unda, uolat uapor ater ad auras.

> As when a flame, fed by twigs, noisily rises within a bronze pot, and the liquid contents froth up: a smoky stream of water rages within and rises high, and the liquid can no longer contain itself as black steam shoots into the air.

And yet the differences are more dramatic than the similarities, and it may be that, in this one passage, Vida has surpassed his master.

Ultimately Vida, like most Neo-Latin poets, and despite his flawless channeling of the spirit of Vergil in his hexameter verse, does not attain to the highest ranks of poetry. Why this should be true of Neo-Latin poetry in general is, perhaps, something of a mystery. It is certainly true of Petrarch, who probably knew Latin better than Italian and appears to have valued his Latin poetry, especially his epic *Africa*, above his efforts in the vernacular. To be sure, some of the finest prose of the sixteenth century, by men like

Sir Thomas More and Desiderius Erasmus, was written in Latin. But in poetry, more essentially than in prose, the highest goal of the Neo-Latinists was to achieve the most perfect imitation of the ancients. Because of this, Vida was engaged in a fundamentally different linguistic act from that of Vergil, whom he so studiously imitated: Vergil was trying to write the best poetry that he could, whereas Vida was trying to be as Vergilian as he could.

Though there may or may not be an *a priori* reason why this act of fealty, of surrender really, to another's style, can never attain to the highest levels of poetry, the empirical evidence would seem to suggest that such is the case. The predictable result in a man of Vida's intelligence, diligence and devotion to his source is that he, like Maffeo Vegio one hundred years earlier, achieves the greatest possible simulacrum. But he fails to reproduce or perhaps even to notice those non-Vergilian quirks that are so constitutive of Vergil's poetry. He could never reproduce, perhaps he could not even hear, the resigned despair with which Vergil ends the fifth book of the *Aeneid*:

> Multa gemens casuque animum concussus amici:
> 'o nimium caelo et pelago confise sereno,
> nudus in ignota, Palinure, iacebis harena.' (5.870–871)

> Groaning deeply and stricken by the fate of his friend, [Aeneas said]: Oh Palinurus, who trusted too much in clear skies and calm seas, you will lie naked in unknowns sands.

This tincture of sadness, this resistless awareness of the *lacrimae rerum*, in short, this tragic sense of life, was something that a Christian cleric by calling and Vida, perhaps by character, could not entertain. Let it also be said in passing that Vida's Christ and Vida himself evidence no conspicuous sense of humor in the *Christiad*, even though the protagonist of the Gospels clearly possessed that quality in abundance.

Another fault that vitiates Vida's verse is, on occasion, an inexcusable wordiness. Instead of saying something like "it was dawn," Vida must inform us that

Iamque dies pulsis tenebris invecta rubebat,
et face sol rosea nigras disiecerat umbras. (3.254–5)

And now the dark shadows of night were driven off, and approaching day glowed red, and the sun's rosy torch had routed the nightly shades.

What Vida can achieve is a purity and smoothness in his diction that generally match the level of Vergil in his steadiest and most workmanlike mode. Rare indeed are such lines as "Tum piceo disclusa volat glans ferrea fumo" (2.210; "Then amid pitchy smoke, the iron bullet dislodges"), describing the discharge of the cannon ball mentioned above; or, better still, "procul undique circum / scintillae absiliunt radiis vibrantibus aureae" (3.383–4; "and wherever [the wind] passed, gold sparks leapt forth in all directions"), in which Vida achieves that perfect marriage of sound and meaning that constitutes poetry at its most delightful and most effective.

For the most part, the sonorities of the *Christiad* are of a far different kind, less imaginative and characterized more by oratorical propriety than by visual power. An oratorical element was one of the defining features of the ancient Roman epic, compared with its Greek sources. This oratorical element may not represent Vergil at his best, but it represents him at his most typical. But such oratorical efficiency as Vida clearly possesses can be put to excellent effect in passages like Christ's triumphal march into heaven, at the end of the *Christiad* (6.701–28), as well as in the thrilling sequence in which Vida relates the tensions that almost break out into open conflict in heaven, as half of the angels, indignant at Christ's Crucifixion, take up arms to save him (5.510–691).

That latter passage points up the profound influence that the *Christiad* was to have on later poets, for the scene in question was to prove an indispensable inspiration for John Milton's description of the battle that Satan and his rebel angels waged against God in Book 6 of *Paradise Lost*. But it was hardly the only influence that Vida exerted on *Paradise Lost* or on other poems by Milton, and certainly not his only influence on several generations of European poets, both in Latin and in the vernacular languages. This influence took two forms: first in the infernal machinery, if you will, that Vida made available to numerous poets of succeeding generations. His figure of Satan, though anticipated in earlier Neo-Latin verse, was clearly the direct template for similar passages in Tasso's *Gerusalemme Liberata* and Marino's *La Strage degli innocenti*, as well as for the figure of Satan in *Paradise Lost*. So numerous are the borrowings of these later poets that it suffices to read one passage from the *Christiad* for parallels to leap to mind:

> quo subito intonuit caecis domus alta cavernis
> undique opaca, ingens; antra intonuere profunda
> atque procul gravido tremefacta est corpore tellus.
> Continuo ruit ad portas gens omnis et adsunt
> lucifugi coetus uaria, atque bicorpora monstra:
> pube tenus hominum facies, verum hispida in anguem
> desinit, ingenti sinuata uolumine cauda.
> Gorgonas hi Sphingasque obscoeno corpore reddunt,
> Centaurosque Hydrasque illi ignivomasque Chimaeras.
> centum alii Scyllas ac foedificas Harpyias,
> et quae multa homines simulacra horrentia fingunt. (1.136–146)

Into the royal chambers he ordered his dire brethren and all his kind, that horrid council. A trumpet sent forth the mighty summons. At once his dwelling, lofty, massive and dark, shook to its darkest caverns. As the deep caves echoed back, the great womb of earth was set trembling afar. The entire horde came running, changeful, twyform monsters that flee the light: human down to the groin, they ended in the form of a serpent, with a huge barbed and coiling tail. Some transformed their obscene bodies into Gorgons, Sphinxes and Centaurs, others into Hydras and fire-breathing Chimaeras, a hundred more into Scyllas and fetid Harpies—all the horrid shapes that human beings have ever imagined.

Compare this with the following lines from Book Four (ll. 25–40) of *Gerusalemme Liberata*, which at points read almost like a translation of the earlier poem:

Tosto gli dèi d'Abisso in varie torme
concorron d'ogn'intorno a l'alte porte.
Oh come strane, oh come orribil forme!
quant'è ne gli occhi lor terrore e morte!
Stampano alcuni il suol di ferine orme,
e 'n fronte umana han chiome d'angui attorte,
e lor s'aggira dietro immensa coda
che quasi sferza si ripiega e snoda.
Qui mille immonde Arpie vedresti e mille
Centauri e Sfingi e pallide Gorgoni,
molte e molte latrar voraci Scille,
e fischiar Idre e sibilar Pitoni,
e vomitar Chimere atre faville,
e Polifemi orrendi e Gerioni;
e in novi mostri, e non piú intesi o visti,
diversi aspetti in un confusi e misti. (4.25–40)

At once in varied troops the gods of the abyss run from all directions to the lofty gates. Oh, what strange and horrible forms! What terror and death are in their eyes! Some strike the ground with bestial gait, their human faces covered with twisting snakes: a massive tail coils behind them, furling and unfurling like a whip. Here you could see a thousand vile Harpies, a thousand Centaurs, sphinxes and pale gorgons, countless Scyllas, whistling hydras and hissing pythons, chimeras vomiting forth dark flames, horrid Polyphemus and Geryon, as well as varied creatures, confusedly mingled together to form monstrosities never since heard of or seen.

Or this more sententious rendering from Milton:

> . . . all monstrous, all prodigious things,
> Abominable, inutterable, and worse
> Then Fables yet have feign'd, or fear conceiv'd,
> Gorgons and Hydras and Chimeras dire. (*Paradise Lost*, 2.625–
> 628)

The other form of influence that the *Christiad* exerted over later poetry consisted in establishing the *Christiad* itself, that is, a narrative poem about Christ and his Passion, as something that very nearly rose to the status of a self-contained genre. Its popularity is reflected in a *Christiad* by the German Latinist, Johannes Klockus (1601), in *Jesus Crucifié*, by the French poet Nicolas Frenicle (1636), and in Diego de Hojeda's Spanish poem *La Christiada* (1611). Also noteworthy is the cento poem to which I have already referred, *The Christiad of Vergil the Evangelist* (*Vergilii Evangelisantis Christiados*), by the Scottish cleric Alexander Ross. Other such works are Michel Foucque's *Vie, Faictz, Passion, Mort, Resurrection, et Ascension de Nostre Seigneur Jesus Christ* (1574) and Friedrich Gottlieb Klopstock's well-known *Der Messias*, completed in 1772, which so aroused the admiration of Young Werther. Early in the nineteenth century, the short-lived Henry Kirke White wrote a *Christiad*, as did William Alexander, a native of Philadelphia, in the middle of that century. But the best of these *Christiads* was perhaps that of Robert Clarke, an Englishman who in 1650 completed a 17,000 line poem on Christ, published in 1670. None of these poets, however, surpassed Vida in consequence or inventiveness.¹²

It is a pleasure to acknowledge my deep thanks to James Hankins, the general editor of the I Tatti Renaissance Library, for the kindness, erudition, and efficiency he has exhibited at every stage of this project. I must also express my immeasurable gratitude to Professor Richard Tarrant of Harvard University's Classics department for the indefatigable energy he has displayed in examining my translation and making many deeply insightful suggestions and corrections that I have eagerly adopted. Any surviving errors and inadvertences are, of course, fully my own. Finally, I would like to thank John Gagné for collating the 1535 and 1550 editions of the Christiad as well as for preparing a bibliography of Marco Girolamo Vida, and Justin Stover for his learned help with the notes.

This translation is dedicated to the memory of my dear friend Tanya Hanley (1968–2007), a woman of profound intelligence and humanity, who loved both Vergil and Christ.

J.G.

NOTES

1. See the Bibliography for editions and full references to works cited in these notes.

2. "Rogo ne a nobis vitae nostrae, aut rerum nostrarum . . . commentarios expectes ullos. . . . Ego certe opus tam arduum, atque adeo periculosum non spe immortalitatis, aut gloriae adortus sum." Quoted in Di Cesare, *Vida's Christiad*, 1. Botta later composed a commentary on Vida which was published in 1569; see Bibliography, under "Other Latin Editions."

3. Di Cesare, *Bibliotheca Vidiana*, 242.

4. Kallendorf, "From Virgil to Vida," 62.

5. Maffeo Vegio, *Short Epics*, edited by Michael C. J. Putnam with James Hankins (Cambridge, Mass.: Harvard University Press, 2004). This may be the earliest Christian epic of the Renaissance.

6. Edited by James Hankins in *Humanism and Platonism in the Italian Renaissance*, 2 vols. (Rome: Storia e letteratura, 2003–2004), II, 375–483.

7. Bruère, "Review Article." For other Vergilian and post-Vergilian parallels, see the Notes to the Translation.

8. Alexander Ross, *Virgilii Evangelisantis Christiados libri XIII, in quibus omnia quae de Domino Nostro Jesu Christo in utroque Testamento vel dicta vel praedicta sunt, altisona divina Maronis tuba suavissime decantantur* (London: E. Tyler, 1659).

9. Alberson, "Lo Mio Maestro," 194–5.

10. Ibid., 206.

11. Quoted in Bruère, "Review Article," 29: "Lectissimae quidem inventiones ad comparationes. . . . In eis vero est et venustas, et robur, et candor, et efficacia. Tametsi nollem Iesum Eridano comparare, ita ut ille fecit, auctum fluviorum accessione; de comitatu verum est, de Christo impium."

12. An excellent account of the influence, as well as the antecedents, of Vida's *Christiad* may be found in Barbara Kiefer Lewalski, *Milton's Brief Epic*, chapters 2 and 3.

CHRISTIAD

LIBER PRIMUS[1]

Qui mare, qui terras, qui coelum numine comples,
spiritus alme, tuo liceat mihi munere regem
bis genitum canere, e superi qui sede parentis
virginis intactae gravidam descendit in alvum,
5 mortalesque auras hausit puer, ut genus ultus
humanum eriperet tenebris et carcere iniquo
morte sua manesque pios inferret Olympo.
Illum sponte hominum morientem ob crimina tellus
aegra tulit puduitque poli de vertice solem
10 aspicere et tenebris insuetis terruit orbem.
Fas mihi te duce mortali immortalia digno
ore loqui interdumque oculos attollere coelo
et lucem accipere aetheream summique parentis
consilia atque necis tam dirae evolvere causas.
15   Iam prope mortis erant metae finisque laborum
Christo aderat, Solymumque ideo haud ignarus ad urbem
Phoenicum extremis remeans de finibus ibat.
Illum ingens comitum numerus iuvenesque senesque
sponte sequebantur, rerum quos fama trahebat
20 undique collectos. Nam magnas sive per urbes
ferret iter seu desertis in montibus iret,
olli se innumeri iungebant, usque parati
iussa sequi, vellet quascunque abducere in oras,
atque novos erat hic semper fas cernere coetus,
25 pinifero veluti Vesuli de vertice primum
it Padus exiguo sulcans sata pinguia rivo;
hinc magis atque magis labendo viribus auctus
surgit latifluoque sonans se gurgite pandit
victor; opes amnes varii auxiliaribus undis

BOOK I

Gentle spirit, who fills with your divine presence the sea, the earth
and the sky, help me to tell of the twice-born king who, from his
Father's throne in heaven above, descended into the womb of an
untouched virgin and, as a mere infant, drew mortal breath; so
that, by his death, he might avenge the human race, rescuing it   5
from darkness and sinful durance and leading the souls of the pious into paradise. The grieving earth bore him as he died willingly
for the sins of men. From the height of heaven, the sun was
ashamed to look on and harrowed the earth with a strange darkness. I am only a mortal man, but I pray that, with your help, I   10
might sing a worthy song about immortal things. Lifting my eyes
to heaven, may I receive, for a time, the ethereal light, to reveal the
counsels of the celestial Father and the causes of so piteous a
death.

Already Christ was approaching the end of his life and of his   15
labors. Hardly unaware of his fate, he arrived from the distant
borders of the Phoenicians at the gates of Jerusalem. Following
him was a throng of young and old alike, who had heard of his
miracles and had come running from all directions. For whether   20
he traveled through populous cities or deserted mountains, a
countless multitude of followers joined him, ready to do his bidding no matter where he led them. And their numbers kept growing, like the Po that rises in a little stream from the pine-rich summit of Viso, cutting a path through the abundant cropland and   25
strengthening as it flows, until with mounting clamor trium-

30   hinc addunt atque inde, suo nec se capit alveo,
turbidus haud uno dum rumpat in aequora cornu.
    Tum vero numero socios seiunxit ab omni
bis senos, sibi quos olim delegit, ut essent
tantorum memores operum testesque laborum
35   atque, ubi secretos nemora in seclusa vocavit,
procerae[2] innitens cedro, moestissimus ore
eque imo rumpens suspiria pectore fatur:
'Ventum ad supremum, socii; data tempora vitae
exegi in terris. Lux nunc infanda propinquat
40   meque pii manes expectant. Illius ergo
en ultro infensam Solymorum ascendimus urbem.
Illic informis leti mihi dira parantur
supplicia; immeritum me nunc coniurat in unum
saeva sacerdotum manus, ut non inscius ipse
45   praedixi toties ac vobis cuncta retexi.
Ibo: morte mea veterum scelus omne piabo.
    'His me prime malis oneras pater: ipse tulisti
dulcia poma; mihi sed nunc tua furta luendum.
Cum tamen expulerit tenebras lux tertia rebus,
50   aereas caede abluta revocabor in auras.
    'Vos etiam, quos non pertaesum denique nostri,
funera acerba manent. Audete, et lucis amori
istius aeternum vitae immortalis honorem
mecum omnes praeferte. Domus non haec data, non hae
55   sunt vobis propriae sedes. Vos aetheris alti
lucida templa vocant, stellis florentia regna,
pax ubi secura ac requies optata laborum:
hic domus, hic patria. Huc omnes contendite laeti
angustum per iter; vestras hic figite sedes.'
60   Dixerat. At socii defixi lumina moestis
haerebant animis ac tristia multa putabant.
Tum senior Petrus haud linguae vocive pepercit,

phantly it pours forth in a roaring flood. From all directions the 30
various tributaries add their waves until the muddied river, no
longer contained within its banks, splits and bursts forth into the
sea.

And now from among all his followers Jesus singled out the
twelve men he had already chosen to be the witnesses of his labors
and to remember his great deeds. In a secluded grove, he leaned 35
against a tall cedar. Tears welled up in his eyes, and a great sigh
rose from the depths of his heart. "I have reached the end, my
friends. My time on earth is over. A sad day approaches, and the
spirits of the just await me. That is why I have come to the hostile 40
city of Jerusalem. Dire punishments and a shameful death have
been prepared for me. The cruel band of priests conspires against
me, despite my innocence. Hardly was this unknown to me. I have
often foretold it and revealed all these things to you. And I will go 45
to them. By my death I will wipe away the sins of our forebears.

"Father Adam, you burden me with these sufferings. You were
the one who bore away the sweet apples. And now it falls to me to
expiate your crimes. When the third dawn chases the darkness
from the earth, I shall be called home to my ethereal abode, the
gore of my execution washed away. 50

"And for you, as well, who have never wearied of my company,
a harsh death awaits. But take heart and join with me, all of you,
in preferring to the love of this world the eternal honor of immortal life. This house is not your true abode. This earth is not your
true home. The shining temples of high heaven call to you, the 55
star-filled realms above, where there is perfect peace and long-
sought rest from toil. There lies your dwelling, your country. Hasten with a happy heart along the narrow path. Make that your
home."

Thus he spoke. But his disciples stood with heavy spirits, their 60
eyes fixed upon the ground as they weighed many sad thoughts.
Peter, who was older than the rest, did not hesitate to speak, but

et tali divum affatus sermone precatur:
'Nate deo, quae tanta deum te denique coeli
65 vis agit, ut libeat letum crudele pacisci
pro quoquam aut certis ultro te offerre periclis?
Quin age, te incolumi potius (potes omnia quando,
nec tibi nequicquam pater est qui sidera torquet)
perficias quodcunque tibi nunc instat agendum,
70 non adeo exosus lucem ingratusque salutis.
Hos animos, hanc confestim precor exue mentem.
Ipse tui miserere, tuum miserere, nec ultro
proiice nos, qui te, tendis quocunque, sequemur.'
    Sic ille, increpuit dictis quem talibus heros:
75 'Non pudet, o nunquam sapiens, mortalia semper
volvere, nube oculos pressum, coelestium inanem?
Nec potis es vanis unquam desuescere curis?
Haecne tibi consulta mei suasere labores?
Non hoc consiliis, non hoc auctoribus istis
80 tempus eget; genitor iussis haud mollibus urget.
At vos o, rebus spretis mortalibus, omnes
ferte viri et duros animo tolerate labores,
oblitique hominem, coelo altas tollite mentes,
et cum mortales linguas in iurgia solvent
85 vos contra, falsis onerantes nomina vestra
criminibus, gaudete ac firmo pectore ferte
indignamque ignominiam contemnite laeti.
Hinc fortunatos vos dicite, praemia quando
certa manent oriturque ingens hinc gloria vestra.'
90   Haec fatus, montes aditum fert tristis in altos.
Incedunt una socii cum rege parati
cuncta pati et iuvenis sortem indignantur iniquam.
Et iam palmosae subit Hierichuntis ad urbem.
Zacchaei excipitur tecto mensisque paratis,
95 cui quondam componere opes per fasque nefasque

thus besought his divine companion: "Son of God, what force of heaven so works upon you, a god, that you would wish to suffer a   65
cruel fate for the sake of others, that you would willingly surrender yourself to certain perils? Since you can do anything at all, since it is not in vain that your Father moves the stars, why not finish what remains to be done while saving your own life, rather than hating life and giving no mind to safety? Set aside these   70
thoughts at once, I pray you. Take pity on yourself and on your friends. Don't throw us heedlessly aside, who will follow you wherever you might go."

Thus he spoke. But the hero upbraided him with these words: "Aren't you ashamed, you who are never wise, to have your eyes al-   75
ways clouded by mortal things, never to be thinking of heaven? Can you never rise above idle cares? Surely my actions have not taught you such notions. This is not the time for such witnesses and counsels. My Father urges me on with no mild command-   80
ments. Rather, my friends, look with contempt on worldly things and bear your sufferings with courage. Forget humanity and fix your minds on heaven. And when every man berates you, heaping   85
calumnies upon your fair names, rather rejoice in fortitude and show contempt for such ignominy. Count yourselves fortunate, when such treasure, such glory lies waiting for you."

So speaking, he made his way solemnly to the top of the moun-   90
tain. His followers went with him, prepared to suffer at the side of their king, even as they lamented the young man's unjust fate. Next he went to the city of Jericho, rich in palms. He was received in the house of Zacchaeus, where the dinner table was set. Once this man had been consumed by a fierce love of wealth, whether acquired by fair means or foul. But then he saw the light, and with   95

immensas amor acer erat, sed luce recepta
hospitis adventu coepit male parta luendo
reddere, cuique suum partiri caetera egenis.
Tot facti infectique auri congesta talenta!
100   Hic subito non laeta ferens gravis impulit aures
nuntius atque animum rumore momordit amaro.
Lazarus haud procul hinc Bethanes regna tenebat,
dives opum, clarus genus alto a sanguine regum.
Nam pater ingentes Syriae frenaverat oras
105 vique sibi captas quondam subiecerat urbis.
Nemo illo hospitibus facilis magis; omnibus illa
noctes atque dies domus ultro oblata patebat.
Huc etiam persaepe ipsum succedere Christum
haud piguit creberque domus indulsit amicae
110 hospitio atque deum posita se nube retexit.
Hunc igitur postquam morientem accepit et acri
vix morbo correptum, auras haurire supremas
et quasi iam leti portas luctarier ante,
demisit lachrymas sociisque haec edidit ore:
115 'Cedamus. Leto actutum revocandus amicus
in lucem, modo me summus pater audiat ipse
atque suas velit hic, ut saepe, ostendere vires.'
Haec ait, et gressum Bethanae tendit ad urbem.
Prosequitur comitum manus ingens atque videndi
120 innumeri studio socios se protinus addunt.
    Interea longe mundi regnator opaci,
infelix monstrum, penitus non inscius illam
iam prope adesse diem, superi qua maximus ultor
imperio patris infernis succederet oris
125 manibus auxilio ac sedes vastaret opertas.
Sollicitus partis animum versabat in omnes,
si qua forte potis regno hanc avertere cladem
molirique deo letum meditatur; ea una

the arrival of his guest, he began to expiate his ill-gotten gains by returning them to their rightful owners and giving the rest away to the poor. So many piled talents of gold, ingots and bars!

All at once a grave messenger appeared. He brought no glad 100 tidings for their ears, but troubled their spirits with a bitter report. In nearby Bethany ruled a wealthy man, Lazarus, whose distinguished lineage was descended from kings. His father had once conquered the huge coast of Syria and subjected its captive cities by force. No one was more hospitable to visitors than Lazarus. 105 Night and day his home lay open to all who came. Nor did Christ himself disdain to go there, but often, setting aside the cloud that concealed his deity, he delighted in the hospitality of that friendly home. And so, when he learned that Lazarus was breathing his 110 last, stricken with a harsh ailment, that he was already struggling at the gates of death, Christ shed tears and spoke thus to his disciples: "Let us go to him. Lazarus, our friend, must be called back 115 from death into the realms of light. If only the Supreme Father will hear my words and wish now, as often in the past, to manifest his power." So speaking, he made his way to Bethany. A great multitude followed him, and many more joined his ranks in their eagerness to see the man. 120

Meanwhile far off, the lord of the benighted realms, that baleful monster, saw that the day approached when the great Avenger, at the behest of his Supreme Father, would descend into the lower regions to succor the departed souls and lay waste to that dark region. Anxiously he searched in all directions for some way to avert 125 this disaster from his kingdom and contrive the death of God.

9

denique cura animo sedet, haec saepe una resurgit.
130 Demens, qui id propter tantum non viderat ipsum
demissum coelo iuvenem, quo sponte piaret
morte obita veterum culpam et scelus omne parentum.
    Protinus acciri diros ad regia fratres
limina, concilium horrendum, et genus omne suorum
135 imperat. Ecce igitur dedit ingens buccina signum,
quo subito intonuit caecis domus alta cavernis
undique opaca, ingens; antra intonuere profunda
atque procul gravido tremefacta est corpore tellus.
Continuo ruit ad portas gens omnis et adsunt
140 lucifugi coetus varia atque bicorpora monstra:
pube tenus hominum facies, verum hispida in anguem
desinit, ingenti sinuata volumine cauda.
Gorgonas hi Sphingasque obscoeno corpore reddunt,
Centaurosque Hydrasque illi ignivomasque Chimaeras,
145 centum alii Scyllas ac foedificas Harpyias,
et quae multa homines simulacra horrentia fingunt.
    At centumgeminus flammanti vertice supra est
arbiter ipse Erebi centenaque brachia iactat
centimanus totidemque eructat faucibus aestus.
150 Omnes luctificum fumumque atrosque procaci
ore oculisque ignes et vastis naribus efflant.
Omnibus intorti pendent pro crinibus angues
nexantes nodis sese ac per colla plicantes.
In manibus rutilaeque faces uncique tridentes,
155 quis sontes animas subigunt atque ignibus urgent.
Nec minus illi etiam diversis partibus orbis
conveniunt properi, qui terris omnibus errant
hortantes scelera ac variis mortalia ludunt
pectora imaginibus rectique oblivia suadent.
160 Necnon ventorum tempestatumque potentes,

The thought obsessed him and kept coming back. Foolish soul! He did not see that God, to this very end, had sent the youth down from heaven to wash away with his death all the crime and guilt of our first parents.

Into the royal chambers he ordered his dire brethren and all their kindred, that horrid council. A trumpet sent forth the mighty summons. At once his dwelling, lofty, massive and dark, shook to its darkest caverns. As the deep caves echoed back, the great womb of earth was set trembling afar. The entire horde came running, changeful, twyform monsters that flee the light: human down to the groin, they ended in the form of a serpent, with a huge, barbed and coiling tail. Some transformed their obscene bodies into Gorgons, Sphinxes and Centaurs, others into Hydras and fire-breathing Chimaeras, a hundred more into Scyllas and fetid Harpies — all the horrid shapes that human beings have ever imagined.

Raised above the rest on a fiery summit stood the hundred-handed lord of Erebus, flinging about his hundred arms and belching fire from his hundred maws. The entire host sent forth glowing smoke and hideous fire from their eyes, noses and rabid mouths. Instead of hair, they all had snakes that contorted themselves into knots and writhed around their necks. In their hands they held fiery torches and bristling pitchforks that pushed down the souls of the guilty and stuffed them into the fire; also present were those who wander to every corner of the earth, enjoining men to sinful deeds, beguiling human hearts with seductive forms that make them forget righteousness. Also in attendance was the cloudwandering race that controls the winds and storms: having

130

135

140

145

150

155

160

nubivagum genus, haud certa regione locati,
nimborum in media consueti nocte vagari.
    Ergo animis prompti atque opibus coiere parati
una omnes; fremitu vario sonat intus opaca
165   regia, rex donec nigram igne tricuspide dextram
armatus coetu in medio sic farier orsus:
'Tartarei proceres, coelo gens orta sereno,
quos olim huc superi mecum inclementia regis
aethere deiectos flagranti fulmine adegit,
170   dum regno cavet ac sceptris multa invidus ille
permetuit refugitque parem. Quae praelia toto
egerimus coelo, quibus olim denique utrinque
sit certatum odiis, notum et meminisse necesse est.
    'Ille astris potitur, parte et plus occupat aequa
175   aetheris ac poenas inimica e gente recepit
crudeles. Pro sideribus, pro luce serena
nobis senta situ loca, sole carentia tecta
reddidit ac tenebris iussit torquere sub imis
immites animas hominum, illaetabile regnum,
180   haud superae aspirare poli datur amplius aulae.
Ingens ingenti claudit nos obiice tellus;
in partemque homini nostri data regia coeli est.
Nec satis. Arma iterum molitur et altera nobis
bella ciet regnisque etiam nos pellit ab imis.
185   'Id propter iuvenem aetherea demisit ab arce
seu natum sive alitibus de fratribus unum.
Iamque aderit fretusque armis coelestibus ille
sedibus exitium vehet his et regna recludet
infera concessasque animas nostro eximet orbe.
190   Fors quoque nos, nisi non segnes occurrimus, ipsos
arcta in vincla dabit vinctosque inducet Olympo
victor ovans; superi illudent toto aethere captis.

no certain abode upon the earth, they were wont to wander at midnight amid the clouds of the sky.

Eagerly and with every resource in readiness, they now rushed into council. The dark palace rang with their varied clamor. Finally their king rose among them, his black hand armed with three-fold 165 fire. And thus he began to speak: "Princes of Hell, a race born in the serenity of heaven, whom once along with me the supreme King in his cruelty cast down with a flaming thunderbolt and drove to this place. Guarding his kingdom and fearing for his very scepter, he trembled and fled from me, his equal. Well known and 170 well worthy of remembrance are those battles we fought throughout heaven, and the contentious hatred on both sides.

"Now he rules the stars, holding sway over a more than equal share of heaven and exacting harsh penance from us, his foes. In 175 place of stars and open air, he has given us this harsh desert and these dwellings that never see the sun. And he has charged us, in this dark and dismal realm, to torture the wayward souls of men, with no hope of ever regaining the lofty halls of heaven. An im- 180 mensity of earth imprisons us here with an immense barrier. Our share of heaven has been given to mankind as their lot. But that is not all. Once more he takes up arms against us, once more he intends to wage war. Surely he will expel us even from these nether realms.

"For this reason he has sent a young man down from his airy citadel, either his Son or one of the winged brethren. And soon he 185 will come. Relying upon the weaponry of heaven, he will bring an end to this realm, throw open the underworld, and carry away those souls conceded to our care. Unless we take action, it may be that the victor will bind even us in tight chains, and carry us in tri- 190 umph up to heaven. There, throughout its entire breadth and length, the angels will mock us in our captivity.

'Iste autem, quanvis mortalia membra caducus
induerit, tamen est nostris imperditus armis.
195   Nempe ego saepe adii coramque interritus urgens
tentavi insidiis nequicquam. (Non ea me res
falsum habuit, neque enim nunc primum talia cerno.)
Quas non in facies, quae non mutatus in ora
accessi incassum? Semper me reppulit ipse,
200   non armis ullis fretus, non viribus usus,
sed tantum veterum repetito carmine vatum
irrita tentamenta, dolos et vim exiit omnem.
        'Ergo quae mihi nunc surgit sententia pandam.
Ille iter antiquas Solymorum instaurat ad arces,
205   sit licet invisus magnae primoribus urbis;
quippe sacerdotes odiis ingentibus illi
infensi insidias, ut cuique est copia, tendunt,
solliciti veterum pro relligione parentum,
ut ferro incautum superent et funere mulctent,
210   quandoquidem ille novos ritus, nova sacra per urbes
instituit priscasque audet rescindere leges.
Hic opibus vestris opus. En nunc confieri rem
tempus adest! In eum cuncti maioribus illos
inflammate odiis et vera et prava canentes
215   pestiferumque animis furtim inspirate venenum.
Ne victi oblitique iras corda aspera ponant,
sed saevi magis atque magis stimulisque subacti
acribus absistant nunquam, nisi caede peracta.
Si vero, si quis sociis ex ipsius unum
220   bis senis capere atque dolis pervertere possit,
res confecta; metus penitus sublatus et omnis.
Praecipitate moras; fluxis succurrite rebus.
Nunc tectis opus insidiis, nunc viribus usus.'
        Vix ea fatus, ubique ruentes iussa facessunt
225   auctores scelerum portisque ex omnibus alte

"And though this young man has taken on mortality and human form, he is impervious to our arms. I myself have gone to him often, fearlessly and urgently tempting him face to face with 195 every feint I knew. But in vain. This fact did not escape me, nor do I realize it only now. What forms, what faces did I not put on, and all in vain! Each time he repelled me, not with force or arms: simply by repeating the scriptures of the prophets of old, he es- 200 caped each seduction, each stratagem and assault.

"So I will now unfold the plan that has risen within me. He has undertaken a journey to the ancient gates of Jerusalem, though he is loathed by the leaders of that great city. The priests, full of 205 hatred for the man, have set against him all the snares that each has at his disposal. To guard the religion of their ancestors, they mean to throw him unawares in irons and punish him with death. For he has established new rites and sacraments throughout the cities of Judaea and he dares to revoke the ancient laws. In this I 210 need your help. Now is the time to act! I want all of you to inflame the priests with ever greater hatred for this man. Tell them truths. Tell them falsehoods. Go secretly and fill their hearts with pestilent poison. Do not allow them, vanquished and forgetful of 215 their wrath, to set aside their hard hearts. Ever more savagely, ever more driven by your sharp goads, may they never give in until his death has been compassed! But if someone could capture one of his twelve followers and seduce him with deceit, the problem 220 would be solved and all fear would be lifted from us. But brook no delay. Come to the rescue while all is in an uproar. Now is the time for covert stratagems and outright force."

No sooner had he spoken than these authors of crimes hastened to do his will, bursting in all directions through every gateway in their ascent. The underworld trembled in all directions at 225

diversi rumpunt; tremit abdita murmure tellus.
Incubuere auris, crinitas anguibus alas
obscurum per inane movent terrasque capessunt.
Non tam olim densa sublimes nube per auras
230 florilegae glomerantur apes aestate serena
nubifugo Borea et madidis cessantibus Austris,
si quando exorta est inter discordia reges
saevaque collatis invadunt praelia signis.
Vae,³ quibus institerint terris, quibus orbis in oris
235 dira cohors! Quantas populis feret illa ruinas?
     Iamque emensus iter multis comitantibus heros,
vera dei soboles, Bethanes moenibus instat.
Cernit ibi moestas crinem laniare sorores,
munera fraterno tumulo suprema ferentes:
240 expertem thalami Marthan atque urbis avitae
Magdali dictam de nomine Magdalenam.
Progreditur bustumque petit. Moestissima Martha,
hunc simul ac vidit, comites fratrisque sepulcrum
deserit ac multo venienti occurrit honore;
245 insequitur soror inde, oculos ambae imbre madentes,
foemineis ambae plangoribus indulgentes.
'Ut te post cari germani funera tandem
accipimus venientem! Ut te saepe ille vocabat,
magne hospes, gelidi perfusus frigore leti!
250 Atque equidem credo, tunc sors te si qua dedisset
nobis, nunc etiam vitales duceret auras.
Nunc quoque (nil quando clari tibi rector Olympi
abnuit) haud penitus nobis spes omnis adempta est.'
     Talibus orabant; comites simul omnia luctu
255 miscebant; moestis resonabant cuncta querelis.
Ast heros tristes dictis solatus amicis,
spondet opem, superas rediturum ad luminis auras

the sound. Riding the winds, through the dark void they beat
their wings, bristling with snakes, and eagerly seized upon the varied lands. So dense a cloud was never formed aloft by the flower-
culling bees, when, in the serenity of summer, cloud-clearing   230
Boreas and rainy Auster cease to blow, and the discordant kings of
the hives rush into battle with their clashing standards. Woe unto
those lands, woe unto those shores where this dire cohort alights!
And what ruin will they visit upon the nations of the earth!   235

Together with a multitude of his followers, the hero, true
offspring of God, completed his journey and reached the walls of
Bethany. There he saw two weeping sisters who tore their hair as
they brought the final offerings to the tomb of their brother. One
of them, Martha, was unmarried. The other went by the name of   240
Magdalena, since her family was from the town of Magdala. As Jesus approached the tomb, the disconsolate Martha saw him. She
left her companions and the grave of her brother and with much
reverence, met him as he came. Her sister followed her and now
their eyes filled with tears as they gave way to a woman's lamenta-   245
tions. "Finally you came, but only after our poor brother died.
Good friend, how often he called to you as he lay in the cold grip
of death. And I am certain that, if somehow chance had brought
you to us sooner, he would still be drawing breath now. And be-   250
cause the lord of bright heaven denies you nothing, even now all
hope has not been taken from us."

So they besought him. Their friends threw all into confusion
with their weeping and the place resounded with lamentation. But   255
with kind words the hero consoled them in their sadness and
promised to help. He assured them that their brother would soon

actutum fratrem incolumem, quem faucibus haustum
telluris quarto iam sol non viderat ortu.

260   Diditur haec totam confestim fama per urbem,
quae cunctis incredibilisque et mira videri.
Vicinis populi passim de montibus omnes
concurrunt studio visendi atque omnia complent.
Ventum erat ad tumulum; stat circunfusa iuventus.

265 Ipse autem in medio duplices ad sidera palmas
iandudum tendens oculosque immobilis heros
orabat tacitusque parentem in vota vocabat.
Orantem observant taciti, intentique tuentur
quid iubeat, quae signa ferat, quo deinde cadat res.

270 Bis toto color ore abiit; bis pectore anhelo
infremuit nutuque caput concussit honestum.
Ecce autem tumuli tremere hostia[4] visa repente.
Omnibus extemplo subita formidine sanguis
diriguit penitusque invasit pectora frigus,

275 cum tandem deus has effudit ad aethera voces:
'Summe parens, quamvis precibus nil abnuis unquam
ipse meis quaecunque petam, tamen hoc tibi grates
munere semper agam. Tua quanta potentia vidit
circunfusa manus, populi videre frequentes.

280 Vos autem famuli, properate, recludite marmor,
saxum ingens auferte viroque exolvite vittas.'

    Nec mora praeceptis; patuerunt claustra sepulcri.
Concursu accedunt magno attonitique pavore
inspectantque videntque intus deforme cadaver,

285 vixque sibi credunt nullo cogente moveri.
Nec mora; clamantis ter voce vocatus amici
erigitur loquiturque et coeli vescitur auris.
Obstupuere omnes, nec sat vidisse loquentem
aut audisse semel, dum cuncta ex ordine narrat

290 conventu in medio: quae funere passus in ipso est,

return unharmed to the light and breezes of this world, even though the sun had not shone upon him for four days, swallowed up as he was by the jaws of earth.

At once the rumor of these words spread through the town, words that seemed incredible, even miraculous to everyone. From all the neighboring mountains the entire population came running and filled the city in eagerness to see what would happen. They converged upon the tomb, which was now surrounded by the town's youth. For some time, the hero stood motionless in the very center, his hands and eyes raised to heaven, and in the silence of prayer he called to his Father. In equal silence and tension the townspeople observed him, wondering what he might command, what signs he might make, what the outcome would be. Twice his face went white. Twice he groaned in his breathless chest and nodded his noble head. And lo, the doors of the tomb suddenly seemed to tremble. All at once, a sudden fear froze the blood in each of the onlookers and a chill invaded the depths of their hearts. Finally, the Son of God addressed these words on high: "Father in heaven, until now you have never denied my prayers, whatever I asked. But for this favor especially, I will be eternally grateful to you. This small group, and this great populace have seen how vast your power is. Now, you servants, make haste and remove the marble lid of the tomb. Lift up the huge stone and remove that man's cerements."

Without delay the sepulcher was opened. The crowd rushed forward and looked in, stricken with fear. When they saw the misshapen cadaver, they could hardly believe that it was moving on its own. Without delay, after his friend Jesus called to him three times, the man arose and spoke, breathing in the air of heaven. Everyone was dumbstruck. It was not enough to see him or hear him speak only once as he stood among them, repeating everything he had experienced in death and the pain his soul felt when, shut out

260

265

270

275

280

285

290

quanto anima instantis vi leti exclusa dolore
terrenosque diu eluctata reliquerit artus,
quas facies moriens, quam obscoena aspexerit ora
terrentum iuxta furiarum irasque minasque,
295   ut vix siderea volucres missi arce ministri
auxilio possent avidas inhibere rapinis.
His addit scelerum poenas ac laeta piorum
praemia quaeve animas miseras subiisse necesse est
arbitria aeternosque nigris fornacibus ignes.
300   His actis deus orantis vicina Simonis
tecta subit, quem tota olim lacerum ulcere membra
eripuit morbo atque in pristina reddidit ipse.
Dum vero mensas grati dignatus amici
accubat in medio procerum urbis, protinus ecce
305   ingreditur forma insignis cultuque puella,
picta peregrinas tunicasque sinusque crepanti
argento saturos atque auro intertexto,
cui caput implicitum gemmis. It flexile collo
aurum ingens mixtis onerosa monilia baccis,[5]
310   propexique nitent electro molle capilli,
nexilibus quos in nodos collegerat hamis,
aureaque ex humero demissam fibula vestem
Eois opibus gravidam et Gangetide gaza
subnectit. Media micat ardens fronte pyropus,
315   crebraque consertis pendent redimicula gemmis,
qualis laeta sinus cum tellus veris honorem
pandit opesque suas gremio explicat alma virenti.
     Haec olim amissis utrisque parentibus orba
restitit, et proles in opes successit avitas
320   unica, quas pater immensas praedives habebat.
Dumque aetas rudis, una illi super omnia cordi
relligio fuit et servandi cura pudoris.
Mox autem paulatim annis fervente iuventa

by the force of imminent death, it struggled relentlessly to free itself from its earthly body. Lazarus described the faces he had seen
in dying, dread forms of furies standing terrifyingly close, with
such angry menace that even the winged messengers sent down
from the starry citadel could scarcely stop their rapine. He spoke   295
of the penalties for sins and the joyous rewards for virtue, the
judgments that sad souls must undergo, the eternal fires in their
black furnaces.

After this miracle, God was invited into the nearby house of Si-   300
mon, whose entire body, wasted and ulcerated, he had once freed
from sickness and restored to health. As he deigned to sit at the
table of his grateful friend, together with the leaders of the town,
suddenly a girl entered, striking in beauty and attire, resplendent   305
in her foreign robes. She was girt round with tinkling silver inter-
mingled with gold and her head was adorned with gems. Her neck
was encircled by a large and heavy chain of gold curiously wrought
with pearls. Her hair, combed downwards, gleamed with pliant
amber and was tied in knots with pins. From her shoulders a robe   310
descended, held fast by a golden fibula and laden with the wealth
of the East and the treasures of the Ganges. A flaming ruby
gleamed in the middle of her forehead and many a ribbon was
hung with gems made fast. She was like the earth that, from its   315
fertile breast, discloses the grace of spring and of its goodness
pours forth the favors of its green lap.

Orphaned of both her parents, she was the only heir to the ancestral wealth that her father had in great abundance. When she   320
was still young, she cared more for religion than anything else,
and she was intent upon preserving her maidenhood. But as the
years went by, in the heat of youth, the misguiding passion of

sensibus illapsa est Veneris malesuada cupido,
325   quae mentem immutans furiis subiecit iniquis,
ah miseram! Abiecto non obstat cura pudori;
non species, non fama movet. Cessit timor omnis,
relligioque oblita, domo iam nubilis exit;
iam convivia, iam spectacula laeta frequentat,
330   vinclaque contemptis rectoribus omnia rumpit,
ac veluti ratis Aegaeo sine remige in alto,
sublatos simul ac fluctus inflaverit aura,
nunc huc incerto, deinde illuc fluctuat aestu,
quo ventique undaeque urgent spoliata magistro.
335   Et iam freta opibus praedulces ambit amores
florentum iuvenum, si quis spectabilis ore
egregio formaque alios supereminet omnes.
    Ergo laeta virum praestanti corpore postquam
accepit venisse, deum quem fama ferebat,
340   nullam passa moram studio correpta videndi
venerat. Ast, ubi conspicuos deperdita vultus
hausit et egregiae divinum frontis honorem
divinosque oculos, ardentis pabula amoris,
diriguit penitusque animo sententia versa est
345   atque alias longe concepit pectore flammas.
Ecce autem subito visae spirantis ab ore
septem adeo circum offusa caligine et atra
nube exire faces, veluti cum torris obusti
ultima sursum flamma fugit fumumque relinquit.
350   'Haec,' deus, 'haec,' inquit, 'capitum foedissima septem
correptam miserae mentem vexabat Erinnys.'
Tum Maria (hoc illi nomen) mutata, nec illa
argento quae illusa sinus modo venerat aureos.
    Iam capiti crinale aurum colloque monile
355   detrahit et tunicas squalentes exuit auro.
Iamque sui piget et curis mordetur honestis.

Venus insinuated itself into her senses, altering her mind and sub- jecting her, poor thing, to shameful passions. She gave no care to 325 her abandoned chastity. She thought nothing of appearances or ill- repute. All fear was abandoned, all piety forgotten. Now, though unmarried, she left her house, frequenting feasts and gay specta- cles. Showing contempt for her guardians, she abandoned all re- straint. She was like an oarless vessel on the Aegean: once the 330 wind has vexed the high waves, it is tossed this way and that upon the deep without a pilot, buffeted by the wind and the waves. Even so did she, with her great wealth, crave the sweet love of 335 young men in their prime, men whose handsome face or form sur- passed all others.

So it was that when she heard that a handsome man had ar- rived, who was rumored to be a god, without delay she eagerly hastened to see him. But when she, lovestruck, saw his noble face 340 and the godly beauty of his fine forehead and divine eyes, the food of burning love, she stiffened and deep down she had a change of heart, and a passion of a very different kind seized her. All at once, 345 as she exhaled from her mouth, seven torches were seen to depart, suffused with the darkness of a black cloud, as when the last flame of a spent firebrand shoots up and leaves only smoke behind. "Be- hold!" Jesus said. "This foul, seven-headed Fury seized the mind 350 of this poor woman and vexed her." Suddenly Mary, for such was her name, was a changed woman, no longer the one who had just entered, her golden robes tricked out with silver.

At once she removed the golden chaplet from her hair and the pendant from her neck, and took off those clothes stiff with gold. 355 Soon she grew ashamed of herself and was vexed by cares, but honorable ones. She asked the Lord to pardon her and fell to her

Inde deum orabat veniam genibusque volutans,
ut canis ad mensam procumbere suetus herilem,
lambebatque pedes nudos lachrymisque rigabat,
360   veste fovens, alios tulerat quam nuper in usus.
Tum de marmoreis varios deprompsit odores
thesauris, casias et nardi mollis aristas
aut thuris lachrymam atque auram fragrantis amomi,
pronaque permulsit nudas liquido unguine plantas;
365   suavis in aereas diffugit spiritus auras.
Cuncta deus placida quae mente accepit et illam
dignatus venia, monitis implevit amicis.
    Interea circumpositis ex urbibus aegrum
cernere vulgus erat conventu accedere magno.
370   Multi ibant oculis clausis, multi auribus orti
indociles, fandi ignari, quique aegra trahebant
membra, ferebantur, quosve exagitabat Erinnys
captos mente, sui immemores, deus ipse iuvabat
auxilio validique omnes laetique redibant.
375   Tandem hinc digrediens Solymorum tendit ad arces.
Hanc fundasse Semes, soboles tua, dicitur urbem,
vitisator pater, exactis simul imbribus ingens
cessavit vastis stagnare paludibus orbis
plurimaque immensi compressa licentia ponti.
380   Tum venere suo bellis qui gente subacta
urbem appellarunt de nomine Iebusaei.
Protinus hinc reges, a prisco sanguis Iuda,
Finitimis late dominam coluere subactis.
Hic templum Solomon per terras omnibus aris
385   eversis ope barbarica rex condidit olim
templum opulentum, ingens, eductam ad sidera molem.
Huc mensas arasque sacras et ahenea labra
transtulit et veteris vestes ac munera templi,
ostro perfusas vestes auroque rigentes;

knees. Like a dog accustomed to sit beside her master's table, she began to kiss his naked feet, drenching them in warm tears and wiping them with the robe that, until recently, she had worn for other ends. Then from a marble casket she brought forth sundry 360 perfumes, cassia, stalks of delicate spikenard, odorous gums and a whiff of fragrant balsam. Bending forward, she anointed his feet with gleaming unguent. A sweet smell rose through the air. The 365 lord accepted all of these things with a happy countenance and, deigning to pardon her, he filled her with kindly advice.

Now from the surrounding cities, a dense multitude of sick people approached. Many were blind. Many were mute, or they were deaf and could not be taught. Those whose limbs were too 370 weak to bear them were carried by others. Those whom the Erynnis had maddened, those who scarcely knew themselves, the Son of God helped personally, and they returned home happy and hale.

Finally he left the town and hastened to Jerusalem. O patriarch 375 and sower of the vine, your son Shem is said to have founded this city when the rains ended, when the great earth ceased to stagnate in vast swamps and the ungoverned force of the immense ocean was finally contained. It was then that the Jebusites arrived: having worsted the indigenous nation in war, they named the city after 380 themselves. Soon there emerged kings, the blood of ancient Judah, who developed the city into a capital, having conquered the neighboring lands far and wide. Here King Solomon built his temple with barbaric opulence, once he had overturned all the altars throughout his dominion. It was a vast and opulent temple, a pile 385 rising to heaven. Hither he brought tables and sacred altars and basins of brass. From the old temple he brought sundry adornments and embroideries dyed purple and stiff with gold. Lamps as

390 tum lychnos lancesque cavasque invexit acerras
cymbiaque et tripodas fulvoque ex aere lebetas
inclusasque sacro leges ac foedera ligno,
quae gemina in silice omnipotens pater ipse notarat.
Hic gentis rex atque omni cum gente sacerdos
395 sacra ferens pecudum fundebat rite cruorem;
victima non alias maculabat sanguine sedes.
Undique mos erat huc populos ter adire quotannis
et proprios genus Isacidum instaurabat honores.
Ipse etiam huc heros crebro se ferre solebat.
400   Iamque viis plenis multis cum millibus ibat,
unde urbis poterant turres atque alta videri
culmina. Laeti omnes ramos viridantis olivae
quasque manu gestent, palmas a stirpe refringunt.
Praecedit peditum late manus omnis; it ingens
405 pone equitum globus; in medio pulcherrimus heros
haud acri provectus equo phalerisque superbo
eminet. At sibi pauperiem ut placuisse beatam
admoneat socios, rex quadrupedantis aselli
terga premit, vates quondam ut cecinere futurum.
410 Nudus erat vertex; humeris demissa fluebat
ad talos vestis, quam festinaverat olim
ipsa parens pueroque dedit gestare, nec illa est
ullo attrita usu, nulla consumpta senecta.
Taurea nudatis circundat tegmina plantis.
415 Talis iter tendit recipitque ad moenia gressum.
        Ante urbem pueri occurrunt mixtaeque puellae
floribus ac variis ornatae tempora sertis.
Omnibus in manibus palmae, omnes carmina laeti
laeta canunt, tonsis et inumbrant ora coronis,
420 certatimque dei gaudent placida ora tueri.
Tum demum portis urbem ingrediuntur apertis
et propius regem servatoremque salutant

well he brought and plates and hollow censers, cups and tripods   390
and cauldrons of gleaming bronze. Finally, in a sacred tabernacle
of wood, he brought the laws and covenants that the omnipotent
Father himself had engraved in stone on twin tablets. Here the
kingly priest, with all his people, carried the holy objects and ritu-
ally spilt the blood of sheep. No other altar was stained with the   395
gore of victims. It was traditional for the people to come here
three times a year, the sons of Isaac having established the prescribed rite. The hero himself used to come here often.

Now the roads filled with many thousands of his followers, and   400
as he approached the city, its towers and roof-tops came into view.
Joyously all the citizens tore branches from flowering olive trees
and pulled palm-fronds from their stalks to carry in their hands.
Far in advance of the rest came the ranks of citizens on foot, followed at a distance by a huge number on horseback. In their midst   405
the hero stood out splendidly. But he was hardly borne upon a
proud horse dazzlingly caparisoned. To teach his followers that he
preferred blessed poverty, the king sat upon the back of a four-
legged ass, as the prophets had once foretold. Jesus's head was
bare. From his shoulders to his feet, a robe descended that his   410
mother had busied herself making for him when he was a boy —
though it was not frayed by any use nor worn away with age — and
leather shoes covered his feet. Such was his appearance as he approached the city's walls.   415

Boys ran out of the city to greet him and girls as well, their hair
adorned with colorful flowers. In every hand was a palm-leaf. All
the people were overjoyed, singing songs and shading their faces
with trim garlands, as they competed ecstatically to look upon the
serene features of the Son of God. Finally they entered the city   420
through the opened gates, and from up close they hailed their king
and savior, holding out to him their thyrsi and waving their olive

praetenduntque manu thyrsos oleasque coruscant
frondentis. Superas ingens it clamor ad auras.
425 Spargitur hic rumor subito ac tota urbe vagatur.
Consurgunt gentis primi. Procul ecce per auras
pulveream cernunt tolli super aethera nubem;
ignari penitus rerum causasque requirunt
tam subiti motus, quem nam tam multa sequantur
430 millia ductorem, quis tantus clamor ovantum.
Ast illi, quibus est divi haud incognita fama,
occurrunt alacres regi plausumque sequentes
ingeminant, quaque ingreditur, passim ecce rubenti
insternunt ostro sola barbaricisque tapetis
435 intenduntque vias sertis et floribus augent.
    Vix ingressus erat, cum densam respicit ecce
in bivio turbam clamoremque auribus haurit
ingentem et secum admirans vestigia pressit.
Vallis erat circum frondosis undique septa
440 collibus; in medio rivis atque imbribus humor
collectus semper stabat laticesque perennes,
quo solitae innuptae praedivitis urbis aquari,
et potum pariter pecudes compellere prisci
pastores lymphaque gregem curare salubri,
445 unde Lacum fama est Ovium[6] dixisse minores.
    Huc concursus erat certis de more diebus
turbaque adibat, inops, variis exercita morbis.
Nanque videbatur magno quandoque moveri
cum sonitu, medio unda lacu et perculsa repente
450 sublato ad coelum spumabant coerula fluctu.
Sed vulgo subiti quae motus causa latebat.
Impubes pueri tantum innuptaeque puellae
signa prius manifesta dabant seseque canebant
cernere pennatum puerum fulgere per auras
455 undanti chlamyde atque auro radiantibus alis

28

branches. A huge roar went up to heaven. Suddenly word of his
arrival spread through the city and the leaders of the people rose   425
into action. From afar, they could see a cloud of dust rising
through the air. Having no idea what was happening, they eagerly
sought the cause of such a sudden commotion. They also wanted
to know the identity of this man whom so many thousands followed and greeted with a clamorous ovation. But others, recogniz-   430
ing his divinity, ran eagerly to their king, redoubling their cries
as they followed. Wherever he went, behold, they strewed the
ground with dazzling red cloth and carpets from barbarian lands,
and they embowered the streets with richly woven flowers!   435

Scarcely had he entered the city when at a crossroads he saw a
dense crowd and heard their loud clamor. Marvelling to himself,
he checked his steps. There was a valley covered on all sides with
leafy hills. In its midst were perennial streams and a pool always
fed by rain water and springs. Here the unmarried maidens of this   440
wealthy city went to fetch water. Here shepherds of old drove
their flocks to drink, nourishing them with its salubrious waters,
which is why subsequent generations called it the Sheep Pool.   445

It was the custom on certain days for people to gather here, a
luckless crowd afflicted with sundry ailments. For a wave seemed
at times to bestir itself with a great noise in the middle of the
pool, and suddenly the blue waters would rise into the sky. But the   450
people were ignorant of the cause of this movement. Beardless
boys, however, and unmarried maidens told of clear portents of
the event, and claimed they could see a winged youth, with
flowing robes and golden wings, shining aloft. Descending from   455

delapsumque polo tranquilla impellere utraque
stagna manu lateque viam signare cadentem.
Qualis stella pater superum quam misit Olympo
aut nautis signum aut populis in castra coactis,
460   praecipitat flammis longe lateque coruscis
scintillans: corda ignaris mortalibus horrent.
      Ergo expectabant denso miseri agmine circum
e coelo signum intenti laticesque quietos
servabant oculis atque omnes auribus auras,
465   auditum ad signum subito ut se primus in undas
quisque daret stagnoque sonanti immergeret artus.
Quippe erat inde salus semper non pluribus, uni
qui subito impulsum prior exiliisset in aequor.
Sicut ubi vacui tendunt medio aequore campi
470   viribus et rapido iuvenes decernere cursu,
arrexere animos cuncti signumque parati
expectant. Pulsat pavor intus pectora anhelus
omnibus atque locum spondet sibi quisque priorem.
      Hos inter longo detentus brachia morbo
475   brachiaque et plantas, omnes et inutilis artus
Ietrus erat, cui quondam et opes et avita fuere
praedia opima, sed, ut iuvenili e corpore morbum
pelleret, heu! nimium mendaci credidit arti,
dumque vias omnis medicaeque explorat opis vim,
480   pauperiem morbo adiecit miserandus iniquam,
ossibus ad vivum qui iam persederat imis.
Iamque fere denum in luctu quater egerat annum
innumeris circunventus morbisque fameque,
quem postquam aspexit propius stellantis Olympi
485   rege satus, sic est ultro placido ore loquutus:
'Infelix, quae te segnis mora detinet unum
servantem has frustra ripas et tristibus undam
praesentem morbis, alii cum scilicet omnes

heaven, he would agitate the pond with both hands and mark his
path as he descended. Like a star that God sent down from heaven
as a sign to sailors or soldiers in their camps, he fell headlong,
glowing far and wide with radiant flames. And the hearts of igno-   460
rant men shuddered.

And so the poor people crowded together, eagerly awaiting
some signal from heaven. Each man watched the still waters and
listened to all the breezes, so as to be the first to jump into the
sounding waters. For health was granted not to all, but only to the   465
first to jump in as the water stirred. Just as young men hasten to
the level ground of an open field to compete in strength and speed
of limb, so all who were present at the pond aroused their souls   470
and awaited the signal. Vowing to be first, every one of them stood
there breathless, with fear in his heart.

Among those afflicted with chronic illness was Jethro, who
suffered ailments in his arms and feet, indeed, in his entire body.   475
Once he had been wealthy in his ancestral farms. But in order to
expel the illness from his young body, alas, he had trusted too
much in the lies of quacks. And so, as he explored every possible
solution as well as the force of medicine's power, the poor man
undeservingly added poverty to the illness that had lodged itself in   480
the very marrow of his bones. For nearly forty years he had been
afflicted by hunger and illness of every sort. After the Son of God
looked more closely at the man, he spoke softly to him. "Unhappy   485
man, why do you alone linger here in vain, beside the salubrious

protinus hinc abeant laeti oblitique laborum
490 accipiant solitas reparato in corpore vires?'
    Ille sub haec largoque genas simul imbre rigabat.
'Non hoc crimen aquae, non vis mihi fontis iniqua est,
verum ego dum motum opperior salientis aquai,
praecipites dant saltu alii se in stagna priores
495 ad sonitum; invalidis nequeo ipse insistere plantis,
nec me tunc opis externae dignatur egentem
in stagno quisquam ante alios mersare salubri.'
Talia narrantem placido deus ore tuetur
atque ait: 'Ipse tuis pedibus subsiste valensque
500 carpe viam, nec cuncta undis debere necesse est.'
Vix ea, cum subito cernentibus omnibus ecce
erigitur stratumque humeris, mirabile visu,
ipse suis referens pedes omnes passibus aequat,
atque suo solidae respondent robore vires.
505 Sicut ubi in silvis, dum ramos colligit, anguem
frigore sopitum pastor brumaque rigentem
frondibus implicuit admovitque inscius igni,
nulla mora est, propius flammas vix pertulit et iam
attollitque caput iamque ignea lumina torquet
510 perque domum serpens micat arduus ore trilingui.
    Parte alia ante fores templi mediaque ministri
ingenti strepitu testudine dona sedentes
vendebant, quae plebs aeratae imponeret arae,
lanigeras pecudes taurosque paresque columbas,
515 voti ut quisque reus rerumque ut copia cuique.
Quos simul atque heros ingressus vidit et omnem
discursu et clamore locum resonare profano,
haud tulit, et verbis graviter commotus acerbis
reppulit, intortum vibrans per terga flagellum,
520 verberaque insonuit sacroque a limine abegit.
Qualis ubi Arctois Boreas erupit ab antris,

water's edge? All the others depart in joy, forgetting their afflictions and reclaiming the wonted vigor of their bodies."   490

At this the man wept and tears streamed down his cheeks.
"This is no fault of the water. Its power is not unjust to me.
Rather while I wait for the water to leap up, others jump in before
me. My feet are too weak to stand. And because I need another to   495
help me, no one is willing to immerse me in the health-restoring
waters before others can jump in." The god looked at him kindly.
"Rise up on your on two feet and go your ways, restored to health!
You need not owe everything to the waters." Scarcely had he spo-   500
ken when everyone saw an extraordinary sight: the man stood up
and, regaining his former strength, he placed his mat on his shoulders and walked steadily and without difficulty. As when a shepherd, foraging for branches in the woods, picks up a serpent en-   505
tangled in the leaves that is overcome with cold and stiff with
frost, then heedlessly brings it home and sets it near the hearth.
All at once, it lifts its head and whirls its fiery eyes, until it crawls
throughout the house, rising up and flashing its forked tongue.   510

In another part of the city, servants of the temple were sitting
before its doors, under the portico. Clamorously they sold offerings to place on the brazen altar: woolly sheep, oxen and paired
doves, according to each man's trangression and his means. But as   515
soon as the hero entered and found the place bustling with profane commerce, he could hardly bear it. Deeply moved, he sharply
rebuked the sellers and struck their backs with a twisted scourge,
driving them from the sacred doorstep to the sound of the lash.   520
He was like Boreas bursting from its arctic caves, its swift blast
sweeping through the fields of air: passing wildly across the heav-

aereos rapido perverrens turbine campos,
it coelo ferus et piceas toto aethere nubes
insequitur; dant victa locum et cava nubila cedunt.
525   'Sacra deo domus haec,' inquit, 'haec numinis aedes;
vos autem versam indignos scelerastis in usus.
Sanguine respersum est aras animaque litatum
hactenus antiquis concesso more sacrorum.
Indultum satis atque ovium iam caedis abunde est.
530   Nunc pater omnipotens pecudum volucrumque cruori
parcere vos posthac iubet ac fumantibus extis.
Vos diversa manent mutatis orgia sacris.
Discite iustitiam tantum puraque litate
mente deumque piis precibus placate volentem.
535   Hi vestri ritus, ea deinde piacula sunto.'
Sic ait, et supplex demisso poplite ad aram
cernuus arcana prece patris numen adorat.
     Iamque sacerdotum primis exarserat ingens
tristi in corde dolor, flammaeque iraeque coquebant.
540   Nec novus hic primum furor, haec odia aspera surgunt.
Antiquae irarum causae antiquique dolores
haudquaquam exciderant animis fixique manebant.
Non tamen hic ausi sunt illum surgere contra,
sed veriti ultricem plebem turbamque sequentum,
545   excessere adytis, nequicquam indigna minati.
Quales nocte lupi stabulis cum forte reclusis
appetiere gregem, verum custodia pernox
obstitit et canibus vocalibus inde revulsit;
olli (dira fames stimulis agit intus) abacti
550   cedunt et montes nequicquam ululatibus implent.
     Dum vero affatur genitorem divus ad aram,
mirantes socii templum per singula lustrant,
suspectu molem vasto artificumque laborem:
Cautibus excisas centum, centum aere columnas,

ens, it drives the dark clouds from the sky until, vanquished and insubstantial, they yield and give way. "This house is sacred to 525 God," he said, "This is the house of the Lord. But you profane it and pervert it to base uses. Until now the altars have been strewn with blood and you have worshipped in the manner permitted by your ancestors. But enough of that. More than enough sheep's blood has been spilt. The Almighty Father commands you hereaf- 530 ter to spare the blood and smoking entrails of birds and sheep. Only learn justice and worship with a pure mind, seeking to placate an indulgent God with pious prayers. Let these be your rites and your atonements!" So he spoke. And then with bended knee 535 he approached the altar and, bowing his head, offered up a secret prayer to his Father's divinity.

Now great pain and anger burned in the aggrieved hearts of the chief priests. Nor was that the first time they had felt this rage or sharp hatred. Hardly had they forgotten their inveterate anger and 540 ancient pain, which remained fixed in their hearts. For now, however, they dared not rise against him. Fearing the vengence of the citizens and his mob of followers, they left the temple, vainly threatening reprisals. They were like nocturnal wolves: if by 545 chance the stable doors are left open, they hungily eye the flock within. But they are held at bay by barking dogs that steadfastly keep watch throughout the night. Though spurred by sharp hunger, they yield and are driven back, vainly filling the hills with their baying. 550

While the Son of God prayed to his Father at the altar, his followers wandered through the temple, marveling at each detail of the building, gazing up at its huge mass and the labors of its artisans: one hundred columns of stone, a hundred more of solid

555 omnes e solido, omnes altis montibus aequas,
     tignaque et aeterna ex cedro laquearia, ahenoque
     aeratas porro stridentes cardine portas,
     sectilibusque minutatim sola levia saxis.
     Tum puro ex auro postes mensasque metallo
560 e simili et fixos alta ad donaria currus
     distinctos ebeno et candenti elephanto.

       Quae dum cuncta legunt, perfectis ordine votis
     improvisus adest tacitusque supervenit heros,
     atque ait: 'Haec moles, adeo haec immania templa,
565 protinus ut vento radicitus eruta pinus,
     versa repente dabunt labem ingentemque ruinam,
     et tibi digna tuis, Solyma, instant praemia factis,
     quae vates ad te missos divinitus ausa es
     tot ferro petere aut duris detrudere saxis.
570 Ipse tuos quoties, praesens ut vera monerem,
     tentavi cives incassum cogere in unum,
     ceu cristata suos dispersa examina foetus
     singultu volucris vocat et plaudentibus alis!
     Ferro excisa cades; iam iam labentia regna
575 protinus arma ruent tua, vindexque hauriet ignis,
     et passim haec largo sudabit sanguine tellus.
     Nonne vides iam ut nunc res procubet inclinata
     et tibi iam votis non prosit nectere vota?
     Longe alias pater omnipotens sacra transtulit oras;
580 longe alia vult ipse coli et placarier urbe.
     Atque adeo hic alte depactus terminus esto.'

       Sic fatus, monstrat miras in marmore formas,
     argumentum ingens, senum monimenta dierum
     magna quibus magni compacta est machina mundi,
585 et veterum eventus et prisca ex ordine avorum
     facta, haud humanis opus enarrabile verbis.
     Non illic hominum effigies simulacrave divum,

bronze, tall as lofty mountains; beams and coffers hewn from ever- 555
lasting cedar; bronze doors that resounded on brazen jambs;
smoothed floors painstakingly inlaid with cut stone. They also saw
door-posts fashioned from pure gold, as well as golden tables and
chariots, placed upon the altars as votive offerings that gleamed 560
with ivory and ebony.

No sooner had they made their tour than the hero appeared
suddenly and silently, having completed his prayers. "This massive
building," he said, "like a pine tree uprooted by the wind, will be 565
overturned in an instant, bringing with it great ruin and collapse.
O City of Solomon! A retribution awaits you that is worthy of
your deeds, you who dared to stone and slaughter so many prophets sent to you by the divine will! How often have I come here,
vainly seeking to bring the citizens together to teach them the 570
truth, like the crested bird that beats its wings, sobbing for its
scattered young! But you will fall by the sword. Soon, soon your
tottering realms and all your arms will run aground, consumed by
avenging fire. Far and wide this land will be covered in blood! 575
Don't you see this peril lying before you already? Don't you understand that there is no more use in stringing prayers together? The
Almighty Father has transferred his sacraments to a distant land.
He wishes to be worshipped and prayed to in another city far off.
Let this end be fixed and immutable." 580

So speaking, he pointed to the dazzling forms sculpted in marble, which gave a noble account of the six days in which the great
machine of the world was created. They also told of great events
in the distant past, relating in order the ancient deeds of the patriarchs. It was a story that could hardly be contained in human 585
words. There were no representations of men or gods. Rather the

arcanis sed cuncta notis signisque notavit
obscuris manus artificis, non hactenus ulli
590 cognita, non potuere ipsi deprendere vates.
    Hic superum sator informem speculatus acervum,
aeternam noctemque indigestumque profundum;
prima videbatur moliri exordia rerum
ipse micans radiis ac multa luce coruscus.
595 Iamque videbatur fulva de nube creare
stelligeri convexa poli terrasque fretumque
et lucem simul undivagam, mox unde micantes
et solis radios et coeli accenderet ignes.
Ipsi iam denso crepitare examine circum
600 auctoremque ducemque suum plausuque sonare
aligeri fratres supera arce, volatile vulgus,
lucis opus primae. Necdum tamen aethera ab imis
flammiferum terris, terras discreverat undis,
sed tantum confusa iacebant semina rerum.
605 Nec mora: vix coeli extuderat septemplicis orbem,
ordine cui vario rutilos affigeret ignes,
et iam cuncta novam incipiebant sumere formam
paulatim coelumque sua compage teneri.
    Cernere erat sicca in medio iam mole relicta
610 littoribus curvis circum maria humida fundi,
illisosque vadis spumare ad sidera fluctus.
Nondum pontivagae curvabant ampla carinae
carbasa, nec liquido lentari in marmore remi,
lata sed innocui verrebant aequora Cauri.
615 Ecce autem iam fagiferi capita ardua montes
attollunt, infraque iacent humiles convalles.
Continuo tellus summittens daedala germen
flore renidescit et frondis explicat arbos.
Iam videas viridi vestiri gramine campos,
620 iam colles densis frondere cacumina silvis

hand of the artificer had recorded everything with arcane notations and obscure signs, which to that day had never been deciphered by any man, not even by the priests. 590

Here the Creator of angels looked down upon the shapeless mass, the endless night and the lifeless deep. Radiant himself and suffused with light, he could be seen animating the most elementary particles of nature. From a dark cloud, he created the earth, 595 the sea and the vault of starry heaven. Also he brought forth the light upon the waters, from which he presently ignited the sun's gleaming rays and the fires in the night sky. Bustling in a dense throng around their Maker and their Lord, the winged multitude, 600 that airborne flock, hailed from the height of heaven the labors of the first day. But he had not yet separated the flaming sky from the lower earth or the earth from the waters. Rather, the seeds of nature remained confounded. No sooner had he hammered out the vault of sevenfold heaven, affixing to each sphere in varied order its 605 golden fire, than the universe began gradually to take shape and the heavens to remain fixed in place.

Now it was possible to see the dry land left in the midst of the mass, the watery seas rushing off it around the curving shores, and 610 the waves dashing among the shallows, their foam rising towards the stars. Not yet had sea-faring barks raised their swollen sails, nor were oars bent in the clear waters, but harmless north winds swept across the broad expanse of water. Behold how mountains, covered in beech trees, raised up their lofty heads and steep valleys 615 lay below! Suddenly the daedal earth planted seeds and burst into flower as trees shot forth leaves. Soon you might see the fields dressed in green grass and the hills, their summits covered with dense forests of oak, olive and coniferous cypresses. Straightway 620

ilicibusque oleisque et coniferis cyparissis.
Nec mora: coeruleo flammis duo lumina coelo
incipiunt teneris primum lucescere rebus,
et sibi ceu mundi vigiles statione vicissim
625 succedunt certoque suum dant foedere lumen.
Nam lucis fons dimensum sol ambit Olympum
ipse die terrasque novo splendore colorat;
nocte suas vultu pallenti servat in umbris
luna vices, fundens auratis cornibus ignem,
630 lucidaque exornant nocturnis aethera gemmis
sidera, perpetuo circunlabentia motu.
Tum bifidis passim verrebant marmora caudis
squamigerum mutae pecudes pelagoque natabant,
at pictae volucres librare per aëra pennis
635 corpora et inter se curvis decernere rostris.
Nec procul hinc errant latos armenta per agros,
lanigerique greges persultant pabula laeta.
Iam latebras videas meditari dira ferarum
semina, iam longos per humum reptare chelydros.
640 Desuper hortari clara de nube putares
coelicolum regem laetasque expromere voces:
'Crescite, propagate genus, mea semina, vestrum,
seclaque perpetuis generatim iungite seclis.'
Tandem nudus homo emicuit tellure creatus,
645 quem superum sator affarique et dicere leges
ore videbatur coram ac praeponere regnis,
qui terras immortalis ditione teneret.
Mansisset dictis, servasset foedera pacta!
At campum arboribus iuxta ac viridantibus herbis
650 lucentem aspicias, stellantia floribus arva,
poma ubi coeruleo multum vigilata draconi.[7]
In medio fons perspicuis argenteus undis,
quattuor adversis volvens regionibus amnes,

the two lights of blue heaven began for the first time to shine down with their flames upon a tender young nature, each succeeding the other in turn, like the guardians of the world, as they brought forth their light by fixed agreement. For by day the sun, 625 the fount of light, traversed the heavens, adorning the earth with new splendor. Amid the shades of night the pale moon preserved its wonted course, pouring fire from its golden horns, while the shining stars adorned the sky with their nightly jewels, gliding 630 around in a perpetual motion. Next the voiceless schools of scaly fish swept through the white-capped waters with forked tails and swam the seas, while parti-colored birds balanced their bodies on wings through the air, quarreling amongst themselves with their curved beaks. Nearby, herds of cattle wandered through wide 635 fields as woolly flocks frolicked over the luxuriant grass. Next you could see the harsh offspring of wild beasts seeking their lairs, while long serpents crept along the ground. Above the rest you could almost hear the King of Heaven exhorting them from a 640 shining cloud and declaring in happy tones: "Grow and increase your races, my offspring, and may your generations endure throughout the ages."

Finally man, still naked, was made from the earth. The Heavenly Father seemed to address him in person, laying down laws 645 and giving him, immortal, dominion over the earth. Would that that man had obeyed those commandments and kept that compact! But you could see a nearby field, resplendent with trees and green grass, and spangled with flowers, where the apples were 650 closely watched by a dusky dragon. In the middle of the field was a fountain. Its pure, silvery waters gushed in four streams over many lands, broadly irrigating the fields as it bathed the lap of the earth.

qui terrae gremio infusi late arva rigarent.
655 Atque hic cernere erat malesuadi fraude draconis
deceptum iuvenem vetitos ex arbore foetus
gustare, edicti immemorem legisque severae,
et iam (vix pomum infelix admoverat ori)
poenituisse putes se frondibus involventem,
660 nec iam coelituum regis gravia ora ferentem.
Nanque videbatur fulvae inter vellera nubis
horribili super impendens mortalibus ore
dura redarguere et saevas indicere poenas
pro meritis, quas ille olim, quas omnis ab illo
665 progenies lueret lucis ventura sub auras.
Interea coniux, quae capta libidine dira
iura prior legesque datas ac foedera solvit,
infelix fruticum frustra per densa latebat.
At victor, factusque potens iam fraudis, ahena
670 effulget squama teretique volumine serpens,
ter superans stirpem, spirisque ingentibus ambit
tortilis, et motis insultat desuper alis,
virgineo irridens deceptos improbus ore.
    Nec procul hinc ideo videas late infera circum
675 regna, subobscuras sedes lucemque malignam
solis, ubi casti manes animaeque piorum
sedibus exclusae quondam debentis Olympi
unius ob scelus expectabant ordine longo.
Stabant hic cani proceres vittataque vatum
680 agmina tendebantque manus ad sidera passas,
quos omnes humeris pater alte extantibus Abras
amplificam pandens chlamydem protentaque late
brachia subnixus dextra laevaque tegebat.
Orantes illos credas superumque parentem
685 supplicibus dictis affari, parceret irae,
parceret unius noxa omnes perdere gentes.

Here you could see the young Adam, deceived by the trickery and
evil counsel of the serpent, tasting the forbidden fruit of the tree, 655
forgetful of God's commandment and stern law, and now he had
scarcely brought the fateful apple to his mouth when you would
think he had repented his action, as he was wrapping himself in
leaves. No longer could he bear to look on the grave face of the 660
king of the heavenly host. Upon a golden, fleecy cloud, God
loomed over the mortals, sternly correcting Adam and pronounc-
ing the sentence, harsh but fair, to be paid by him and all his sons
who thereafter would emerge into the light of day. Meanwhile Eve, 665
who had earlier been seduced by savage desire into breaking the
laws and covenants of God, tried sadly and in vain to hide herself
among the thick leaves of the bushes. But the victorious serpent,
having now succeeded in his deceit, flashed his copper scales and 670
wrapped his soft tail thrice about the tree as he ascended. Twisting
around it his massive coils, he beat his wings and, looking down,
shamelessly mocked those whom he had deceived with his innocent appearance.

Nearby you could see the broad nether realms, shadowy regions
lit by a meager sun. Here chaste ghosts and pious souls waited 675
in long array, excluded from the heaven they deserved because of
one man's transgression. Here stood the white-haired elders and
the belaureled flock of prophets, raising their suppliant hands to
heaven. Spreading wide his arms and his large cloak, Father Abra- 680
ham, with his broad shoulders covered them all with both his
hands. You would think they were praying, beseeching the Almighty Father to mitigate his anger and not to destroy all the peo- 685
ples of the earth for one man's sin. Christ paused at this point and

Substitit hic imo suspirans pectore divus,
atque ait: 'En nostrum deposcunt ista laborem.
In me nulla mora est; ego tantae debitus irae
690 morte mea eripiam hos tenebris et claustra refringam.
Quin ea quae subito paucis deprensa sequuntur
sublegite, infandum mihi portendentia letum.'
    Omnibus hic pauci extinctis mortalibus ibant
inclusi ligno summas impune per undas.
695 Ingens lativago fluitabat machina ponto
et vix extabant immani corpore montes,
quos procul abruptus collisis nubibus ignis
ingeminans creber coelo rutilante petebat.
Hic natum senior nudo Isacon ense petebat,
700 infelix pater, exequitur dum tristia iussa.
Aspiceres illum toto iam corpore niti
dextram attollentem; nondum respexerat, et iam
nuntius ecce aderat coeli demissus ab arce
iussa ferens primis contraria; victima iuxta
705 pascebat pueri ignari pro caede parata
candidus et villis aries argenteus albis.
Hinc fratrem invisum narrata ob somnia fratres
vendebant, misero mentiti dira parenti
funera discerptumque feris; pater ipse cruentam
710 versabat gnati tunicam lachrymisque rigabat.
    Hic etiam, Phariis dum cives ducit ab oris
post longa exilia in patriam promissaque regna
legifer, auxiliis fretus coelestibus heros,
orta lues populum errantem miseranda repente
715 serpentum afflatu leto dabat, atque iacebant
corpora tabifico passim morientia morsu.
Dux vero in medio campi suspendit ahenum
ingenti e malo colubrum stratosque iubebat
dirigere huc aciem intentos lignumque tueri,

sighed deeply. "Alas, see how these woes compel me to suffer. I will not delay. By my death I will settle the debt owed to my Father's anger and rescue them from darkness, breaking open their 690 jails. Indeed, unravel the scenes that follow, understood by few, that presage my unspeakable death."

When the rest of humanity perished, some few passed unscathed through the flood enclosed in a wooden boat. The massive ark floated upon the broad sea. Scarcely could the mountains, de- 695 spite their massive size, be seen above the waves. In the fiery sky, clouds collided and let forth redoubled thunder and lightning that, from far off, battered the mountain-tops. Elsewhere, the patriarch had drawn his sword upon his son Isaac. How sad the father was to obey the unhappy commands! You could see him raise his right 700 hand, striving with all his strength. He had not yet turned round when an angel from heaven appeared, repealing the harsh orders. There grazed a resplendent ram with a silvery white coat, to be sacrificed in place of the unsuspecting boy. Further on, Joseph was 705 sold into slavery by his brothers. Angered by his dream interpretations, they lied to their father and told him that the young man had been slain by wild beasts. And here the father himself examined the robe of his child and watered it with his tears. 710

And there was Moses the lawgiver, the hero who with the help of heaven was leading his people after long exile from the land of Pharaoh home to the promised land. But suddenly a terrible pestilence, contracted from the breath of serpents, slew the wandering tribe; they lay all about, dying from the serpent's poisoned bite. In 715 the middle of the field Moses hung a brazen serpent from an enormous pole and bade those who lay on the ground to fix their gaze upon the wood. This was the only means of certain salvation for

720 quae miseris erat haud dubiae via sola salutis.
Parte alia rostro terebrans sibi viscera acuto
foeta avis implumes pascebat vulnere natos.
Stant olli circum materno sanguine laeti
et pectus certatim omnes rimantur apertum.

725 His animadversis portis bipatentibus ibat
multa putans, necdum gradibus descenderat heros
omnibus, et magno iam longe urgente tumultu
ecce trahebatur passis per terga capillis
pallida longaevi coniux Susanna Manassei,

730 quoi pater egregiam forma et florentibus annis
haud placitis taedis invitam aegramque iugarat.
Nanque fidem ob thalami foedatam ad iusta vocabant
supplicia ingenti iuvenum sectante caterva.
Et iam saxa manu pueri vulgusque tenebant.

735 Ipse sed antevolans prohibebat tela sacerdos,
donec porticibus Christum conspexit in amplis,
ad quem, ubi concessit miseramque ad limina traxit,
ingressus versare dolos, 'Haec prodidit,' inquit,
'coniugium thalamique fidem deprensa fefellit.

740 Sontem iura neci tali pro crimine dedi
nostra iubent duris (sed quae inclementia?) saxis.
Teque ideo vatum interpres mitissime adimus,
et tua, quaenam sit, sententia quaerimus omnes.

Dixerat atque animo iam spes pascebat inanes,

745 his captum implicitumque putans sermonibus hostem,
praeclusos abitus, non effugia ulla relicta.
Illam quippe neci si solveret interceptam
miti animo miseratus, eum turba omnis in ipsum
saxaque et ultrices raptim converteret iras,

750 quod sanctas gentis leges everteret illex;
si vero ad poenam iusset pro crimine duci,
sese odiis vulgi obiiceret crudelis acerbis.

those sadly afflicted. Elsewhere on the wall, a mother bird pierced   720
her own vitals with her sharp beak as she fed her offspring from
her own wound. They stood around her, rejoicing in their
mother's blood as all hastened to peck at the open wound.

After he had inspected the sculptures, Jesus, the hero, left   725
through the twin doors, and many things weighed on his mind.
He had not yet reached the end of the stairs when a large and
noisy crowd dragged forward the pale and disheveled Susanna,
wife of the aged Manasseh. Beautiful and young, she was given to
him by her father in a joyless marriage, though she was unwilling   730
and sick at heart. Now the crowd called for her to receive the just
punishment for adultery. Following closely behind was a huge mob
of youths. Already the crowd, young and old, held stones in their
hands.

A priest, rushing forward, prohibited them from throwing the
stones when he spotted Christ standing under the spacious por-   735
tico. He came up and delivered the unhappy woman to him. And
then, to lay a trap, he said, "This woman was caught committing
adultery and betraying her marriage bed. Our laws have ordained
that anyone guilty of this crime should suffer a cruel death by
stoning (but what cruelty is there in that?). And so we come to   740
you, gentle scholar of scripture, and wish to know your opinion in
the matter."

So speaking the man was filled with vain hopes. He imagined
that his enemy had been caught and bound by these words, that   745
all exits were shut. For if, with his tender heart, Christ took pity
on the captive and sought to rescue her from the death sentence,
then the entire crowd would turn their anger and their vengeful
stones against him for having subverted the sacred laws of their   750
nation. If, on the other hand, he upheld the sentence, he would
appear cruel and expose himself to the vengence of the mob. With

Haec agitans iam victorem se mente ferebat,
pectora laetitia multum tumefactus inani.
755 Ac veluti in somnis olim sibi visus arator,
dum terrae attrito suspendit vomere terga,
auri ingens pondus campo effodisse subacto,
gaudia vana fovet. Cernet somno ille relictus
pauperiem, duros et adhuc sibi adesse labores,
760 somnia fortunamque animo execratus inanem.
     Ipse viam deus invenit (fallacia numen
nulla humana valet contra) qua legibus illi
parceret illaesis. Nempe ut defixa tenebat
ora solo, tandem attollens turbamque paratam
765 aspectans ait: 'haud dubium quin crimine letum
sit merita; id prisci quondam sanxere parentes.
Ergo agite, o vestrum quicunque est criminis expers,
saxa manu primus rapiat feriatque merentem.
Ecquis erit tanto e numero, qui vulnera prima
770 dirigat et sceleris purum se proferat ultro?'
Sic memorans, omnis servabat lumine pronus
obliquo horrendumque tuens illumque paratus
inscripsisse solo, cui mens interrita nullum
esset ob admissum foede securaque culpae.
775 Stabat conspectu in medio tremebunda puella,
iam suffusa oculos mortis nigrore propinquae,
et positis terram genibus submissa petebat,
non minus exanimata metu quam in retia cerva
acta canum latratu et longo exercita cursu,
780 cum iam consumptae vires, cum se undique cinctam
hoste videt mortemque instantem certa moratur.
His autem auditis responsis, omnibus ingens
confestim cecidit furor et vis fracta quievit.
Quisque suam tacito versant in pectore vitam,
785 inque vicem spectant sese atque adversa tuentur,

this in mind, the priest, imagining he had won a victory, was
puffed up with baseless joy. He was like the farmer who dreams
that he has tilled a field with a well-worn plough and dug up a   755
mass of gold in the field. He becomes senselessly joyous, even
though, when he awakens, he will see that his poverty and hardship remain. And with all his heart he will curse his dreams and
his illusory wealth.   760

But because no human deceit is a match for a god, Christ
found a way to spare her without harming the laws. For some time
he stared at the ground. Then he raised his eyes and looked at the
waiting crowd. "Without doubt," he said, "she has merited death
for her crime. This is the law sanctioned of old. And so, let him   765
among you who is free of any transgression hurl the first stone and
strike her as she deserves. Is there anyone in this large crowd who
will inflict the first wound, who will stand forth willingly and
claim he is free of sin?" So speaking he lowered his head and, with   770
a terrible regard, he watched all of them with a sidelong glance,
ready to write his name on the ground whose mind was guiltless
and undisturbed by any base deed. In the midst of them all stood
the frightened girl, her eyes made somber by imminent death.   775
Kneeling upon the earth, she meekly implored them. She was no
less petrified with fear than a deer exhausted by a long chase and
driven into the nets by barking dogs: with all strength gone, it sees
itself surrounded by the enemy and awaits certain death. But   780
when the crowd had heard the words of Christ, suddenly each
man's anger, though great, left him and his violence subsided. As
each of them silently looked into his own heart and considered
what his life had been, and then glanced over at his neighbors, no   785

nec quisquam turba in tanta se prodidit ultro.
Saxa cadunt manibus furtim labentia et omnes
quisque sui memores abeunt templumque relinquunt.
Ut vero deus aspexit vacua atria circum,
790   linea detraxit pavitanti vincla puellae,
atque illam verbis monitam dimittit amicis:
'I melior, veterum famam iam extingue malorum.'
    Talia dein socios fatur conversus ad ipsos:
'Heu durum genus; haud possunt desistere victi.
795   Nil linquunt intentatum, nil prorsus inausum.
Nempe ego nunc festis fas contra et iura diebus
affero opem invalidis aegrosque in pristina reddo;
nunc sontes et sponte sua commissa fatentes
accipio noxaque animos et crimine solvo.
800   Nunc socii fruges tractant et vina, priusquam
dent manibus lymphas; cum victu corpora curant
nec dapibus parcunt et quae in nos plurima iactant.
Quin etiam me fraude petunt furta irrita adorti
vel cum Romanis astu me opponere tentant
805   incautum quaeruntque dolo, an fas pendere regi
per capita argentum, edicto quod quisque iubetur.
Nec caecos mea facta movent ingentia, quae non
humanis fierent opibus, non artibus ullis.
Nec qua vi haec agitem spoliati lumine cernunt,
810   consiliisque audent supremi obstare parentis.
Nec priscos tollo ritus legesve refigo;
quippe alia arcanis longe sententia dictis
indeprensa latet. Longe altera sacra teguntur
nube sub obscura verborum. Ut caetera mittam,
815   quid suis horretis vetitis imponere mensis
viscera? Non animis labem sublimibus affert
aut his aut illis ieiunia solvere rebus.
Vobis intus obest mens ipsa et dira cupido.

one in all that mob was willing to come forward. The stones slipped out of their hands and all of them, mindful of themselves, skulked away from the temple. But when the god looked around him now and saw an empty court, he undid the hemp cords that bound the frightened girl and he sent her on her way, admonish- 790 ing with these gentle words: "Go forth a better person. Rid yourself of the infamy of past sins."

After that he turned to his disciples. "What a hard race of men! Even in defeat, they can scarcely give up! There is nothing they won't attempt or dare. To be sure, even on the days of rest, 795 contrary to sacred and human law, I minister to the sick and restore them to health. I welcome those who willingly admit their guilt and I absolve their souls of the taint of crime. My disciples handle fruit and wine before washing their hands. They feed their 800 bodies and indulge in feasts and do much besides that the priests charge me with. In fact, the priests falsely accuse me and invent all kinds of crimes for me, but in vain. Or they deceitfully try to embroil me unawares with the Romans, asking whether our religion permits us to pay taxes to the Emperor, as each man is bidden to 805 do. In their blindness, they remain unmoved by my miracles, which are impossible through human powers or magic. My great deeds move these blind men not at all, deeds done neither by human resources nor by any deceptive tricks. Sightless, they do not perceive the power through which I accomplish my deeds, and they dare to obstruct the designs of my Almighty Father. But I do 810 not abrogate the ancient rites or annul the laws. Surely these obscure sayings have a very different meaning that remains hidden. Far other rites lie concealed beneath a dark cloud of words. Leaving aside the rest, why does it disgust them to set pork on the table? It hardly defiles our sublime souls to be rid of our hunger 815 with one food rather than another. What harms us within is the mind itself and its dangerous desires. But because the bristly pig

Sed quoniam gaudet coeno immundaque palude
820   setigerum genus et pecori huic innata libido est,
in sue adumbrantur veneris mala gaudia foedae.
Quin etiam, ut iussis animos coelestibus auctor
paulatim assuescens posset mollire colendo
nec nulla inciperet sub relligione tenere
825   indociles primum populos obtusaque gentis,
pectora iussit oves iugulare et sanguine terram
imbuere immeritosque aris mactare iuvencos.
Quae tamen omnia erant, si cui mens alta vigebat,
venturae speculum mox relligionis et umbra.'
830   His actis iam devexum cum vesper Olympum
clauderet, egrediens malefida cessit ab urbe.
Tum genitorem obitus affarier ante propinquos
exoptans coramque arcanas promere voces,
ignaros socios Taburi ima in valle reliquit;
835   ipse autem ascensu superans capita ardua montis
constitit, aereae feriunt ubi sidera cedri.
Addiderant comites se tantum ex omnibus illi
fidus Ioannes cum fratre Petrusque vocati.
Stabant orantes taciti pariterque supinas
840   tendebant sine voce manus ac lumina coelo.
Ipse autem his magno genitorem affatur amore:
'O pater, en insons nunc dira ad funera pergo,
progenies tua, nec tot ferre indigna recuso,
quando certa tibi mens atque haec fixa voluntas,
845   et tanti mortale genus. Nil demoror; adsum.
Hos saltem qui me patriaque suisque relictis
per varios casus lectissima corda sequuntur,
aspice, et immeritos caecis averte periclis.
Haud vereor quod se his homines, gens impia passim
850   opponunt. Nil facta hominum mortalia terrent.
Ipsi etiam (nihil hoc moveor) moriantur ad unum,

enjoys lying in mud and unclean swamps, because it is libidinous
by nature, in the pig are shadowed forth the wicked joys of foul   820
lust. Rather, the Heavenly Father, in order to tame the human
soul by gradually accustoming it to religious observance and divine
commandments, and to soften the insensate hearts of a primitive
race that had no traditional observances, first ordered that sheep   825
be slaughtered and that their blood be spilt upon the earth, while
innocent cattle were sacrificed upon the altars. But to any high-
minded person, all of these things were a reflection, a foreshadow-
ing, of the faith to come."

   After these events, Christ left the faithless city, just as evening   830
was covering up the heavens. He resolved to address his Father
about his approaching death and speak to him directly about secret matters. So he left his unsuspecting disciples in the valley of
Mount Tabor and ascended the steep summit, coming to a halt   835
where the lofty cedars strike the stars. Of all the disciples, he
asked only the faithful John, his brother James, and Peter to accompany him. They stood praying in silence, raising their hands
and eyes to heaven. But Jesus with great love addressed his parent   840
in these words: "Father, though I am innocent and your Son, I go
now to a cruel death. I do not refuse to suffer these indignities,
since you have made up your mind and your will is fixed; and the
race of men are worthy of it. I will not delay. Here am I. Only   845
look upon these men, these rare souls who follow me. They have
left their homes and families and suffered so much. Protect these
innocent people from unseen perils. I fear not at all that impious
men will everywhere oppose them. No mortal deeds frighten me.
Let each man die in his turn—that does not move me at all. Or, if   850
you choose, destroy them with your dread thunder and thoroughly

aut potius saevo, si vis, tu fulmine perde
correptos igni et penitus res attere fractas.
Tu, genitor, tanto finemque impone labori,
855   si tantae est genus humanum coelo addere molis,
seclaque mutatis in pristina reddere rebus.
Tantum oro (scelus!) inferno summissa barathro
gens, pestem meditata viris, nil improba furtis
officiat, non infando praevertat amore
860   insidiis captos nec corda improvida fallat,
dum scelera hortatur nostrique oblivia suadet.
Iam iam aderunt infandi hostes, armata dolis gens,
nondum animos satiata, graves nondum ulta dolores.
Has fraudes iamque has fraude artesque movebunt.
865   Quas non mentiti simulato corpore formas,
ut capiant genus innocuum vertantque venenis
pestiferis? Tu frange dolos ferque irrita in auras
cuncta, pater; tandem victis edice quiescant.
Sint qui per terras gentes post funera nostra
870   iustitiam erudiant et relligionis amorem.
Hanc veniam concede; id gnati cedat amori.'
    Filius haec. Genitor contra cui talia reddit:
'Nate, patris virtus nostrique simillima imago,
nulla tuis fraus (solve metum) nullaeve nocebunt
875   insidiae, quas nunc regni molitur operti
arbiter. Incepti frustra irritus omnia tentat.
Induat in facies centum, centum ille figuras.
Ipse adero, retegamque dolos foecundaque fraudis
agmina disiiciam et magna virtute resistam.
880   Unus erit tantum, cui mentem insania vertet,
infelix, iam nunc devoto pectore versat
infandum scelus atque tui iam poenitet aegrum,
secum indignantem, tua quod praecepta sequutus
exuerit blandum vitae mortalis amorem

shatter and obliterate their world. Put an end to your great labors, if it is so arduous a thing to lift the human race into heaven and by 855 revolution to restore the purity of the first days. This alone I ask: that the race that inhabits the pit of hell, that always contrives pestilence, effect no stealthy harm against the race of men, that it not ensnare them and pervert them to base loves, deceiving their unguarded hearts and enjoining them to sin and to forget my teach- 860 ings. Surely this unspeakable enemy will come armed with wiles, insatiable souls who have not yet avenged their grave sufferings. They will contrive every cunning and treachery. What shapes will they not put on, changing their bodies as they seek to capture an 865 innocent race and pervert it with their poison? Undo those wiles, Father, and scatter all of them, useless, to the wind. Once and for all, command your vanquished enemies to be still. After my death, may men remain on earth who pursue justice and love of religion. 870 Grant this one mercy, for the love of your child."

So spoke the Son. To him his Father thus replied: "O Son, virtue and image of your Father, fear not. Your friends will not be harmed by any treachery or deceit contrived by the lord of the 875 hidden realm. All his undertakings are vain. Though he should put on a hundred faces and a hundred forms, I will lay bare his wiles and scatter his troops, so fertile in fraud, and repel them with great strength. There will be one man alone whom madness 880 will pervert. The miserable creature even now contrives an unspeakable crime in his accursed heart. Already this sick man repents having joined you. He berates himself because, in following your teachings, he had abandoned the sweet love of mortal life and

885   malueritque graves sub te tolerare labores —
    omnia quae mecum mundi ante exordia nosti.
    Hunc tamen indignum numero coetuque piorum
    addidimus memores vatum, qui talia quondam
    praedixere, tuis exemplum insigne futurum.
890   Evadent alii insidias meliora sequuti.
    Omnes te propter contempto lucis amore
    haud mortem horrescent pergentque in funera laeti,
    innumeramque suo parient tibi sanguine gentem
    proiectu vitae et mortis amore superbi.
895   Efficiam coelo dignos post aspera tandem
    funera, deserti magnum aetheris incrementum.
    Quos tu olim aspicies hac relligione nepotes
    surgere, nate, tibi! Quam pectora certa videbis!
    Tu modo, tu perge et coeptum decurre laborem.
900   Hi, quos cernis enim vix nunc tua iussa sequutos
    indociles, fandi ignaros (mora non erit), altos
    pectore concipient sensus doctoque verendas
    ore canent leges, afflati numine nostro,
    et vastum in melius referent hortatibus orbem.
905   Succedent aliis alii sacrique nepotes;
    victores tua signa ferent trans ultima claustra
    Oceani, latas undis cohibentia terras,
    clarescetque tuum passim per secula nomen.
    Sponte sua invicti reges tibi sceptra, tibi arma
910   subiicient sua per terras arasque sacrabunt.
    Atque adeo gravida imperiis Roma illa superba,
    Apenninivagi quae propter Tybridis undam
    ingentes populos frenat, pulcherrima rerum,
    summittet fasces et, quas regit, orbis habenas.
915   Illic relligio, centum illic maxima templa,
    centum arae tibi fumantes centumque ministri,
    quique viris late atque ipsis det iura sacerdos

chose to suffer great labors under you. But all this you knew as   885
well as I did from before the beginning of the world. Unworthy
though he was, I added him to your band of pious men. In this I
was mindful of the ancient prophets, who had predicted as much.
I wished him to serve as an example to your followers. The others,   890
choosing a better course, will avoid such snares. For your sake
scorning the love of life, none of them will fear death and they will
meet their doom with gladness. Made proud by their disregard of
life and their love of death, they will bring forth from their blood
countless new followers for you. And after such bitter deaths I will   895
make them worthy of heaven and greatly increase its numbers.
How many, yet unborn, will you one day see rising to join this religion. And what stout hearts! Only carry on and see your labors
to their end. These resistant souls whom you see here, ignorant of   900
speech and scarcely able to follow your example, will soon understand in their hearts. Inspired by my Spirit, they will learnedly in-
tone the sacred laws and by their teachings they will turn the great
world to a better state. One generation will follow another and   905
your sacred sons will carry your standards victoriously beyond
the furthest barriers of Ocean that engirds the lands with its waters, and through the ages they will make your name glorious.
Throughout the world, unvanquished kings will eagerly set before
you their scepters and their arms and raise altars to you. Even   910
Rome, that proud city laden with empire, the most beautiful of all
things, which governs great nations from beside the waters of the
Tiber as it flows down from the Apennines, even she will subject
to you her fasces and the reins with which she rules the world!
There, in that city, is religion and a hundred great temples. One   915
hundred smoking altars, one hundred priests, and one above all
who will lay down the law, not only to all men, but even to kings,

regibus et summo te in terris reddat honore.
Si qua tamen paulatim annis labentibus aetas
920 decolor inficiet mores versisque nepotes
degeneres surgent studiis, per dura laboresque
exercens lapsam revocabo in pristina gentem.
Illa malis semper melior se tollet ad astra.
Saepe solo velut eversam excisamque videbis,
925 quam modo praedixi, populorum incursibus urbem.
Verum quo magis illa malis exercita, semper
altius hoc surgens, celsum caput inseret astris,
moeniaque in melius semper recidiva reponet,
nec nisi subiecto passim sibi desinet orbe.
930 Sic placitum. Nostri sedes ea numinis esto.'
    Haec ait, et natum dextra complexus inhaesit.
Ecce autem subito rubra vibratus ab aethra
cum sonitu fulgor micat, et polus intonat ingens.
Nam pater omnipotens manifestus ab aethere nubem
935 ostendit radiis illustrem lucis et igni.
Omnia collucent late loca. Turbine Christus
corripitur rapido mediaque in nube refulsit,
verus et aspectu patuit deus atque per auras
divinum toto spiravit vertice odorem
940 luminis aetherei specimen, genitoris imago.
Nec secus emicuit roseo pulcherrimus ore
insolita circum perfundens omnia luce,
quam cum mane recens lucis fons aureus ingens
lumine sol coelum exoriens rigat omne profuso,
945 Oceani in speculo longe resplendet imago,
et croceae effulgent aurata cacumina silvae.
Talem se sociis mirantibus obtulit heros,
amborum in medio vatum, quorum alter adivit
flammifero quondam invectus coeli ardua curru,
950 et tranavit equis insultans aeris auras.

and cause you to be honored throughout the world. And if in the
course of years a lesser age will coarsen men's morals, if a degener-
ate progeny turns away from such pursuits, then I will impose   920
harsh labors upon that fallen race and so recall them to their earlier piety. Ennobled through such ills, that race will ever raise itself
to the stars. Often you will see the city I have just mentioned
overturned and cut down by incursions of barbarians. But verily,   925
the more harshly that city is wrought upon, so much the higher
will it raise its head among the stars. And though its walls may
fall, they will always rise stronger than before, not resting until the
entire earth has been subdued by it. For such is my will. This be
the dwelling place of my divine spirit."   930

So speaking, he embraced his son. Suddenly a clamorous thunderbolt shivered and flashed through the rubied air, and the great
firmament resounded. In heaven the Almighty Father manifested
himself in a cloud of fire and radiant light. Far and wide, the earth   935
shone. Christ was caught in a rushing whirlwind and, clearly a
god, he glowed amid the clouds. Throughout the heavens, this vision of ethereal light, the image of his Father, shed a divine fra-   940
grance. Bathing the sky in a strange glow, he shone forth bril-
liantly; just as when at earliest dawn the rising sun—that great,
golden source of day—floods the entire sky with light, its reflection shines afar in the mirror of Ocean and the golden summit   945
of the saffron-scented woods is set ablaze. Such was the form in
which the hero offered himself to his astonished followers. He was
flanked by two prophets, one of whom climbed to the heights of
heaven in a fiery chariot, drawn in triumph through the fields of
air by a team of horses. The other led the wandering sons of Isaac   950

Isacidum Phariis genus alter duxit ab oris,
dux profugum, legesque dedit moremque sacrorum.
Necnon coelicolum propius tum maxima pandi
visa domus coelique ingens apparuit aula.
955 Tum genitor nubis fulgens candentis amictu
oscula libavit nato, et vox lapsa per auras.
'Hic mea progenies; hic est mea magna voluptas.
Uni huic mortales omnes parete volentes.
Nec plura his. Toto assonuit chorus omnis Olympo
960 coelestum cantu vario plausumque dedere.
    Tum demum in faciem consuetam redditus heros,
attonitos socios monstrisque metuque sepultos
excitat atque hominis mortali apparuit ore.

out of the lands of Pharoah, giving them laws and religion. And near at hand, the great palace of the angels seemed to open its gates and the massive hall of heaven came into view. Then God the Father, clad in the mantle of a gleaming cloud, bestowed a kiss upon his son, and his voice glided downward through the air: "Here is my child. Here is my great joy. Let all men willingly obey him alone." He said nothing more. Throughout heaven, a great chorus of angels applauded and gave their assent in varied song. 955

960

Finally the hero resumed his wonted shape. Rousing his followers, who were awed and thunderstruck by what they had just witnessed, he appeared once more in the form of a mortal man.

LIBER II

At Solymi, trepidi rerum et formidine caeci,
noctem illam patrum primi templique ministri
insomnem duxere. Animis adeo addita cura
incubat ac nullam attonitis dat dira quietem.
5   Omnibus ante oculos urbem ingredientis imago
laeta dei festique manus impubis honores
illiusque vident late increbrescere nomen.
Fama volat passimque canit miracula rerum.
Quid faciant? Magis atque magis iam vera patescunt,
10 quae quondam prisci vates cecinere futura,
terras coelesti regem de stirpe manere,
cuius in adventu templum Iudaeaque tandem
regna ruant, Solymeque eversis desinat aris
antiquo de more sacros imponere honores.
15 Ergo infracti animis omnes, terrore subacti,
tectis quisque suo septi clausique manebant.
Quales quae solitae florentia rura volantes
carpere apes, ubi saevit hyems coelumque profusos
solvitur in nimbos et aquosus regnat Orion,
20 ocia lenta terunt clausisque alvearibus aegrae
cunctantur circumque fores ac limine mussant.
    Tempus erat per membra quies cum grata soporem
irrigat ac positis affert oblivia curis,
et iam noctipotens manus, imo emissa barathro,
25 horribiles visu formae furialibus omnem
coetibus obsedere urbem. Pars turribus instant,
pars apicem templi et fastigia summa coronant.
Caetera perque vias legio, perque alta domorum
tecta volant tractimque haerent per culmina tignis.

BOOK II

Frightened by what was happening and blinded by foreboding, the leaders of Solomon's city and the priests of his temple passed a sleepless night, so grievous was the care that occupied their troubled souls and gave them no rest. They had all seen the joyous spectacle of God entering the city. They had seen as well the festive honors bestowed on him by the city's youth. And they perceived that his fame was spreading abroad, carrying everywhere the news of his miracles. What should they do? Each day made clearer the truth of the ancient prophecies: that the earth would soon see a king of heavenly descent; at his coming the temple and kingdom of Judaea would finally collapse; and once the altars were overturned, the city of Solomon would cease to observe its ancient rites. Broken in spirit and prostrate with terror, the elders remained shut up in their houses and locked the doors. They were like bees that fly here and there, pollinating the flowering fields: but when winter rages and the heavens dissolve in showery clouds and watery Orion is in the ascendant, they pass their days in idleness, lingering inertly in their enclosed hives or buzzing about the entranceways.

It was that time of night when care is set aside and welcome rest brings sleep and oblivion to weary bodies. This was the moment when that nocturnal cohort, horrible to look on, emerged from the depths and laid siege to the city with their raging packs. Some occupied towers, others the roofs and summits of the temple. The rest of the legion flew through the streets, swooped up to the lofty roofs and hung in long rows upon the wooden rafters.

30　Haud secus Italiam repetunt ubi vere tepenti
　　coerula aves longo fessae super aequora cursu,
　　quae prior occurrit tellus, hanc agmine denso
　　certatim arripiunt procurvaque littora complent.
　　　　Principio spargunt occultum in pectora virus
35　vipereamque viris animam caecumque furorem
　　inspirant odiumque animis et crimina linquunt.
　　Multi etiam in facies hominum vertuntur et omnem
　　protinus incendunt variis rumoribus urbem.
　　Irrepunt tectis alii somnoque solutis
40　somnia dira ferunt varia sub imagine rerum
　　atque hominum falsis simulacris pectora ludunt.
　　Iamque huius subeunt iamque illius alta potentum
　　limina et attonitos dictis hortantur in hostem
　　terrificantque animos facta atque infecta canentes.
45　Christum inferre faces arisque instare bipenni
　　armatum aerata atque adytis extrema minari,
　　et iam semusto in templo dominarier ignem.
　　　　Quin ipsos templi mentiti veste ministros
　　singula tecta adeunt patresque ad limina sacra
50　conciliumque vocant. Nigri dux agminis ipse
　　impulit aerisono stridentes cardine portas.
　　Hinc atque hinc delubra petunt, concurritur ultro
　　undique, nec tenebris nox obstat euntibus atra.
　　Non aliter captam si rumor nuntiet urbem
55　nocte dolis intempesta atque latentibus armis
　　hostem inferre acies et iam summa arce receptum
　　culminibusque immissa voret fax atra penates,
　　plenis cuncta viis fervent, trepidoque tumultu
　　huc atque huc itur, nec sat rationis eundi est.
60　Praecedunt dirae facies, facibusque nefandis
　　sufficiunt lucem et summo dant vertice lumen
　　terrificas capitum quatientes undique flammas.

They were like the birds that in the warmth of spring grow weary 30
of their long journey across the blue sea and seek again the shores
of Italy. Multitudinously they vie to seize on whatever land lies
first in their path and fill the curving shore.

First the hellish cohort distilled an unseen poison and a viper-
ous mood in men's hearts, inspiring them to blind rage, and leav- 35
ing thoughts of hatred and violence in their path. Many assumed a
human form and inflamed the city with their varied rumors. Others crept into bedchambers and brought manifold dire dreams to
sleeping souls, thus deluding human hearts with false semblances. 40
Then, entering the lofty home of one powerful citizen after another, they frightened them with rumors true and false, and
roused them against the enemy. They told them that Christ had
come with torches, that armed with a brazen axe, he menaced the 45
altars. They intimated that he threatened to destroy the very
building, that already fire was raging in the temple half-destroyed.

Moreover, they deceptively donned the vestments of the temple's priests, then ran to each of their homes and called the elders
to council on the sacred ground. The leader of this dark band 50
himself pushed open the doors, which screeched upon their brazen jambs. In every direction they ran, seeking the shrines. Black
night with its darkness was no obstacle to them. As when a rumor spreads that a city has been captured by guile in the dead of
night, that the enemy is waging a battle with covert arms and has 55
already seized the heights, that a fire has been loosed from the
summit and is already destroying homes, suddenly the streets are
filled with activity and, amid the general clamor, everyone runs
thoughtlessly to and fro. The dire forms led on, providing light
with their evil brands. Light as well they provided from the crown 60
of their heads, shaking a terrifying fire in all directions. As for the

Nec miseri tamen agnoscunt; furor omnibus intus
eripuit mentem lapsumque in viscera virus.
65 Nec minus interea bis seni ex agmine missi
bis senos Christi ad socios, evertere si quem
possent et furiis deceptum incendere iniquis.
Illi autem pleni monitis ducis (ante futura
praescius ista suis praedixerat omnia) servant
70 invictos animos inapertaque pectora fraudi,
quanquam hostis species sese transformet in omnes
nequicquam expertus mentesque indagine captet.
        Unus non valuit sese his subducere vinclis,
Iscarius pesti infandae devotus Iudas,
75 lectorum procerum labes et pestis Iudas!
Hic se olim addiderat socium vestigia divi
ingressus, patria atque opibus carisque relictis,
incerta exilia, incertas quacunque paratus
ire vias, talique necem pro rege pacisci.
80 At mox coeptorum piguit durique laboris
paulatim pertaesum. Animo tum volvere secum,
noctes atque dies tacitus, si qua potis arctis
legibus exolvi et priscae se reddere vitae,
indignans longum incassum cecidisse laborem.
85 Hos abitus iamque hos abitus et furta parabat,
impatiens operum, rebus non laetus egenis.
        Talibus undantem curis animoque labantem
iampridem nigrae reperit dux ipse cohortis.
Haud minus exultans animis quam monte sub alto
90 cum procul aspexit tendentem in pascua cervum
Gaetulus leo, quem siccis exercet hiantem
faucibus ex longo collecta insania edendi.
Ac prius in faciem Galilaei versus Iorae,
ipsi qui fuerat coniunctus sanguine Iudae,
95 insomnem aggreditur verbis: 'Tu nocte silenti

others, the poor souls did not understand. Their reason had been vanquished by madness and by the poison that had entered their vitals. Meanwhile, twelve of them were dispatched to the twelve 65 disciples of Christ to try to win over and deceive them with their resentful ravings. But the disciples were armed with the teachings of their leader who in his foreknowledge had predicted to them that all these things would occur. And so their minds were unvanquished and their hearts impervious to fraud. And even though 70 the enemy took on all shapes and tried to capture their minds through treachery, it was in vain.

Only one man, Judas Iscariot, given over to unspeakable vileness, was not strong enough to resist these snares. Judas, that pox, that pestilence among the chosen apostles! Once he had aban- 75 doned wealth, country and friends, choosing to join with the others and follow in the footsteps of the Lord. He had been prepared to go anywhere, into perilous exile and on perilous journeys, even to suffer death for so great a king. But soon he grew weary of 80 these undertakings and gradually wearied of harsh efforts such as these. Night and day, he wondered in silence how he might free himself from the hard laws and return to his earlier life. For he was indignant that all his efforts turned out to be useless. Impatient of these labors and unhappy in his straightened circum- 85 stances, he stealthily planned one means of escape after another.

His mind long prone to waver, Judas was being buffeted by cares like these when the leader of the dark cohort himself found Judas out. Exulting in his heart, the devil was like a Gaetulian lion, its dry jaws gaping wide, driven by long-gathering hunger, 90 who beneath a high mountain sees far off a deer heading for the fields. But first the devil changed himself into the semblance of Jora the Galilean, a blood relative of Judas, who approached the sleepless Judas with the words: "In the silence of night you wander 95

montibus in solis erras, insane, potesque
ultro saeva pati sub nudo frigora coelo,
atque tibi alterius sub nutu degitur aetas,
dum sequeris (quis te tantus furor incitat?) istum
100   elatumque animis eversoremque sacrorum,
quem tantum illuvies adeunt teterrima gentis
foeminei coetus et semiviri comitatus?
Primi omnes infensi odiis concordibus ardent
sacrilegoque necem intentant. Iamque ille furorem
105   vesanum expendet, cedet fiducia tanta.
Non illi auxilio magnarum gloria rerum,
quas mentitur, erit. Nil contra obtendere densa
nubila, nil solitas accingi proderit artis.
Rumpe moras. Eia instanti te surripe cladi!'
110   Sic ait, ardentemque odiis instigat acerbis.
Tum mutata acri percussit pectora thyrso
et subito nocti ablatus se immiscuit atrae.

    Hinc miserum invadens praecordia ad intima sese
ingerit atque imis dirum implicat ossibus ignem.
115   Olim etiam in mentem veniunt quaecunque sub illo
iussus dura tulit, quaecunque exhausta pericla.
Et piget atque nefas polluto volvit amore,
immeritumque animo sedet hosti prodere regem.

    Ah miser, ah male sane, deum non pectore sentis?
120   Non oculis numen praesens, non auribus hauris?
Quis te mutavit tantus furor? Aspice quo nunc
culmine praecipitas, quanam trahis arce ruinam!
Nec qualis sentis tibi menti insederit error?
Quid struis aut quo te raptat tam dira cupido,
125   quae nunc te male habet mentisque et lucis egentem?
Quam nunc amittis sortem, irreparabile donum,
optabunt seri post secula mille nepotes.
Atque adeo quae vota foves, quam mente secas spem,

crazily amid the lonely mountains. You willingly withstand harsh cold under the open sky and all your days are spent at the behest of another, while you follow (what madness!) this braggart, this destroyer of all things sacred, who is surrounded only by a rank 100 pollution of eunuchs and womenfolk. The leaders of the city are all united in their hatred for this irreligious man and are plotting his death. Soon he will pay for his madness and his arrogance will give way. He will find no succor in his famous miracles, which are 105 all lies. It will do no good to call forth dense clouds or to wrap himself in his wonted arts. Don't waste time. Run from this impending disaster!" So he spoke, provoking the angry man to bitter hatred. Striking his altered heart with a sharp rod, the demon 110 vanished suddenly into the darkness of the night.

From this point on, the devil invaded the wretch's inmost heart, inflaming him to the marrow of his bones. Judas was thinking of all the harsh things he had suffered under the command of Jesus and all the perils he had endured. He felt repugnance. His love 115 now polluted, he conceived an outrageous act: betraying the king he did not deserve to the enemy.

Poor, sick wretch! Don't you feel God moving within your heart? Can't you sense his presence with your eyes and ears? What 120 madness has perverted you? Look at the cliff from which you jump headlong! Look at the high citadel from which you are falling! Don't you recognize the folly that has laid siege to your mind? What are you plotting? Whither are you ravished by this baleful 125 desire that holds you in thrall, blinded and out of your mind? For a thousand generations to come, men will long to possess that irreplaceable good fortune that you now throw away. Meanwhile, all

laetitia elatos animos inflatus inani,
130 omnia discerpent rapientque per aera venti.
Excute dum licet, infandam de pectore pestem
quaeque imis te nunc est addita cura medullis!
    Iamque sacerdotes totaque ex urbe senatus
secretam in templi sedem concesserat omnis.
135 Ipse sacerdotum primus, cui tempora sacra
infula cingebat, Caiphas in sede sedebat
celsior aurata; inde alii longo ordine cives,
quos omnis circunsiliunt acuuntque furorem
Tartareae haud ulli visae sine corpore pestes —
140 nec mora, nec requies — sublapsae in pectora cunctis
eripiunt mentem atque animis incendia miscent.
Multa illi inter se vario sermone serebant
solliciti; vasto strepit ingens murmure templum.
Sunt qui ipsum iubeant utcunque absumere Christum
145 seu vi sive dolo, iuvenemque invadere ferro
qui rursum in lucem nuper revocatus ab umbris
venerat et totam monstro concusserat urbem.
Ast alii plebem metuunt vulgique furorem,
nanque sibi ingentis populos devinxerat heros,
150 hos meritis, illos divino affabilis ore.
    Hic Nicodemus erat pesti impenetrabilis unus,
primores inter gentis non ultimus ipsos,
cui longe menti melior sententia, sed non
audebat dictis contra omnes tendere solus.
155 Ille deo quondam sese inscius intulit hostem
atque dolis frustra contra stetit. Inde ubi numen
admonitus sensit, veluti de nocte profunda
in lucem revocatus, ei se iunxit amore,
clam tamen, infensae vitans odia aspera gentis.
160 Tum vero illius de vita et sanguine cerni
ut vidit letumque insonti triste parari,

the prayers you now foster, all the hopes you now conceive, in a
mind swollen with empty dreams, all of them will be gathered up
by the wind and scattered through the air. While you still can,   130
drive this disease from your heart and this anxiety from the marrow of your bones!

Now the priests and all the leaders of the city had convened
within the hidden recesses of the temple. The archpriest Caiaphas,
his temples girt with the sacred chaplet, sat above the rest on a   135
golden throne. Beneath him stood a mass of citizens whom the
hellish vermin, incorporeal and unseen, encircled and goaded to
fury without pause or rest. These demons insinuated themselves
into each man's heart, seizing hold of his mind and inflaming his   140
soul. As the citizens began nervously to debate among themselves,
the massive temple resounded with their vast clamor. Some
wanted to take Christ himself, whether by force or treachery, and
to attack the young man who was recently recalled to the light   145
from the shades of death, convulsing the city with the miracle. But
others feared that that might incur the rage of the people, whom
the hero had bound to him in great numbers, some through his
deeds, others through the eloquence of his divine words.   150

Hardly the least among the leaders of the city, Nicodemus
alone remained untouched by such demonic pestilence. He was far
wiser than the others, but being only one man, he did not dare
to raise his voice against all the rest. Once he had thoughtlessly
stood in enmity to Christ, treacherously contending against him.   155
But when, with greater wisdom, he sensed the man's holiness,
Nicodemus was like one who has been brought back from deepest
darkness into light: he came to love Jesus, but secretly, in order to
escape the bitter hatred of his angry race. Now when he saw that
it was a question of Jesus' life and limb, that a sad fate was being   160
plotted against an innocent man, Nicodemus could no longer con-

non tulit ulterius latebras haecque edidit ore
in medio: 'Non obscuram, non lucis egentem
rem ferimus, neque enim vereor iam vera profari
165   pro patria, quanvis mihi sint extrema ferenda.
Cernitis hunc omnes manifesto numine ferri
maioremque homine et, nosmet nisi fallimus ipsi,
vera dei patuit soboles, verus deus, ille
olim quem toties afflati numine vates
170   venturum cecinere, nefas quo triste piaret,
commendans genus aeterno mortale parenti.
Hoc liquet, hoc ultra non in discrimen agendum.
    'Huius ope innumeri, quos nox obscura premebat
luminibus captos, iucunda luce fruuntur.
175   Multi etiam voces obstructis auribus orti
accipiunt redduntque. Aegris quot reddita venit
insperata salus, qui lenta aut membra trahebant
victa lue aut subito correpti corpora morbo?
Tris etiam (nostis) obita iam a morte reduxit
180   elatos idem in lucem; modo Lazarus omnem
perculit et monstro ingenti permiscuit urbem.
Pro laevas hominum mentis, pro pectora caeca!
Non haec paeoniis succis, non artibus ullis
confieri possunt. Maior deus intus agit rem,
185   maius numen inest. Quoties divina loquentem
incassum contra stetimus, verbisque dolisque
instructi? Quoties ausi vim tendere inermi
aut ferro aut duris nequicquam perdere saxis?
Nube cava eripuit caput ex oculisque recedens
190   aligerum se coelesti subito agmine sepsit.

ceal himself, but openly spoke thus: "The matter we debate is not obscure. It does not need clarification. I do not fear to speak the truth for the sake of my country, even though I might be punished with death. You all see that this man is guided by a manifest and superhuman divinity, that he is greater than a man, and that, unless we are deceiving ourselves, he stands revealed as the true offspring of God, indeed as the true God. He is the very one whose coming was often foretold by the divinely inspired prophets of old, in order that he might atone for grievous sins, commending the race of men to his Eternal Father. That much is clear and now beyond controversy.

"Through his powers, many whose vision had been covered up in dark night now savor once more the light of day. And many who were born deaf now can hear and speak. And how many have been restored to unimagined health whose bodies had either been paralyzed by chronic disease or struck down by sudden affliction! Three times, as you know, he brought the dead back into the light of the living. And only recently, Lazarus has stirred up the entire city with just such a miracle. O wayward minds and blind hearts of men! Such miracles cannot be performed by medicinal drugs or by any craft. A greater god is at work within, a greater spirit dwells inside him. How often, while he was speaking divine truths, have we vainly opposed him, armed as we were with stratagems and words. How often have we tried to attack him unarmed, to destroy him with swords and stones, all in vain. Immediately he covered himself in mist and, withdrawing from human sight, hid himself amid the heavenly host. And who would not adore his di-

165

170

175

180

185

190

Et quisquam illius certum non numen adoret?
Quid molimur adhuc? Quid nobis deinde relictum?
Quin potius, quando nobis demissus Olympo
auxilio venit, una omnes adeamus, ab ipso
195   suppliciter pacem oremus commissa fatentes.'
     Talia perstabat repetens. Violentia cunctis
gliscit et accensus semper per viscera sensus
conflatur magis et saevos furor aggerat aestus,
paulatimque animi turgescunt tristibus iris.
200   Exarsere omnes. Pestis latet intus et omnem
eripuit miseris lucem victisque veneno
pestifero nebulas offudit mentibus atras.
Tum demum erumpit quae cunctos ira coquebat;
infremuere omnes contra gemitumque dedere.
205   Qualiter aere cavo, dum sulfura pascitur atra,
inclusus magis atque magis furit acrior ignis
moliturque fugam, nec se capit intus anhelans,
nulla sed angustis foribus via, nec potis extra
rumpere, materiam donec comprenderit omnem;
210   tum piceo disclusa volat glans ferrea fumo.
Fit crepitus: credas rupto ruere aethere coelum.
Iamque illa et turres procul ecce stravit et arces;
corpora et arma iacent late et via facta per hostes.
Haud illi secus accensi meliora monentem
215   excludunt adytis atque extra moenia trudunt.
     Tum vero Caiphas, ubi facta silentia linguis,
sic orsus sibi, quae sedeat sententia, pandit.
'Haud equidem moror, o cives, quod versus ad hostes
iste etiam infando captus perfugerit astu,
220   qui toties summa pro re, pro legibus olim
obiecit patriis caput ultro, ipsumque premebat
obnitens contra nuper sermonibus hostem.
Tanta est artificis pellacia, vis ea fandi,

vinity as a thing certain? What do we do now? What remains for
us to attempt? Sent down from heaven, he comes to help us: How
much wiser, then, for us all to go to him and, admitting our sins,
seek peace as suppliants." 195

So he spoke, standing his ground. But a violent mood arose in
all who heard. The mob's wrath grew ever more visceral and madness intensified their savage anger. By degrees their souls swelled
with bitter wrath. A deep and hidden pestilence blotted the light 200
from their poor eyes, poisoning their minds and wrapping them in
dark clouds. Then at last the rage that was burning in all of them
erupted. Everyone roared and groaned against Nicodemus. As
when poisonous sulfur consumes itself within the chamber of a
bronze cannon, the confined fire rages with ever greater force. 205
Hissing and seeking to break out, it can no longer contain itself,
yet it has no avenue of escape through the narrow channels of the
bore, no means of freeing itself until all the matter is consumed.
Then amid pitchy smoke, the iron bullet discharges and takes
wing with a thunderous sound. You would think that the sky had 210
split open and the heavens were falling! And behold, the cannonball has laid waste to distant towers and fortifications, bodies and
weapons lie scattered everywhere, and a path has been cut through
the enemy camp! Even so were the elders in Jerusalem incensed
against Nicodemus, though he gave them wiser counsel. And so
they expelled him from the temple and harried him beyond the
walls of the city. 215

Once there was silence again in the temple, Caiaphas began to
speak his mind. "Fellow citizens, I do not care that Nicodemus
has gone over to the enemy, ensnared as he was by their unspeakable wiles. He who so often had exposed himself to danger will- 220
ingly for the sake of the ancestral laws and matters of highest im-
portance, and who was recently attacking our enemy, pressing him
hard in debate, was himself seduced. Such is the seductive power,
such the eloquence of this imposter that he can convert anyone he

ut quoscunque¹ velit vertat superetque venenis.
225 Scilicet hunc credam coelo divinitus actum
nobis venisse auxilio, quo se impius ortum
patre deo canit ac leges abolere parentum
antiquas cupit atque novos inducere ritus?
Seque ultro excidio templi venisse fatetur,
230 quod nostri monitis olim coelestibus acti
impensis tantorum operum struxere parentes.
Quae novitas aut relligio, qui denique mores?
Ille etiam, ne quid sceleris sibi restet inausum,
sacrilegus sontes et quorum crimina nota
235 prosequitur venia, haud veritus scelerata subire
limina, nec festis parcit de more diebus.
Ergo agite atque illi insidias letumque merenti
maturate viri! Crescentem extinguite flammam,
ne mox subsiliat victrix ad tecta domorum,
240 degustetque trabes perque ardua culmina regnet.
Subvertet solitis aliter totam artibus urbem,
seditione potens; populos captabit et omnem
subiiciet sibi prodigiis fallacibus oram.
Hinc quae tot nobis annos tam prospera cessit
245 relligio eversis actutum desinet aris.
Tum metuo ne Romulidae, non talia passi,
quicquid adhuc iuris superest, a gente reposcant
et profugos patria iubeant decedere terra.
Unum pro multis detur caput, unius omnes
250 expiet ac tutos mors tanto in turbine praestet.
Hoc habet. Haec melior superet sententia, cives;
haec illi ob numen dona, hunc reddamus honorem.'
Talia fatus erat. Furiis stimulantibus intus
experti passique senes eadem ore fremebant.
255 Omnibus idem animus, sed qua ratione quibusve
id fieri occulte queat artibus, exquirebant.

chooses and overcome that man with his poison. Am I to believe
that he was sent from heaven to help us — he impiously claims to   225
be the Son of God — when he seeks to abolish the ancient laws of
his ancestors and establish new rituals? He openly avows that he
has come to destroy the temple, which our fathers, at the behest of
heaven, built up with so much labor. What innovation is this?   230
Where is his reverence, his moral standards? Lest any outrage remain unattempted, this unholy man has presumed to pardon even
notorious criminals. He does not scruple to enter the homes of
lawbreakers, even on the traditional Sabbath days. Run then, men,   235
and lay your traps for him, for he deserves death. Put out this
growing fire or it will soon leap up and sweep victoriously through
our houses, consuming the rafters and overwhelming the lofty
rooftops! Otherwise he will seditiously employ his wonted arts to   240
subvert the entire city, take captive the entire population and make
every region submit to him through his dissembling trickery. On
account of him, our religion, which has favored us so greatly
through so many years, will instantly perish as our altars are destroyed. At that point I fear that the sons of Romulus, intolerant   245
of such developments, will take from us what remains of our au-
tonomy and exile us from our fatherland. May one life be sacrificed that many might be saved. Let the death of one man requite
the sins of all the rest, and may his death win safety for us all in
the midst of turmoil. He is done for. Let my better wisdom pre-   250
vail, citizens. Let these be the rewards and this the honor that we
render unto his divinity!"

So he spoke. Having felt the spur of fury within themselves,
the elders roared their assent. They were all of one mind, but they
wanted to know on what pretext and by which arts they might   255
covertly achieve this goal. Just then, to the astonishment of all,

Cum subito, ecce suis clam se furatus, Iudas
improvisus adest cunctis mirantibus. Illum
excipiunt trepidi spirantem immane, locantque
260　sede inter primos farique hortantur et ardent
quid veniat dubiis animis audire silentque.
　　　Ille autem torquens huc flammea lumina et illuc
sic fatur: 'Scio vos Galilaei facta furentis
formidare, patres, patriae qui legibus affert
265　exitium; moliri ideo vos plurima cerno.
Si mihi quae posco promittitis, omnia solus,
quae nunc vos frustra exercent, dispendia tollam.
Ille manus faciam in vestras hodie incidat ultro.'
Dixerat. Argenti laeti pepigere talenta
270　ter dena, egregii pretium memorabile facti,
dimittuntque alacres atque extra limina ducunt.
Ille petit montes iterum sociosque revisit.
　　　Forte propinquabat genti solennis et orae
festa dies, veterum cum relligione parentum
275　immunes operum ducunt septem ocia soles,
perque domos ovium foetus epulantur et acri
fermento parcunt iussi, properataque liba
expediunt mensasque onerant agrestibus herbis,
laetitiae veteris memores. Hac luce ferebant
280　Aegyptum priscos olim coelestibus actos
prodigiis magna cum praeda exisse parentes,
ingressos pede iter salsas impune per undas.
Ergo ingens tum sceptriferam concursus ad urbem
undique erat, populique omnes ad sacra fluebant.
285　Non effusa tamen turba huc sine more ruebat,
verum quisque ducemque suum gentemque tribumque
una ibant comitati. Etenim licet omnibus idem
sanguis cognataque, orti sint stirpe nepotes
omnes Isacidae, paribus sub legibus omnes,

Judas unexpectedly appeared, having stolen away from his brethren. In their alarm they admitted him and his frightful designs. They placed him in a seat of honor and bade him speak. And then, still in doubt and burning to hear why he had come, they fell silent. 260

His flaming eyes shooting in all directions, he thus began: "I know, fathers, that you fear the deeds of the mad Galilean, who brings ruin upon the laws of the fatherland. I see you plotting many things. Promise me what I ask and single-handedly I will lift the burden that weighs upon you. I shall deliver him this day into your hands of his own free will." So he spoke. Gladly they fixed upon thirty talents of silver, the famous price for that infamous deed. Then they eagerly let him go, leading him out of the temple. Once more he went to the mountains to visit his brethren. 265 270

It happened that the festive day was approaching, a day of great solemnity for the nation and the land, when the religion of the fathers prescribed that seven days be passed in leisure and inactivity. In every home men feasted on young lamb and, according to the law, ate only unleavened bread. Laying out hastily made cakes in memory of their ancient happiness, they covered their dinner tables with bitter herbs. This was the day, they said, when their forefathers, inspired by divine portents, went out from Egypt and journeyed on foot, unscathed, through the salt sea. For that reason, there was now a great rush from all directions into the sceptered city, as everyone streamed to the altars. But there was nothing disorderly in their coming. Rather each man accompanied the leader of his race and tribe. For though all were of the same blood, descended from Isaac along the same lineage, their race 275 280 285

290   scindit se tamen in bis senas una tribus gens
      atque Palaestinam late est diducta per omnem.
      Libera gens olim multa munita virum vi
      florentesque urbes populis opibusque vigentes.
      Tunc autem patriis de finibus exturbati,
295   pene omnes aberant et Caspia saxa colebant.
      Vix de bis senis tribus una intacta manebat
      alteraque et patria sese tellure tenebant,
      Beniamidum gens aque ipso domus inclyta Iuda,
      ambae tunc etiam populis opibusque vigentes.
300   Tantum autem imperio adiectam ceu caetera passim
      contuderat bello et victricibus hauserat armis,
      hanc quoque servitio partem Roma alta premebat.
      Sceptra urbi tantum sublataque ademerat arma,
      linquens sacra viris ac leges victor avitas.
305   Nunc tellus deserta iacet. Tot clara fuere
      moenia, tot populis pariter cum fortibus urbes,
      hae bello, hae validis quassatae viribus aevi!
      Usque adeo saevas superum pater arsit in iras
      nimbipotens natique necem non passus inultam est.
310   Non tamen indecorem tantae solatia cladis
      ipse sinam antiquam (superent modo carmina) terram,
      ne penitus seclis obliviscentibus aetas
      deleat extinctam pariter cum nomine gentem;
      regem illis superum prosit regionibus ortum
315   vagisse et coelo primum reptasse sub illo.
        Vos ideo aligeri coetus, gens aetheris alti,
      qui levibus magnum pedibus pulsatis Olympum,
      nam vos saepe polo missi peragrastis et oram
      et gentis crebri hospitio indulsistis amicae,
320   este duces mihi, dum tota regione vagantem
      raptat amor. Longum vos mecum ferre per aevum
      nomina, quae cecidere, iuvet deletaque gentis

had divided into twelve tribes and spread out across the breadth of   290
Palestine. They were once a free race of valiant men, whose flourishing cities abounded in people and wealth. But then, exiled from
their ancestral home, almost all of them were scattered and dwelt
among the Caspian rocks. From twelve tribes, scarcely two re-   295
mained intact in their fatherland, the race of Benjamin and the famous house of Judah himself, both conspicuous in wealth and
population.

Just as lofty Rome had vanquished and exhausted so many   300
other nations through force of arms, this nation as well was en-
slaved and added to the empire. But the victor had taken from the
inhabitants only their sovereignty and their arms, leaving them
their religion and ancestral laws. Today the land is a desert. So
many walled towns, so many cities, together with their brave pop-   305
ulations, laid waste by war and the destructive powers of time!
Such was the fierce fury of the heavenly Father above, who would
not suffer the death of his child to pass unavenged. But as a solace
for such great destruction, I will not allow this ancient land to be   310
without renown — if only my poem survives — so that time in forgetful ages to come may not blot out this people along with its
name! Let it not be for nothing that in these regions the king of
heaven was born a babe, that he first crawled beneath this sky and
first uttered here his infant cries.   315

O winged assembly, race of high heaven, you who tread great
Olympus with a light step, you who have often come down to tra-
verse these shores, tasting the hospitality of its kindly denizens:
lead me now as I wander through this land, driven onward by   320
love. For the sake of future ages, may you recite with me this
race's vanished towns that have fallen, as well as its ancient cities

oppida et antiquas antiqui nominis arces.
Post autem vestra sublatus ad aethera penna
325 carmine mortales oras visusque relinquam.
Vos me sublimi sistetis tramite vectum
avia per superum loca. Me iuvet alite curru
aurea nubifugo mulcentem sidera cantu
intactas primum ire vias mortalibus aegris
330 et petere insolitam coeli alta e rupe coronam.
Haec olim, audentem ni deserat aetheris aura.
    Nunc mecum populos percurrite templa petentes.
Non alias illuc aditum est maioribus unquam
et numero et studiis. Nec tantum sacra petebant,
335 quantum avidos Christi visendi traxerat ardor.
Orti autem a magno primi ingrediuntur Iuda,
per multos ductum reges genus. Haec tribus usque
et numero et virtute caput super extulit omnes,
tantum alias superans quantum leo cuncta ferarum
340 semina inexhaustis animis et viribus anteit.
    Littorea innumeri Gaza venere Sabeque.
Engada deseruere racemiferosque recessus,
urbis Adulaeae sedes humilemque Raphean.
Hic Lyde atque Selis ventosaque Iamnia et Hippa,
345 Ascalo Azotique arces Acharonque Sochonque,
quaeque fluentisonis Iope perfunditur undis
proiectae rupes pontoque minantia saxa.
Parte alia antiquam cives liquere Damascum,
primus ubi (ut perhibent), limo felice creatus,
350 natus homo est coelique novas erupit in auras.
Deseriturque Emaus Nepseque exhausta silescit,
quaesivitque suos Aegypti proxima regnis
Anthedon, natique dei cunabula, Bethle.
    Tum deserta silent et Galgala Bessuraque omnis
355 arvaque qua Marethon, qua proxima nubibus Erme,

of ancient fame. Hereafter, lifted to heaven on your wings and
borne aloft by my song, I shall leave behind all mortal lands and
sights. As I ascend along a lofty road, bear me aloft through the 325
hidden recesses of heaven. Charming the stars with my cloud-dis-
pelling song, may I be the first to journey in a winged chariot
along a path untouched by weary mortals. At the pinnacle of
heaven, may I claim a crown no one has claimed before. And so I 330
shall one day, unless the breath of heaven abandon my attempt.

Now help me to recite the names of the tribes that came to the
temple. Never before had the city seen so great or so eager a
crowd. But they had come not so much for the sacred service as
for the chance to see Christ. First came those who had been born 335
into the tribe of great Judah, a clan rich in kings. Both in size and
in courage, this tribe surpassed all the others, even as the lion sur-
passes all the other beasts in its inexhaustible courage and enduring strength.   340

Many came from Sheba and the shores of Gaza. They deserted
Engedi and its wine-bearing thickets, Adullam's city and lowly
Raphaim. And here were the citizens of Lydda and Shilhim, of
Hippa and windy Jabneel, of Ascalon and the cliffs of Ashdod, of
Ekron, Socoh and Joppa, watered by mellifluous waves, promon- 345
tories and bluffs that menace the sea. The citizens abandoned ancient Damascus as well, where, they say, man was first created
from the fertile soil and sprang up amid the new breezes of
heaven. Emaus was emptied and Nibshan stood silent. Hard by   350
the kingdom of Egypt, Anthedon besought its citizens, and Bethlehem too, the cradle of God born man.

Deserted Gilgal fell silent and so did all Bethsura. Likewise the
fields of Maarath and Hermon nigh the clouds, and Zoar, won- 355

qua Sigoris mirata nurum, dum incendia versa
respicit, humanos servasse in marmore vultus
concretique salis subitum traxisse rigorem,
qua calet Asphaltis flammis infamibus unda
360   ingentesque palus ad coelum exaestuat aestus,
aera contristans graveolenti sulfuris aura.
Quondam hic laeta seges riguisque rosaria campis;
nunc stat ager dumis obductaque sentibus arva.
Crimen, amor malesuade, tuum, vim tendere adorti
365   infandam indigenae pueris coelestibus olim,
divina capti facie et florentibus annis,
fecissentque, fuga nisi se illi ad sidera lapsi
remigio nixos rapuissent praepetis alae.
Non tulit altitonans pater atque ultricibus omnem
370   involvit flammis tractum immersitque profundo.
Squalet adhuc cinere et putri late ora favilla;
infoecunda ideo terra et sine frugibus agri
difficilesque aditus et inaccessi secessus.
Illic, ut fama est, nitidum florem educat arbos,
375   quem cupiunt iuvenes, cupiunt decerpse puellae.
At simul atque gravi perflante evanuit Austro,
succedunt poma hirsutis asperrima barbis,
quae nulli iuvenes, nullae cupiere puellae.
Haec tamen aspectu solida et syncera putares,
380   foeda sed illuvies intus subitoque fatiscunt,
ad tactum cinefacta, hominum nihil usibus apta.
Pallida item flavis cum vix seges albet aristis,
dira immaturas messes interficit aura.

    Protinus hinc subeunt populi Symeone creati,
385   qui Saroen Molodamque viri Sicelegidaque[2] oram

dering at the young wife when she turned to see the raging fires:
she preserved her human features in a statue that assumed at once
the hardness of caked salt. Silent as well were those lands where
the Dead Sea boils with infamous flames: the swamp belches up to
heaven its huge eruptions, making the air gloomy with the fetid
breath of sulfur. Once this region had abounded in fertile harvests 360
and rose bowers throughout its well-watered meadows. But now
its fields are thick with bramble, its plains with briar. This was the
penalty for your crime, O casuistical love, when the inhabitants attempted unspeakable violence against the angels, enchanted as 365
they were by the angels' heavenly beauty and flourishing youth:
and they would have had their way, had not these youths hastened
to heaven on the oarage of their swift wings. But God the Father,
thundering from on high, grew indignant, consuming the entire
land in avenging flames and flooding it with the sea. Even now the 370
land is a desolation of ash and stinking ember, its fields fruitless
and sere, its approaches parlous and its recesses difficult of access.
Legend has it that here a tree brings forth a lovely flower, which
youths and maidens long to cull. But no sooner has it vanished 375
under the blasts of sultry Auster than it is replaced by apples bristling with shaggy barbs, which neither youth nor maiden ever desired. In appearance it looks solid and good. But within lurks a
filth that is no sooner touched than it turns to ash, useless to hu- 380
mankind. No sooner has the pale crop bloomed upon its golden
stalks than the baleful breeze blasts the immature harvest.

Next came the sons of Simeon, who dwelt in Sharuhen,
Molodah and the shores of Ziklag, its fields rich in fruit and vines. 385

felicem frugum laetosque uligine campos,
qui Sipabota colunt Asanesque biverticis arces,
quique Atharin, quondam generosos palmite colles,
Remmona qui cultisque erectam in collibus Ain,
390 et quos thurilegae pascunt centum oppida Idumes
ruraque odoriferas Arabum vergentia ad oras.
    Ecce autem Isachari[3] magno clamore nepotes
ingressi delubra petunt aramque salutant.
Gens victu facilis contentaque finibus arctis.
395 Hic adsunt quos Hermonius sub vertice pascit,
Hermonius generator apum, generator equorum;
qui Taburi capita alta tenent, quibus ardua rupes
Carmeli domus. Haec rapido gens turbine quondam
sublatum vatem coeli per aperta repente
400 vidit flammifero ferri super aethera curru.
Sensena quos misit, quos Hennada, quos alit Affra
nobilis, in summis sitientes rupibus urbes;
qui Senum et Reboten liquere Remethiaque[4] arva,
vitibus et variis intersita littora pomis.
405   At taciti incedunt gens Dani e sanguine creti
deiectique oculos deiectique ora per urbem
templa petunt. Qualis cum frigora prima lacessunt
autumnum nec dum ramis decussit honorem
bruma suum, coluber latebras meditatur iterque
410 fert tacitum lapsu repens per saxa quieto
sibilaque ora premit neque caudae surrigit orbes.
Iamque viros tristes credas, quod sanguine ab illo
praedixere ducem fore pleni numine vates,
qui genus humanum Christi sub imagine falsa
415 terreat atque hominum vitas et crimina quaerat,
deterior fas atque nefas ubi verterit aetas
et rebus feret exitium mortalibus ignis.
Protinus at multis aderit cum millibus ultor,

Here as well were the inhabitants of Sipabota and the twin mountains of Ashan. Also the inhabitants of Ether whose hills once
brought forth palms, of Remmon and Ain, rising amid the tilled
fields. Here too were those who dwelt amid the hundred towns of
Edom, rich in incense, and the fields bordering the fragrant lands   390
of the Arabians.

And now the famous sons of Isaac, entering the temple, sought
the altars and hailed the ark. Their race live well, content within
their limited borders. Some were present who lived beneath the   395
peaks of Hermus, nourisher of horses and bees. Others inhabited
the lofty summits of Tabor, whose steep cliff is Mount Carmel;
once this tribe saw a prophet carried suddenly in a whirlwind
through the open sky, up to the ether in a flaming chariot. Also   400
present were the denizens of Sansannah, Enhaddah and noble
Haphraim, cities that thirst atop their cliffs, as well as those who
left Shunem behind, and Reboth, and the Remethian fields, coasts
planted with vines and brightly colored fruit.

But the race born of the blood of Dan entered in silence. With   405
downcast eyes and downcast faces, they passed through the city to
the temples. As when the first chill besets the autumn season and
winter storms have not yet shaken off the adornment of each
branch, then the snake seeks a hiding place, silently passing among
the rocks with a soundless fall, muting its hissing tongue and rais- 410
ing not even the coils of its tail. You would say that these men
were sad because the divinely inspired prophets had foretold how,
from their blood, a leader would arise to terrorize the human race
under the false image of the Christ; how he would inquire into the
crimes and lives of men, in a more corrupt age when good and ill   415
would be reversed and fire consume all things mortal. But then an
avenger would suddenly appear, backed by many thousands of

vera dei soboles, verus datus arbiter orbi.
420 Illum nequicquam pugnantem et vana moventem,
turbine corripiens, terrae ima in viscera trudet.
  Insequitur iuvenum nimbus genus Asere ductum,
spicea quis capita obnubit de more corona
omnibus et nexae ludunt per tempora aristae.
425 Hi Betagumque Hormamque serunt; his Aphega sedes;
illos Ama dedit, illos misere Robaeae.
  Non numero Arctipus Labanae, non Aziba cessit.
Hos iuxta seram in noctem soliti urere myrtos
littoreas ponti gens accola Zabulones
430 dona ferunt. Pars Ieptaphiles ab sede profecti;
pars Iedaba venere. Canam hi liquere, modo atra
miratam puras in vina rubescere lymphas.
  Hos Nazara tulit, tulit illos ardua Sembros,
quaeque modo aerias iterum venisse sub auras
435 vidit morte obita puerum, Galileia Nais
millia multa tulit, totidemque huberrima Dotha;
aque suis Nalole Cathetiaque alta relicta est.
  At quis Nephthalidum numeraverit oppida et arces
innumeras, quas et Cedar,[5] quas et sacer altis
440 fert humeris Libanus coeli confinibus aequus?
  Qui celsam Nasona habitant, qui Nephthalis urbem,
gens oris fandique potens foecundaque veri,
nascentem gemino Iordanem fonte salutat.
  Omnis iit Galilaea, omnis Samarea penates
445 deseruit, studio gens tantum accita videndi.
Saepe hac rege satus superum tellure moratus
sponte deum se detexit. Miracula rerum
asseda nunc etiam meminit, meminere Caperna,
et vetus amisit quae nomen[6] Graia Sebaste.
450 It Bethole eductaque ad sidera Bessais arce
et quos piscosis Gennesara proluit undis.

men. This true Son of God, sent down to judge the world, would
fling him, flailing and scheming in vain, into the deepest entrails of   420
the earth.

Next followed the throng of youths, the race of Asher. All their
heads were covered, according to their custom, with crowns of
wheat, and they sported stalks of wheat in their hair. Some tilled
the fields of Betan and Ramah. Others came from Aphek or were   425
sent by Amad and Rehob. As many came from Lebanese Arctipus and Achzib. Following them was the gift-bearing tribe of
Zebulun, who dwell by the sea and are wont to burn, late into the
night, the myrtles of the shore. The sons of Japhtahel and Idalah,   430
likewise, came from their homes. Others came from Cana, which
so lately had marveled at the clear water turned to dark wine.
Then followed the sons of Nazareth and lofty Shimron. Thousands came from most fertile Dothan and and equal number from
Nain in Galilee, that lately saw a boy returned to life after he'd en-   435
countered death. Likewise Nahallal and lofty Katteh were abandoned by their sons. But who can number the towns of the sons
of Naphthali, with its countless castles, or the children of Kedar,
or those whom holy Lebanon, as high as heaven itself, carries   440
upon its lofty shoulders? And the inhabitants of Enhazor and of
Naphtil came, a race rich in eloquence and truth, that hails the
Jordan at its twofold source. All of Galilee and Samaria came, too,
drawn by an avid desire to look on Christ. Often the Son of God,   445
dwelling upon the earth, willingly revealed his divinity in this
place. Even now did Ziddim and Capernaum recall his miracles,
and Greek Sebaste, which lost its ancient name. Bethol came, and
Bethsaida whose city rises to the stars. Present too were those   450
whom Gennesaret bathes in its waters, rich in fish. The house of

Levigenae vero sacrum genus omnibus ibant
immixti, neque enim propria his regio ulla colenda
sorte data est, sed diversas dux legifer olim
455 huc illuc oras aeque est partitus in omnes,
praefecitque sacros aris, proque hubere glebae
et iugulare dedit pecudes atque exta cremare.
    At non contentus regnis sceptrisque Manasseus,
sortitus quae trans fluvium sibi iunxerat ampla,
460 protulit imperium qua Nepheca Bersaque surgunt,
venatrix pecorumque altrix et Dora ferarum.
Olli etiam parent Tenachos nemorosaque Iebla
et Magedos nulli populis opibusque secunda,
quasque rigat Taphua claris argenteus undis,
465 ver ubi perpetuum scatebrisque recentia prata.
Succedunt qui trans Iordanis flumen opima
arva serunt, tribus ipso etiam deducta Manasseo.
    Necnon Gade sati, necnon Rubene creati
belligero, fratrum cunctorum maximus aevo
470 qui fuit, una omnes urbem ingrediuntur, ut olim
una etiam sedem optarunt trans flumen eandem,
indigenis quondam regnata gigantibus arva.
Argobiae qui rura colunt Basanidaque oram,
qui saltus Galadina tuos, Ogique subactas
475 sexaginta urbes Galaticaque oppida: Iabin
et Sebamam Balmenque Ramotha Golanque Nabenque
Edrenque Selcamque et semirutam Cariathen.
Haec tunc nomina, nunc alio sunt nomine terrae.
Tum qui cedriferae pascunt asperrima Arimnes,
480 omnes fronde caput tecti, omnes terga veruti.
Qui Bosorim Rabathenque tenent, qui Gaulida et omnem
fortibus exercent tauris Bathaltidos oram,
et quos humectat praeceps de montibus Arnos.
Nec vos transierim, qui prata feracis Abillae,

Levi, a holy tribe, came forth, mixed among the others. For this
race alone was allotted no place of its own. Rather the Lawgiver
distributed them here and there among the lands. Yet he gave   455
them jurisdiction over the altars, and in place of fertile earth, he
taught them to sacrifice sheep and burn their entrails.

But Manasseh, not content with the ample realms and scepters
allotted her on the other side of the river, extended her rule to in-
clude Nepaca and Bersa, as well as Dora, the huntress and nour-   460
isher of flocks and beasts. Under her sway fell Tenaach as well,
and wooded Iblea, and Meggido, second to none in wealth and citizens. So too came Entappuah, silvery amid its sparkling waves,
where spring is eternal and the fields are always renewed by the   465
waters. Next came those who sow the fertile land beyond the Jordan, a tribe descended from this same Manasseh.

Then came the sons of Gad and warlike Ruben, oldest of all
the brothers. Now they entered the city together and united, since   470
they had chosen to live in the same place beyond the river, in fields
once ruled by native giants. So too came those who dwell in the
fields of Argob and the land of Bashan, and those who inhabit
your forests, Gilead, and the sixty vanquished cities of Og and the
towns of Gilead: Jabesh and Shibmah, Baalmeon, Ramoth, Golan,   475
and Nebo, Edar and Salcak and Kirjathaim half-destroyed. Such
were your names then; but now these lands have another name.
They were followed by those who live amid the harsh terrain of
Aram, rich in cedar, their heads covered with leaves and javelins
on their backs. After them came the inhabitants of Bezer, Rabath-   480
Ammon and Golan, and all who plow the lands of Bethalto with
their strong oxen, or drink the waters of the Arnon that falls
headlong from the mountains. And let me not forget you men

485 quique Eleale viri metitis viridemque Aserota,[7]
    Seoniamque Esebon, saxis horrentia regna,
    desertasque Cades, quas Phasga habet arduus et quas
    hinc atque hinc Hermus praeruptas sustinet urbes,
    quas Abaris, cuius nimboso e vertice quondam
490 pastores admirati videre morantem
    Iordanem ingenti subsidere mole coacta
    undarum et cursu cedentia flumina retro,
    dum domus Isacidum promissa capesseret arva.
       Postremi subeunt advecti e sede propinqua
495 Beniamidae, data sorte quibus laetissima tellus,
    maxima ubi et Solyme totius regia gentis,
    altaque Iarephile Luzaeque binominis arces,
    quaeque modo quarta regem iam luce sepultum
    Bethane obstupuit revocari ad munera vitae,
500 et Tarela et Samare et lentisciferae Gabaothae,
    gens infesta feris: ideo exuviasque luporum
    induti incedunt iuvenes, canibusque fatigant,
    quas sepire plagis iuvat usque et frangere, silvas
    atque adeo assiduo venatu mane recentes
505 convectant humeris praedas, quas vesper Olympum
    claudit ubi, gaudent partiri epulisque fruuntur
    atque inter sese per agros convivia curant.
    Hic adsunt, quis Maspha domus, quibus arduus Hemen[8]
    difficiles colles ac scabra crepidine terga,
510 qui liquere Recen celsasque Berothidos arces
    atque Sylum quondam gaudentem paupere templo,
    qui longumque Helephon Avinque Amosamque Selamque
    atque ululata Rhamae passim Rachellidos arva.
       Qui Gabeone domo quique Hierichunte profecti.
515 Indigenas est fama, viae assiduique meatus
    oblitum, vidisse diu considere solem
    imperio ducis atque diem decedere serum.

who till the fields of fertile Abel, of Elealeh, green Ashteroth and   485
Sionian Heshbon, bristling with rocks; also deserted Kadesh, the
cities of steep Pisgah, and those shattered towns, here and there,
upon the heights of Hermus or of Abaris: atop its cloud-capped
summit once the shepherds marveled to see slow Jordan halt, its   490
great quantity of water stilled, and the yielding streams flow backwards until the house of the sons of Isaac could take possession of
the promised fields.

   Last came the sons of Benjamin from their nearby home. To
them was allotted the most fertile land of all, with great Jerusalem,   495
the royal dwelling of the entire race, and lofty Japheti, the two-
named fortresses of Luz, and Bethany which, on the fourth day after its king's interment, marveled to see him return to the tasks of
life. Next came the inhabitants of Taralah and Zemaraim and
Gibeah, rich in mastic trees, a race bestial to beasts: hence its   500
youths entered, wearing the fur of wolves. With their hounds they
weary the woods, which it pleases them to tear up and fence with
netting. And so, up early after a diligent hunt, they carry their
new-caught prey on their shoulders. And when evening descends
upon the heavens, they delight to divide the meat and have a feast,   505
filling the fields with their convivial talk. Also present were those
who dwell in Mizpah and steep Hammon, hills difficult of ascent
and rugged mountain chains. Then too came the inhabitants of
Rakem and the lofty summits of Beeroth, and Siloh that once re-   510
joiced in its humble temple, as well as the inhabits of Heleph,
Aven, Mosa, Selah, and the fields of Ramah, echoing everywhere
with Rachel's lamentations.

   Then there were those who came from the house of Gibeon
and of Jericho. Legend has it that they beheld the sun, its wonted   515
course and journey forgotten, standing still at their general's behest and drawing out the day. Among them one youth of noble

Hos inter facie egregia puer altior ibat,
qui prisco genus a Saulo nomenque trahebat.
520 Iam tum illum vates uno omnes ore canebant
praestanti clarum eloquio factisque futurum.
Quantis ille tamen mentem caligine pressus
in nostros odiis primum furiisque feretur!
Omnipotens aderit pater et se pectore toto
525 altius infundet iuveni excutietque furorem.
Protinus afflatus divinitus aetheris aura
implebit terras monitis, latumque per orbem
mortales meliora docens ad sacra vocabit,
nec letum horrescet pro relligione cruentum.
530 Iam duodena tribus magnae successerat urbi.
Ipse etiam templo ut solitos inferret honores
munere nec tali tam laeta luce careret,
affatur socios Christus: 'Lux sacra propinquat.
Omnis se dapibus festa domus apparat urbe.
535 Ecquis erit vestrum, primus qui ad moenia tendat,
si quis forte opibus fessos invitet abundans,
nos quoque ut ante meos obitus ac funus acerbum
solennes epulas celebremus et annua sacra?
Nec longe quaerendus. Erit puer obvius ultro
540 urnam humero lymphasque ferens de fonte recentes.
Quo tendat gressus aut quo sese ille receptet,
observate, locumque acie capite usque sequendo.
Limina vos eadem accipiant, tectumque subite.
Tum dominum affati coram hospitiumque rogantes,
545 exiguam sacris sedem, nostrum edite nomen.
Tectum auratum ingens pictisque insigne tapetis
protinus ostendet. Structas ibi ponite mensas.
Ipse adero atque eadem socios ad limina ducam.'
Dixit. Ioannes mandata Petrusque facessunt,
550 et moesti magnae succedunt moenibus urbis.

countenance walked taller than the rest, bearing the name and lineage of Saul. All the prophets sang of him with one voice, as destined to achieve fame through eloquence and action. But how great will be the rage and hatred that he will bear against our people, his mind clouded by darkness! The Almighty Father will appear and pour himself deep into the young man's heart and drive out his fury. Then infused all at once with the divine breath of heaven, he shall fill the lands of the wide world with his teachings, instructing mortals and calling them to a better form of worship. Nor will he shrink from a bloody death for the sake of religion.

Now the twelve tribes had reached the great city. Jesus was determined to perform the customary rites in the temple and not to omit the duties of this blessed day. He addressed his disciples thus: "The sacred day is near. Throughout the festive city, each house prepares a feast. Is there one of you who will run ahead and ask if some rich man might invite the weary into his house? Thus before I am harshly put to death, we too might celebrate the solemn meal and the annual rites. It will not be hard to find the man. You will come across a boy carrying an urn on his shoulder, full of water newly drawn from a fountain. Mark where he passes and his destination. Follow him and make a note of the place. Let the same house invite you in and enter it. When you speak to the owner, ask for the hospitality of a meager place to hold the sacred feast and give him my name. He will at once show you a huge, golden chamber, resplendent with colored tapestries. Set the meal there. Then I myself will come and bring my disciples into that house."

So he spoke. Full of sadness, John and Peter hastened to do his bidding and reached the walls of the great city. Their path was uncertain and they observed everything from afar. Then a servant-

Ibant incerti atque oculis procul omnia obibant,
cum puer urnam humero gestans lymphamque recentem
vicino veniens de fonte occurrit. Eum usque
servantes gressum ferret quacunque sequuntur,
555   quasque subit, subeunt ipsi quoque protinus aedes.
Huc atavis clarusque Simon et prole beatus
septena sese semper referebat ab agris,
si quando caris cum gnatis viseret urbem.
Nanque illum potius campis rurique iuvabat
560   degere civilesque procul contemnere honores.
Umbrae illi nemorum cordi rivique secantes
praedia, quae centum dives vertebat aratris.
Iam gravis argutasque fides et carmina amabat
fluminis in ripis aut fontem propter amoenum;
565   norat enim coeli numeros mensusque viasque.
Saepe deo plenus porro ventura canebat
agricolis quid sol, quid menstrua luna pararet,
sudique pluviaeque docens praenuntia signa.
Tum sacris intentam igitur concesserat urbem,
570   ut de more dies festos celebraret avito.
Dumque alia famuli mensas et dona pararent
parte domus, veterum facta ipse canebat avorum,
nunc citharae levibus digitis, nunc pectine eburno
percurrens molli attactu vocalia fila.

575   Praecipue a prima revocabat origine, quaenam
has ex more epulas atque haec solennia priscae
relligio intulerit genti. Verum ecce canenti
improvisus adest Petrus et sacra carmina rumpit.
'Rex,' ait, 'est nobis, quo nusquam iustior alter
580   aut pietate prior; Christum omnes nomine dicunt.
Is tua nos ultro supplex ad limina mittit.
Exiguam sacris sedem mensisque rogamus.'
His ille auditis gavisus nomine tanto,

boy appeared carrying on his shoulders the water he had just
drawn from a nearby fountain. Eagerly they followed him, keeping
him in their sights, wherever his step should lead. And soon they
entered the very house he had entered. There they were ap-   555
proached by Simon, illustrious in ancestors and rich in his seven
children. He would always come here from the country whenever
he visited the city with his beloved sons. For he preferred to dwell
in the fields and on the land, holding civil honors in contempt.
Rather this wealthy man loved the shady glen and the streams that   560
cut through the farmland that he tilled with a hundred plows. A
serious man, he loved both song and musical skill as he played
along the river banks or beside a pleasant spring. He knew the
movements, the courses and the paths of all the heavens. Inspired   565
by God, he often sang to the husbandmen of things to come, telling them what the sun and moon held in store and teaching them
the portents of rain and fair weather. And so he had come then to
the city as it readied the sacred rites, to celebrate the feast days according to ancient custom. And while his servants, in one part of   570
his house, were preparing meals and gifts, he sang the deeds of his
ancient ancestors, lightly touching the lyre with swift fingers or
passing an ivory pick across its singing strings.

Especially he related the very beginnings of the tradition that   575
had established these feasts and yearly rites among their ancestors.
As he was singing their true origin, Peter appeared suddenly, in-
terrupting his sacred song. "We have a king," he said, "second to
none in justice or piety. Everyone calls him the Christ. We ask of   580
you a little room for the holiday feast and rites. As a suppliant, he
has sent us to your doorstep." As soon as Simon heard these
words, he rejoiced in the great name. Without hesitation, he or-

imperat haud haerens animo tectum omne recludi;
585 hinc hilares totis adolere penatibus ignes
et pingui suffire Arabum iubet atria silva,
interiusque viros media in penetralia ducit.
Inde locum ostendit mira testudine pictis
aulaeis circunvelatum ostroque rubenti.
590 Luxuriant sola strata; nitent argentea eburnis
fulcra torisque scyphique auroque e simplice lances,
et passim domus argentoque auroque renidet.
    Atque haec deinde refert: 'Non hoc mihi nomen ad aures
nunc primum venit, illius sed cognita fama
595 iam pridem virtus, neque enim mihi cernere coram
fas fuit aut vocem divinam hausisse loquentis.
Adveniat. Placidus tectis assuescat amicis.
Vos hic expectate. Viros, qui exacta reportent
omnia, dimittam meaque illum ad limina ducant,
600 atque utinam libeat longum his in sedibus olli
degere et hospitii dignetur nomine tectum,
quod nostros iuvet interdum memorare nepotes
hospitibusque locum felicem ostendere seris.
Interea adventu vestro intermissa sequamur
605 carmina et antiquos patrum repetamus honores,
dum nigra roriferis nox terras obruat umbris.'
    Sic ait, ac nervis socians concordibus ora
obloquitur numeris. Quae concinit, ordine picta
cuncta putes aut textilibus simulata figuris.
610 Nempe Paretoniis cantu deducit ab oris
Isacidum genus, arrepta maris aequora virga
ut profugum dux findat aquasque impune per altas,
ut sine navigiis ierint pelagique profunda
sicco calcarint pede. Nanque induruit humor
615 aridus et liquidas late est via secta per undas.
A tergo tota ex Aegypto curribus hostes

dered that his entire home be opened, that festive torches be lit throughout the house, and that the halls be perfumed with the   585
fragrances of Arabia. He invited the two men into the innermost parts of the house. There he showed them a wondrously vaulted room hung round with brightly colored tapestries and glowing purple. The paved floors shone and the couches gleamed with silver and inlaid ivory. The cups and dishes were of pure gold. Indeed, the house was radiant throughout with silver and gold.   590

Simon spoke thus: "This is not the first time that I hear his name: his virtue has long been known to me by reputation, though I never had the right to meet him face to face or to hear   595
his divine voice. Let him come and stay under my roof as long as he likes. You wait here. I will send my men to explain all that has been decided and lead him to my home. I hope he will wish to remain a long time, honoring my house with a reputation for hospitality. May my progeny fondly recall his coming and show this   600
happy place to visitors many years from now. Meanwhile, let me resume the songs I broke off at your coming, songs that relate the ancient honors of our fathers. I will sing until black night covers   605
the earth in clouds and dew."

So he spoke. And singing in verse, he harmonized his voice to the lyre's strings. His song was like a finely composed painting or like figures rendered in a tapestry. In song he led the sons of Isaac out of the lands of Pharaoh. Waving a wand, the leader of the refugees divided the waters, so that, without boats, they could walk   610
unharmed through the depths of the sea. For the sea had hardened and dried up, cutting a path through the clear waves. Behind   615
them, from every part of Egypt, the enemy was pursuing them

quadriugis vecti instabant fulgentibus armis.
Iamque pios canit emenso pelago alta tenere
littora littoreisque metu se condere silvis.
620   Nulla mora est: iterum telo tellure recussa
divino, redeunt in se maria ecce refusa,
quae media ingenti dirimebat semita tractu.
Inde hostes ruere et salsis in fluctibus arma,
armaque quadrupedesque et corpora mersa virorum
625   aspiceres magis atque magis subsidere in undis
semper et absumptos velut evanescere currus;
qui medii extabant, medios salis hauserat aestus.
      Addit, ut omnipotens rerum sator aethere ab ipso
paverit in vasta gentem regione locorum
630   errantem, dape coelesti miseratus egenos.
Cernere ibique putes epulas nivis instar ab aethra
defluere ad terram subitas coetusque paratis
accinctos dapibus latis epularier arvis.
Proinde etiam duras cautes pulsabat eadem
635   dux coelum aspectans virga, cum protinus amnis
prosilit et dulcem saxa erupere liquorem,
atque hausere novis populi de fontibus undam,
quos sitis ex longo collecta urebat hiantes.
Tum canit, ut primus Solymorum conditor arcis
640   dona laboratae frugisque recensque reperti
pocula plena meri obtulerit campestribus aris,
cespite quas viridi sectaque extruxerat orno.
      Atque ea dum intentis hauribant auribus omnes,
haud rerum ignarus, Christus de montibus altis
645   cesserat infensaeque iterum successerat urbi.
Et iam declivi cum sol properaret Olympo,
hospitis intravit sociis comitantibus aedes
regifico instructas luxu dapibusque paratis.

with gleaming weaponry, riding in four-horse chariots. Next Simon sang of how the chosen people crossed the sea and, reaching
the opposite shore, hid themselves in fear along the wooded litto-
ral. Once more the earth was struck with the divine rod of Moses
and suddenly the sea, which had been divided by a path straight   620
down the middle, closed up again. Midway through the huge, exposed passage, you could see the enemy's army rushing headlong,
and amid the salt waves, weapons, horses, and the bodies of the
drowned sank deeper into the sea, while ever more chariots sank   625
down and vanished into its brackish waters.

   Next Simon told of how, from heaven itself, the omnipotent
Creator of the universe took pity on his people and fed them celestial manna as they wandered, destitute, through the vast desert.
You could almost see the manna, like snow, falling swiftly from   630
heaven to earth, as the assembled people, in the broad meadows,
prepared to feast on the meal that had been prepared for them.
Then, gazing up at heaven, their leader struck the hard stone with
the selfsame rod and presently a spring gushed forth. As the rocks   635
unleashed a torrent of sweet water, the people, who had been
thirsting for so long, drank up the draughts from this unexpected
source. And then he sang of how the first builder of the citadel of
Jerusalem had offered the hard-won harvest and cups full of the
newly-discovered wine on those rustic altars that he had built with 640
green grass and cut ashwood.

   While everyone listened intently, Christ was well aware of what
was taking place. Coming down from the mountaintop, he once
again entered the city of his enemies. With the sun hastening   645
along the downward-sloping sky, he and his disciples arrived at his
host's house, which was laid out in regal luxury. As they all re-

Discubuere omnes. Una inter dirus Iudas
650 dissimulans sedet, et vultu mentitur amorem.
  Iamque heros puras fruges properataque liba
accipiens, frangensque manu partitur in omnes.
Inde mero implevit pateram lymphaque recenti
et laticis mixti dium sacravit honorem,
655 spumantemque dedit sociis, mox talia fatur:
'Corporis haec nostri, haec vera cruoris imago,
unus pro cunctis quem fundam sacra parenti
hostia, ut antiquae noxae contagia tollam.
Vos ideo, quoties positas accedere mensas
660 contigerit sacrasque dapes libamina iussa,
funeris his nostri moestum referetis honorem
et nunquam istius abolescet gloria facti.'
  Nec plura. Ex illo mox servavere minores
hunc semper ritum memores, arisque sacramus
665 synceram cererem et dulcem de vite liquorem
pro veterum tauris, pecudum pro pinguibus extis.
Ipse, sacerdotum verbis eductus, ab astris
frugibus insinuat sese regnator Olympi,
libaturque dei sacrum cum sanguine corpus.
670 In summos haec relligio successit honores.
  Ergo ubi pulsa fames sociis, sese ocius heros
exuit insignem tunicam et mantilibus albis
succinctus, poscit flammis undantia ahena.
Tum gelidam irrorans dextra laevaque sonoris
675 pertentans labris, ferventem temperat undam.
Hinc genibus positis Petro reliquisque suorum—
plurima quanquam ille attonitus novitate recuset—
dat pedibus lymphas et molli siccat amictu
accurvus, sociis linquens imitabile factum.
680 Mox gemitus imo ducens de pectore fatur:
'En mihi summa dies, socii, quamque ipse propinquam

clined for the meal that had been set before them, the baleful Judas dissimulated his true feelings and in his face he feigned love.   650

Now the hero received unleavened bread and the quick-baked
loaves, and he broke the bread and distributed it to them all. Then
he filled a cup with wine and fresh water and consecrated the holy
goodness of the mixed drink. With these words he gave it, frothing, to his disciples: "This is the true image of my body, this the   655
true image of my blood. Though but one man, I will spill my
blood for the sake of all men, a sacred offering unto my Father, to
remove the stain of ancient sin. And as often as you sit down to
such meals, to this consecrated food and wine, you will relate the   660
sad honor of my death, whose glory will never fade."

He said no more. But since that time, all subsequent generations have faithfully preserved this rite. And so we hallow our altars with simple bread and with the sweet juice of the vine, in   665
place of the bulls and fatted sheep that men used of old. The lord
of Olympus himself, drawn down from heaven by the words of
the priests, enters into the meal, as the sacred body and blood of
God are offered up. This holy tradition has long been held in the
highest reverence.   670

When the disciples had satisfied their hunger, Jesus quickly removed his fine tunic and, girt with white linens, asked for a
bronze vessel boiling from the fire. With his left hand he poured
the cold water and tested it with his right, cooling the liquid that
frothed around the sounding basin of the bowl. Then he knelt and   675
began to wash the feet of his disciples. Peter was astonished by
this strange act and kept refusing. But Jesus bent over and dried
their feet with his soft cloak, providing them with an example to
be imitated.

Then a sigh rose from the depths of his heart. "Behold,   680
friends," he said, "the final day has come, which I often said was

praedixi toties; nox illa advenit acerba.
Vos linquam et moriens genitoris iussa capessam.
Unus erit vestrum (vix, o vix credere tantum
685 fas scelus) insidiis prodet qui me hostibus ultro.
Haud me animi fallit. Furias iam perfidus ille
concipit insidiasque animo meditatur avaro.
Id pietas mea magna, mei meruere labores.
Non tamen ipse diu pulchro laetabere facto,
690 quisquis eris. Satius si nunquam lucis amorem
gustasses, dulcis nec vitae limen inisses.
At vos este pii inque vicem (quae exempla reliqui)
inter vos aliis alii parete volentes,
summissisque animis fastus abolete superbos.
695 Non Erebi in tanto cessabunt cardine dirae
vestra potestates praevertere corda timore.
Pervigiles quaeso iam custodite proculque
consulite. Hic animos atque illos promite sensus,
quos toties mihi polliciti, ne cedite pesti;
700 vos servate, viri, noctem non amplius unam.'
  Extemplo turbati omnes gemitumque dedere,
suspensi quem caecum adeo furiisque subactum
ore premens signet venturi praescius heros.
Quem senior tali aggreditur sermone precando:
705 'O coeli decus, in quenquam tam immane putandum est
posse scelus cadere? Quisnam foedissimus ille?
Faxo hodie nunquam nobis illudat inultis.
Non adeo effugit cum sanguine vivida virtus
pulsa annis, nec dextra mihi tam frigida languet.'
710 Sic ait, et pariter vagina liberat ensem.
Dux autem signis manifestis prodidit hostem,
sed cunctis mentem eripuit voluitque latere,
donec res perfecta. Dehinc haec edidit ore:
'Immo omni ex numero mihi nemo hac nocte suprema

close at hand, and the bitter night. I shall leave you and go to my
death, to satisfy the commandments of my Father. For one among
you (O, it is almost wicked to believe in such wickedness!) will
come forth to betray me treacherously to my enemies. But I know   685
already what he intends. The traitor even now is devising his mad
scheme, trying to trap me in his greedy heart. Such is the reward
of my piety and all my labors! But whoever you are, you will not
enjoy for long the rewards of this noble deed! Rather it would be
better for you never to have felt the love of daylight, never to have   690
crossed the threshold of sweet life. As for the rest of you, be pious
and, imitating those examples I have set for you, serve one another
willingly, casting pride and luxury from your humble hearts. At
such a critical moment, those baleful powers of Erebus will not
cease trying to corrupt your hearts with fear. I bid you to be ever   695
vigilant and think of the future. Show the world that heart, that
feeling which you always promised me you would; be on your
guard and resist their plague for just this one night."   700

At once everyone was astonished and began to murmur, wondering whom the prescient hero could possibly mean, who could
be so blind, so vanquished by madness. The oldest of them, Peter,
besought him thus: "Glory of heaven, can it be that such a mon-   705
strous crime could occur to anyone? Who is this utterly evil man?
I will make sure that no one can ever trick us and evade vengeance.
Though I may be weighed down by years, courage has not fled my
blood. My hand is not so cold or weary."

So speaking he unsheathed his sword. But though Christ re-   710
vealed his enemy by manifest signs, he also confused their minds,
wishing to conceal the truth until the deed was done. Then he
said: "Truly, from all your number, there is not one of you who

715 vestrum non infidus erit, solusque relinquar.
Tu quoque, magnanimo cui nunc ea copia fandi
sub tecto atque amplis tendis super aethera dictis
omnis irritans ventos omnisque procellas,
hinc atque hinc circunfusos ubi videris hostes
720 me capto, quaeres latebras iaciesque salutem
mendaci in lingua pedibusque fugacibus acer.
Atque ubi curriculo mediam nox humida metam
attigerit, ter me tibi notum ille ipse negabis
futilis, incutietque metus tibi foemina inermis.'

725 Dixerat. Ille animi robur magis usque magisque
spondebat turpique metu impenetrabile pectus.
'Foeda alios servet fuga; nec tu me ante timoris
argue quam terga urgenti dare videris hosti.
Quo te cunque feres, adero. Sequar ultima tecum.
730 Nulla tuis poterit me vis abiungere rebus.'

His deus exactis mensas urbemque reliquit
et secum sociis pura sub nocte virentes
transtulit in colles olea et loca sola petivit
atque omnes secum iussit vigilare; sed illi,
735 assiduis noctisque dieque laboribus hausti,
haud poterant invictum oculis defendere somnum,
et gelidi in summo recubantes aequore saxi,
infusum toto proflabant ore soporem.

Interea curis confectus tristibus heros,
740 coelesti velut oblitus se semine cretum,
indignos animo eventus, indigna labanti
supplicia atque genus leti versabat acerbum,
horrebatque. Id enim matris de corpore traxit,
ut quaecunque hominum mortalia pectora terrent,
745 ipse etiam haec eadem mortali corde paveret.
Mens immota tamen virtusque invicta manebat.
Ergo iterum atque iterum genitorem affatus et ambas

will not betray me. I will be left alone. And you, who have spoken 715
so nobly under this roof, you who reach the heavens on your lofty
words and rouse all the winds and storms, when you shall see me
captive and yourself surrounded by enemies, you will seek a place
to hide, finding safety in lies and in the swiftness of your feet. By 720
the time the humid night has reached the midpoint of its career,
thrice will you deny in vain that you ever knew me, and a harmless
girl will strike fear into your heart."

So he spoke. But Peter swore ever more vehemently that he 725
possessed strength of mind and a breast impervious to shameful
fear. "Let other men find safety in base flight. Don't accuse me of
cowardice until you see me turn my back on the approaching enemy. Wherever you go, there will I be. I will go to death itself with
you. No force will ever tear me from your service." 730

After this exchange, the Son of God rose from the meal and
left the city. In the serenity of night, he retired with his disciples
to the green hills, seeking a secluded olive grove. Here he instructed his disciples to keep watch. But they were so wearied by 735
the labors of the previous day and night, that they couldn't stave
off all-mastering sleep. And so they lay down on the cool surface
of a rock and slept deeply.

Meanwhile, Jesus was consumed by sharp cares, as if he had
forgotten that he was born of celestial seed. As his wavering soul 740
reflected on the shameful events to come and the torments and the
harsh manner of his death, he felt fear. For he had from his
mother a mortal body and in his mortal heart he feared all that
frightens the hearts of mortal men. Yet his mind remained un- 745
moved and his virtue unvanquished. Over and over he called on

ad coelum tendens palmas, hac voce rogabat:
'Omnipotens talin Pater o me funere obire?
750   Mene aliena malis tantis commissa piare?
Eripe me informi leto et tua flecte severa
consilia in melius durosque averte dolores.
Si tamen id fixum sedet atque haec certa tibi mens,
nec generi humano gnati nisi morte sequestra
755   placaris, non fas orbis⁹ me deesse saluti.
Ibo ultro: crimen generis commune refellam.'

    Dixerat, atque graves curas sub corde premebat,
multa agitans. Toto simul ibat corpore sudor
proruptus, simul et sanguis vel sanguinis instar.
760   Ecce autem effulgens subito dilapsus ab axe
stelligero pictis iuxta puer astitit alis,
dicta ferens patris in tanto solatia rerum
turbine, mulcebatque aegrum curasque levabat,
abstergens toto fluidum de corpore rorem.

765   Hortator vero scelerisque inventor Iudas
composito interea vocat hostes vertice ab alto,
seque ultro comitem atque ducem venientibus offert.
Ergo adsunt improvisi, illum in vincla petentes;
longius aera micant tremulai lumine lunae.
770   Iam clypei resonant, iam ferri stridit acumen,
pinguiaque exuperant noctem funalia longo
ordine multifidaeque faces, quas unguine supra
obduxit manus et ferro inspicavit acuto.
Fit strepitus; vasto circum mons undique pulsu
775   armorum sonat atque virum clamoribus omnis.

    Quos his nil trepidus compellans vocibus heros,
'Heus,' inquit, 'iam state, viri; quem quaeritis adsum.
Quo ferrum flammaeque? Palam conspectus in urbe
conventu cecini magno praecepta parentis.
780   Cur non una omnes vos tunc tenuistis inermem?

his Father, raising both hands to heaven and speaking these words: "Almighty Father, is this the fate that I am doomed to suffer? Must I undergo such suffering to expiate the sins of others? Save me from a horrid death and turn your harsh thoughts to mildness. But if this is decided, if your mind is made up that you can be propitiated towards the race of men only by the death of your own son, then it is not right that I should be found wanting in the salvation of the world. I go willingly. I will undo the common sin of mankind." 750

755

So he spoke. Though greatly agitated, he suppressed his deep sorrow. Suddenly he broke out into a sweat and his entire body was covered in blood, or something like blood. At once a radiant child with brightly-colored wings descended from starry heaven and stood beside him in his anguish, bringing him the consoling words of his Father. The angel calmed his troubled mind, comforting him and wiping the perspiration from his whole body. 760

Meanwhile Judas, the instigator and deviser of the crime, summoned Christ's enemies from the hilltop, as agreed. When they arrived, he eagerly offered his services as a companion and guide. And so it was that they came upon Christ suddenly, intending to throw him in chains, their armor gleaming far off in the tremulous moonlight. You could hear the clash of shields and the hiss of swords. Long rows of greasy flares vanquished the night, as did split torches smeared with pitch and sharpened with knives. Suddenly there was a noise and everywhere the hills resounded with the clash of arms and men. 765

770

775

Undaunted, Jesus enjoined them with these words: "Here, men, stop! I am the one you want. Why these torches and knives? Before a great crowd, in full sight of the city, I recounted the teachings of my Father. Why didn't you seize me then, unarmed? Why do I see these troops assembled under cover of night? But if 780

Ista sub obscurum noctis cur agmina cerno?
Quod si me tamen ad mortem deposcitis armis
insontem et vobis adeo obstat gloria nostra,
hos sinite illaesos. Nihil hi meruere nec ausi.
785   Tantum dilecti comitis mandata facessunt.
Unus ego vestras explebo deditus iras.'
    Haec ait, et bis se quaerentibus obtulit ultro.
Illi autem ad vocem toties (mirabile visu)
procubuere soloque ingentem fusa dedere
790   arma sonum atque oculis subito nox plurima oborta est.
Consurgunt tandem, somno vinoque gravatis
assimiles, haerentque obliti, donec Iudas,
qui nusquam somno noctu se straverat illa,
signa dedit manifesta hostique obiecit amicum.
795   Nanque pii scelus id praetexens nomine amoris,
composuit sese et ficto dedit oscula vultu.
    Ille dolum praesensit et haec presso edidit ore:
'Haec vero meruit, comitum fidissime, noster
oscula amor? Tanton scelere ulla ad praemia tendis?
800   Haud equidem haec tecum pepigi commercia quondam.'
Vix ea fatus erat, cum circunfusa iuventus
caeca ruit, densaque omnes indagine cingunt.
Non aliter quam coniectum cum in retia rara
cervum aut fulmineis metuendum dentibus aprum
805   pastorum circum saevit manus, ilicet hastas
comminus agglomerant certatim, ad sidera voces
undique eunt, reboant montes clamore propinqui;
sic iuvenem obsessum longe fulgentibus armis
saeva cohors premere atque omnes incumbere inermi.
810   Hi prensare manu, hi stupea vincula collo
iniicere, et nunc huc, nunc illuc ducere captum.
    Perfurit ante alios et sese turbidus infert
Malchus, Idumaeis missus captivus ab oris.

you are coming in arms to kill me, an innocent man, because my fame is such a provocation to you, I ask only that you not harm my disciples. They have done nothing wrong; they have not even tried to do so. Their only crime was to do my bidding out of affection for me. I surrender: Let it be me alone who shall appease   785 your anger."

So speaking, he twice surrendered willingly to those who sought him. But each time they fell prostrate in response to his words—an amazing sight!—and loudly threw down their arms. Suddenly their eyes were covered up in dark night. Finally they   790 rose, as if groggy from sleep and wine, and milled about bewildered until Judas, who had not slept all night, gave the sign and betrayed his friend to the enemy. Feigning a devoted love he did   795 not feel, he masked his crime and kissed his friend.

Jesus foresaw the betrayal and said softly: "Most faithful of friends, is this kiss truly what my love has earned? What reward do you seek for this crime? Surely this was not the bargain I struck with you before?" Scarcely had he spoken when a group of   800 young men rushed blindly forward and thronged around him. As when a band of shepherds falls fiercely upon a stag thrust into thin mesh or a boar with its terrifying, lighting-swift tusks: From up close they eagerly compete to throw their spears at it. And from   805 every direction their cries rise to the heavens and the surrounding hills reecho with the noise. Even so did this savage pack oppress the young man, who was unarmed, and their weapons gleamed far off. Some seized him, other threw rope around his neck, leading   810 him captive one way and then another.

More ferocious than all the rest was Malchus, who had been sent as a captive from Edom. But he was unused to fighting or

Nulli ferre manum, nulli contendere suetus:
815 non ea vis illi, non tanta in pectore virtus.
Verum ut se Caiphae praestantem ostendat in armis,
cui datus haerebat famulus, nam tuta videbat
omnia et audenti nullum hic obstare periclum,
audet, cedentemque ultro petit improbus hostem,
820 ventosam nequicquam acuens in iurgia linguam,
et vix ille suas tumefactus corde capit spes.
Non tulit hoc praeceps animi Petrus; arripit ensem,
et super incumbens inhonesto vulnere tempus
occupat ac patulam dicto ocius amputat aurem.
825   Quod deus aspiciens, subito dextramque tetendit,
decisamque ab humo madido cum pulvere partem
sustulit applicuitque manu medica, unde resecta est,
affixitque loco; nullo haesit fixa dolore,
ulla nec apparent vestigia vulneris usquam.
830 Mox socium increpitans, vim dextra arcere volentem
condere tela iubet, vetito neque fidere ferro.
Ni faciat, senior nequicquam magna locuto
strictum ardens illi per costas exigat ensem.
'Non istis opibus, non istis nitimur,' inquit,
835 'viribus. Est genitor, qui me si funere acerbo
eripere et fuso nati sine sanguine vellet
placari generi humano, centum agmina posset
coelicolum, mihi centum acies summittere ab arce
siderea, infensum qui coetum hunc ense trucident.
840 Militiamne adeo superum pugnataque bella
atque potestates varias et nomina nescis?
Nunc sine me imperiis magni parere parentis,
quae me sola premunt. Hominum nil demoror arma.'
    Talibus auditis senior vix desinit irae
845 invitus, veluti aspexit si forte magistri
assuetum imperiis cervum media urbe Molossus,

raising his hand against anyone. He had neither the strength for it nor the courage. But to show his master Caiaphas that he was an 815 experienced fighter — he also saw that he was exposing himself to no real danger, that everything was safe — he suddenly became bold. And so this scoundrel eagerly set upon his unresisting foe, assailing him with vain and baseless threats. All puffed up, he 820 could scarcely contain his ambitious heart. This was more than the headstrong Peter could bear. He drew his sword and, coming near, he smote the temple of Malchus, creating an ugly wound, and cut off his exposed ear faster than you could speak.

As soon as the Son of God saw this, he held out his hand and 825 lifted up the severed ear, which lay in the dirt on the damp earth. Then, with a physician's hand, he fixed it where it had been cut off, leaving no pain or scar. Then he rebuked his friend, who had wanted to retaliate against this violence. He told him to sheathe 830 his sword and not rely upon forbidden weaponry. If Jesus had not spoken thus, Peter, burning with anger, would surely have driven the man through with his drawn sword. "We have no need of weapons or violence," Jesus said. "If my Father wished to rescue 835 me from harsh death and make peace with men without spilling my blood, he could dispatch from heaven a hundred battalions, a hundred legions of angels to slaughter this savage crew. Surely you have heard of those angelic armies and the wars they have fought, 840 with all their varied ranks and titles? Suffer me now to obey my great father's commands, which alone guide me. I have no use for the arms of men."

Even at these words the older man found it hard to set aside his rage, like a Molossian hound that sees a tame stag in the midst of 845

silvestrem ratus insequitur. Vix voce coercet
venator rabido instantem cervicibus ore.
Ergo sponte sua victum nec viribus usum
850 corripiunt cuncti (heu species indigna) trahuntque
invalidum et dictis lapsantem immitibus urgent.
    Haec, pater omnipotens, superum regnator Olympo,
tam lentus cernis nec coelo tartara misces?
Ecquando horrificum dextra iaculabere fulmen,
855 si nunc immoto facies innubila mundo est?
Foedere iam rupto rerum confusa laborent
atque repente elementa ruant; ruat arduus aether.
Cur tua dextra vacat? Cur non face terra trisulca
iam fumat? Quos flamma vorax servatur in usus?
860 Non genus humanum, non tanti regia coeli
alitibus supplenda choris, non aurea gens, quae
mox hinc se tollet pietate insignis ad astra.
Ne nostri tanto te cura incendat amore,
iactari ut tali patiaris turbine natum
865 unigenam desertum, inopem atque extrema ferentem.
    Diffugere metu comites silvisque teguntur,
spumiferi ut suis adventu saevique leonis
semianimes. Passim insequitur ferus hostis euntes.
Aspiceres hunc iam captum, iam veste relicta
870 elapsum manibus rapido petere ardua cursu,
illum speluncas et sicubi operta subire
per silvam loca, saxorumque in fornice condi.
Nec mora, nec requies: cursu nemora avia fervent,
et vasto intonsi colles clamore resultant.
875   Iamque sacerdotis summi tecta ampla subibant;
protinus huc tota passim concurritur urbe.
Primores adsunt procerum poenasque reposcunt,
uni infensi omnes, atque illum torva tuentes
perterrent vinctumque minis crudelibus urgent.

a city and immediately lunges after what it thinks to be a woodland creature. The voice of the hunter can scarcely contain the animal as he hangs over his prey with rabid mouth. At that point all of Christ's assailants set upon him—a disgraceful spectacle—since 850 he had given up willingly rather than fight back. And so they dragged the weakened man, and when he fell, they heaped scorn upon him.

Almighty Father, who rule over the angels in heaven, how can you bear to witness these acts and not confound heaven and hell? When will you unleash your terrifying thunder if you look on serenely now, and the earth remains unclouded and unmoved? Let 855 the natural order be violently disturbed! Let all its elements forget their bonds and run promiscuously into one another! May high heaven itself come tumbling down! What stays your hand? Why is the earth not yet aflame with your forked fire? To what end do you spare your all-devouring flames? The human race is not worth 860 your Son's suffering, nor the kingdom of heaven and its angelic choruses, nor the golden race, notable for its piety, that soon will raise itself hence to the stars. Blaze not with such love for us as to suffer your only-begotten Son—abandoned, destitute, and near death—to be so afflicted. 865

Now the disciples of Jesus scattered in fear and hid in the woods, like frightened creatures at the approach of a foaming boar or savage lion. Everywhere the merciless enemy pursued them. You could have seen one man, already captured, throw off his clothes and, slipping his captors, run headlong for the wilds, while an- 870 other sought out caves or woods that might provide cover, hiding in the rocky arches. Suddenly the secluded thickets were alive with activity and the leafy hills reechoed loudly.

Now the enemies of Christ arrived at the spacious dwelling of 875 the archpriest and all the citizens rushed there as well. The leaders of the city, all together, angrily demanded punishment for this solitary bound man, whom they eyed fiercely and cruelly threatened.

880   Tum gentis primus Caiphas ita denique fatur:
'Res hodie bene gesta, viri. Non artibus ullis
infandum evasit caput; illi nulla supersunt
effugia. Instaurandi animi et, quod restat, agendum.
Nunc est illa dies, qua gloria maxima sese
885   ostendit nobis. Sed opus properantibus astu.
Accipite et linguis omnes animisque favete.
Nulli fas nostrum quenquam demittere morti;
Romani ducis arbitrio stat quisque caditve.
Quaeramus leti causas et crimina primum,
890   inde ducem instructi verbis adeamus, ut ipse
audiat et morti indefensum destinet hostem.'
Sic ait. Hinc captum alloquitur: 'Tune ille supremi
vera dei soboles, verus deus, aethere ab alto
quem vates oriturum orbi cecinere priores?
895   Per patris obtestor numen qui sidera fulcit,
fare age, ne te dissimula quaerentibus ultra,
discussisque palam qui sis, nunc nubibus ede,
ne te divino ignari fraudemus honore.'
    Dixerat. Ille autem in medio defessus, inermis,
900   conspectu paulum sustollens lumina fatur:
'Sum quod ais. Quid me studio tentatis inani,
haec eadem toties scitati? Parcite tectis
insidiis victique dolis desistite tandem.
Ipse palam fateor. Nec iam mora longior obstat,
905   cum mihi sublimis cedet plaga lucida Olympi
regnanda; aetherea iam iam cernetis in aula
amplexum dextram patris omnipotentis, et inde
mox iterum terras petere aspicietis eundem
fulgentem clara in nebula, quem mille sequuti
910   coelicolae auratis impellent aethera pennis.'
    Vix ea dicta, humeris sibi cum de more sacerdos
abscindens tunicam inquit: 'Eget quid lucis adhuc res

Finally Caiaphas, their leader, spoke thus: "You have done well 880
today, men. No tricks have let this unspeakable villain evade capture. And now he has no further means of escape. Take heart,
then, and do what remains to be done. This is the day when the
greatest glory is revealed to us. But in our haste, we must remain
alert. Listen to my plan in silence, all of you, and approve it in 885
your hearts. None of us is permitted to condemn any man to
death. Rather it is by the will of the Roman governor that a man
lives or dies. First let us find evidence of his crimes and reasons to
urge his execution. Then we will approach the governor, armed
with arguments. When he hears them, he will condemn our en- 890
emy, who has no legal defense, to death." Having thus spoken, he
turned to address his captive. "So you are the true Son of God,
the true God, who the ancient prophets foretold would descend
from heaven and inhabit the world? By the soul of God the Father
who upholds the stars, speak to me. Do not hide yourself any 895
longer from those who seek you. And, all clouds dispersed, tell me
plainly who you are, lest, in our ignorance, we defraud you of the
honors due a divine being."

So he spoke. As all of them looked on, Jesus, weary and unarmed, began to speak, barely raising his eyes. "I am as you say. 900
Why do you make trial of me in vain, since you have learnt the
truth many times over. You have been beaten. Spare me your hidden stratagems; have done at last with deceit. I will tell you everything plainly. Soon, very soon, the radiant shores of heaven will 905
yield themselves to my rule and you will see me both returned to
earth and in the heavenly palace, holding the hand of my Almighty Father. And once again you will see me return to earth, resplendent in a shining cloud, followed by a thousand angels, beating the air with their gilded wings!" 910

Scarcely had he spoken when the priest, according to custom,
rent the garment from his shoulders, and said, "What further evi-

indiciis tot clara? Palam scelus ipse fatetur.
Nonne, deo quicunque audet se fingere natum,
915　fas et iura iubent mulctari funere acerbo?
Tollite, ferte moras! Romani ad praesidis aedes
abripite hunc iubeo meritasque reposcite poenas.'
　　Interea casu Petrus perculsus iniquo
prosequitur moerens longeque observat amicum.
920　Iamque sub ingentis devenerat atria templi,
tecta sacerdotis magni, solusque sedebat
tristis, inops animi, ante fores nocturnus apertas.
Olli serva, domus cui curae ianua herilis,
id quod erat rata, 'Tune etiam fugis,' inquit, 'et isti
925　iunctus eras scelerum consors, ideoque per umbras
explorator ades, quando omnia nocte quiescunt?'
　　Diriguit Petrus ad vocem formidine turpi.
Oblitusque sui est (quae vitae tanta cupido?),
nec iam scit, subita turbatus imagine rerum,
930　quid faciat, quo se vertat, quas advocet artis.
Qualis ubi dulci virgo decepta sopore
parvula, quam mater campis ignara reliquit
in solis abeunte die sub tecta revertens,
confestim rupto circuntulit humida somno
935　lumina, nec comites nec matrem conspicit usquam,
sed loca sola metu videt exanimata viarumque
immemor atque horrere nigra circum omnia nocte.
　　Talis erat miser ille animo confusus et haerens.
At cari nomen tandem abiuravit amici,
940　pro quo sponte neci modo se devoverat ardens.
Quin etiam, quo se tegeret, succedere tecto
hostili tulit et famulis se immiscuit amens.
Nec latuit tamen. Illum omnes inimica tueri
suspectum et latebras verbis urgere foventem,
945　terque adeo obiectum nomen patriamque magistri

dence do we need when the matter is so clear? He himself con-
fesses the crime. Is it not fitting, it is not law, that any man who
dares to call himself the Son of God should be punished with
death? Take him without delay! Take him, I order you, to the   915
house of the Roman governor and seek the penalty he deserves."

Meanwhile Peter watched his friend from a distance and was
moved to tears by this injustice. Already he stood at the entrance
to the great temple, the dwelling of the archpriest. It was night   920
when he sat down before the open doors, sad and alone, without
hope. A servant woman who guarded the entrance to her master's
home understood the truth. "So you too are fleeing the punishment he has received, being a partner in his crimes? Is that why   925
you are spying here, in the shadows, when all the world is at rest?"

At the sound of her voice, Peter went rigid, prey to base fear.
Forgetting himself—but why should he want to live so much?—
and suddenly frightened by his circumstances, he no longer knew
what to do, where to turn, what trick he might play. He was like a   930
little girl lulled to gentle sleep, whom her mother, returning home
at day's end, has thoughtlessly left behind in the deserted fields.
Suddenly awakened, the girl's eyes well up and dart in all directions. She cannot see her mother or her friends anywhere. But   935
breathless with fear and having forgotten how to get home, she
looks out at the deserted fields and shudders at everything in the
black night.

Thus was Peter dismayed, his mind wavering. And yet at last
he renounced the name of the friend for whom, only a few hours
earlier, he had so willingly and ardently vowed he would die. In-   940
deed, he even hid in his enemy's dwelling, foolishly mingling
among the household. But he could not hide. Everyone looked angrily at him and spoke harshly as he sought a place to hide. Thrice
he heard the name and country of his teacher being flung at him,
and thrice he feigned ignorance. At that moment, the crested birds   945

audierat, ficto ter dissimulaverat ore,
cum matutino mediae iam noctis abactae
edebant cantu cristatae signa volucres
auroram in tectis solitae acri voce vocare.
950   Tum monitus verborum heros quae extrema canebat,
ingemuit rupitque imo suspiria corde,
et penitus duris tristi dolor ossibus arsit.
Tum sese miser incusans turpemque timorem,
erepsit furtim foribus, solusque per urbem
955   totam illam ingemuit somni sine munere noctem,
menti caniciem demissam in pectora vellens.
Quin illum hanc perhibent mox semper flesse sub horam
admissi memorem dum vixit. Eum aethera pandens
saepe oriens solis, saepe ater vesper in antris
960   invenit luctu indulgentem eademque querentem,
dum nulla admittit moesto solatia amori.
Deserti subeunt monita usque novissima regis,
ac se perculsum muliebri voce recursat.
        Et iam tempus erat, cum nondum Aurora relato
965   orta die albentes coeli discriminat oras.
Iamque deum vinctis manibus post terga trahebant
praesidis ad sedem, quo crimina quaereret ipse,
quem penes arbitrium et morti damnaret acerbae.
Illo Iudaeam frenabat tempore missus
970   Caesaris imperio Tiberi Pilatus opimam
Pontius, insigni Romanus origine gentis,
quem furibunda manus trepido est aggressa tumultu
vociferans, 'Hunc dede neci! Trabe fige merentem
infami, auctorem scelerum fraudumque potentem!'
975   Haec crebra ingeminant densique ad limen inundant.
Ille autem iuvenis procero in corpore fixos
intentusque oculos intentusque ora tenebat
(nondum illi dulcis flos prorsum evanuit aevi),

that are wont shrilly to call forth the dawn from the roof tops
sounded their morning song and signalled that midnight had
passed. Then, remembering the last words he had heard from his
teacher, Peter groaned and a sigh escaped his heart. He was so sad   950
that he felt a sharp pain in his very bones. As the poor man re-
proached himself for his base cowardice, he crept furtively from
the doors of the house. Alone in the city, he spent the whole night
weeping, without benefit of sleep, tearing at the white beard that   955
hung down his chest. Indeed, they say that afterwards, as long as
he lived, he would always weep at that hour in memory of what he
had done. Often the rising sun or the darkening evening found
him indulging his grief and lamenting these same actions of his;
but he allowed his remorseful love no solace. For he remembered   960
the final words of the king he had forsaken, and the memory of
how he had been laid thus low by a woman's voice preyed on his
mind.

It was now just before sunrise, when Aurora had not yet
marked out the pale corners of the sky. Already God was being   965
led, his hands tied behind his back, to the throne of the governor,
who had jurisdiction in the matter. His captors wanted Pontius
Pilate to inquire into the allegations and impose the harshest sentence. For at that time Pilate, a Roman of distinguished family,
governed wealthy Judaea at the command of Tiberius Caesar.   970
Now a furious mob besieged his palace with fearful tumult, shouting: "Put him to death! Nail him to that infamous cross! He deserves it after all the crimes, all the fraud he has committed!"

Repeating these cries, they gathered in force at his doorstep. Pi-   975
late however fixed his gaze intently on the tall form of the young
man from whom the tender flower of youth had not yet vanished.
Marveling at his fine appearance and at the extraordinary nobility

insolitam speciem, insolitos miratur honores
980 oris et expleri nequit. Hunc e stirpe fatetur
aut divum aut saltem magnorum e sanguine regum,
et secum sortem capti miseratur iniquam,
iamque favet tacitusque agitat, si qua potis illum
impune eripere et ruptis exolvere vinclis.
985 Quem sic alloquitur: 'Quae te commissa fatigant,
fare age, qui casus? Unde haec effusa repente
tempestas tibi? Num tantis scelera impia mersum
implicuere malis? An divum tristior ira?
Unde domo? Quo te memoras e sanguine cretum
990 aut quibus aspiras sceptris? Quae debita regna?'
    Christus ad haec paucis: 'Non huc ego criminis ergo
protrahor. Haud turpi mihi mens obnoxia facto,
sed patris, immensi coeli cui regia paret,
iussa sequor, nec regna moror mortalia, quanvis
995 haud equidem clara me regum e stirpe negarim.'
Haec tantum. Ille autem[10] admirans decus oris honesti,
nunc hoc, nunc illo[11] sermone affatur et omnem
Explorat. Sed responso non amplius heros
dignatur, saevo curarum exercitus aestu.
1000 Tandem illum dux, ut turbam compescat acerbam,
servari iubet atque domo interiore recondit.

of Jesus' face, Pilate couldn't get his fill of looking. Certain that the captive must be descended from the gods or at least of the blood   980 of great kings, Pilate took pity on the unjust fortune of the captive. He took his side and silently exerted himself to find some way to spare him from punishment and release him from his bonds. Then he addressed him: "Tell me, what are the actions and misfortunes that hound you? Why has this storm been suddenly   985 unleashed against you? Can some wicked crime really have entangled you in these great misfortunes? Or is it the stern anger of the gods? Tell me where you come from and who your parents are. To what scepters do you aspire, what kingdom is your due?"   990

Christ responded in few words. "I am not being dragged here because of any crime. My mind is not involved with anything base. Rather I follow the commandments of my Father, whom the entire kingdom of heaven obeys. I seek no earthly rule, though I would not deny that I am born of the race of kings." That was all   995 he said. As Pilate marveled at the beauty of his noble face, he broached one subject after another, trying to sound the hero out. But Jesus did not deign to respond further, wrought upon as he was by cruel and seething cares. Finally, to calm the hostile mob, the governor ordered that the captive be taken into custody and   1000 concealed within his house.

LIBER III

Fama volans iam finitimas impleverat urbes
exceptum insidiis heroa dolisque suorum;
obscurus tamen atque incerto auctore vagari
rumor adhuc, necdum matris penetrarat ad aures,
5   cuncta licet nunquam illa animo secura timeret
praesago. Nempe audierat vatumque tremenda
terrebant monita, pro libertate piorum
natum sponte sua subiturum funus acerbum.
   Ast ubi Iosephus senior praesensit (ei olim
10   alma parens fuerat superum concredita iussis),
Nazaren linquens Solymorum se intulit urbi.
Vix introgressus videt omnia fervere multo
concursu populi sublustri nocte per umbras,
moeniaque ingenti misceri tota tumultu.
15   Ecce autem, elapsus manibus telisque cohortis,
fidus Ioannes pallenti tristior ore
occurrit. Sed vix amens agnovit amicum,
dum trepidat, casusque animo ducis haeret acerbus.
Cui senior: 'Heus, siste gradum. Quo te rapis?' inquit.
20   'Quo res nostra loco? Sine te nunc vester ubi dux,
patre deo satus? Aut strepitus quis tantus in urbe?
Hei, mihi non fallunt pavidam praesagia matrem!'
   Sic ait. Illum autem iuvenis complexus et haerens
tantum fundebat lachrymas gemitusque ciebat.
25   Tandem pauca refert: 'Nostra heu spes occidit omnis
atque absumpta salus. Dux foede carcere captus
clauditur. Invidia primores urbis in illum
conspirant poenasque graves cum sanguine poscunt.
Fidi omnes petiere fugam terrore subacti.

BOOK III

News spread to the neighboring towns that the hero had been captured through the deceit and treachery of his companions. But this rumor was as yet vague and the identity of its author was unknown. Though it had not yet reached the ears of Jesus' mother, she feared everything, since her prophetic soul was never free from 5 care. She had surely heard and dreaded the awful predictions of the prophets, that in order to free the souls of good men, her son would willingly meet a terrible end.

For his part the aged Joseph (to whom the mother of God had been entrusted by divine commandment) sensed that something 10 was wrong, so he left Nazareth for Jerusalem. On entering that city, he found everything in an uproar. Crowds hastened to and fro, clamoring about the walls in the dark of a moonless night. Presently he came upon the faithful John. Having escaped the hands and spears of the mob, the young man looked very pale and 15 grim. In agitation and fear for the fate of his leader, he scarcely recognized his friend. The older man said to him, "Wait! Where are you running? How do things stands with us? And why aren't you with the Lord, the Son of God? Why isn't he with you? Do 20 you know the reason for all this uproar in the city? Alas, his mother's forebodings have come true!"

So he spoke. The younger man simply embraced him. For some time he could only weep and sigh. Finally he spoke a few words: 25 "All our hope is dead. All our salvation has vanished. The Lord has been taken in a shameful way and thrown in prison. Out of envy, the leaders of the city are conspiring against him, asking for harsh and bloody retribution. All of the faithful are terrified and

30 Mater ubi est? Miseraene adeo iam nuntius aures
perculit? Hic utinam tecum nunc afforet ipsa:
Pontius, aspiciens lachrymas gemitusque parentis,
forsitan indigni casus miseresceret ultro.
Ire tamen libet ac pacem veniamque precari,
35 et populi invidiam atque odium crudele profari.'
      Sic memorans gressum Syriae rectoris ad aedes
tendit. Ei senior comitem se iungit et ambo
incedunt pariter tristes, ceu forte boves cum
agricola amisit pauper, quos hostis abegit
40 depopulatus agros, quaesitum protinus illos
longum iter ingreditur; natorum maximus olli
it comes. Hic illic saepe ambo ignota per arva,
si quos forte suis similes videre vagari,
subsistunt flentes atque avia questibus implent.
45   Haud illi secus, et iam ventum ad limina tecti,
quod regum quondam fuit antiquissima sedes,
cum res incolumi regno Iudaea maneret,
sed tum Romulides orae moderator habebat.
Fervere cuncta vident strepitu patresque sub ipso
50 vestibulo ante fores dissensu tendere magno,
iamque sacerdotes paulatim cedere ab aula
Romano velut infensos ac dira minantes.
      His animum arrecti paulum lenire dolorem
incipiunt, rebusque aliquam sperare salutem,
55 atque ita Ioannes: 'Mihi se nonnulla aperit spes.
Solve metum atque virum pro nato affare deique
dissimula sobolem et causas innecte precandi.'
His dictis, pariter succedunt aedibus ambo,
atque ducem senior, qui re suspensus eadem
60 his super in medio procerum consulta rogabat,
alloquitur genua amplexans supplexque precatur:
'Optime Romulidum, quem clari rector Olympi

have taken flight. But where is Jesus' mother? Has someone told 30
her the news? I wish she had come with you. If Pilate could see
her tears, if he could hear her sighs, perhaps he would be moved
to pity at this injustice. Still, someone has to go and seek his pardon. Someone has to explain to him the jealousy and cruel hatred
of the people."   35

With that he began to make his way to the palace of the ruler
of Syria. The older man went with him, his equal in sadness. Joseph was like a poor farmer whose cattle have been stolen by an
invader laying waste to the land. As the farmer goes in search of 40
them, his oldest son joins them and they hasten in all directions
through unknown fields. And if, by chance, they see some cattle
wandering by that remind them of the ones they have lost, they
stand weeping and fill the fields with their lamentation.

And so it was with these two men. Soon they had reached the 45
palace that long before had belonged to the kings of Judaea, while
yet the kingdom stood. But now it housed the Roman governor of
the province. Everything there was in confusion. The city elders
stood in the entrance, before the doors, arguing among themselves. 50
Eventually they left, angry with the governor and making dire
threats.

The two men noticed and took heart. They were slightly less
grief-stricken, in hopes that the life of Jesus might yet be spared.
John said, "I find some hope in this. Take courage and speak to 55
the man on behalf of your son. But don't mention his divine birth.
Only tell the governor the reason for your suit." With that they
entered the building. The older man addressed the ruler, who was
himself in some doubt how to proceed and, surrounded by the
city leaders, sought their advice in the matter. Joseph clasped the 60
man's knees in suppliant fashion and besought him: "Noblest of
Romans, whom the lord of bright Olympus chose to subdue

iustitia voluit Syriam frenare superbam,
parce piis saevumque hominum compesce furorem.
65 Hinc ratio penitus sublata est; vi geritur res.
Illi ego sum genitor, quem primi gentis in unum
coniurant omnes et ficto crimine terrent.
Iamque tibi, ut scelere ante omnes immanior unus,
traditus, immeritas quo pendat sanguine poenas.
70 Illum autem virtus tantum et benefacta per orbem
his mersere malis sua, dum gens effera laudi
invidet eximiae, nec fert surgentis honorem.'

    Talibus orabat; largo simul imbre rigabant
ora senis lachrymae, placido quem Pontius ore
75 accipit atque ambos verbis solatur amicis,
depositumque senem molli locat ipse sedili
atque haec deinde refert: 'Ut vos hic tempore adestis
optati! Nec enim forsan venisse pigebit.
Tu modo vera mihi scitanti edissere pauca
80 nunc, pater, haud veritus; fidei te credere fas est
omne meae. Coelum et coeli vaga sidera testor,
sollicito mihi cura tui est nunc maxima nati,
quem tibi mente agito incolumem servare, furoremque
et rabiem, ut potui, compressi gentis iniquae.
85 Fare age (nanque mihi haud nunc primum venit ad aures)
quae fortuna viro, unde domo, quo sanguine cretus.
Ede tuum matrisque genus; non ille creatus
stirpe humili, mihi si verum mens augurat. Ut se
incessu gerit! Ut vultuque et corpore toto est
90 humana maior species! Ut lumina honorum
plena! Ut regifici motus! Verba inde notavi,
nil mortale sonat. Sensi illo in pectore numen.
Aut certe deus ille aut non mortalibus ortus.
Dicite vos; nam me scitantem avertitur ipse

proud Syria with justice: take pity on the pious and curb the raging fury of men. For fury destroys their reason and they know
only violence. I am the father of the man whom the leaders of the   65
city conspire against and persecute with false accusations. Now he
has been remanded to your custody as the basest of criminals, to
be punished with death on a trumped-up charge. But nothing
other than his virtue and good deeds throughout the world has re-   70
duced him to this misfortune. This barbarous nation envies the
praise he receives and they cannot stand to see him grow in
honor."

As the old man spoke, tears covered his face. With a gentle expression, Pilate received him and consoled both men with kind
words. Then he himself placed the old man in a soft chair and   75
spoke thus, "How glad I am that you have come here in time! And
perhaps you will not regret having come. Speak to me, father,
without fear and in few words, for I only wish to learn the truth.
You can have complete confidence in my good faith. I call the   80
heavens and the stars to witness that your son is now my greatest
concern. I mean to save him for you and, as far as I can, I have
checked the fury and rage of this unjust race. So speak to me, for
this is not the first time I have heard of him. Tell me about his lot   85
in life. Where does he come from and who were his ancestors? I
wish to know your lineage and his mother's as well, for I suspect
that he comes from no humble stock. How well he carries himself! There is something more than human in his face and form.
How full of nobility are his eyes! How regal his movements! And   90
there is nothing mortal in his speech. I sensed that there was
something divine in his heart. Even if he is not a god, surely his
was no mortal birth. Tell me then, for he turned away from me
when, as a friend, I inquired of him. He kept silent and scarcely

95   et vix responso tacitus dignatur amicum,
      contemptorque illi est animus lucisque meique.
        His dictis, senior paulisper substitit anceps,
      sene ultra tegeret quaerenti, an proderet illi
      et divi genus et verum sine fraude parentem.
100 Cum breviter comes admotus sic fatur ad aurem:
      'Regia progenies, nymphae dignate superbo
      coniugio, quid adhuc haeres? Absiste vereri.
      Omnia sublatis aperi iam nubibus ultro.
      Pone metus et rumpe moras; video omnia tuta.'
105   Dixerat. Ille igitur missa formidine coepit:
      'Dicam equidem nec, dux, tibi magna arcana silebo.
      Sed quando genus insedit cognoscere nostrum,
      id primum, neque te suspensum ambage tenebo.
      Quanvis res inopes opera ad fabrilia versum
110 exercent, tamen est mihi regum a stirpe propago,
      admotumque genus superis clarique parentes.
      Principio innumerae pater Abras gentis et auctor
      maximus ille tuas non, ut reor, effugit aures,
      qui generi legesque tulit moremque sacrorum.
115 Isacon hic dedit; Isacides Iacobus ab illo,
      bis senos qui mox proceres genuit, quibus omnis
      nostra domos in bis senas gens secta tribusque est.
      Hos inter pietate olim quam maior Iudas,
      tam sese sobole egregia super extulit omnes,
120 Iudaeamque suo dixit de nomine terram.
      Hinc (licet in medio series longissima patrum)
      Davides ortus, regum pater, unde meorum
      per bis septem exit genus actum ab origine reges.
        'Verum longe aliud iuveni genus. Ille parentes
125 quanvis mortales mortalibus editus oris
      dignatur, tamen est divo coelestis origo,

deigned to answer my questions, though I wished to be his friend. 95
In his soul he holds me and life itself in contempt."

So he spoke. For a time the old man was uncertain whether to
conceal the truth from the governor any longer or to divulge the
divine parentage of his son. But then John approached and whis- 100
pered briefly in his ear, "Scion of kings, you who were deemed
worthy of high marriage to the maiden, why do you hesitate?
There is no reason to be afraid. Scatter all mists and reveal everything without delay! Clearly it is safe."

He spoke, and so, putting aside his fears, Joseph began. "I shall 105
speak, Excellency, and I shall reveal great mysteries to you. But
since you are determined to know my origins, I will tell you that
first. Straitened circumstances may have forced me to turn to
manual labor, but I am of royal blood, a race dear to heaven, with 110
distinguished ancestors. Surely you have heard of the first and
greatest of our ancestors, Abraham, the patriarch of our numerous
race, who gave us laws and religious observances. He sired Isaac,
who sired Jacob, through whose twelve sons our entire race is di- 115
vided into twelve houses and tribes. Among them Judas, distinguished as much by piety as by his noble sons, rose far above the
rest and named this land Judaea, after himself. Many generations 120
later, David was born, the father of kings. From his to mine is
fourteen generations more.

"Very different, however, is the ancestry of my son. Though he
deigned to be born of mortal parents in the lands of mortal men,
his origin is celestial. He was sired by God the Father and he re- 125

estque deo genitore satus gaudetque parente,
cui mare velivolum, cui tellus paret et aether.
Illum autem aereas in luminis edidit auras
130 nunquam mixta viro mulier, foetaeque remansit
virginitas, olim ut vates cecinere futurum.
Nam pater omnipotens foecunda desuper aura
afflatam implevit; tumuit divinitus alvus.
Quod vero genitor vulgo sum creditus ipse,
135 haud ita res, mihique alma parens accredita tantum,
qui cum animi posset curas durumque laborem
partiri; mox me famae niveoque pudori
permetuens, eadem dignata est nomine veri
coniugis immeritum, nec tali munere dignum.
140 'Haec erat (ut revocans rem cunctam ab origine pandam)
Iudaeas inter virgo pulcherrima nymphas,
centum optata procis (Mariam dixere) parentum
unica progenies urbe edita Nazaraea.
Ipsa autem aeterno prae virginitatis amore
145 oderat et thalamos et se sacraverat aris.
Anna tamen grandaeva parens, haud nescia vatum
plenaque venturi, e gnata praeviderat olim
egregiam factis sobolem regemque futurum,
qui populos magnos magna ditione teneret;
150 id coelo fixum esse, pios id prodere vates.
Saepe illam in somnis monuit vox missa per auras
iungere connubio natam generosque vocare;
iamque erat apta viro, iam nubilis. Hactenus autem
distulerant superum monitis parere parentes,
155 cum media, ecce! iterum sublimes luce per auras
vox audita: "Viro, properate, o iungere natam.
Nec generi longe optandi; de sanguine vestro
quaerantur de more. Omnis mora segnis abesto."

joices in him who rules the earth, the air and the ship-filled sea.
But he was brought forth into the light by a virgin mother, whose
maidenhood remained after his birth, as the prophets had once   130
foretold. For the Almighty Father breathed down upon her, filling
her with seminal breath until miraculously her womb began to
grow. I am assumed to be the father, but that is not so. His dear
mother was merely entrusted to me, to share in her hard labors   135
and the cares of her soul. Only subsequently, fearing for her good
name and spotless modesty, did she honor me, unworthy though I
was, with the name of husband.

"So that you might know everything from the beginning, she   140
was the fairest maiden in Judaea, sought by a hundred suitors.
Her name was Mary and she was the only child of parents from
Nazareth. But in her enduring love of maidenhood, she despised
marriage and devoted herself to religion. Her aged mother Anna,   145
who knew well the prophets and was herself full of portents, had
foreseen that her daughter would bring forth a son destined for
greatness, a future king who would hold great nations in his powerful sway. For such was the will of heaven and so the prophets
had foretold. Often in dreams a voice from above had bidden her   150
to give her daughter in marriage and to summon suitors. For she
was already of marriageable age. Hitherto her parents had put off
obeying the divine commandment, until, behold! in broad daylight
a voice was again heard in heaven: 'Give your daughter in marriage   155
now! Do not seek far abroad for your son-in-law; let him be chosen from your own blood, according to custom. But tarry not!'

'Continuo parvam vulgatur fama per urbem.
160 Tum consanguinei pulchrae spe coniugis omnes
conveniunt iuvenes; complentur virginis aedes.
Ipse etiam patri consanguinitate propinquus
accessi, quanvis aevi maturus, ut ipsi
aequaevo natae ob thalamos gratarer amico.
165 Stabant innumeri, forma atque aetatibus aequis
florentes, coelum cui munera tanta pararet
incerti, et sortem sibi quisque optabat amicam.
'Dum spes ambiguae, dum turba ignara futuri,
in secreta domus omnes evasimus altae
170 tecta, ubi Ioachides numen placare solebat
virginis ore pater. Fuit ara veterrima, nostrae
quam gentis primi posuere metuque sacratam;
ter centum totos atavi coluere per annos.
Hanc humiles circum et prostrati fundimur omnes,
175 orantes pacem superos superumque parentem,
det signum coelo placidus quem poscat ab alto.
In medio astabat lachrymans pulcherrima virgo,
flaventis effusa comas demissaque largo
rorantes oculos fletu. Pudor ora pererrans
180 cana, rosis veluti miscebat lilia rubris.
Qualis, virgineos ubi lavit in aequore vultus,
luna recens stellis late comitantibus orta,
ingreditur gracili coeli per coerula cornu,
talis erat virgo, iuvenum stipata corona,
185 multa deum verbis testata deique ministros
aligeros non sponte sua haec ad munera flecti.
Hortatur pavidam pater et lachrymantia tergit
lumina, iussa docens superum, simul oscula libat.
'Ecce autem, ut praesens aderat quoque pronuba, coetu
190 in medio Anna parens, subito correpta furore,
plena deo tota (visu venerabile) in aede

"At once the news ran through the small town. All the young men of her lineage converged on the girl's house and filled it, in hopes of winning this beautiful wife. Being a close kinsman of her father, I too came forward (though I was of advanced age) to congratulate him, a friend and coeval, on the marriage of his daughter. Unnumbered young men were present, flourishing in beauty and youth. Though no one knew on whom heaven would bestow this great gift, each man hoped that fortune would smile on him.

"While their hopes were still uncertain and none of the young men knew the outcome, we all went to the back of the lofty house, where the girl's father Joachim used to offer prayers and sacrifices to God. Here was an ancient altar, built by remote ancestors and consecrated in fear. Our awed forebears worshiped here for three hundred years. Humbly kneeling around it, we poured libations and asked God and his angels to grant us peace and to signal from above which of the suitors he would choose. The beautiful young woman stood weeping in our midst, her hair disheveled and her tearful eyes downcast. A blush flashed across her pale face, like red roses among lilies. As when the new moon, surrounded by stars, bathes its virginal face in a stream and rises through the deep-blue heavens with delicate horns, even so did the maiden, surrounded by a crowd of young men, attest before God and his winged ministers that she did not willingly submit to these duties. To encourage the timid girl, her father wiped and kissed her weeping eyes and recalled to her the commandment of heaven.

"All at once the girl's mother, Anna, who was also present as a matron of honor, was inspired by God to dance madly through the house—a holy sight!—and raise a great noise to heaven. And

160

165

170

175

180

185

190

bacchatur tollitque ingentem coelo ululatum.
Unum in me conversa oculo, me fertur in unum,
nil minus hoc ducentem animo, nil tale verentem,
195   corripiensque manu, "Solus tu posceris," inquit.
"Annuit hoc uni superum tibi connubium rex."
Obstupuere omnes, nec tunc ex agmine tanto
exortem quisquam seniori invidit honorem.
Ipse, aevi quod eram seris minus integer annis,
200   multa recusabam, multa huc venisse pigebat.
Aequales aderant fidi, simul et renuentem
hortari atque animum mihi blandis addere dictis.
Cedo igitur victus tandemque uxorius illam
accedo et lachrymans lachrymantem ad limina duco.
205   'Et iam nox aderat stellis fulgentibus apta,
suffundens umbras mundo nigrantibus alis.
Secretis thalamis pariter succedimus ambo.
Flebat sponsa; solum lachrymis iuxta omne madebat,
ac veluti, cum vere subest huberrimus humor
210   arboribus, lentae vitis si forte cacumen
falce putans stirpem feriat male providus unca
agricola, immeritam et violarit vulnere matrem.
Ipse aderam et dictis solabar mitibus aegram,
virginis haud cupidus primum decerpere florem.
215   Cum sic longa trahens suspiria pectore ab imo, est
orsa loqui: "Non relligio mihi vana suasit
et thalamos odisse et virginitatis amorem
aeternum colere. Intus agit vis aetheris intus,
longaevam responsa licet contraria matrem
220   sollicitent vatumque minae, sunt et mea contra
vatum iussa mihi, nulli succumbere labi,
nullis virgineam taedis summittere mentem.
Ante retro primos properet revolutus ad ortus
Iordanis, sistantque suos vaga sidera cursus!"

then she turned her eyes on me alone and approached, though I was least expecting this or hoping for it. She seized my hand and said, 'You alone have been chosen. The king of heaven has conceded this marriage to you alone.' Everyone was dumbstruck. But no one in all that crowd begrudged me, an old man, this honor that was more than I deserved. Because I was not in the best health, due to my advanced age, I repeatedly demurred. I was irked that I had even come to the house. But good men of my own age encouraged me to accept, inspiring me with kind words. Finally vanquished, I yielded and approached my new wife. Then weeping, I led her weeping over the threshold.

"Soon the starry night on black wings spread its shadows over the world and we went together to the seclusion of the bedroom. My wife wept and the ground grew moist with tears. Just as in spring, when the sap rises in abundance on the trees, if an improvident reaper, as he prunes the top of a winding vine, happens to wound the stalk with his curved scythe, he violates the innocent mother-plant as well. Standing near her, I consoled the poor girl with gentle words, hardly eager to take her maidenhood. Finally she sighed deeply and began to speak. 'No empty superstition caused me to hate marriage and wish to remain a virgin forever. Rather a heavenly power drives me from within. Though the prophets' ambiguous words and portents have moved my aged mother, against them I have my own prophetic commands that urge me to resist any taint or to bend my virgin mind to marriage. Sooner would the Jordan flow back to its source and the wandering stars cease their orbits!' So she spoke. And tears, a warrant of

195

200

205

210

215

220

225 Haec ait, inque genas stillantes undique honestae
ex oculis simul incipiunt turgescere gemmae.
     'Nec mora, deinde mihi insinuans quatit ima repente
ossa timor. Genua aegra labant; nox plurima oborta
ante oculos. Ter sum conatus pauca profari,
230 ter frustrata sono lingua est, nec verba sequuta.
Tum quoque vox audita: "Toro thalamisque paratis
parce; tamen concessa tibi connubia serva."
Exurgo, atque oculos iam dudum in virgine fixus
horrenda, tali sum tandem voce loquutus:
235 "Quis mihi te virgo invito coniunxit Olympo?
Quis tantis (non hos equidem quaesivi hymenaeos)
immeritum implicuit monstris? Haud talia quondam
praedixit puero genitor ludibria vates,
iam senior vates idem templique sacerdos.
240 Ille quidem aut nullos thalamos, mihi nulla manere
connubia, aut certe clarum fore me inde canebat.
Verum age, quae menti surgat sententia pandam,
quandoquidem superi mihi te iunxere, sed idem
absterrent monstris, licet et mox usque licebit
245 virgineum serves intacto corpore florem.
Haud tamen ipse ausim iniussus dissolvere sacri
connubii vincla ista. Domo degemus eadem,
ipse tibi ut genitor, mihi tu ceu filia semper,
teque adeo casus iam nunc complector in omnes.
250 Hoc tua relligio velit, hoc mea serior aetas."
Annuit his aliaque domus in parte puella
secubuit. Mitto totam quae monstra per illam
sum passus, quam mira horrens insomnia noctem.
     'Iamque dies pulsis tenebris invecta rubebat,
255 et face sol rosea nigras disiecerat umbras.

her sincerity, welled up like jewels in her eyes and flowed down her   225
cheeks.

"Suddenly, deep within me, a great fear arose. My knees grew
unsteady and I could no longer see. Three times I tried to speak,
but each time my tongue vainly strove to form a sound, a word.
And then I heard someone say, 'Spare the bed and the bridal   230
chambers. But preserve the marriage rites that have been allowed
you.' I rose up and stared for some time at the awe-inspiring young
woman. Finally I said, 'Who joined me to you in marriage against
the will of heaven? Who has involved me, innocent of any wrong,   235
in such unnatural events—for I certainly never sought this marriage? This was hardly the claim that my father, an aged seer, a
priest of the temple, made about me when I was a boy, that I
should become a laughingstock. For he predicted either that no
marriage-chamber should be in store for me, or that I should be   240
famous for my marriage. Come then: I will tell you what I have in
mind, since heaven, which has joined us, frightens me with por-
tentous signs. And so you are and ever shall be allowed to preserve
your body and virginity intact. As for me, I would never dare to   245
dissolve, unbidden, the bonds of this sacred union. We shall live
in the same house and I will be like a father and you like a daughter, and in that sense I now embrace you for better or worse. This
is what is called for by your piety and my advanced age.' She   250
agreed to that and slept in another part of the house. I will leave
out the portents and extraordinary visions that I saw, all a-tremble
throughout the night.

"And now the dark shadows of night were driven off, and approaching day glowed red, and the sun's rosy torch had routed the
nightly shades. I rose from bed and went to my wife. Scarcely had   255

Corripio e stratis artus sponsamque reviso.
Vix thalami impuleram bipatentis cardine portas,
cum lux ecce oculis ingens offusa[1] repente.
Collucent summi radiis laquearia tecti,
260 collucentque trabes, visumque ardere cubile.
Ipsa autem thalami in medio sedet aurea virgo
attonitae similis, nec enim me multa rogantem
dignatur. Nihil illa meo sermone movetur.
Tantum fixa oculos coelo palmasque tenebat
265 aut stellae similis aut puniceae aurorae.
O illa a solita quantum mutata figura!
Quantus honos oculis, quantus decor additus ori!
Haud aliter quam, cum simulacrum excidit acernum
artificis manus e silvis in sede locandum
270 sacrata, quod plebs dehinc supplex omnis adoret,
si, postquam effigiem poliens trunco extudit arte,
extremum super imposito decus induat auro.
Immotam penitus circundat lucida nubes
solis inardescens radiis, stellaeque videntur
275 lucentes capiti circum aurea tempora pasci,
sub pedibusque deae lumen dare candida luna.
      'Pertimui, et mira stupefactus imagine rerum
talia voce dabam: "Pater, his o me exue monstris,
omnipotens. Non haec superi sine numine vestro.
280 Vestra haec portenta agnosco manifestaque signa.
Aspirate animo placidi dubiumque monete
quid sequar aut quaenam vobis sententia constet."
Tantum effatus eram. Tandem pulcherrima virgo
ad sese redit, abrupto velut excita somno
285 suspirans, lachrymisque sinus humectat obortis.
Accedo atque rogo nova per connubia supplex
atque illum aeternae per virginitatis amorem,
unum quem niveo colit intemerata pudore,

I thrown open the doors of the chamber when my eyes were filled with a blast of light. The coffers of the ceiling, like the floors, were filled with light. The whole room seemed to be inflamed. For her 260 part, the young woman, gilded by the light, sat in the middle of the room like one amazed and she did not deign to answer my questions to her. She was not moved by my words. She merely fixed her eyes on heaven and held up her hands, like stars or like the rosy dawn. How changed she seemed from her wonted form! 265 What nobility shone in those eyes, what beauty in her face! She was like some statue carved in maple that the sculptor's hand has brought from the forest and set in a temple to be venerated thenceforth by a crowd of suppliants; once he has artfully shaped 270 it from the wood and polished it smooth, he gives it a final adornment by gilding it with pure gold. She sat immobile, surrounded by a cloud glowing with sunlight. Blazing stars seemed to graze her temples, while the feet of this goddess were set upon a glow- 275 ing, silvery moon.

"I was terrified. In my astonishment at this vision, I called out, 'O Father Almighty, spare me such portents. The angels have not contrived these things without your will. I know that these are your portents and clear signs. Gently inspire and instruct me, in 280 my doubt, as to what I should do and what you intend.' So I spoke. Finally the beautiful young woman returned to herself and sighed, as though abruptly awakened from sleep. She bedewed her breast with the tears that welled up. I went to her. By our recent 285 marriage rites and by the love of everlasting maidenhood that she cultivated alone, with her snow-white modesty intact, I besought

admittat socium curarum et magna recludat
290   rerum arcana, nihil metuens, mihique omnia credat.
     'Illa solo vultum atque oculos deiecta nitentis,
rore velut demissa caput rosa matutino,
cunctatur; demum incipiens sic ora resolvit:
"Dicam equidem pater. Haud patiar te nostra latere
295   gaudia. Sed quae nunc aut unde exordia sumam?
Nam quis narranti rerum miracula credat
tantarum? Per ego has lachrymas quas excutit ingens
laetitia, obtestor, quae fabor, pectore condas,
ne prius incipiant in vanum serpere vulgus
300   quam deus ipse aliis vulgaverit omnia signis.
     '"Iam monitrix operum stellas Aurora fugarat,
et sol pallentes lustrabat lampade terras.
Ipsa revolvebam vatum monimenta priorum,
dicta animo recolens. Sed prae tunc omnibus unum
305   forte mihi ante oculos (neque enim sine numine certo
oblatum reor) immotum fixumve manebat,
quod cuncti pariter super omnia praedixere
affore, concubitu nullo cum regia virgo,
impatiens exorsque viri (mirabile dictu),
310   coelicolum regem sub luminis ederet auras,
cuius in adventu laetentur cuncta per orbem
protinus et toto surgat gens aurea mundo.
     '"Illam felicem tacite mecum ipse[2] vocabam
quam pater omnipotens tanto cumularet honore,
315   iamque dei matrem venerabar mente futuram,
infantique deo, si forte his ille diebus,
his si forte oris nascatur, dona parabam.
Talia dum mecum eventus ignara voluto,
ecce mihi nova lux oculis oblata repente.
320   Suspicio; liquidas sine nube remetior auras.
Mira loquar: video medium discedere coelum

her on bended knee to make me a partner in her cares, to open up
to me her great secrets and confide everything.   290

"She paused and looked down, fixing her shining eyes on the
floor, like a rose encumbered by the morning dew. Finally she began to speak. 'I will tell you, father. I could hardly bear to conceal
from you my joy. But where should I begin? Who would believe   295
me if I spoke such marvels? By these very tears, the product of
great joy, I ask you to bury within your heart what I am about to
tell you, lest it spread among the people before God himself
chooses to disclose everything through other signs.   300

"'Already dawn, the revealer of deeds, had put the stars to flight
and the sun shone down on the pale earth. For my part I kept recalling the teachings of the ancient prophets. But one above all remained fixed in my mind, placed there surely by some higher   305
power. All the prophets had predicted that a royal virgin, who was
without taint of the marriage bed and remained, astonishingly, a
virgin, would bring into the light of the world a king of angels;
and that, immediately upon his coming, there would be happiness   310
everywhere and a golden age would arise throughout creation.

"'Silently I used to call her blessed whom the Almighty Father
himself chose for such an honor. In my mind I worshipped her
who was destined to be the Mother of God. I even made gifts for   315
the infant god, in case he were to be born in this age and in this
land. And I was thinking such thoughts, with no idea of what
would happen, when suddenly a strange light filled my eyes. I
looked up and found no cloud in the clear skies. Then I saw an   320
amazing thing: the heavens were split down the middle and a host

pennatasque acies populos felicis Olympi
exultare polo superumque applaudere regi.
Non obstant clausi postes, non pariete tectum
325   marmoreo circunseptum. Video ignea coeli
sidera sidereosque globos superum aurea tecta.
Tum mihi se puer ante oculos allapsus Olympo
ora deo propior radiantibus obtulit alis,
et placidus tendens candentia lilia dextra,
330   me sic affari laetasque expromere voces:
'O una ante alias coelo acceptissima matres,
magnus adest tibi praesenti regnator Olympi
numine. Tu nuribus felix magis omnibus una.'
   '"Hic mihi vix paucis auditis talibus ingens
335   miranti gelidos subito tremor alligat artus.
Tum sic ille animum divino pignore firmat:
'Parce metu virgo. Placuisti ex omnibus una
coelituum regi, faciat quam prole parentem.
Et iam concipies puerum gravis; ille erit ingens,
340   progeniemque patris summi secla omnia dicent,
et quoniam multis olim feret ipse salutem
servabitque pios, patrio dic nomine IESVM,
sedibus infernis iam nunc lachrymabile nomen.
Supra homines, supra aspicies se tollere et ipsos
345   coelicolas fama insignem ac praestantibus ausis.
Nam pater omnipotens atavorum in sceptra reponet
pristina regnantem late, regumque sedebit
in solio, neque enim metas neque tempora regni
accipiet; toto aeternum dominabitur orbe.'
350   Dixerat. Ipsa autem paulatim abeunte timore
subiicio: 'Sed qua vero ratione, quod inquis,
confieri poterit? Nam mens mihi denique fixa
atque immota manet nunquam violare pudorem
virgineum semperque virum commercia fugi.'

of winged angels rejoiced in the sky as they gloried in their king!
Neither closed doors nor a roof hemmed with stone was any obstacle to them. I saw fiery stars in the sky and the starry spheres   325
that are the golden homes of the heavenly ones. On radiant wings,
a child with a face like a god's descended from heaven and stood
before my very eyes. Then, offering me the whitest callow-lilies, he
gave me these happy tidings: "Of all mothers, you are the dearest   330
to heaven. The great lord of Olympus is come to you, his spirit is
near at hand, most fortunate of all the daughters of men."

"'Scarcely had I heard and marvelled at these few words, when
a sudden fear gripped my cold body. Then, with this token of di-   335
vine favor, he gave me encouragement: "Don't be afraid. Above all
the other women of the earth, it has pleased the King of Angels to
make you the mother of his child. And so you will conceive a son.
He will be a great man, whom all ages to come will hail as the Son
of his supreme Father. And since he himself will bring salvation to   340
many, being the savior of pious souls, you will call him by the ancestral name of JESUS, a name that even now is causing much
lamentation in the nether realms. You will see him rise above all
men, even above the angels, through his reputation and outstand-
ing deeds. For his Almighty Father will bestow on him a kingdom   345
over the whole earth, such as his ancestors held of old, and he will
sit on the throne of kings, accepting no term or limit to his rule
over all the earth." So he spoke. As my fear gradually diminished,   350
I asked, "But how could this happen as you say? For I have made
up my mind never to lose my virginity, always to flee the company
of men."

355 '"His ego finieram paucis, his ille sequutus:
'Te superum pater afflabit coelestibus auris
desuper, afflatu quo solo plena sine ullo
concubitu, exacto gravis edes tempore partum.
Atque ideo, quem foeta dabis, deus ille feretur
360 aeterno genitore satus, qui temperat orbem.
Quae, ne vana putes, scis quae tibi sanguine iuncta est,
Helisabe sobolis, ut degerit hactenus exors,
ut sterili seclis iandudum effoeta senectus
spem cunctam abstulerit partus prolisque creandae,
365 plena viro pariet tamen illa, et tempore luna
perfecto gravidae iam sextum circuit orbem.
Cuncta potest etenim qui me tibi mittit ab alto
aethere, siderei rex idem atque auctor Olympi.'
Haec ait, et paribus se in coelum proripit alis.
370 '"Quem supera aspiciens tali sum voce sequuta:
'Quisquis es, o coeli iuvenum pulcherrime, praepes
obsequor ac votis, quod rex iubet, omnibus opto.'
Interea nubes maculoso discolor auro
demissa ad terram croceis me amplectitur alis.
375 Diffulgent intus radiique ignique coruscae
scintillant veluti squamae vario ordine circum,
squamaeque stellaeque auri fulgore micantes,
adverso quales imitantur³ sole colores,
cum picturato coelum distinxit amictu
380 nubicolor liquidis effusis imbribus arquus.
Hanc simul omnipotens genitor perflavit ab alto,
continuo ruit ecce voluta liquentibus astris
aura potens, quaque illa venit, procul undique circum
scintillae absiliunt radiis vibrantibus aureae.
385 Turbine corripior rapido, visque illa per omnes
aurai, vis omnipotens mihi diditur artus,
aethereusque vigor toto se corpore miscet,

"'With these words I finished and he continued. "The Father   355
of Angels will fill you with heavenly breath from above. Through
this alone, without having to lie with a man, you will be with
child. When the child is brought to term, you will give birth. And
for this reason he whom you bring forth will be esteemed a god,
sired by his Heavenly Father, ruler of the universe. And lest you   360
think this an empty promise, know that your cousin Elizabeth,
she who has lived so long without offspring, she from whom, after
many years of sterility, depleted age had removed all hope of children, even she is now big with child. Indeed, the moon has already   365
passed through six cycles since the time of the child's conception.
All things, then, are possible for the King and Creator of heaven,
who has sent me to you from on high." So speaking, he flew off to
heaven on paired wings.

"'I looked up into the skies and called after him, "Whoever you   370
are, fairest of heavenly youths, I eagerly obey and, with every vow,
wish for what the king commands." Meanwhile a cloud spotted
with gold descended upon the earth and covered me with its
saffron wings. The rays of its light shone within, glittering with   375
fiery sparks all around like the shimmering scales of a fish. But
these scales and stars gleamed like glowing gold and imitated the
hues of the low-lying sun after clear rain, when the misty rainbow
throws across the sky its pied mantle. As soon as the Almighty   380
Father had breathed upon this cloud, behold, a powerful wind
rushed down from the bright stars, and wherever it passed, gold
sparks leapt forth in all directions. Suddenly I was carried away
upon a whirlwind, and the force, the all-mastering force of that   385
wind spread through my entire body, as a heavenly power entered

visaque praedulci mihi corda liquescere amore.
Qualis secreto naturae foedere tellus
390 concipit et vario clam foetu plena gravescit,
matris ubi in gremium descendit plurimus aether,
auraque foecundos afflavit verna tepores.
His actis clarum sonuere per aethera coetus
aligeri cantu vario plausumque dedere.
395 Hinc tonitru ingenti tremuerunt ardua Olympi,
crebraque per coelum hic illic rima ignea fulsit."
    'Talia narrabat virgo; simul ora rigabat
laetitia illachrymans. Tum tendo ad sidera palmas,
multa orans animi ambiguus. Nec credere quibam
400 (mens adeo mihi laeva fuit) tam mira ferenti,
quandoquidem iuvenes plerunque innectere fraudes
virginibus soliti incautis et fallere furto,
ah! faciles dictis aurem praebere puellas.
Quin etiam hanc volvi (scelus) olim linquere demens.
405 Verum eadem in somnis pueri redeuntis imago
visa mihi vultusque habitusque simillimus illi,
ipsa sibi modo quem memorabat sponsa loquutum.
Nudus erat roseos humeros; tantum aureo laevo
pendebat demissa chlamys quam fibula subter,
410 ilia tergemino mordebat rasilis auro,
rubraque compactis pendebant cingula bullis,
molles a tergo tractim succrescere plumae,
ac sensim geminas humeris assurgere in alas.
Tum suras gemmis inclusit, caetera nudus.
415 Oris multus honos gratique in corpore motus
haud nostri puerum generis testantur adesse,
sed coeli sobolem atque aulae stellantis alumnum.
Nec minus ipsa etiam mira spectabilis arte
vestis erat baccis[4] superas illusa per oras.
420 Textile Maeandro duplici infra circuit aurum

me and my heart seemed to melt with the sweetest love. It was as when the earth conceives, through some occult pact of nature, and covertly becomes pregnant with its varied young, while an abun- 390 dant wind descends into the womb of mother earth and the vernal breeze blows fecund warmth. At this the angelic choruses rejoiced, their clear voices resounding through heaven. Thereupon the heights of Olympus shook with huge thunderclaps, and many 395 bolts of lightning flashed throughout the sky!'

"So the virgin spoke and tears of joy covered her face. I was not certain what to feel, so I prayed for some time and raised my hands to heaven. I was not able to believe her as she told such marvels, so blinded were my thoughts, given that young men often 400 lay plots like these for unsuspecting maidens and, alas, by stealth deceive young women all too eager to lend an ear to such dis- course. Though it would have been a crime to do so, I madly thought of leaving her. But then, in a dream, I saw a youth return- ing, in face and habit like the angel with whom my wife had just 405 claimed to speak. He was half-naked and his shoulders, the color of roses, were bare. From his noble left shoulder a robe hung down, held from below by a clasp. His loins were girt by a golden sash with tight bosses. Soft feathers grew at his shoulders, broad- 410 ening steadily to form a pair of wings. Though his calves were cov- ered in gems, his thighs were bare. The beauty of his face and the grace of his movements revealed that he was not human, but a 415 child of heaven, raised in the starry palace. No less conspicuous was his splendid cloak, its upper fringes embellished with pearls, admirably encircled by a golden hem in a double meander. Therein 420

admirabile opus. Tres hic impune per ignes
laeti ibant pueri intexti pariterque canebant
coelicolum regi conversi ad sidera laudes.
Cernere erat mediis acres fornacibus ignes
425　parcere corporibus longeque absistere flammas.
　　　'Mirabar tacitus, cum sic pulcherrimus ore
affatur trepidum iuvenis: "Sate sanguine regum,
quod tantum irrepsit menti scelus? Omnia non te
signa movent haud haec fieri sine numine certo?
430　Ne dubita, nam vera canit sanctissima virgo.
Iam nunc congressus nunquam perpessa viriles
concepit, gravis aetherea divinitus aura,
nam pater omnipotens coelesti afflavit ab arce
atque uterum implevit dilapsum numen ab astris.
435　Casta fides nobis colitur. Desiste vereri.
Haec vates olim vestri cecinere futura,
cuncta sed obscura implicuere ambage tegentes.
Nanque haec illa quidem coeli in penetralibus altis
porta ingens, clausa aeternum, nec pervia gressu
440　ulli hominum. Tantum omnipotens deus ipse per illam
itque reditque viam, nec claustra immota resignat.
Hanc tibi commendat summi regnator Olympi,
coniugio adiungens stabili, sed coniugis usum
effuge. Securum tecum sponsa exigat aevum,
445　quanvis tuta deo iam nunc sit praeside virgo."
　　　'Sic fatus, subito in tenues evanuit auras,
pernici liquida arva fuga per nubila carpens,
et simul incussit mihi blandum in pectus amorem,
utque rigor ferri rutilo lentescit in igne,
450　sic mihi cor rapido sensi mollescere motu.
Consurgo et veniam conversus ad aethera posco,
meque ipsum incuso amens et lux reddita menti.
Inque dies magis atque magis coeli alta patescunt

three boys were depicted, happily passing unscathed through the fire. As they turned to the stars, they sang praises to the lord. You could see hot fires in the furnaces sparing their bodies, as the flames stood far off.   425

"All afraid, I marveled in silence as the beautiful youth addressed me: 'Scion of royal blood, what great crime has stolen into your mind? Do all these signs not move you to believe that such things could come about only if God willed them? Have no doubt that the saintly maiden spoke the truth. Now indeed has she con-   430
ceived a child without carnal knowledge of men. Rather she was impregnated by the ethereal force of Almighty God, who breathed upon her from heaven, as the Holy Spirit glided down from the stars, filling her womb. We reverence her faith and chastity. Do not fear. Your prophets once foretold these things, but concealed   435
all in the obscurity of their diction. For she is the massive gate before the innermost sanctum of the heavenly palace. It is eternally shut and no man may enter. Almighty God alone passes through it, without opening the closed doors. The lord of Olympus com-   440
mends this woman to you, to be joined in eternal wedlock. But do not consummate the marriage. Let your wife spend her days in peace by your side, though even now she is safely guarded by God.'   445

"With these words he suddenly vanished into thin air, swiftly fleeing through the clouds to the fields of pure sky, and as he went he filled my soul with sweet love. Just as stiff iron bends in the glowing fire, so I felt my fast-beating heart grow soft. I arose and,   450
turning to heaven, I prayed for pardon. As the inner light returned to my mind I was ashamed of my folly and, with each day, I saw

consilia, antiquis quae vatibus omnia quondam
455 obscuris vera involvens deus ostendebat.
Haec virgo est rubus ille, procul quem in monte videbat
ardentem vates igni crepitante cremari
corniger, attactu cum nullo innoxia flamma
lamberet et frondes illaesae in stirpe virerent.
460 Haec eadem niveae quondam impenetrabile lanae
nimbis vellus erat, cum late cuncta maderent
imbribus effusis circum, tellusque nataret
humida, ni veterum vana est prudentia vatum.
Haec mecum et toto penitus nox pectore abacta est.
465   'Haud mora, prodigiis tantis facit ipsa fidem res.
Iam diffusa canit Galilaea per oppida fama
inventam (portentum ingens) in montibus altis
nuper anum, quae suprema iam affecta senecta
plena viro attulerit sobolis spem, cum tamen acta
470 infoecunda illi fuerit sterilisque iuventa.
Tum mihi sponsa: "Puer coeli demissus ab oris
hoc," inquit, "mihi praedixit, nam cuncta recordor.
Haec anus est, haec Helisabe mihi sanguine iuncta,
cui sextum luna gravidae iam circuit orbem."
475 Nec plura. Extemplo placet ire et stirpe propinquam
visere anum, gradimurque ambo super alta locorum,
tectaque Zacchariae petimus procul ardua vatis.
Vix primum attigeram limen (mirabile dictu)
occurrit tremebunda anus, intrantique puellae
480 optatos dedit amplexus. Deus amplexantem
invasit, subitusque sub ossa repente cucurrit
ima calor, talesque dedit venerata loquelas:
"Longe una ante alias tu fortunata parentes
tuque uterique tui virgo sanctissima pondus.
485 Unde repente mihi tanta indulgentia coeli?
Unde haec affulsit serae tam clara senectae

more clearly the high designs of heaven. God made manifest all
the truths that the ancient prophets had obscurely foretold. The   455
maiden was that bush that the horned prophet saw burning on the
mountain, though the harmless flames did not consume it and the
leaves were still green upon their stalk. She was the fleece of snow-
white wool, impermeable to torrential rain, even as everything   460
around was flooded with the rains and the moist earth seemed to
be swimming—unless the foresight of the ancient prophets prove
false. As I meditated thus, night vanished from the depths of my
heart.

"At once, great portents revealed the truth of what I had seen: 465
throughout the towns of Galilee it was reported (a great marvel)
that in the high mountains a woman of very advanced age, though
sterile in youth, had lately become pregnant and was expecting.
My wife said to me, 'The youth who descended from heaven pre-   470
dicted as much to me, for I remember everything. The aged
woman is Elizabeth, my blood relative, who is now six months
pregnant.' She said nothing more. At once she desired to see the
aged woman, her close relative. We both journeyed across the   475
hills, seeking the lofty dwelling of the seer Zachariah. We had no
sooner reached the threshold when, to our surprise, the trembling
old woman came forward and gave the young maiden the embrace
she desired. God filled Elizabeth in that embrace. A heavenly fire   480
reached into her bones and she reverently spoke these words. 'You
are more blessed by far than all other women, holy virgin—you
and the child you carry in your womb. Why did heaven suddenly
look down so favorably on me? Why did such a brilliant spring-   485
time shine upon me in advanced old age? I am allowed to look on
the Mother of God, to speak face to face with her who was se-

tempestas? Fas ecce dei vidisse parentem,
et coram affari lectam de millibus unam
dignantem has sedes meaque ultro in tecta profectam.
490   Nam mihi (vix primum attigeras haec limina) pectus
emicuit, saliensque utero signum edidit infans.
Felix diva parens superum gratissima regi,
syncera spectata fide, quae credere veris,
dum tua nondum animo praesagis gaudia, dictis
495   haud verita es. Promissa manent pueri alitis ecce
certa tibi. Iam nunc ades, orbisque aspice casus,
o coeli regina, hominum miserata labores."
Dixerat, at teneri qualis rosa plena pudoris,
haud animis elata tumentibus aurea virgo
500   coelicolum regi laudes laetata canebat,
quod se tam prope sidereo aspexisset Olympo
indignam bonus atque humilem, nil tale merentem,
exultansque suos sibi vaticinatur honores
promissos atavis priscisque parentibus olim.
505   'Ex illo quanta immensum portenta per orbem
terruerint hominum mentes praesagaque signa,
limina dum vitae omnipotens attingeret infans,
longa renarrare est mora. Iam tunc Caspia regna
responsis vatum horrebant, iam Nilus et omnis
510   Aegyptus trepidare, omnes orientis et urbes.
Vestri etiam audierant (si vera est fama) per oras
Ausonias iam iam venturum lucis ad auras
invictum regem, cui passim cederet orbis
regnandus, qui se patria virtute potentem
515   seque suumque genus sublimi inferret Olympo.
'His tandem certus signis ego numinis instar
plenam utero supplex sponsam venerabar, et ultro
parebam. Victum gravidae et divina ferebat
pocula de coelo volucer puer. Illum ego saepe

lected from thousands and has chosen to come into my house and grace it with her presence. Scarcely had you come when I felt my heart quiver—the infant moved in my womb and gave a sign! 490 Blessed Mother of God, most pleasing to the King of Heaven, you were found to be pure of faith because you did not hesitate to believe the truth of the angel's words even before you knew what joys awaited. But the promises of the winged boy are certain. Come 495 now and consider the sorrows of this world, queen of heaven, and take pity on the trials of men.' So she spoke and the resplendent maiden, like a rose full of tender bashfulness, did not become proud, but joyously sang praises to the King of Angels: of his 500 goodness he had looked down from the height of heaven upon her, all unworthy and base and deserving no such reward. In her exultation, she foretold the honors that awaited her, honors that had been promised by her ancestors.

"It would take too long to relate all the portents and all the 505 presentient signs that, from that time forward, terrified the minds of men throughout the wide world, as the almighty infant was approaching the threshold of life. Already the Caspian realms trembled at the responses of their oracles. So too the Nile and all of Egypt and all the cities of the east. It was even rumored through- 510 out your Ausonian land—if report is true—that an unvanquished king would be born, to whose reign all men would yield. Fortified by his father's strength, he would raise himself and his people to heaven. 515

"Finally I was persuaded by these unerring signs. Honoring my pregnant wife like a suppliant before God, I willingly obeyed her. Descending from heaven, a winged boy often brought food and divine drink to the laboring maiden. Often I saw him enter her

520 intrantem thalamum manifesto in lumine vidi.
Iamque optanti animo divini tempora partus
expectabam ardens, sed spem mora iniqua trahebat,
et saepe haec cupido repetebam pectore mecum:
"Si modo, si mihi coelestis se ostendere coram
525 non fugiat puer ante obitus, quando omnia de se
rettulit ipsa mihi virgo pulcherrima vera.
Purpureos flores metite et candentia plena
lilia ferte manu, venienti ad limina lucis
dona parate deo puerumque invisite regem.
530 O mihi si quoque tam longe suprema senectae
pars maneat, quantum valeam tua cernere facta,
sancte puer, cum sublata formidine mundum
pacabis, patrioque deus regnabis Olympo.
Tum pax alma colet terras pietasque fidesque,
535 quaeque labat nunc relligio atque resurgere ubique
iustitiam in melius versus mirabitur orbis.
Tum ferus in falces curvas conflabitur ensis,
aureaque incipient mundo succedere secla."
Sic ego saepe moras mecum lenire solebam,
540 et magis usque animo mihi spes accensa vigebat.
    'Forte recognoscens populos numerare iubebat
Augustus Caesar, rerum cui summa potestas.
Ipse igitur veteris repetebam moenia Bethles,
unde genus duco, quo me quoque civibus urbis
545 insererem nomenque meum nomenque meorum.
Sponsa sequebatur Nazarae ab sede profecta.
Vix patriae intraram muros et rara domorum
tecta, soporiferis cum nox coelum abstulit umbris.
Est sedes deserta humilem ingredientibus urbem
550 horrenti culmoque et carice tecta palustri,
agricolis olim statio gratissima, si quos
rure procul patrio nox deprendisset in urbe,

chamber in broad daylight. Now with a hopeful heart I eagerly 520
awaited the hour of the divine birth, though I chafed at the delay.
I reasoned thus with my eager heart. 'If only that heavenly child
would reveal himself to me before I die, since every word was true 525
that the lovely maiden spoke. Pluck flowers of many hues and fill
your hands with pure white lilies. Bring gifts to the boy king as he
reaches the threshold of light. May I live long enough, despite my
old age, to witness your great deeds, as you bring peace to a world 530
freed from fear and reign as a god in the heaven of your Father!
Then faith, piety and nourishing peace will reside on the earth,
and religion as well, though now faltering. And an ennobled world 535
will marvel to see the return of justice in every land. Then will the
cruel sword be beaten into plowshares, and a long sequence of centuries, a golden age, will ensue upon the earth.' In this way I often
found solace in spite of long delays, as hope grew ever greater in
my heart. 540

"Now it so happened that Augustus Caesar, supreme in power
over the world, ordered that a census be taken. And so I returned
with my family to Bethlehem, the home of my forefathers, the origin of my clan, to enroll myself, my own name and my family
among the citizens of the city. My wife followed me as we set out 545
from Nazareth. Scarcely had I entered the walls of my ancestral
village with its scattered houses, when the darkness of night covered the heavens and made us sleepy. As you enter that humble
city, there is a deserted dwelling covered with shaggy thatch and
sedge from the swamplands, a place that once was most welcome 550
to farmers who found themselves in the town, far from home, at

nanque aliis procul a tectis summota recedit.
Huc igitur fessi pariter succedimus ambo
555 seu casu seu sic rector sortitus Olympi,
ut potius reor et potius fas credere duco.
Natum etenim non solum extrema per omnia vitam
ducere et in terris indignos volvere casus,
verum etiam tecto voluit sub paupere eundem
560 nasci humilique domo miserabilem et omnium egenum.
    'Principio in stabulis pandum ad praesepia sisto
quadrupedem auxiliumque viae onerumque levamen,
quem iuxta in stipulis sese locat inclyta virgo,
quippe alia interior domus ulla haud parte vacabat.
565 Bos erat a laeva, tepidum flans ore vaporem,
quem pauper campis luce exercebat arator,
pauca soli curvo suspendens iugera aratro,
nec sera nisi nocte domum repetebat ab agro
conducto, vitam ut posset tolerare labore
570 ipse suo atque famem parvis avertere natis.
Et iam nox medium spatium confecerat horis,
cum mihi, qui saxo haerebam iam lumina victus,
somnus abit, neque enim mersum tunc me altus habebat.
Ecce oculos fulgore novo lux occupat ingens.
575 Diffulgent intus late magalia, quaeque
stramina tetra modo horrebant, nunc aurea cernas.
Exurgo. Aspicio iuxta praesepia nudum
infantem radiis illustrem ac luce coruscum,
quem virgo tenerum in duris modo pauper avenis
580 ediderat nullo nixu, nullo aegra dolore.
Astabant taciti bos hinc, hinc tardus asellus,
pabulaque obliti pariter capita alta tenebant.
Ipsa etiam radiis fulgebat mater utroque
poplite subsidens, oculos demissa nitentis.

nightfall. It was far from most of the other houses. Wearily we went there together, either by chance or, as seems to me more likely and fitting, by the will of God. For he wished his son to live 555 a life marked by harsh circumstances and to suffer indignities on earth, but also to be born beneath a pauper's roof, in a poor dwelling and wanting for everything. 560

"First I stabled the stooped mule, who had lightened our load and helped us on our journey, and then the noble maiden lay down near it in the straw. For there was no room for us at the inn. On our left was an ox, exhaling his warm breath. During the day 565 the humble farmer used him in the fields to drag the curved plough over his meager allotment of land, and did not bring him home from the rented fields until late at night; in this way he could make a tolerable living from his work and stave off hunger from his young children. Already it was the middle of the night. I 570 was lying wearily on the stone floor when suddenly sleep left me — for I'd not yet sunk into deep slumber — and a mighty burst of light filled my eyes. The inside of the stable shone, and the straw 575 bed, which had just now seemed so wretched, gleamed as if made of gold. I got up and saw beside the stables a naked child gleaming and radiating light. The poor girl had just delivered the delicate child without pain of labor, in the rough straw. The ox and the 580 sluggish ass stood nearby in silence and looked on, forgetting their fodder. Sitting with her legs under her, Mary herself seemed to glow, her brilliant eyes cast down. Ah, how she gazed at the naked

585 Ah, nudum lachrymis parvum spectabat obortis,
tendebatque manus suffuso lumine iunctas.
'Astrorum qualis facies rorantibus umbris
post imbrem, siccis Boreas ubi frigidus alis
ingruit ac coelum populans cava nubila differt,
590 talis virgineo species accesserat ori.
Quid facerem? Partem subieci ambobus amictus
ipse mei atque olidae substravi terga bidentis
pro picturatis cunis, pro murice et auro.
Caetera pauperies noxque intempesta vetabant.
595 Necdum clara dies merso diluxerat orbi,
iam conferto aderant pastores agmine et antri
floribus ac variis auxerunt limina sertis,
rustica multifori fundentes sibila canna.
Ut stabula ingressi, ad praesepia lumina vertunt
600 summissi terramque petunt et numen adorant.
'Mirabar mecum tacitus, fama unde per agros
haec subito exisset deque ipsis quaerere coepi.
Unus quaerentem sic est affarier orsus:
"Pastores sumus; in vicinis saltibus omnes
605 pascimus. Insomnem ut nobis mos ducere noctis
haud partem exiguam atque gregem servare coactum,
nocte fere media vigilantibus astitit ingens
lux cunctis supra caput, attonitisque pavore
ingenti talis vox est audita per auras:
610 'Ne trepidate, viri, vobis nova gaudia porto.
Ille piis toties promissus vatibus olim
finibus his hodie natus deus. Eximet ille
e tenebris hominum genus atque in pristina reddet.
Illum vicina fas vobis cernere in urbe
615 effultum stipula atque humile ad praesepe iacentem.'
His moniti vicinam oculos torquemus ad urbem.
Ecce autem volucer pictis exercitus alis

child with tears in her eyes! Suffused with light, she held her   585
hands together in prayer.

"Her maidenly face was like the starry heavens after a shower,
when cold Boreas, on his parching wings, invades the skies and
routs the hollow clouds. What was I to do? I set beneath them   590
both a part of my cloak, and laid down the unclean hide of a sheep
in place of a painted cradle, of purple sheets and gold. Indigence
and the cold night prohibited my doing anything else. Bright daylight had not yet illuminated the earth, still sunk in darkness,   595
when a band of shepherds came and adorned the cave's entrance
with flowers and particolored wreaths, as they played a rustic tune
on their pierced reed-pipe. Entering the stable, they turned their
downcast eyes to the manger and, kneeling on the ground, they
adored the divine child.   600

"I wondered to myself how word could have gotten out so
quickly through the fields. When I asked, one of them answered
thus: 'We are shepherds who graze our flocks in the neighboring
groves. We spend a good part of the night awake, keeping our   605
flocks together. Around midnight, while we all kept watch, a huge
light appeared overhead. We were stricken with a great fear when
suddenly, through the air, we heard a voice. "Be not afraid, men,
for I bring you new tidings of joy. A god has been born this day, in   610
this land, who was often promised to you by the prophets of old.
He will lead the race of men out of darkness and restore them to
their former purity. You may visit him in the nearby town, where
he lies upon a bed of straw, in a humble manger." So instructed,   615
we turned our eyes to the neighboring town. And all at once a
host of celestial youths with many-colored wings filled the sky

coelestes supra pueri toto aethere visi
nubibus impositi liquidas equitare per oras
620 et mirum in morem celeri proludere coetu.
Atque ubi ter coelum ternis toto agmine versi
lustravere choris, ter lustravere choreis,
concentu petiere polum. Longe ardua Olympi
responsant; laetis dissultat plausibus aether."
625 'Talia narrabant, nec sese explere corusci
infantis facie poterant, fixique manebant
haerentes oculis, haerentes pectore toto.
Fulgebat puer ore, oculis ac corpore ab omni
divino longe circum loca lumine complens,
630 qualis puniceo se pandens ore, rosarum
cum primum dias flos visit luminis oras,
aut ubi sole novo roseis orientis in oris
enituit verni species patefacta diei.
Nos vero interea, quanquam indubitabile numen
635 novimus atque deum, nec opis nec lactis egentem,
parvum alimus tamen, ut mortali semine cretum;
hubera siccantem matris tenerumque fovemus
invalidumque artus. Mortalem quippe creatus
mortali matris traxit de corpore partem,
640 atque ideo, ut veterum mos est antiquus avorum,
imprimimus generis signum, Samiaque putamus
exiguam testa pellem genitalia circum;
addimus et nomen, memoresque vocamus IESVM,
ut quondam admonuit puer actus ab aethere praepes.
645 Idem etiam, quod sit regum de stirpe sacerdos,
gentibus est Graio dictus de nomine Christus.
'Quin etiam, quanvis nullo intemerata remansit
concubitu mater, tamen intra tecta morata est,
usque quater denos dum solis cerneret ortus.
650 Tum demum sacram Solymorum advenimus urbem

above, riding on clouds through the clear air, their swift band re- 620
joicing in marvelous fashion. And when all their number had
thrice orbited the skies in threefold chorus and threefold dance,
they returned to heaven all together. Far and wide the heights of
Olympus echoed with the sound. The air rang with joyous music.'

"So the shepherd spoke. They could not satisfy themselves with 625
looking at the face of the radiant infant, but stood with their eyes
and their entire souls fixed on him. As the divine child glowed in
his face, his eyes and his entire body, he filled the surrounding
lands with a divine light, as when the rose that first opens to the 630
day spreads wide its ruby mouth, or when the first rays of the sun
appear in the chambers of the east, and the beauty of the spring
day shines forth. We knew that he was a divinity, a god, needing
neither help nor food. But still we nourished him as if he were a 635
mortal child. As he drank his mother's milk, I kept the delicate,
weak-limbed child warm. Having been created human, he took on
the mortal nature of his mother's mortal body. And so, following 640
the custom of our ancestors, we marked him with the sign of our
race, and circumcised him with a shard of Samian pottery, and
named him JESUS, as the heavenly angel had bidden us. And 645
since he is a priest of royal blood, his name among the Gentiles is
the Greek word 'Christ.'

"Though his mother remained a virgin, unstained by the bridal
bed, still she stayed within the house, watching the rising of the
sun for forty days. Only then did we go with the boy to Jerusalem
so that the royal maiden could purify herself. According to cus- 650

cum puero, quo se lustraret regia virgo,
torquatasque arae attulimus de more columbas.
Stabat sacra ferens altaria ad ipsa sacerdos
succinctus lino albenti capitisque bicorni
655   tegmine, pervigilem adservans penetralibus ignem.
Hunc circum ante aram natorum intonsa corona
fundebant pateris vituli, ut tunc forte, cruorem,
quem pater, ut sontis populi commissa piaret,
mactarat superum regi veniamque precatus
660   suppliciter solitos aris adolebat honores.
Circunfusi aderant primores gentis et omnes
tempora tangebant dextris vittata iuvenci.
Iamque levi fusum delibans ille cruorem
terque quaterque sacram digito irroraverat aram,
665   araeque impositam flammam, et septem ordine lychnos,
linteaque ampla, quibus sacrorum arcana teguntur.
   'Et iam finis erat sacris, fessusque sacerdos
cum gnatis dapibus sese accingebat opimis.
Tunc humili gressu virgo procedit ad aram,
670   infantem laeva gestans dextraque volucres.
Quid memorem quae signa polo pater edidit alto
testatus veram sobolem? Quantum ipse sacerdos
horruerit pueri aspectu? Quam mira repente
ignibus insolitis lux circunfulserit aram?
675   Ter thura accensos venerans coniecit in ignes;
ter subiecta tholo subito ingens flamma reluxit.
Ille tamen collo patrio de more volucres
immolat intorto atque effundens rite cruorem;
porricit et plumas et aperti gutturis exta,
680   solis ab occasu nitidos conversus ad ortus,
diffringitque alas; tum sacros suggerit ignes
visceribus. Grato vapor it super aethera fumo,
araque panchaeos flagrans exhalat odores.

tom, we also brought two doves with colored necks and set them
on the altar. At those altars stood a priest dressed in white linens
and a two-cornered hat, bearing sacred vessels. Within the temple,
he tended the eternal flame. Around him before the altar stood the   655
unshaven circle of his sons, who, as it happened, were spilling
from shallow bowls the blood of a young bull. To atone for the
sins of his guilty race, he had sacrificed the bull to the King of Angels and as a suppliant he was burning the wonted offerings upon
the altars. All the leading men of the race stood round him in a   660
circle, placing their right hands on the garlanded head of the bull-
ock. Now he poured the blood on the altar, three and four times
aspersing with a light finger the sacred altar, the flame, a lamp
with seven candles in a row, as well as the sheets that conceal the   665
holy things.

"And now these sacred rites were over and the wearied priest,
together with his sons, sat down to an excellent meal. Then with
humble step the virgin proceeded to the altar, carrying the child in
her right hand and the doves in her left. Why should I repeat to   670
you the signs the Supreme Father gave as he acknowledged his
true Son or how the priest himself trembled at the sight of the
child or how a miraculous light glowed with strange fire around
the altar? Three times he reverently tossed incense into the lit   675
fires, and three times a massive flame flared up beneath the
domed-roof. Having first twisted their necks and poured out the
blood, he sacrificed the birds according to the traditions of his nation. Then, turning from the setting sun to its dazzling birth, he   680
offered up the feathers and entrails of the doves. He tore off the
wings and placed them in the sacred flame. An odor rose up
through the air in pleasing smoke, and the altar was filled with
Arabian incense.

'Ecce hominum subito turbantur pectora casu.
685 Nomen avi Simeon referens erat obsitus annis,
quo nemo tota urbe fuit servantior aequi.
Huic, ut erat longe venturi praescius, olim
aethereae vis omnipotens promiserat aurae
visurum sese ante deum auctoremque salutis
690 expectatum orbi, quam lucis linqueret auras.
Iamque erat hunc vitae pertaesum aegerque senectae
optabat duros leto finire labores,
sed spes illa animo cupido usque infixa manebat.
Ergo ubi adesse deum praesensit numine plenus,
695 qualis ubi gressum per agros comitatus herilem
forte canis leporem vi longe sensit odora,
continuo intenditque aures atque aera captat
naribus, et coeptum rumpens iter avius errat
atque oculis incerta ferae vestigia lustrans,
700 nunc hos, nunc illos cursus fert atque recursus
incertus; longe latratibus arva resultant.
Talis erat senis in templo exultantis imago.
Tum puerum tremulis correptum amplectitur ulnis
atque arcte premit. Hinc lachrymis ita fatur obortis:
705 "Macte infans virtute, dei indubitata propago,
mundi opifer, qui nostra venis veterumque parentum
sponte admissa tui largo lavere amne cruoris
et liquidas aperire vias ad sidera coeli.
Exoptatus ades, nec me tua maxima fallunt,
710 summe pater, promissa. Mori me denique fas est.
Nunc o me nunc ad requiem finemque laborum
corporis exutum vinclis dimittis, ut olim
pollicitus; iam viderunt mea lumina quem tu
auxilium mundo misisti, ut gentibus esset
715 in tenebris lux, Isacidos nova gloria prolis."
His dictis, matrem versus mox fatur ad ipsam:

"All at once human hearts were disturbed by a surprising event. There was a man who bore the name of his ancestor, Simeon, 685 stooped with years. In the entire city, no one was more steadfast than he in observance of what was right and fair. Since he could see far into the future, it had once been promised to him by the almighty power of heaven that before he left the lighted air he would see God, the source of salvation, long awaited by the world. Though he was weary of life and weakened by old age, though he 690 wished to end his hard labors with death, still that hope remained fixed in his avid soul. Thus filled with divine presence, he had a presentiment that a divinity was near, as when a hound that accompanies his master through the fields and with his keen nose 695 senses far off the presence of a hare. Immediately he pricks up his ears and sniffs the air, and as he shoots from the intended path, his eyes survey the uncertain tracks of the hare, now darting this way and now that, and, baffled, fills the fields with barking. Such 700 was the exultation of that old man in the temple. He gathered up the infant in his trembling arms and held him tight. He wept as he declared, 'O child, mayest thou be blessed for thy goodness, undoubted Son of God, Creator of the universe. You have come of 705 your own volition to wash away our sins and those of our forefathers in the river of your blood, and to open up the shining paths to starry heaven. You have come in answer to my prayers and you, Supreme Father, have not deceived me in your promises. Now, finally, I can die. Now you deliver me, freed from these bodily 710 chains, to rest and an end of toil, as once you promised. For my eyes have seen him whom you send into the world to help it, to be a light unto the benighted Gentiles and a new glory for the sons of Isaac.' Then he turned to the mother and addressed her. 'To 715 whom shall I compare your beauty? Who shall I say rivals you in

"O cui te forma assimulem? Cui laudibus aequem?
Quasve tibi referam grates, quae sola salutem
felici peperisti utero mortalibus aegris?
720 Quanquam etiam exitio multis hunc affore partum,
et tempus fore praedico, illaetabile tempus,
cum tibi cor gelidum gladius penetrabit acutus
ah miserae! et magno virgo dotabere luctu,
mutataque fluet Iordanis decolor unda.
725 Tum serus segnisque dies nascetur, et aegre
lutea vix terris ostendet pallidus ora,
atque gravi tellus optabit mole relinqui
ipsa sua et rupto per inania foedere labi."
'Haec ubi, confestim veluti cedentia somno
730 lumina demisit, placidaque ibi morte quievit.
Obstupuere alii, sed nos, quis caetera nota,
terremur magis, inque vicem disquirimus ambo
solliciti quosnam matri denuntiet enses,
aut quibus exitio tantum⁵ puer ipse futurus.
735 Haud longum fuit in medio dehinc tempus; utrunque
exitus edocuit dubiosque ambage resolvit,
ni nobis maiora etiam nunc vulnera restant,
atque alia ex aliis semper graviora parantur.
'Illis extremo quippe ex oriente diebus
740 tres adeo magni reges ditione profecti,
huc sese intulerant puero dona ampla ferentes,
aurumque et thuris glebas stactaeque liquorem.
His vis astrorum ac ratio volventis Olympi
monstrarat regem nostris in finibus ortum,
745 quoi coeli terraeque paterent debita sceptra.
Sancti igitur partus studio huc venere videndi.
Stella facem ducens venientibus usque coruscam
dux erat atque viam signabat lumine largo,
ceu quondam patribus deserta per avia nostris

praise? How can I thank you, who alone through your fertile womb have brought salvation to weary mortals? But I foresee that this birth will bring death to many and that the time will come, an 720 unhappy time, when a sharp lance will pierce your cold heart. Alas, Mary, you will be afflicted with great sorrow and the muddied Jordan will reverse its course. Then that day will dawn late and slow, and unwillingly show the world its face of sickly pallor. 725 And the earth will wish to throw off its heavy mantle, break its pact and glide through the empty void.'

"As soon as he had spoken these words, his eyes seemed to close in sleep and he died a peaceful death. Others were aston- 730 ished. But we, the parents, were frightened, since we knew the rest of the prophecy. Repeatedly we asked ourselves with what swords the boy will threaten his mother, and to whom he would bring death. We were not long in doubt. For the outcome resolved both 735 of our doubts, unless, that is, still greater wounds are still to come, and ever greater sorrows are being prepared.

"In those days, from far to the East, there appeared three kings of great wealth, bearing the child abundant gifts of gold, frankin- 740 cense and myrrh. The power of the stars and the pattern of heaven in its revolutions had taught them that a king had been born in our land, to whom heaven and earth would yield their scepters due. And so they came, eager to see the blessed birth. A star 745 served as a shining lamp to guide them as they came, marking their way with its great light. It was like that fiery lamp that shone from above upon our fathers as they wandered through the wilder-

750 in patriam tandem Pharia redeuntibus ora
praecurrens monstrabat iter nocte ignea lampas
desuper et mirum spargebat lucida lumen.
    'Iamque urbem ingressi sedes adiere tyranni
Herodis causamque viae docuere, rati olli
755 hanc sobolem, quod erat rex his in finibus, ortam.
Obstupuit simul atque animo perterritus ille est.
Nec mora, permetuens sibine succederet haeres
quaesitus puer in regnis externus avitis,
indigenas vates iubet intra moenia cogi
760 regia scitarique omnes tempusque locumque
nascentis pueri, patriamque domumque requirit.
Illi autem Bethlen veterum monimenta minari
cuncta docent, dux unde ortus se tolleret olim
fama ingens, claris ingens super aethera factis.
765 Tum magis atque magis curarum fluctuat aestu
sollicitamque gerit cassa formidine mentem.
    'Tandem his affatus reges dimittit Eoos:[6]
"Quae vos causa, viri, nostris nunc applicat oris,
haec eadem longe spe nos suspendit, aventes
770 cernere promissos pueri tot vatibus ortus.
Haud procul hinc saxo Bethle fundata vetusto
urbs colitur nostris. Natum illuc quaerite regem.
Mox iubeo, inventum nobis qui nuntiet, inde
mittite, nostro etiam puer accumuletur honore."
775 Sic ait, et falso simulat nova gaudia vultu.
Verum longe aliud male amico pectore agebat
demens, qui coeli regem, cui sidera parent,
crederet in terris mortalia regna morari.
    'Ergo iter instaurant conspecto sidere laeti.
780 Iamque propinquabant magna stipante caterva,
cum subito supra tectum ingens substitit astrum
irradians largoque mapalia lumine complens,

ness at night, showing them the way and guiding them from the   750
land of Pharaoh back to their homeland.

"Presently they entered Jerusalem and approached the palace of
the tyrant Herod. They told him the reason for their journey,
imagining that the child had been born to him, since he was king
of this land. At once he was dumbstruck and terrified. Fearing   755
that his successor would be some foreigner occupying his ancestral
throne, he immediately called the local seers into the palace, seeking to learn from them when and where the child was being born,
what his race and lineage were. They informed him that all the re-   760
cords of the old prophets had foretold that Bethlehem would
bring forth a leader great in fame and in his superhuman deeds.
And Herod became ever more overwhelmed with anxiety as his
tormented mind was beset by baseless fears.   765

"Finally he dismissed the kings from the East with these words:
'Men, the very same cause that brought you to our land has made
me yearn to witness the birth of this boy whom so many prophets
have promised us. Not far from here is a town settled by those of   770
our race, on the old rock of Bethlehem. There seek the newborn
king. Then I ask you to send me word that you have found the
child, that I might heap honors upon him.' So he spoke, feigning
joy. But in his malevolence, this madman was moved by anything   775
but a kind heart: foolishly he imagined that he who holds sway in
heaven would care about a mortal kingdom.

"The three kings happily resumed their journey, guided by the
star. Already they approached, accompanied by a great multitude,
when suddenly a great star shone above the roof, filling the hovel   780
with an abundance of light, like comets that portend imminent

quales cum belli motus aut funera regum
portendunt, crinem irato sparsere minacem
785 aethere, ni diri rubeant lugubre cometae.
    'Tris adeo angusti subter fastigia tecti
pauper ego excepi reges in rebus egenis.
Vidi illos auro illustres ostroque decoros
ante pedes pueri sese demittere pronos
790 suppliciter, genibusque piae procumbere matris,
dum sua quisque facit sortiti ex ordine dona.
Barbarici ante fores expectabant comitatus
interea, tyrioque instratus murice terga
stans sonipes teres exercebat dentibus aurum.
795 His dehinc perfectis abeunt laetique sequuntur
quod longo irradians aperitur tramite sidus.
Sed non inde via moniti referuntur eadem
regia linquentes a laeva moenia longe,
rursus Idumaei sedemne regis adirent.
800   'Ille autem, ut sese delusum denique sensit,
accensus furiis suspectam misit ad urbem
mille viros ferro instructos, qui moenia furto
per noctem ingressi teneros, quicunque reperti
infantes matrum iugularent hubere raptos,
805 quo numero in tanto caderet quoque regius haeres.
Ipse sed in somnis visus sum voce moneri
praecipitem celerare fugam, loca linquere nota.
"Surge, age, rumpe moras, puerum tecum arripe matremque
et septengemini cursu pete flumina Nili;
810 hinc terram cole quae procul his haud dissidet oris,
nec refer inde pedem, nisi te prius ipse vocaro:
rex etenim letum infanti molitur acerbum."
    'Consurgo, et plenus monitis matri omnia pando.
Vidisses visu exanguem exanimemque puellam
815 huc illuc trepidare fuga et vix fidere nocti.

war or the death of kings, scattering their menacing tails in the angry air, unless they turn a baleful red.   785

"And so it happened that, poor as I was, I received the three kings under my humble roof. I watched them, splendid in their robes of purple and gold, bowing in suppliant fashion at the feet of the child and at his mother's knees, while each in the allotted   790 order gave the child the gift he had brought. Meanwhile, before the doors a crowd of their barbaric retinue waited for them, while a steed stood by, caparisoned in imperial purple and chewing on his golden bit. Once they had accomplished their mission, they   795 left in joy, following the star that illuminated their long journey. Yet they did not return along the same path by which they had come. Forewarned, they kept the royal palace far to their north, lest they should once more reach the seat of the Idumaean king.

"When the king perceived that he had been deceived, he be-   800 came enraged and sent a thousand swordsmen to the suspect city. Their instructions were to enter it by stealth at night. They were to rip all the youngest male infants from their mothers' breasts and slaughter them. Among so many deaths, he assumed, the royal heir would be felled as well. But in a dream a voice warned me to   805 take flight at once and leave the places I knew. 'Arise without delay,' it counseled, 'and take the boy and his mother with you. Run to the streams of the Nile, with its seven heads. Live there henceforth, far from this town, and do not return until I myself shall   810 summon you. For the king is plotting a cruel death for the child.'

"I arose and unfolded to my wife all I had been bidden to do. She looked pale and breathless as she fled to and fro, scarcely trusting in the darkness. Even then, alas, a sharp sword had   815

Iam tum illi pectus gladius traiecit acutus,
ah miserae! ingenti labefactaque corda dolore.
Cedimus, et taciti malefidam linquimus urbem
per noctem ac propero petimus nemora avia gressu.
820 Et iam palmosae saltus atque ardua Idumes
praetervectus eram, veteris iam moenia Elusae,
quaque Asiam Libycis disiungit finibus omnem
Mapsa, ferax oleae. Ingredior pluviae inscia regna,
regna Phari, quibus est coeli vis cognita primum
825 astraque lunaique globus solisque meatus.
Ignotos passim montis, ignota saluto
flumina turrigerasque legens praetervehor urbes.
Iamque papyriferi ripis Anthedonis ibam.
'Aurae omnes terrent pavidos, capitique timentes
830 tam caro. At puero blandiri murmure silvae
lauricomae et ramis capita accurvare reflexis,
aurarumque leves animae indulgere susurro.
Ipsae etiam nobis cautes, ipsique videntur
verticibus leviter motis alludere montes,
835 signaque laetitiae dare stagna loquacia circum.
Audires blandum fessas erroribus undas
perstrepere et molli lapsu per saxa sonare
humida saxa super nitido viridantia musco.
Praecipue ripis volucres et fluminis alveo
840 assuetae liquidis mulcebant vocibus auras,
et iactu alarum resonabant corpora plausa.
Sese etiam omnifero gremio venientibus offert
laeta dei aspectu tellus. Flant gramina odorem
cuncta suum et mollem praetexit amaracus umbram.
845 Nec vero incerta latebrosus origine Nilus
non manifesta dedit salienti flumine signa
adventante deo; laetis se sustulit undis
stagna arcana ciens fundoque apparuit imo.

pierced her chest, the poor girl! and her heart was weak with sorrow. But we obeyed. We quietly left the untrustworthy city by night and sought in haste a pathless wood. Soon we had passed the hills and groves of Edom, rich in palms, and the walls of ancient Elusa, where Mapsa, fertile in olives, separates all of Asia from the Libyan shore. I entered a kingdom that knew no rain, the kingdom of Pharaoh, where men first kenned the powers of heaven, the paths of the stars, the moon and the sun. Here and there I passed unknown rivers and mountains and cities with lofty towers. And now I came to the banks of Anthedon, rich in papyrus.

"Every breeze terrified us, as we feared for the life of our dear child. But the forests of laurel trees murmured softly to the boy, bowing their heads with curved branches, while the gentle breezes seemed to whisper to him. The very cliffs, the very hills seemed to sway lightly before us and the babbling streams signaled their joy. The water, weary of its wandering, murmured gently, echoing with a soft fall among wet rocks, green with shining moss. Above us all the birds that haunted the riverbanks and basin made the air mellow with their clear voices, and their bodies resounded with the beating of their wings. At the sight of God, the happy earth opened its fecund lap to us as we journeyed by. Plants exhaled their perfumes and the marjoram tree provided soothing shade. The Nile as well, hiding the secret of its origins, overflowed its banks and gave clear signs of the coming of the Lord. Rising up in joyous waves, it set its hidden waters in motion and laid bare its riverbed.

820

825

830

835

840

845

'Ad bivias nobis fauces flexusque viarum
850   increpitans clypeo fulgentique ense per auras
ocius usque aderat coelo pulcherrimus ales,
et monstrabat iter sibi per divortia nota,
ne recta regione viae deprenderet hostis.
Coeruleis huic terga notis suffusa rubebant,
855   multum illi assimilis qui me connubia quondam
solventem increpuit tenebrasque a mente fugavit.
Supra nos alii pendentes aere pennis
ibant et noctis resupini infantis ab ore
humorem arcebant lentum plumaque tegebant.
860   'Iamque ego perplexum per iter prope fida tenebam
arva legens sistris bacchata sonantibus, et iam
tutus erat longe nostris a finibus infans,
attamen Aegypti penetro interiora, nec ulla
fida satis tellus mihi visa aut regis iniqui
865   sat sceptris divisa. Animo timeo omnia tuta.
Nec placet Hermopolis, nec centum pervia portis
visa satis Thebe tanto procul esse periclo.
Nos igitur regum turritis clara sepulcris
accepit Memphis; hac demum sede quievi
870   paupere sub tecto veteris securus amici.
    'Iam vero Pelusiacas vulgata per oras
fama Palaestinum subito serit undique regem
florentem teneris orbasse nepotibus urbem,
quos frustra insontes passim ferro impius hausit,
875   dulcia linquentes vagitu lumina vitae.
Palluit applicuitque sinu perterrita mater
infantem atque animum sceleris perstrinxit imago.
Quos ibi tum gentis fletus qualive per urbem
funestam credis matres errasse ululatu!
880   Sanguine diluta est tellus; cava tecta natarunt.
Non si forte olim incautis pastoribus orta

"We had come to a fork and a turn in the road; suddenly a resplendent angel appeared in the sky, his shield and gleaming sword
resounding. He led us on a winding path known to him, so that   850
our foe could not seize us along the more accustomed road. The
angel's entire back gleamed with celestial markings, very much like
those of the angel who had berated me for wishing to abandon my
marriage and who banished darkness from my mind. Soon other   855
angels flew to us, and hung aloft in mid-air. At night they covered
the sleeping child with their feathers and kept the cool dew from
his face.

"By now I had taken a meandering path to safer fields that re-   860
sounded with the joyous clash of cymbals. And though the boy
was finally safe, far from our own land, still I ventured deeper into
Egypt and did not yet feel secure or sufficiently far from the tyrant's kingdom. My heart was fearful even in lands that were safe.   865
Neither Hermopolis nor Thebes with its hundred gates seemed to
me far enough from peril. So we settled in Memphis, famous for
the towered tombs of its kings. It was here that finally I could rest,
secure in the humble dwelling of an old friend.   870

"Now report reached the Pelusian lands that the Palestinian
king had bereaved the flourishing town of its young sons, impiously slaying the innocent. With a wail they had abandoned the
sweet light of life. Mary grew pale with fear and drew the child   875
closer to her. She could not stop thinking of the crime that had
been committed: the wailing of the people, the lamentation of
mothers wandering through the fateful city, the earth and the
empty houses swimming in blood! When a sudden storm rises in   880
the fields and thickets and takes the shepherds by surprise, all the

ingruerit subito tempestas omnibus arvis,
omnibus et silvis, tot fusi grandine dira
spectentur per humum afflictis cum matribus agni,
885 corpora quot passim puerorum abiecta iacebant
per fora perque vias urbis. Sic denique multis
exitio fuit, ut vates praedixerat, infans;
nunc etiam lugent orbae sua pignora matres.
Non tamen ille diu scelere est laetatus ab illo,
890 nam membra immundo correptus tabida morbo,
illaudatam animam parvo post tempore fudit.

    'Ipse iterum in somnis divina voce coactus
linquere monstriferi septenflua flumina Nili,
in patriam redeo, atque memor vestigia retro
895 observata legens pignus cum matre reduco.
Forsitan et puero fuerit quae cura requiris,
quae mens, an virtus illi maturior aevo,
ecquid non puerile annis puerilibus ausus.
Si tibi nunc, quaecunque olim admiranda notavi,
900 primaevo dum flore virens adolesceret aetas,
enumerare vacet, me vox prius ipsa relinquat
defessum atque diem clauso nox condat Olympo.
Nam quoties dictis tener haud mortalibus ambos
terruit! Aut quoties sanctos expavimus ignes
905 flammarumque globos et terrificos fulgores,
saepe quibus visus puer est ardere nitentem
caesariem, coeli dum splendet luce corusca!
Nec referam quoties genitorem audivimus illum
affari solum arcanasque expromere voces.
910 Alma parens, tenues arguto pectine telas
percurrens, saepe humana sub imagine coetus
coelituum tectum intrantes exterrita vidit
blandiri puero et pictis colludere plumis,
aut violis tegere et nimbo vestire rosarum.

lambs that lie scattered with their mothers on the earth are not so numerous as were the bodies of the infant boys that lay scattered everywhere in the public places and the roads! And so it was, as   885 the prophets had foretold, that one child caused the death of many children. Even now mothers lament the bereavement of their young. But Herod would not exult for long in his crime. For his limbs were afflicted with a loathsome wasting disease, and very   890 soon thereafter, lamented by none, he gave up the ghost.

"Once again in a dream I was driven to leave the seven-headed Nile, source of prodigies. Retracing my steps, since I had noted well the path, I returned home with my wife and son. Perhaps you   895 are wondering what interested the boy, what mind or virtue he demonstrated beyond his years, and whether, even as a boy, he attempted things that no boy would. If there were time and I told you all the astonishing things I remember him doing while still in the first flower of youth, I would sooner lose my voice from weari-   900 ness and dark night would cover the sky. How often did he astound us both with words that surpassed human understanding! How many times were we frightened by those sacred flames, those balls of fire, that terrifying lightning that seemed to blaze from his   905 long hair as he shone with the gleaming light of heaven! I won't tell you how frequently we heard him speak in private to his Father in a secret language. Often as she was nimbly weaving fine cloth upon her loom, his dear mother shuddered to see hosts of   910 angels, in human form, enter the house to entertain the child and divert him with their painted wings, as they covered him in violets and rained down roses on him. Us, his guardians, he treated with

915 Nos tamen interea custodes ille vereri
summissus, carae et mandata facessere matris
nostraque, et implebat veri genitoris amorem,
dum membris habilis vigor et vis firma veniret.
 'Et iam bis senos crescens exegerat annos,
920 necdum se populis signo detexerat ullo.
Tum primum coepit Iudaea per oppida vulgo
illius apparere palamque est prodita virtus.
Forte dies aderat genti solennis, et urbi
huic magnae sacer ante alias, quo regia mecum
925 venerat et virgo, atque sequens sese aureus illi
implicuit dextrae puer. Et iam rite litatis
ipse domum sacris magna cum matre redibam.
Iamque labore viae fessis lux prima peracta,
et piceam clauso nox coelo involverat umbram.
930 Defuit hic puer et genitricem meque fefellit.
 'Tum consanguineos frustra et scitatus amicos,
terque quaterque viam repetens clamore replevi.
Flebat se incusans unam pulcherrima mater,
flaventem fusa crinem per eburnea colla.
935 Ora decent lachrymae, disiecti colla capilli,
qualis virginea cum mollis amaracus urna
et pluviam et ventos pariter perpessa procaces
demisit turbata comas, iterumque resurgens
extulit os coelo ac priscum meditatur honorem.
940 Dumque viam relego, invitum comes aegra sequuta est.
Tris adeo incerti soles erravimus urbe
nequicquam; quarta est vix demum luce repertus.
Nanque mihi et miserae cum spes sublata parenti
cuncta foret penitus, in mentem venit utrique
945 templa iterum petere atque preces effundere ad aram.
Vix ingressus eram limen, cum protinus ambo
ecce sacerdotum in medio conspeximus illum

humble respect, and he did the bidding of his dear mother and 915
me. And as his limbs took on a more mature strength, he fulfilled
the love of his true Father.

"He was already twelve years old and still he had not revealed
himself to the people by any sign. Then for the first time he began 920
to appear commonly throughout the towns of Judaea and to give
open signs of his power. It was on that solemn day, the holiest of
the year in this great city, and royal Mary came with me. The
blessed boy followed, holding her hand. After I had performed the 925
prescribed rites of supplication, I was on my way home with his
blessed mother. Already the first day had passed. We were wearied
by the journey, and night had covered the heavens in pitch darkness. Suddenly the boy was not with us, having slipped free of his
mother and me. 930

"After inquiring in vain among relatives and friends, I ran
through the streets calling for him. Filled with self-reproach, his
lovely mother wept, her blond hair spilling down her ivory neck.
But tears became her, as did her disheveled hair. She was like a 935
tender marjoram plant in a young girl's vase: struck by rain and
strong winds, it throws down its leaves; but as it rises up again and
shows its face to heaven, it reclaims its former beauty. While I re-
traced my steps she accompanied me, though I asked her not to do 940
so. For three whole days we searched the city in vain; it was on the
fourth day when he was finally found. When all hope was taken
from me and from his unhappy mother, it occurred to each of us
to go to the temple and offer up prayers at the altar. But we had 945
scarcely entered when we saw him, surrounded by priests. As the
first rudimentary signs of his future powers, he was reciting the

(prima rudimenta et virtutis signa futurae),
alta recensentem vatum monimenta patrumque
950 primores ultro scitantem obscura docentemque.
    'Illum omnes admirari haud vulgata canentem
supra aciem captumque hominis mentemque vigentem,
humana non vi edoctum, non arte magistra,
maturumque animi nimium puerilibus annis.
955 Nec minus insigni cunctis spectantibus ore
gratus erat. Neque enim poterant se explere tuendo
flagrantesque dei vultus blandosque serena
luce oculos magis aut propexum verticis aurum
et florem grati, qui vix inceperat, aevi.
960 Nam quocunque caput circum torsisset honestum,
luce recens orta vel sidere pulchrior aureo,
laeta serenato ridebant omnia mundo,
et toto dulcem iactabat corpore amorem.
Inculti qualis nitet inter gramina campi,
965 purpureus secum primum foliis narcissus
exeruit ruptoque caput detexit amictu,
aut qualis nitidi species micat alma smaragdi,
cum tenui argento tenuive includitur auro.
    'Prima mali fuit hinc nobis scintilla, puerque
970 ex illo formidata primoribus urbis
virtute invisus fuit, et corda aspera movit,
atque hoc deinde ingens succensa est fomite flamma,
inque dies gliscens furor atque insania crevit.
Omnia quae porro ipse videns metuensque futuri
975 orabam impavidum, ne vitae prodigus hosti
obiiceret, ne se perdendum proderet ultro.
Verum luce prius lateant in montibus arces,
aut nocte in summis celetur turribus ignis,
obruta quam longum iaceat sine nomine virtus.

teachings of the prophets, asking and instructing the elders about obscure matters. 950

"They all marveled as he revealed secrets beyond the grasp or ken of humankind. They marveled at a mind taught by no human power, no teacher's skill, and a maturity that far surpassed his years. No less were they amazed by his fine features. They could 955 scarcely get enough of looking on his face, infused with deity, his eyes that charmed with their serene light, and his golden hair and the first flowering of his gracious youth. Wherever he turned his noble head, lovelier than the rising sun or a golden star, everything 960 around him seemed to laugh with delight. His entire body inspired sweet love. He was like the purple narcissus that first puts forth its brilliant leaves amid the grass, revealing its flower as its 965 sheath falls away; he was like a precious emerald gleaming in a filigree of silver or gold.

"But from this emerged the initial spark of our woes. From that moment, he was hated by many of the leading citizens, who were 970 envious of his formidable virtue, and he provoked their hard hearts. And from that tinder a great fire was ignited. For their rage and madness grew daily. Having foreseen and feared precisely that, I besought him, who was unafraid, not to risk his life and expose 975 himself to his enemies, lest he be destroyed in the process. For truly, sooner would a citadel lie hidden by day on a mountain, sooner would fire be concealed at night atop a tower, than his virtues could remain hidden and unnoted.

980 'Non tamen ille odiis magis ussit pectora acerbis
quam cum terdenis iam vir volventibus annis
fontis aquam latices Bacchi convertit in atros.
Forte Canam mecum Galilaeae advenerat urbem—
mater et ipsa aderat—veteri dum accitus amico
985 obsequor; intactam genero qui iungere natam
conventu procerum magno de more parabat.
Iamque omnes circum positis discumbere mensis
atque alacres epulari et vina reposcere laeti,
necdum finis erat dapibus, cum murmur ubique
990 exoritur totasque auditur triste per aedes,
laetitiae causam exhaustis liquentia vina
defecisse cadis turbarique omnia visa.
Tum res alma parens tenues miserata puellae
innuit, et gnatum summissa voce precata est,
995 ferret opem. Vidi hic iuvenem primum ore moveri
turbatum, carae precibus tamen inde parentis
annuit et fesso rerum succurrit amico.
Sex, ut erant ibi tot numero, carchesia lymphis
impleri iubet actutum, mensisque reponi,
1000 quae simul aspexit propius deus, omnibus ecce!
mutatus subito nigrescere cernitur humor,
vinaque pro pura mirantes hausimus unda.
    'Audisti, dux, et genus et cunabula nati
primitiasque dei. Ne caetera deinde requiras,
1005 hanc omnem erexit factis florentibus oram.
Quae si audire tamen tibi nunc fert corde voluptas,
is longe memoret melior' (simul ore sedentem
signat Ioannem); 'vidit nanque omnia praesens,
errabunda ducis semper vestigia servans,
1010 dum mihi cura domi servandae virginis haeret.'
Dixit, et hic facto defessus fine quievit.

184

"But nothing he did inspired more hatred in those hard hearts 980
than when, as a man of more than thirty years, he converted the
water of the well into draughts of dark wine. It happened that he
accompanied me and his mother to Cana, a city in Galilee, where I
went in obedience to the request of an old friend. According to
custom, before all the leading men of the city, this man prepared 985
to marry his maiden daughter to a youth. Everyone had lain down
by the set tables, eager to eat and drink. But the feast was not yet
ended when a sad murmur ran through the house: all the wine, 990
that source of gladness, had run out and the casks were empty. Everything was in confusion. Mary took pity on the girl's straitened
circumstances and quietly asked her son to help her. I saw that at
first he was disturbed by this request. But finally he obeyed the 995
entreaties of his mother and aided the hapless friend. He asked
them to fill six casks with water and place them on the tables. As
soon as the Son of God approached and looked on them, in each 1000
the water turned to dark liquid. And so it was that all of us, astonished, drank wine instead of water!

"Sir, you have learnt of the race and birth of my son, as well as
the events of the god's youth. To put everything in few words, he
has roused this land with his flourishing deeds. If you wish to 1005
know more about those deeds, this man" (he nodded to the seated
John) "can relate them far better than I can, for he witnessed all of
them first hand and followed Jesus in his wanderings, while I remained at home to care for the maiden." So Joseph spoke. Having 1010
said what he had to say, he wearily fell silent.

'Immo,' ait, 'istius causas ab origine partus
exequere, aut quae relligio, si vera per oram
percepi, Iudaea deum non amplius unum
1015   aeternum colit, haud mortali semine cretum,
indigetesque suis divos altaribus arcet.
Inde tibi noti recolens ex ordine divi
caetera mira refer. Nanque hunc in corpore vires
deficiunt, teque auxilio iubet ipse subire.'
1020   Pontius haec; cuncti intenti simul ora tenebant.

"Certainly," Pilate replied. "Tell me from the beginning the reasons for his birth. Describe to me this religion, since, if I have heard true, only one eternal god is worshiped throughout Judaea, by no means born of mortal seed, while the indigenous gods are 1015 kept away from its altars. Tell me about the other miracles of this god whom you know, for his father is clearly weary and he asks your help." So Pilate spoke. And everyone waited intently for the response. 1020

LIBER IV

Hic iuvenis, facie quo tum non gratior alter,
puberibusque annis erat ingrediente iuventa,
multa prius veniam praefatus, multa recusans
verba diu premit; inde animo mortalia linquens
5 paulatim oblitusque hominem, penetralia divum
mente subit coelum peragrans, fruiturque beato
coelituum aspectu omnipotentique aetheris aura,
admissus superam depasci lumine lucem,
inque deo tota defixus mente moratur.
10 Qualis ubi alta petens terris aufertur ab imis
alituum regina, vagas spatiata per auras,
dat plausum gyro atque in nubila conditur alis.
Aetherea iamque illa plaga levis instat, et acrem
intendens aciem criniti lumina solis
15 suspicit, obtutuque oculos fixa haeret acuto.
     Illum adeo tacitum interea mirantur, in unum
versi omnes velut exanimum somnoque gravatum,
et crebri excutiunt. Demum sibi redditus ipse
cum gemitu ex imo sic fari pectore coepit:
20 'Principio pater omnipotens rerum sator et fons,
ingens, immensus, solus regnabat ubique.
Nondum sidereos mundi procuderat orbes.
Nondum mundus erat, necdum ibant tempora in orbem,
nullaque coeruleo radiabant lumina coelo.
25 Quicquid erat, deus illud erat, quodcunque ubicunque
complexus circum, penitus sese omnis in uno.[1]
Filius huic tantum, quem non effuderat ulla
vel dea vel solito mortalis foemina partu,
ipse sed aeterna genitor conceperat illum

BOOK IV

This most handsome young man, still hardly more than a boy, repeatedly demurred and excused himself, long remaining silent. Gradually his spirit seemed to leave all mortal things behind. Forgetting mortal concerns, he wandered the heavens in his mind, until he reached the innermost sanctuaries of the divine. He delighted in the blessed sight of the angels and in the breath of the Almighty. Allowed to savor the light of heaven, he remained fixed on God with all his spirit. He was like the queen of birds, borne aloft from the depths of the earth as she seeks the heavens. Wandering through the vagrant air, she rejoices in her orbit and hides herself amid the clouds. As she floats up to the ethereal plains, she sets her keen gaze on the gleaming sun and does not release it from her sight.

Everyone turned and marveled at the young man standing there in silence, as though lifeless or weighed down by sleep, and they energetically shook him awake. Finally, returning to consciousness, he sighed and spoke from the depths of his heart. "In the beginning, the Almighty Father, source and creator of the universe, ruled alone, immense, massive and omnipresent. He had not yet forged the starry orbs of heaven. The world did not yet exist, nor had the spheres gone spinning in time, nor did any lights shine in the cerulean heavens. Whatever existed was God. He embraced all time and space, and the whole was entirely in the One. Only his Son existed beside him, brought forth by no goddess or by any mortal woman through ordinary birth. Rather, in the eternity of his mind, the eternal Father—astonishingly—begat his eternal

10

30 aeternum aeternus (dictu mirabile) mente.
    Haud olli terreni artus moribundave membra,
    sed sine corpore erat, patris alta ut mente supremi
    conceptum arcanoque latens in pectore VERBVM,
    quod nondum in volucres vox edita protulit auras,
35 omnipotens verbum, finisque et originis expers,
    quo mare, quo tellus, quo constat maximus aether,
    utque pater deus, aeque etiam deus unica proles.
    At geminos tu proinde deos fuge credere porro:
    numen idem simul ambobus, deus unus uterque est.
40 Quin etiam, quo inter se ambo iunguntur, amorem
    (nanque ab utroque venit conspirans mutuus ardor)
    omnipotens aeque numenque deumque vocamus,
    afflantem maria ac terras coelique profunda,
    afflatu quo cuncta vigent, quo cuncta moventur,
45 trisque unum esse deum, ter numen dicimus unum.
      'Quove magis mirere, deus, quem cernimus ipsi
    factum hominem atque hominum mortali corpore cretum,
    non minus ac prius aetherea nunc regnat in aula
    cum genitore, pari simul omnia numine torquens.
50 Nempe locis nullis, spatiis non clauditur ullis,
    omnibus inque locis idem omni tempore praesens,
    suffugiens nostras acies sensuque remotus,
    cuncta replet deus ac molem se fundit in omnem.
    Lux humiles veluti perfundens lumine terras
55 solis ab orbe venit suppostaque circuit arva,
    non tamen aethereo divisa ab sole recedit
    illa usquam, quanvis longinquas ambiat oras.
    Nec sine sole suo est lux, nec sine luce sua sol.
      'Quid vero impulerit tantos adiisse labores
60 atque haec ferre deum, dum morti obnoxius errat,

Son. This child had no terrestrial form, no mortal shape. He was   30
bodiless, having been created by the lofty mind of his supreme Father. The WORD, hidden in the secret places of his Father's
heart, had not yet been sent forth upon the wandering air, the almighty Word, without beginning or end, through Whom God   35
made the sea, earth and sky. As the Father was God, so too the
only begotten Son was God. But do not believe that these were
two gods. Both possess the same divinity and each of them is the
one God. Furthermore, the Love that joins each to the other (for   40
each breathes forth a love that is returned) we call God, equally
omnipotent and divine, that inspirits the seas, the earth, and the
heights of heaven, that invigorates all things and moves all things.
These Three we call one God, and the one God we call threefold.

"What will truly astonish you is this, that the God whom we   45
ourselves have seen in the form of a man, who grew in the mortal
body of a man, now, no less than before, lives in airy heaven with
his Father, moving all things with his divinity. For no place, no
space can contain him. He is present at all times in all places.   50
Though he flees our sight and avoids our senses, yet does God fill
all things and pour himself into all matter. Even so does the light
that covers the humble earth come from the orb of the sun and
encircles the fields that lie beneath, yet at no point is it divided   55
from the sun, even though it extends to distant lands. Nor is there
light without the sun, nor is there a sun without light.

"I will start from the beginning, from the remotest causes, and
explain what impelled this God to enter upon such great labors
and expose himself to death. Scarcely had the creator of the world   60

dicam equidem, et repetens altas ab origine causas
expediam. Coelum et coeli quos suspicis orbes
vix opifex rerum extuderat terrasque iacentis,
cum simul aligeros populos sanctosque volucres
65   ter ternas acies, celerem et sine corpore gentem,
qui coeli incolerent ipsos septemplicis orbes,
condidit aeterno genitor succensus amore,
ut sua, qua fruitur solus natusque per aevum,
communis foret et multis concessa voluptas.
70   Continuo, fuerat quos aequum dicere laudes
auctorique deoque suo ac persolvere grates,
regnandi vesanus amor (quis ferret inultus?)
haud partem exiguam invasit furiisque subegit,
ut cuperent summo sese praeferre parenti,
75   immemores, animis victi caecique furore.
Non tulit omnipotens sator et meliora sequutos
armavit contra. Nulla hinc mora, talia adortos
indecores coelo sedes detrusit in imas,
noctis ubi horriferae nigror aeternaeque tenebrae.
80   Primus natus homo hinc, terris quem maximus auctor,
et liquidis late dominum praefecerat undis,
quo mox pro superis excussis astra teneret
desertasque domos. Ipse et genus omne suorum
omnigenumque uni subiecit secla animantum,
85   squamigerum pecudes et pennis picta volantum
corpora montivagumque simul genus omne ferarum.
Tantum floriferis dominum cum imponeret arvis,
arboris unius foetu illum parcere iussit.
At vetito captus mali infelicis amore
90   coniugis hortatu, quam fraude illexerat anguis,
immemor, heu! superi violavit foedera regis.
   'Vix avido arreptum pomum foedaverat ore,
cum pater imbripotens iam fulva e nube tonare

formed the heavens and the heavenly bodies and the lands that lay
beneath, when inflamed with eternal love, he created the saintly
race of angels in thrice three ranks, swift and bodiless, in order to   65
inhabit the seven spheres of heaven and to share in the pleasure
that had belonged to him and his Son alone in eternity. Immediately, no small part of those who should have been praising and   70
thanking their creator and God were seized and maddened by an
insane lust for power (and who can bear it and not take vengeance?) to contend with the Heavenly Father, ungrateful and
blind in their madness. This their Almighty Father could not tol-   75
erate. Against them he armed his more obedient angels. Without
delay he flung the base souls who had attempted such outrage into
the pit of hell, a land of horrid night and never-ending darkness.

"Thus it was that man was first created. The Supreme Author   80
made him lord of the earth and shining sea, so that in due course
he and all his issue might occupy the heavens in place of the
routed angels, indeed, that he might dwell in the very homes they
had vacated. To him the Father subjected all the generations of animals, the scaly fish and the birds with brightly painted pennons   85
and the beasts that wander the mountains. Now when God had
given him dominion over the flowery fields, he bade his creation
spare the fruit of one tree only. But sadly overcome by forbidden
desire for the apple, this creature allowed himself to be swayed by
his wife, who had been seduced by the serpent's fraud. And so,   90
heedlessly, he violated his vows to the Supreme King.

"Scarcely had he defiled the fruit with his eager mouth when
the Father of the rains thundered from on high in a thick cloud.

desuper auditus, saevasque indicere poenas
95   iratus quas ille olim, quas omnis ab illo
progenies lueret lucis ventura sub auras.
Continuo ingenti coelo sunt addita claustra;
impia tum primum proles exorta repente
et subito tellus scelere est imbuta nefando.
100   Emersit fraus, emersit malesuada libido.
Hinc durus generi humano labor additus, hinc fons
curarum et tristis patefacta est ianua leti
morbique et dolor atque fames et turpis egestas,
cum genus humanum curis sine degere posset
105   plurimaque in terris vivendo vincere secla.
Ex illo sine more homines, sine lege per agros
degebant; tantum placabant sanguine fuso
coelicolum regem, bonus ut gregibusque sibique
afforet atque satis vim coeli averteret arvis,
110   indociles, rerum ignari ac rationis inanes.
Isque fere status annorum bis millibus orbi
constiterat, iam iamque magis pater optimus iras
oblitus veteres paulum mitescere coepit.
Nondum homini tamen aethereum patefecit Olympum,
115   sed genus humanum fingens acuensque monendo
et leges dedit et ritus moremque sacrorum,
instituitque, genus nostrum discriminis ergo
lege iubens, testa circum praecidere acuta
exiguam, unde viri sumus, omni in corpore partem.
120   Tum vatum implevit venientis pectora veri,
qui populis laetum canerent demum affore tempus,
ianua aperta piis coeli cum sponte pateret.
    'Casti autem interea manes animaeque piorum
sub terram umbrosa expectabant valle sedentes.
125   Iam vatum memores numerabant tempora et ambas
tendebant paribus votis ad sidera palmas,

Angrily he pronounced sentence on him and all his generations   95
who should ever see the light of life. At once heaven was shut off
with gates. Now for the first time impious men arose and filled the
earth with unholy crimes. Now deceit came into the world, and
desire that counsels evil. And so harsh labor was given to men and   100
abundance of cares. The doors of dreary death were thrown open,
and there soon followed disease and pain, hunger and ignoble
want, though the human race might have lived without any cares,
dwelling upon the earth for centuries at a time. From then on,   105
men lived in the fields without civility or laws. All they knew was
to placate the king of angels with spilt blood, so that he might
look kindly upon them and their flocks and spare their fields from
the wrath of heaven. Otherwise they were untutored, unteachable
and bereft of reason. Such was the condition of the world for   110
nearly two thousand years, until gradually the Supreme Father forgot his wrath and began to relent. Though he had not yet opened
heaven to men, he formed them and sharpened their souls by his   115
teaching, giving them laws and sacred rites. To distinguish our
race he made it law that the small part of our bodies where we are
men should be circumcised in each man with a sharp shard. Then
he filled the hearts of the prophets with the truth of things to
come, and they foretold to the people that the blessed day would   120
finally arrive when the doors of heaven would be thrown open to
the pious.

"Meanwhile, in a shady vale beneath the earth, the spirits of the
chaste and pious sat waiting. Remembering the words of the
prophets, they bided their time, raising their hands to heaven in   125
kindred prayer. They asked the king of angels to forgo his anger

coelestum regem orantes, desisteret ira,
parceret unius genus omne extinguere noxa.
"Parce pater, parce omnipotens," vox omnibus una,
130 "nos promisso olim, longe disiungimur unde
luminis expertes blandi, memor assere coelo.
Haud nos eduxti nequicquam lucis ad auras.
Si qua tamen veteris superant vestigia culpae,
dilue rore tuo facilis, fontesque reclude
135 divinos, o quis superum coelestia tandem
flumina, coelestes nobis bonus irriget imbres.
Vos, o flammiferi labentes aetheris orbes,
irrorate. Vagae nobis succurrite nubes;
optatam pluviam, felicem effundite rorem.
140 Tuque adeo, quem iam expectant tot secula votis
promissum, inferni cui nutant moenia mundi,
summi vera patris soboles, coeli aureus imber,
rumpe moras, age, sidereos rumpe ocius orbes,
aetheris huc fractis vi multa allabere portis!"
145 Talibus orabant omnes, eademque canebant.
    'Quos pater omnipotens superum, sarcire ruinas
iam meditans, coeli penitus miseratus ab arce est.
Cum vero aethereas nutu recludere portas
posset et alitibus potius de civibus unum
150 mittere, qui regnis manes divelleret atris
in superum referens sedes, stellantia templa,
ipse sui ut memores magis ac maioribus arctos
vinciret meritis homines, qui cuncta piaret,
factum hominem e summo natum ipsum misit Olympo.
155 Ne tamen ignaris mortalibus appareret
ignotusque novusque suis, neve ilicet illum
finibus arcerent pulsum, quod se ipse deimet
progeniem leges contra memoraret avitas,
praemisit vatem egregium his in finibus ortum,

without destroying the entire race for the sins of one man. "Spare us, spare us, Father Almighty," was the burden of all their prayers. "Be mindful of us and take us to that heaven promised us long ago, from which we are far removed, deprived of the blessed light of day. Hardly in vain did you bring us forth into the light. If there remains any trace of original sin, cleanse it mercifully with your waters and open to us the fountains of heaven. May some benign angel finally irrigate us with those celestial streams and that celestial dew! Oh, bedew us, gliding spheres of flaming heaven! Help us, wandering clouds! Shower down on us that longed-for rain and happy dew. And you whom so many centuries have awaited, you who were promised to us in response to our vows, you to whom the walls of the underworld bow down, true Son of the Supreme Father and golden rain of heaven, come without delay! Suspend your celestial orbit and, breaking open the heavenly gates, glide hither with all your might." Such was the prayer they sang as though with one voice.

"The Almighty Father of angels had already thought to repair the damage and, from the heights of heaven, he was moved to clemency. With a nod of his head, surely, he could have opened the gates of heaven and sent down one of the winged angels to free these souls from their dark kingdom and lead them up to heavenly seats and starry temples. But in order to make men more mindful of him and to bind them to him through ever greater favors, he sent down from heaven his own Son, made mortal, to atone for all. And yet, that this Son might not suddenly appear, a stranger to ignorant mortals, that they should not expel Him from their lands for claiming, contrary to the ancestral laws, that he was the Son of God, God sent before him a worthy prophet, full of divine

160 nomine Ioannem, Helisabe quem numine plenum
Zacchariae extrema parit infoecunda senecta,
gentibus ipse deum ut natum praenuntius ore
proderet atque suas spes fesso ostenderet orbi.
    'Ille hominum primis vitans vestigia ab annis;
165 horridus in solis agitavit montibus aevum,
montibus et silvis et littoribus desertis.
Speluncae tectum horrentes; victum aspera nullo
arbuta terra dabat cultu aut sudantia truncis
mella cavis; liquidi praebebant pocula fontes.
170 Vestis erat pellis hirsutis horrida villis.
Tantum laetificas gaudebat spargere voces,
affatus nemora et montis ac littora ponti.
Tanta sed haud latuit virtus tamen; ilicet ingens
fama viri circunfusas penetravit ad urbes.
175 Iamque illum coelo demissum credere gentes,
qui, tot veridicae ut quondam cecinere sibyllae,
humanum genus horrificis educeret umbris.
Et iam concursu populi illum accedere magno
scitatum, quisnam, unde domo, quid ferret an ipse
180 afforet e coelo, miseris qui gentibus olim
auxilio venturus, eum bis terque rogabant.
    'Ille sed umbrosis repetebat talia ab antris:
"Gaudete o tenebris iandudum ac nubibus atris
obductae gentes! Lux ecce optata propinquat!
185 Ne vero, ne me ignari vos credite lucem
promissam (immeritos neque enim furamur honores);
tantum ego ceu solem nascentem lucifer ante
exoritur nitidoque diem denuntiat astro;
praedico actutum vobis iubar affore vestrum.
190 Iam iam aderit deus, ecce deus mortalibus oris
ceu mortalis adest! Venienti occurrite laeti,
fronde vias festa decorate, tapetibus agros,

power, named John. In extreme age, the long infertile Elizabeth   160
bore him to Zacharias. He was to be a herald who would declare
to the nations the coming of God, thus restoring hope to a weary
world.

"From earliest youth, John shunned the paths of men. Rough
in appearance, he spent his days in the solitary mountains and   165
groves and the deserted shores of the sea. Rough caves were his
home. For food, the untilled earth yielded him harsh berries and
the honey that dripped from broken tree-trunks. The clear springs
gave him drink. For clothes he wore skins bristling with shaggy
hair. His only joy was to raise glad shouts and speak to the groves,   170
the mountains and the shores of the sea. But his great virtue could
hardly remain hidden; the great fame of the man spread at once to
the cities round about. The people believed he had been sent
down from heaven to lift the human race out of its dark ignorance,   175
as truth-telling sibyls had sung before. And so the people went to
him in great numbers to find out who he was and whence he
came. Again and again they asked what tidings he brought and
whether he was the one whose coming from heaven was foretold,
to help the miserable race of men.   180

"From his shadowy cave he continually repeated: 'Rejoice, you
who have long dwelt in darkness and dismal clouds. Behold, the
light approaches! Do not ignorantly suppose me to be the promised light. I do not grasp after honors I do not deserve. I am only   185
like the morning star that precedes the rising sun, the shining light
that foretells the day. Very soon, I prophesy, your glorious light
will appear. Soon, soon God will come! Behold, like a mortal man   190
he is already present in the lands of men. Run to him joyously
when he comes. Strew his path with festive fronds, cover the fields

et numen digno venerati agnoscite honore!
Discite iustitiam interea atque assuescite recto,
195   et duce me scelus infectum lavite amne liquenti.
Ipse autem aetherea divinitus eluet aura
omne malum ac veteris penitus contagia culpae,
seclaque mutato succedent aurea mundo."
  'Talibus auditis, cunctis ex urbibus ibant
200   finitimi, qua Iordanes fluit agmine dulci,
orantes pacem atque ultro commissa fatentes,
quos vates puro nudos lustrabat in amne,
rite cavis capiti invergens sacra flumina palmis.
  'Ecce autem deus ipse etiam, ceu caetera turba,
205   lustrandi sese studio clam tendit ad amnem,
nil ut inexpertum moribundo in corpore linquat,
mortali quod fas homini et subiisse necesse est,
ne pigeat seros imitari facta nepotes.
Abstinuit primum vates tactusque refugit,
210   agnoscensque deum palmas utrasque tetendit
supplex accurvusque vadis mirantibus ipsis.
Paruit inde tamen iussus, divinaque membra
horrescensque tremensque liquenti perluit amne.
Protinus aurifluo Iordanes gurgite fulsit,
215   et superum vasto intonuit domus alta fragore.
Insuper et coeli claro delapsa columba est
vertice per purum, candenti argentea pluma
terga, sed auratis circum et rutilantibus alis.
Iamque viam late signans super astitit ambos,
220   coelestique aura pendens afflavit utrunque.
Vox simul et magni rubra genitoris ab aethra
audita est, nati dulcem testantis amorem.
Interea aligeri iuvenes, gens incola coeli,
missi aderant, liquido pendentes aëre circum,
225   carbaseosque sinus mantiliaque alba ferebant,

with carpets, and reverently avow his deity with honor due. Meanwhile, learn justice and grow accustomed to righteousness. Guided by me, wash your sins in the clear stream. With his heavenly breath he will cleanse all evil, thoroughly removing the taint of original sin, and a golden age will dawn over an altered world.'

"At these words, people came from all the cities that bordered the clear waters of the Jordan. Praying for peace, they willingly confessed their sins. Naked in the pure stream, they were baptized by the prophet, who poured water on their heads from his cupped hands.

"And now behold how God himself, like all the rest of the crowd, hastened in secret to the river to be baptized. He wanted his mortal body to want for no experience that mortal men rightly or necessarily undergo, so that future generations should not hesitate to imitate his deeds. At first the prophet would not baptize him. Recognizing God, he held out his hands in supplication and bowed, and the very waters seemed to marvel. Nevertheless, he did as he was bidden. Trembling and aghast, he poured the clear stream over the divine body. At once the Jordan glowed with golden water and high heaven loudly thundered. From the shining heights of heaven a dove descended through the pure air, its silvery back covered in brilliant plumage, its wings of burnished gold. Tracing a broad path, it hovered above them both, and breathed on each of them with the spirit of heaven. At the same time the voice of the Almighty Father was heard in the glowing sky, attesting to his gentle love for his Son. Winged angels meanwhile, the race of heaven, descended and hung aloft in the liquid air. As commanded, they carried cloths and white robes to dry the wet limbs

195

200

205

210

215

220

225

iussa ministeria, ut nati membra humida herilis
rorantemque sacro siccarent flumine crinem.
His actis deus evasit fluviumque reliquit.
    'Quem vates longo ripam ordine circunfusis
230 ostendit, talique abeuntem est voce sequutus:
"En ego quem terris toties iam iam affore quondam
pollicitus, deus! Ecce deus, qui crimina nostra
thuricremas agnus veluti mactatus ad aras
morte luet superoque volens cadet hostia patri.
235 Hunc optate ducem, hunc vobis optate magistrum."
Ex illo vates, nemora et loca sola relinquens,
urbes per medias ibat populisque canebat
advenisse deum, promissum numen adesse.
    'Credita res paucis, donec se ostendere coram
240 supra hominem coepit deus ipse ingentibus orsis.
Nam primum numero ex omni delegit amicos
bis senos, quiscum curas durumque laborem
partiri et casus posset deducere in omnes;
ante quidem solus terdenos egerat annos.
245 Sed ne forte putes multis e millibus illi
nos ideo placuisse, dolis quod et arte magistra
spectatos longe ante alios deprenderit omnes
aut opibus claraque domus a stirpe potentes,
omnibus obscurum genus et sine luce penates
250 atque humilis fortuna, nec astu praedita vita.
Quinque adeo sumus exigua Bessaide creti.
Nobis ars erat insidias piscosa secundum
flumina squamigerum generi hamo tendere adunco,
atque innare salum foecundaque piscibus arva.
255 Tunc etiam, cum nos ad se primum ille vocavit,
humida littorea sarcibam retia arena;
ipse Iacobus adhuc salientes littore pisces
servabat frater. Nec tum procul inde secabant

of their mortal Lord, as well as his hair, yet dripping from the sacred stream. When that was done, the Son of God arose from the river and departed.

"The prophet pointed him out to those who had formed a long line on the riverbank, and he called after the departing man with these words. 'Behold our God! Behold him whose arrival on earth 230 I so often foretold. By his death, like a lamb slaughtered amid the incense of the altar, he will wash away all our crimes. Of his own volition he will offer himself as a victim, sacrificed to his Almighty Father. Take him as your leader, choose him as your teacher.' 235 From that moment, the prophet left the groves and deserts for the centers of cities, spreading the news that God had come, that the promised deity was among them.

"Few believed him until the god, through his miraculous deeds, began to reveal himself openly as a being more than human. The 240 first thing he did was to select twelve men from among all his friends to share in his cares and hard labors, men he could count on in any eventuality. Before that, however, he lived for thrice ten years alone. But do not imagine that, out of so many thousands, 245 we impressed him because he found us far shrewder and more learned than others or because we were wealthy or born into illustrious families. Know that we are all of obscure origin and undistinguished homes. Our fortunes are humble and we do not live by 250 our wits. Five of us were born in lowly Bethsaida. All our skill was to angle for fish beside the teaming rivers, to ply the watery fields, rich in spawn. Thus, when first he called on us, I was repair- 255 ing damp nets on the sandy shore. My brother James was looking after the fish that were still leaping about on the strand. Not

Andreas parvaque Petrus vada salsa carina
260 isdem acti fratres studiis, eadem aequora circum.
Tum mihi coniunctus patriaque domoque Philippus
accitus pisces et retia torta reliquit.
Addunt se socios Thomas, Thaddaeus eademque
arte Simon, Cana quem genuit Galileia, amicum
265 fluminibus patriis mutisque natantibus hostem.
Nanque Iacobus, ei cognato sanguine fretus,
Alphaeo natus patre se subiunxerat ante.
Ut genus indecores pene omnes, sic quoque nostra
nomina dura vides, insueta atque aspera dictu.
270 Haud facies sola est impexis horrida barbis!
Tres alii, neque enim longe meliore sequuti
fortuna, addiderant sese: Matthaeus, et aevo
iam gravis effoetisque Petri iam proximus annis
Bartholomaeus, et ipse mali fabricator Iudas.
275 'Vix memorem quaecunque oculis, quaecunque sub illo
auribus his hausi repetens miracula rerum
tempore tam parvo (vix terna hyberna peracta,
ex quo illi socii dignatus nomine iungor),
nec me tam vastum nunc currere oporteat aequor.
280 Pauca sed e multis, et ea haud mihi mollia fatu,
ingrediar tamen et breviter tua iussa capessens
expediam. Mitto modo quae monimenta reliquit
finitimas (tibi nota reor) non parva per urbes,
nanque omnem egregiis factis insigniit oram.
285 Quis nescit nuper revocatum ad munera vitae
palmiferae regem Bethanes, lumine quarto
quem vidit sol extinctum impositumque sepulcro,
ut sileam innumeros, quibus ipse in limine leti
affuit et durae de mortis fauce revulsit?
290 Nam prius enumerem quot ponto aquilonibus undae
spumescant vasto, quot inundent littora arenis,

far off Andrew and Peter were plying the salty shallows in a small
boat, two brothers carrying on the same trade in the same waters.
Then Phillip, who came from the same country and the same   260
house as I did, was called by Jesus and left behind the fish and the
twisted nets. We were joined by Thomas, Thaddeus, and Simon,
a fisherman as well, who was born in Cana in Galilee. He was a
friend to his country's streams, but the enemy of its voiceless fish.
His blood relative James, the son of Alphaeus, had already joined   265
his number. Since almost all of us are of humble birth, you see
that our names are harsh, unusual and difficult to say. Not only
our faces are rough with unkempt bristles! Three others, not sub-   270
stantially more favored than we were, joined as well: Matthew and
Bartholomew, already weighed down with years, the oldest after Peter, and Judas himself, the contriver of evil.

"I can scarcely recount all the miracles I saw Jesus perform with   275
my own eyes and ears, and in so short a time — it is scarcely three
years that I have been honored to call myself his disciple. Nor
would it be proper for me to embark on so vast an ocean by trying
to recount them all. Yet I will tell you a few out of many, and even   280
those are by no means easy to recount. Still, I shall try to relate
them briefly, in obedience to your command. I will leave aside the
deeds he recently performed in the neighboring cities. I think you
know them, for he has honored the whole land with his miracles.
Who has not heard of the king of Bethany, rich in palms, so lately   285
recalled to life on the fourth day after the sun beheld him dead
and buried, not to mention all the others whom Jesus succored at
death's door and saved from the jaws of a dreadful demise? Sooner
could I count the waves stirred up by the winds on the vast sea,
the waves that crash against the sandy shores, than I could count   290
the times he helped those who came to him as suppliants in their

quam quot opem morbos varios in corpore passis
supplicibus tulit et validos laetosque remisit.
Multi capti oculis, clausis multi auribus orti,
295 ne possent ullas audire aut edere voces;
claudi alii imparibus vix aegre passibus ibant.
His rigor ex longo immotos sopiverat artus;
illis semeso serpentia corpore hiabant
hulcera et illuvies membris immunda fluebat.
300 Nec deerant tumefacta quibus praecordia et alvus
insyncera sitim miseris adduxerat acrem,
nullae artes poterant, quam nulla extinguere aquae vis.
Tum quibus assiduis concussa tremoribus usque
nutabant tremuloque lababant corpore membra,
305 ignea quos febris aut corrupti corporis humor,
et quos praeterea vis caeci incognita morbi
versabat lecto totos distracta per artus,
quosve animis captos agitans male habebat Erinnys.
Omnibus aspectu solo tactuve ferebat
310 divus opem: subito linquebant corpora morbi,
et stratis ipsi surgebant protinus aegri.
        'Atque ideo quacunque viam observatus agebat,
semper eum opperiens turba ingens strata iacebat
per fora perque vias sanctique ad limina templi.
315 Nondum aliquem tamen infernis revocaverat umbris
morte obita, cum Sidonia remearet ab ora,
et Naim ingressus sociis comitantibus altam est.
Ecce autem ingentem longo procedere pompam
ordine flammarum aspicimus moestamque per urbem
320 audimus luctum, causam tum denique luctus
cernimus: egregii iuvenis miserabile corpus
impositum molli pheretro, quem mersit acerba
morte dies, dulci cum vix pubesceret aevo,
atque omnem vultu florenti dempsit honorem.

sickness. They came to him with sundry afflictions, but went
home happy and healthy. Many were born blind or deaf, and   295
could neither hear nor speak. Many were crippled and could
hardly walk. With some, all their strength had lain dormant for
years, made numb and immobile with paralysis. Half consumed,
these bodies were covered with open sores and exuded a ghastly
pus. And there were those with swollen innards. Their bellies pro-   300
voked a sharp thirst that no medicine and no amount of water
could ever quench. Then there were those afflicted with palsy who
could scarcely stand upright because of the constant tremor of
their limbs; those afflicted with a burning fever or rheum; those   305
afflicted by some unknown disease, who tossed about on their
beds when seizures came. Then there were those who had lost
their minds and were inhabited by an evil demon. This divine being brought help to all of them merely by touching them or looking on them. At once the diseases left their bodies, and they rose   310
from their sickbeds through their own strength.

"And so wherever he went, as soon as he was spotted, a huge
crowd was there to meet him, lying prostrate before him in the
roads and public spaces and on the steps of the holy temple. He
had not yet summoned back any dead man from the nether   315
shades, when on his return from the Sidonian coast he came to
lofty Naim with his disciples. Just then we saw a great procession
advancing, accompanied by a long row of torches, and throughout
the city we heard great lamentation. Finally we learned the cause   320
of sorrow: the pitiable corpse of a fine young man who lay upon a
soft bier. Though scarcely arrived at man's estate, he had died that
very day and all his beauty had vanished, as when a hyacinth wilts

325 Qualis, quem pede pressit agro bos signa relinquens,
paulatim lassa languet cervice hyacinthus,
aut rosa quam molli decerpens pollice virgo,
vepribus in densis lapsam sub sole reliquit.
Urbe furens tota genitrix miseranda, capillos
330 scissa genasque ambas manibus foedata cruentis,
ibat. Eam circum pariter per densa viarum
pulsabant saevis matres plangoribus astra;
ipsi orbam cives miserantur: ei unica proles
ille relictus erat, vidui solatia lecti.

335 Ut deus exanimis iuvenili in corpore vidit
pallorem et molli pictas lanugine malas,
parcere lamentis iubet et considere pompam,
admotusque manu mulcens immobile corpus
rursum animam gelidis membris innexuit. Ecce
340 erigitur puer et (cunctis mirabile visum)
prosiluit raptim in medios vacuumque pheretrum
liquit et amplexans solatus voce parentem est.
Nec vero multis etiam post mensibus idem
egregiam amissa donavit luce puellam,
345 cui calor et toto de pectore fugerat omnis
halitus, aereas penitus dilapsus in auras.
Virginis ipse pater factum testatur Iarus,
largus opum, pollens lingua et popularibus auris.

'Quid repetam, purum vivo cum e fonte liquorem
350 in vinum convertit, opes miseratus amici?
Forte olim aerei spectans de vertice montis,
cum sol emenso depressior iret Olympo,
ingentem vidit numerum affluxisse[2] sequentum,
matres atque viros, quos per deserta locorum
355 duxerat oblitosque sui oblitosque suorum.
Substitit hic miseratus. Eos iam tertia nanque
muneris expertes cereris lux acta videbat.

from its weary neck when trodden on in the field by an ox; or   325
when the hand of some gentle virgin plucks a rose and then aban-
dons it in the sunlight amid the briars. The pitiable mother ran
madly through the city, her hair unkempt, her cheeks defiled by
her bloodied hands. All around her, in the tangle of streets, the   330
other mothers raised their fierce lamentations to the stars. The citizens pitied the mother, bereaved of her only child, the one consolation of her widowed bed. When the Son of God saw the deathly
pallor of the child's body and his cheeks covered with soft down,   335
he bade the funeral procession halt and desist from their lamentations. Then he lightly touched the motionless body and bound its
soul anew to its cold limbs. At once, to universal amazement, the
boy arose and, leaving the bier empty, leapt into the midst of the   340
crowd to embrace and console his mother. Not many months
later, Jesus brought back to life a beautiful young girl from whose
body the vital warmth and breath had floated up to heaven. This   345
deed is attested by Iarus, the girl's own father, a generous and eloquent man, well loved by the people.

"And do I need to repeat how, taking pity on a friend's need, Jesus changed fresh water into wine? Another time, looking down   350
from the summit of a lofty mountain, as the sun was setting in the
heavens, he saw a large crowd of men and women whom he had
led through the desert and who had forgotten themselves and
their families. He looked on in pity. For three days they had gone   355
without eating. Here there was no food, nor could they buy or

Hic neque erant fruges, vicina nec oppida possent
unde dapes petere argento victumque parare,
360 arboreos necdum foetus decoxerat aestas.
Vix tandem inventus puer est ex agmine tanto
quinque, viae auxilium, qui secum liba ferebat
atque duos, dederat quos huc pia mater eunti,
inclusos myrto et bene olenti gramine pisces.
365 Sed quid enim haec adeo tam multis millibus autem?
Et iam diffisi socii mussare querentes,
quos bonus affatu Christus solatus amico,
in coetum vocat ac paucis ita deinde profatur:
"Nemo hodie numero e tanto non laetus abibit."
370   'Hinc supplex tali genitorem voce precatur:
"Summe parens, ope cuius alit terra omnia quique
et sole et liquidis foecundas imbribus agros,
si quondam Isacidum generi per inhospita eunti
divinas epulas coelo es largitus ab alto,
375 semine si nullo constant quaecunque creasti
et nihil omnino fuerant coelum aequora tellus,
adsis obscoenamque famem tot millibus arce."
Haec tantum. Dehinc gramineo discumbere campo
imperat effusos coetus dapibusque parari.
380 Inde in frusta secat laeto cerealia vultu
liba minutatim et populos partitur in omnis.
(Millia quinque hominum campis saturanda sedebant.)
Ecce (incredibile auditu, mirabile visu)
omnibus in manibus visae succrescere partes
385 exiguae, dapibusque epulati largius omnes.
Et frugum pariter laticumque expleta cupido est;
quin et relliquias mensis superantia frusta
vix cava congestas bis sex cepere canistra.
   'Accipe nunc aliud quod paucis ante diebus
390 vidimus. Arbor erat foliis densissima in agro

procure it in any nearby town. Summer had not yet ripened the
fruit on the trees. One boy was found in this great multitude who   360
had a five loaves as provisions and two fish, covered in myrtle and
fragrant herbs, that his mother had given him for the journey. But
what were these to so many thousands? And when his disciples   365
had lost hope and were murmuring, Jesus called them together
and spoke these few, kindly words: 'Today no one in this great
number will go away without good cheer.'

"Then he called upon his Maker. 'Supreme Father, who help   370
the earth to bring forth all things and who make the fields fertile
with sunlight and clear rain, if ever you sent down from on high
your divine sustenance to feed the children of Isaac as they wandered in the hostile desert, if all you create subsists without seed,   375
and if without you the sea, the earth and the sky would be as
nothing, then help me now to drive vile hunger from these people
in their thousands." That was all he said. Then he bade the multitudes lie down on the grass and prepare for the meal. Suffused   380
with joy, he divided the loaves into tiny pieces and distributed
them to all the people. Five thousand sat waiting to be fed. And
though it was incredible to hear and miraculous to behold, each
man saw the scraps grow in his hands, and everyone ate in abundance from the feast. And at once their thirst and hunger were re-   385
lieved. Indeed, the remaining scraps from the meal could hardly be
held in twelve hollow baskets!

"And listen also to what happened only a few days ago. In a deserted field stood a tree covered with leaves. From it in former   390

deserto, unde olim pendentia poma viator
carpebat sitiens. Heros qui hac forte tenebat
pulverulentus iter, quaesivit in arbore foetus
incassum, infoecunda comas nam et brachia tantum
395   luxurians late circum tendebat opaca.
    Non tulit, ac verbis sterilem execratus acerbis.
Continuo (manifesta audis) exarvit arbos,
et folia aereas volitarunt lapsa per auras.
    'Nec minus est olli imperii maris aequora in alta.
400   Uni omnes undae assurgunt fluctusque quiescunt
unius edicto. Vidi, vidi ipse furentes
illius hybernos ad vocem ponere coros
vimque omnem, motas quae flabris asperat undas.
Nondum luna suum ter cursum plena peregit,
405   cum subito in lento deprensis marmore nobis
nocte fere media, dum retia ducimus, orta est
turbida tempestas et pontus inhorruit ater
fluctibus elatis et concursantibus undis,
inflictamque ratem iam iam salis hauserat aestus.
410   Nos trepidare metu leti discrimine parvo,
cum procul ecce ducem, quem nuper liquimus alto
littore spectantem fluctus scopulo illidentes,
ferre iter aspicimus medias impune per undas
suspensum tumidoque pedes haud tinguere ponto.
415   Horruimus visu subito, nec credere quibam
me veram faciem, haud simulatum cernere corpus,
tam celeres egisse vias sine remige in undis,
ni sese, verbis dum nos hortatur amicis,
ultro ostendisset: "Quonam fiducia vobis
420   iam nunc pulsa mei cessit? Timor omnis abesto.
Indubitare meis tandem dediscite dictis."
Sic ait, atque ratem, quae iam superantibus undis
cesserat, insiliens solo tumida aequora nutu

times a thirsting traveler could pluck the apples that hung down. But when Jesus happened to pass it on a dusty journey, he sought fruit from it in vain: it spread out nothing but leaves and dark branches. He could not tolerate this and bitterly cursed the fruit-   395
less tree. At once it shriveled up (you are hearing the plain truth) and the falling leaves flew through the air.

"Nor has he less dominion over the high seas. All the waves rise up for him alone, and at his behest they fall silent again. With my   400
own eyes I saw the raging wintery gusts of the northwest wind be calmed at his command and all the force that churns the waters with its blasts. The full moon had not yet come and gone three times when suddenly, as we drew up our nets at midnight on a calm sea, a roaring tempest arose and the surge grew black and   405
rough. The waters mounted and the waves crashed together and the churning of the salt sea had almost consumed the afflicted raft. We shivered with fear at approaching death, when suddenly, far   410
off, we saw our Lord, whom we had just left ashore watching the waves smash against the rocks. He walked unharmed in the midst of the waves, his feet hardly touched by the waters. We were terrified at the strange sight. So swiftly did he move across the   415
sea, without aid of any oars, that I would hardly have believed I was seeing his true face and form rather than an image, had he not revealed himself to us and spoken these kind words. 'Why has your faith in me flagged? Banish all fear! Learn not to doubt my   420
words.' So he spoke. And jumping onto the ship, which was al-ready wallowing in water, he pacified the waters with nothing more than a nod and the sea forgot its menacing roar. And so, the

placavit, posuitque minacia murmura pontus.
425 Sic terrae in tutum positis adnavimus undis
incolumes celerique volavimus aequora cursu.
    'Nec mora, vix siccum attigerat tellure potitus,
ecce aliud dictu magis ac mirabile visu.
Nanque magistratus aderant in littore missi
430 aera reposcentes, quae pendere lege quotannis
regibus antiqua pro sese quisque iubemur.
Accipit hos placidus quos, dum sermone moratur,
Petrum ad se vocat, et fidam summissus ad aurem,
"Vade," ait, "et iacto quem primum traxeris hamo
435 aequoribus piscem cultro scrutabere acuto.
Intus erit regi quod iussi pendimus ambo."
Iussa facit senior. Trahit hamo ad littora praedam,
argentumque viris dat piscis in ore repertum.
    'Horresco quoties stimulis immitibus actus
440 quidam animo subit, idem illo quem tempore vidi,
dum legerem expositos hoc ipso in littore pisces,
obsessum furiis atque ore immane furentem.
Hunc olim (ut perhibent) vetito genuere parentes
concubitu iuncti atque inconcessis hymenaeis;
445 quippe torum ascendere, dei cum sacra vetarent,
cum scenis gens indulget nostra omnis opacis.
Sed non gavisi scelere illi tempore longo.
Nam subito amplexus interque et gaudia adulter
sacrilegam tenues animam exhalavit in auras
450 infelix, scelerique eadem nox prima nefando,
et pariter suprema fuit discrimine parvo.
Illam autem aethereis flammis divinitus ignis
corripuit, cum iam maturi pondera partus
urgerent, eademque duos leto hora dedisset,
455 infans ni foret exectae genitricis ab alvo
exemptus, parvum patris eduxere sorores.

waters stilled, we sailed swiftly and safely to the security of dry   425
land.

"No sooner had he reached the land and stood on the shore,
when, behold! a more startling event occurred, even more wondrous to relate. For some magistrates were present on the shore,
having been sent to collect taxes. According to an ancient law, we   430
were each of us bidden to pay these taxes yearly to the crown. Jesus received the men affably and while conversing with them,
called Peter and whispered confidingly into his ear, 'Get the first
fish you hook and then examine its innards with a sharp knife.   435
Within will be enough for both of us to pay the king.' The older
man did as bidden and brought the hooked prey ashore. Then he
gave the magistrates a silver coin he had found in the fish's mouth.

"I am horrified each time I recall a man I saw around this time
as I was counting fish that were set out along the shore. Mad-   440
dened by harsh goads, he was beset by demons and was frothing
at the mouth. They say he had been born to parents joined in forbidden love and an illicit marriage. Indeed, they went to bed at a   445
time when sacred ritual forbade it, when all our nation devotes itself to dark re-enactments. But they did not enjoy their crime for
long. Amidst their joyous embraces, the adulterer gave up his sacrilegious soul, and that first night of love was also their last. When   450
the mother was already advanced in labor, she was struck down by
a heaven-sent fever. The same hour would have caused the death
of two human beings except that the child was pulled from her cut   455
womb and was raised by his father's sisters. Though he had done

Ipse etiam mox immeritus scelerata parentum
facta luit, iucunda oculorum luce negata
obstructaeque aures penitus mansere, nec illi
460   aut ullas haurire datum est aut reddere voces.
Quin etiam simul atque adolevit, protinus aegrum
arripuit furor, infernae vis effera gentis.
Centum illum furiae, centum illum (flebile) pestes
victum exercebant, Erebi legio acta latebris,
465   horrendasque hominis singultus ore cientes
edebant voces ac terrificos mugitus.
Illum omnes exclamantem atque insueta frementem
horrebant trepidique fuga se in tecta ferebant,
si quando nodis ruptisque immane catenis
470   incautis liber custodibus evasisset.
Iamque ille oblitus fratres, iamque ille sorores
amplius haud gressum patris intra tecta ferebat,
verum more ferae silvis degebat et antris,
sicubi saxa cava aut aevo consumpta sepulcra,
475   ater, egens corpusque abiecto nudus amictu.
    'Talem igitur nodo manibus post terga revinctis
Christi ad conspectum, si fors miseresceret ipse,
vi multa consanguinei carique trahebant.
Ille autem obniti contra, dum rumpere nodos
480   tendit et horrendos clamores tollere ad astra,
qualis, ubi longis pugnator taurus ad aras
funibus arripitur, saevo fremit ore per urbem
et spumas agit et cornu ferit aera adunco;
instant hinc famuli atque illinc et verbera crebri
485   ingeminant quassantque sudes per terga, per armos;
diffugiunt vulgus trepidum, in tutumque recepti
porticibus gaudent longe spectare periclum.
Talis erat iuvenis species immane furentis,

no wrong, he paid for his parents' sins by being deprived of sight
and sound, so that he could neither hear nor speak. What is more,   460
as soon as he reached adolescence, a madness, the violence of infernal demons, seized the afflicted man. A hundred furies, a hundred plagues assailed him, a legion sent forth out of the depths of
hell. From his mouth these demons emitted ghastly sobs and hid-   465
eous lowings. Horrified by his strange and horrible outbursts, everyone ran inside the house whenever in his rage he broke free of
the chains that bound him because his guards were not watching.
Forgetting his brothers and sisters, he hardly set foot in his father's   470
house. Like a beast, rather, he haunted the woods and caves. His
home he made wherever there was a hollow rock or tombs ravaged
by age. He had thrown away his cloak, leaving his naked body
blackened and destitute.   475

"Such was his appearance when, with his hands tied behind his
back, his relations and friends forcibly dragged him before Christ.
They hoped Jesus would pity the afflicted man. For his part, the
man resisted and tried to break his bonds, shouting horrendous
things to the heavens, just as when a violent bull is being dragged   480
to the altar with long ropes, it bellows savagely through the town,
foaming at the mouth and piercing the air with its curved horn;
attendants come running from all direction and rain down blows
upon it, lashing its shoulders and back with rods, and frightened   485
onlookers flee, happy to watch from the safety of a distant portico.
Such was the inhuman appearance of the raging youth when fi-

quem tandem ante deum fessi statuere rogantes
490 ferret opem, saltem furiis tam tristibus illum
solveret excuteretque animo crudelia monstra.
   'Hic heros palmas in coelum sustulit ambas,
concipiensque preces, genitorem in vota vocavit.
Ecce autem magnum, subitum et mirabile monstrum!
495 Auditi exululare lupi, latrare canes ceu,
tam diras iactat voces lymphatus ab ore.
Non tam immane sonet sese frangentibus undis
rupibus ex altis ingens decursus aquarum,
rumpantur claustra alta lacus si forte Velini,
500 totaque praecipitent valles stagna ardua in imas,
omnis ea ut regio fiat mare et oppida circum
mersa natent metuatque sacris Roma obruta templis.
Nunc coeli crepitus imitantur, cum superum rex
fulminat et tonitru quatit aetheris aurea templa;
505 nunc ferri sonitum aut ruptarum mole catenarum
ingenti horrificum stridorem aut murmura ponti.
Circum omnis tellus, circum coelum omne remugit.
   'Instat vi multa deus increpitatque morantes.
Iamque illi trepidare intus pacemque precari:
510 "Quid nunc, vera dei atque indubitata propago,
concesso in poenas nos o de corpore trudis?
Egressis saltem pecora haec invadere detur."
(Setigeri tum forte sues ea littora propter
pascebant.) "Nosne horrifero sic merge barathro,
515 neve iube terrae inferioris operta subire."
Annuit. Extemplo videas procul ecce nigrantem
mollibus haud stimulis furiarum errare subactum
in diversa gregem nunc huc, nunc protinus illuc.
Nec mora, nec requies: intus vis effera saevit,
520 donec praecipites sese alta in stagna dedere,

218

nally, wearily, his family brought him before Christ, and asked him
to free the man from his terrible madness and dash the demons   490
from his soul.

"Now the hero raised both hands to heaven, and prayed to his
Father. And behold a swift, a great miracle occurred! Like the baying of wolves and the barking of dogs, such were the sounds that   495
the man emitted from his slavering mouth. So great a sound was
never made by the rushing waters whose turbid waves come crashing down from their lofty cliffs, if perchance the high dams of the
lake of Piediluco burst asunder and its waters flood the deepest   500
valleys, leaving the region a sea, the nearby towns submerged, and
Rome deluged, fearing for its sacred temples. Now the man's ravings recalled the roar of heaven's king when he fulminates, rattling
with thunder the golden temples of the air; now it recalled the
clash of iron and the horrifying crash of massive chains breaking,   505
and finally the surge of the ocean. The sound filled the air, extend-
ing to the surrounding fields.

"With great force, God bore down on them and assailed the demons for staying. They became frightened inside the man's body
and sued for peace. 'O true, undoubted offspring of God, why do   510
you now cast us out from this body that has been turned over to
us for punishment? At least allow us, if we leave, to enter those
swine.' (It happened that some bristly swine were feeding beside
the shore). 'Don't hurl us down into the terrifying abyss or dispatch us to the hidden places of the underworld.' He agreed. Sud-   515
denly you could see the black swine, driven by the demons' savage
goad, fleeing in all directions without rest or respite. The harsh
force raged within them until they finally jumped headlong into
deep pools, where they all drowned. But the young man's ex-   520

et cunctis pariter vita est erepta sub unda.
At iuvenis fessos subito collabitur artus
exemptus tandem nodosis brachia vinclis.
Mordicus ora solo impressus cunctatur adhucque
525 singultans pectusque lacessit anhelitus ingens,
expiransque animam pulmonibus aeger agebat.
Quem iuxta genitore deo satus astitit oraque
attingens dextra atque oculos auresque reclusit,
iamque videt loquiturque, et corda oblita residunt.
530 It vulgi clamor super aurea sidera ovantis,
supremique patris sobolemque deumque fatentur.

'Sed quid non ipse evaleat? Quin nos quoque missos
aegris iussit opem ferre auxilioque levare
praesenti. Mortis multos de faucibus atris
535 non opibus hominum, nulla revocavimus arte,
verum implorato ter tantum voce magistri
nomine surgebant stratis ibantque refecti.
Omni autem ex numero sese vix obtulit unus,
quem stimulis actum saevis caecoque furore
540 incassum victi tentavimus; acrior illum
usque adeo magis atque magis vis intus agebat.
Cui cum ferret opem divus mox optimus ipse,
iratus quod parva sui fiducia nobis,
"Corporibus tales facile," inquit, "pellere pestes."
545 "Parcendum dapibus tamen e coeloque petendum.
Nec solis vero haec vobis concessa facultas,
sed nomen quicunque meum vulgaverit, omnia
fas audere, mei modo ne fiducia desit.
Ille etiam iussos immani corpore montes
550 transferet et verso sistet vaga flumina cursu.
Ite animis igitur certi confidite, neve
instabili titubate fide. Iacite aurea veri
semina ubique; orbem vestra perfundite luce

hausted limbs gave out beneath him, as his arms were finally freed
from their bonds. Gnashing his teeth, he remained face down on
the ground, still moaning, as his chest heaved in deep gasps, and   525
he exhaled the breath from his lungs. The Son of God stood next
to him. He touched the man's face, opening his eyes and ears. The
man now saw and spoke and soon his distracted heart was at
peace. The crowd raised up to heaven a great cry, confessing Jesus   530
to be God and the Son of the Supreme Father.

"But what could he not do? In fact, he sent us as well to care
for the sick and alleviate their sufferings. Many we rescued from
the dark jaws of death, through no human powers or medical art.
We had only to speak our teacher's name three times in order   535
for many to rise from their sickbeds and go forth in health. In all
their number, there was only one man we were unable to cure.
Hounded by savage goads and blind fury, he raved ever more violently. Then the best of divine beings himself lent a hand, angered   540
that we had so little faith in him. 'It is an easy thing,' he said, 'to
drive such spirits as these from people's bodies. You must fast and
seek heaven's help. Nor is this power allowed to you alone. But   545
whoever has spread my teachings can attempt anything at all, as
long as he believes in me. He will move the mighty mass of mountains and change the course of rushing rivers. So go forth in confi-   550
dence and founder not in your faith. Sow everywhere the golden
seeds of truth and flood with light a world covered in darkness

obductum tenebris atque alta nocte sepultum.
555 Vos hominum lux, vos squalentis lumina mundi."
Sic fatus, nobis alios subiunxit, ut essent
consortes tantorum operum sociique laborum,
et septem elegit decies, tamen ipse dolebat
exiguum numerum, neque tot satis esse ferebat
560 tanto operi, ac veluti qui centum vertit aratris
tellurem et campos rastris exercet avitos,
cum matura seges iam flavis canet aristis,
si desint qui messem operis (quae plurima) condant,
fluctuet atque viros aliis conducat ab oris.
565 'Quid memorem, ut mentes hominum curasque latentis,
quod fieri certo nequeat sine numine, cernat?
Quippe animis dubios, taciti dum vana timemus,
castigans dictis nos saepe erexit acerbis
mirantes. Quoties ipsis etiam hostibus olim
570 praedixit, quos mente dolos, quae furta pararent
incassum, dum caeci odiis agitantur iniquis?
'Foemina nec latuit bis senos passa per annos
sanguinis immundi manans de corpore flumen.
Illa quidem ardentis morbi confecta dolore
575 pone sequebatur, si qua illum tangere posset,
hanc unam rata nempe viam restare salutis.
Ergo, dum pubes fluit undique et agmina inundant,
illa subit leviterque extremum apprendit amictum.
Ad tactum veter effugit de corpore morbus,
580 iamque abitum latuisse putans clam mente parabat.
Praesensit deus et pavidam seseque tegentem
affatus placide monitis implevit amicis.
'Vidi oculos ante ipse meos mortalia nuper
aut membra exutum aut perfusum luce superne;
585 non infra solis speciem dare corpore lumen.
His multisque aliis, ego quae creberrima vidi,

and buried in deepest night. You are the light of men, lamps unto a sordid world.' With such exhortations he brought others as well to join us in these great efforts, to be the partners of his labors. In all he chose seventy of us. But he was dissatisfied with this number, saying that we were not enough for so great a labor. He was like a man who tills his ancestral fields with a hundred plows; but as the crop ripens and its stalks turn to gold, he worries that he does not have enough hands for the abundant harvest and hires workers from distant lands.

"Do I need to mention that he could read the minds and hidden cares of men, something impossible without divine help? Indeed he often astonished us by sensing our very doubts. When we were full of baseless fears, he would chastise and goad us with bitter words. How often did he foretell even to his enemies what deceits and ploys they would resort to in vain, blinded by base hatred.

"Nor did it escape his notice that one woman had suffered for twelve years from a stream of foul blood coming from her body. Stricken with pain from the burning malady, she followed behind him. She wished to touch him, believing that this was her one remaining hope of health. And so, as all the young people went out to see Christ, as crowds surged around him, she went too, and gently grasped the hem of his cloak. At his touch, the chronic disease fled her body. And now she was about to leave quietly, thinking she had not been noticed. But Jesus sensed what had happened and, as she timidly tried to cover herself, he spoke kindly to her.

"With my own eyes I lately saw him shorn of his mortal body or suffused with a heavenly glow. A light greater than the sun's emanated from him. Through these and many other signs I frequently saw he manifested his deity on earth. But he never forgot

555

560

565

570

575

580

585

per terras patuit signis deus. Haud tamen unquam
sese hominem oblitus moribundo corpore cretum;
multa tulit quoque, mortales quae ferre necesse est,
590　atque id sponte quidem, nobis imitanda relinquens.
Saepe hilares mensas ideo et convivia adivit,
nec coetus bonus est hominum aspernatus in urbe.
Saepe etiam insidias inimicae gentis et iras
suffugiens, ut homo male tuti limina templi
595　exiit obiecitque cavam pro corpore nubem,
nec se in conspectum latebris dedit abditus atris,
dum fremerent hostes nequicquam et saxa pararent.
　　'Atque equidem memini (vix actus volvitur annus)
nuper Ioannis comperta caede recenti
600　quem rex, uxorem praereptam reddere fratri
admonitus, tenebris ferro obtruncarat in atris,
urbibus his abiit cautus populisque relictis
digressus, silvae elapsum accepere profundae.
Nec rex ipse Erebi, generis foedissimus hostis
605　humani, nostras qui recto avertere mentes
nititur, abstinuit dominove deove pepercit.
Forte etenim comitum strepitus turbamque sequentum
dum fugeret quondam, se clam subduxerat heros
coetibus et solus lucis degebat in altis,
610　iamque quater denos frugum sine munere soles
condiderat totidemque famem per inhospita noctes
pertulerat, cum iam tempus ratus ecce nocendi
affuit extemplo multis cum millibus hostis
noctipotens, quos tartareis ducebat ab antris,
615　flammea semiferi capitis gestamina quassans.
Iamque sui frustra spe praemia percipit astus;
ergo illi meditans nequicquam illudere dictis
talibus aggreditur: "Superi tu certa parentis
progenies verusque deus, tibique omnia parent;

224

that he was born a man in a mortal body and he suffered many of
the things that mortals suffer. And he did so willingly as a lesson
for the rest of us to imitate. Often he frequented joyous feasts and 590
drinking parties, nor of his goodness did he spurn the company of
men. Fleeing like a mortal man the snares and ire of his enemies,
he left the unsafe threshold of the temple and hid himself in a hollow cloud, concealing himself in a dark lair as his enemies vainly 595
raged and readied their stones.

"I remember well (for hardly a year has passed) the time when
King Herod—whom John the Baptist had rebuked, telling him
to give back the wife he had stolen from his brother—had the 600
prophet beheaded in the darkness of a dungeon. Soon thereafter,
Jesus prudently left the towns and their peoples, taking refuge in
the deep woods. The lord of Erebus himself, that foulest enemy of
mankind, who always seeks to turn mens' minds from the path of
right, could not resist making trial of the Son of God. Having fled 605
from the noise and crowd of his followers and hidden himself all
alone in the depths of a forest, Jesus suffered hunger for forty days
and forty nights in the wilderness, without any food. Believing 610
that the time was ripe for doing him harm, the hostile lord of
night appeared with his legions, summoned from their tartarean
caves. He shook his bestial head with its flaming locks. He already 615
saw, with empty hope, the reward for his cunning. He imagined he
could deceive Jesus, whom he thus addressed: 'True offspring of
the Heavenly Father, a veritable God yourself, whom all things
obey, why do you persist in afflicting your body with hunger?

620 quid durare fame confecto corpore pergis,
nec subito in totidem convertere adorea liba
haec circum quae saxa vides ingentia tentas?"
Non divum latuere doli atque haec reddidit ore:
"Sunt mihi mortali tostae pro munere frugis
625 sermones patris auditi divinaque verba,
quae, quoties animo repeto memor, effugit omnis
pulsa fames subito mensaeque oblita cupido."
    'Dixerat. His tamen auditis haud destitit hostis
congressu victus primo, pugnamque retentat
630 atque aliis super atque aliis assultibus instat,
terque novos semper coepti irritus integrat astus
nequicquam, nunc regnorum, nunc laudis inani
immotum tentans animum praevertere amore.
Ut cum sollicitum tollunt mare fluctibus Euri,
635 crebra ferit saevitque minaci verbere in alta
littora, sed saxis allisa revertitur unda.
Nec deus, haec subito quanvis praesentiat, arcet
conantem patiturque dolos sibi nectere vanos.
Nunc se marmorei supra fastigia templi,
640 nunc rupem supra scabrumque crepidine saxum
subvectari ultro sinit et spem accendit inanem.
Cum vero vicisse ratus iam gaudia dira
conciperet frustra ille inhians, se protinus heros
ipse deum claro confessus numine coram
645 irrita furta dolosque exibat semper apertos.
Qualis, ubi excussis per plana evasit habenis,
liber equus ludit famulos hinc inde sequentes,
saepe hic dissimulans atque illic improbus haeret,
perque viam oblatas interdum pascitur herbas;
650 ast ubi iam videt instantes, elabitur alteque
emicat et spatia transmittit maxima campi.
Quam speciem expertus nequicquam ubi denique sensit

Why not try to turn these huge stones that lie about you into as 620
many loaves of spelt?' But his treachery did not escape the divine
one, who answered thus: 'In place of the mortal nourishment of
baked bread, I have the divine words of my Father. As often as I 625
repeat them to myself, all hunger flees at once and all desire for
food is forgotten.'

"So he spoke. Though vanquished in the first duel, the enemy
was scarcely stopped by these words, but resumed the battle with
one onslaught after another. Three times in vain he attempted to 630
pervert Jesus's steadfast soul through empty love of praise or
power: he was like the East Wind that roils the rough seas and the
waves that repeatedly pound the shore and lash it with their fury,
but the water is dashed against the rocks and thrown back. Yet al- 635
though the Son of God immediately sensed his treachery, he did
not try to ward off his opponent, whom he suffered to tempt him
in vain, whether from atop marble temples or cliffs or sharp rocks,
filling his enemy with empty hopes. Finally when the devil 640
thought he had won and was already salivating in anticipation of
his foul victory, at once the hero manifested himself in all his divinity and left behind his empty treachery and obvious stratagems.
Jesus was like a horse that has shaken off its reins and is running 645
free across the fields, making sport of the stable-boys that come after him, sometimes pausing mischievously to feed upon the grass
by the way; but as soon as he sees them approach, slips away again 650
and darts through the fields, covering vast distances. When the
atrocious enemy realized he had tried deceit without success, he

hostis atrox, abiit victusque, deumque reliquit,
cui volucres centum pluma pernice ministri
655   astabant missu genitoris opemque ferebant.
     'Si vero causas odiorum ac semina quaeris
tantorum, cur gens omnis opponitur uni,
haec norint ipsi. Certe non talia gessit,
quae capto affingunt odiis crudelibus acti.
660   Non homines inter magis est affabilis alter,
non pietate prior, venia complectitur omnes.
Hostis, civis ei nullo discrimine habentur.
Multi impune ideo digna atque indigna ferenti
obiecere, omnes nutu cum perdere posset.
665   Sera olim cum Sidoniam sub nocte per oram
ferret iter fessus, nos parva exclusit ab urbe
gens fera, nec tecto est dignata heroa precantem.
Nos igitur tristes supremum orare parentem
aspiceret coelo nec gnatum ferret inultum,
670   sed populum immitem coelesti protinus igni
corriperet subitis et inhospita moenia flammis.
Non tulit ac verbis nos indignatus amaris
increpuit, potiusque urbem miseratus iniquam est.
     'Saepe etiam auctores scelerum haud ignarus adibat
675   infamesque domos scelerataque tecta subibat,
quo moniti exuerent fastus moresque sinistros
et secum inciperent paulatim assuescere recto.
Sic Matthaeus, agri dives sic noster et ipse est
Zacchaeus, centumque alii ad meliora vocati.
680   Nec tamen, id faceret dum creber, defuit olim
qui falli ratus incautum, pro crimine magno
obiiceret, quod non fugeret contagia dira.
Ipse sed, ut medicam veluti languentibus aegris
ferret opem, totam quaerebat sponte per urbem,
685   sicubi mortales mentem caligine pressi,

left in defeat and abandoned the Son of God, who was assisted by
a hundred winged angels standing by his side, sent at his Father's
behest to minister to him.   655

"If you seek the cause and origin of that great hatred that in-
duces an entire race to oppose a single man, only they themselves
know it. Surely he is not guilty of the crimes that they, driven by
cruel hatred, impute to him. No man is more approachable, more   660
pious or more forgiving than he is. He treats his enemies no
differently from his countrymen. Many have accused him with impunity and he has borne all of it, when he could destroy them all
with a nod of his head. Once late at night, when he was wearily
traveling through Sidon, the feral inhabitants barred us from their   665
small city and would not offer shelter to the hero when he asked
for it. In our ill humor, we prayed to God to look down from
heaven and not suffer his Son to go unavenged. Rather we besought him to strike these cruel people down at once with a thun-   670
derbolt and set fire to their inhospitable walls. But Jesus would not
stand for it and indignantly rebuked us with harsh words, and
rather took pity on the wicked city.

"Often he associated with criminals, though by no means ignorant of what they had done, and he would enter their notorious
dwellings and wicked homes. He admonished them to shake off   675
their pride and their evil ways, so that, following him, they might
gradually learn the ways of righteousness. So it was with Matthew; so too even in the case of our Zacchaeus, rich in land, and
with a hundred others that he called to a better way of life. Since
he did this often, there was always someone who reckoned that Je-   680
sus had imprudently allowed himself to be tricked, and accused
him, as a great crime, of not shunning evil influences. But in order
to bring medicine to those languishing in sickness, he eagerly went
through the city, wherever men's minds were afflicted with darkness, so that of his goodness and mercy he could rescue them from   685

quos nocte eriperet bonus ad lucemque vocaret,
in tenebris caeco miseratus pectore volvi;
id superis, superum id magno cordi esse parenti,
seque ideo claro missum memorabat Olympo.
690 ‘Insuper et coelum compleret quanta docebat
laetitia, aetherei quanto gens incola regni
acciperet plausu, si quis mortalibus oris
inventor scelerum atque pii contemptor et aequi
iustitiam colere inciperet rectumque tueri.
695 Sicut ovem incautus pastor qui e millibus unam
amisit serae oblitam decedere nocti
cum gregibus, ubi per rupes perque aspera tristis
quaesivit dumeta diu loca cuncta volutis
convisens oculis, demum si forte reposta
700 pascentem valle invenit, subito arripit illam
sublatamque humero stabulis laetissimus infert.
Intranti dulces occurrunt oscula nati
praeripere et reducem plausu domus excipit omnis.
Iccirco neque colloquiis muliebribus heros
705 abstinuit, nuperque legens Samaritidos orae
rura sub antiquis Sicharaeae moenibus urbis,
viderat ad fontem venientem ut forte puellam,
imploravit aquam supplex putealiaque hausit
munera, qui pelago, qui fluminibusque sonoris
710 imperat et vastum largis rigat imbribus orbem,
cuius ad imperium populis sitientibus olim
delicuit rupes atque undis plurima fluxit.
Secreti nos interea mirarier omnes,
ipse sed admonitam atque ultro commissa fatentem
715 in lucem e tenebris altaque e nocte vocabat.
‘Saepe illi pueros aevo et florente puellas
flore comam pressos et molli fronde revinctos
summisere piae, metuunt dum cuncta, parentes,

their benightedness and call them to the light. For he would remind us that this was pleasing to the angels and to their Father,
and that it was for this very reason that he had been sent down
from heaven.

"He taught us how much joy filled the heavens and how much   690
pleasure the angels felt whenever some malefactor on earth, having
rejecting piety and fairness, began to cultivate justice and righteousness. It is as when, out of a flock of thousands, the incautious
shepherd loses one sheep that forgot to return with the herd late   695
at night, and the shepherd's eyes are searching for it in all directions among the rocks and underbrush; if perchance he finds the
sheep pasturing in a hidden vale, he seizes her at once and, carry-   700
ing her on his shoulders, happily bears her back into the fold. As
he enters his sweet children run to kiss him and the whole house
rejoices in the sheep's return. For this reason, our hero did not refuse to converse with women. Recently making his way in the
countryside, beneath the ancient walls of Sychar in Samaria, he   705
saw a woman coming by chance to a well. He begged water of her
and gladly drank the gift of the well—he who commands the sea
and sounding rivers, and waters the vast earth with abundant rain;
he at whose command a rock flowed with water for the thirsting   710
populace, issuing forth in an abundant stream. Secretly all of us
marveled, but after he had instructed her and she was freely confessing her sins, he called her forth out of darkness and deep night
into the daylight.   715

"Often mothers, pious and ever fearful, brought their children
to him, boys and girls in flourishing youth, their hair pressed with
flowers and tied back with pliant garlands. They wanted him to

quo teneris animis pulchrae virtutis amorem
720 insereret stimulisque rudes impleret honestis.
Impubem turbam affatus placido ore monebat
lustrabatque manu, ne carmina dira nocerent,
neve ulla infernis premeret vis edita ab oris.
'Quin etiam elatos animo super omnia acerbis
725 urgebat dictis rebusque exempla reliquit.
mecum olim socii, absentem dum quaerimus illum,
tendebant, fessique via consedimus omnes
speluncae ante fores, densis quam plurima opacat
frondibus et flexu ramorum protegit ulmus.
730 Multum hic inter nos quaerentes vana moramur,
quis nostrum foret e numero praestantior omni,
dilectusve ipsi magis acceptusve magistro.
Mira loquar: nos ut primum ipse in limine vidit,
haesit acerba tuens iterumque iterumque rogavit,
735 quis sermo foret aut quaenam certamina nobis.
Nos contra taciti nihil hiscere, dum piget omnes
verborum memores, fuerant quae plurima vana.
Tum subito ostendens puerum, cui mollibus annis
laudis adhuc erat et tumidi mens nescia flatus,
740 "Nulli fas," inquit, "superum aspirare beatis
conciliis, si non fastus dediscat inanes
et penitus famae exuerit contemptor amorem,
ceu puer hic nullam suspirat pectore laudem.
Non aliter coelum pateat. Prius aequore salso
745 esse queant nubes aut pisces vivere in arvis,
arboris aut stirpes frondescere in aetheris oris."
'Horret adhuc animus, mihi cum fratrique poposcit
illum praecipuos frustra pia mater honores,
scilicet aetherea superi genitoris ut aula
750 coelicolum in medio celsa cum sede sederet
subnixus, propior nostrum resideret uterque

instill in these young souls a love of sweet virtue, to fill their untutored hearts with honorable teachings. He kindly taught the 720
young, and blessed them with his touch so that no evil spell or infernal force could harm them.

"As for those whose minds were filled with pride, he used to rebuke them with especially harsh words, and taught by example as
well as precept. Once while he was away, some disciples set out 725
with me to find him. Weary of the journey, we all sat down by the
mouth of a cave, shaded by the dense leaves and protected by the
bending branches of an elm. We spent much time vainly wondering who among us was best loved by our teacher and most pleasing 730
to him. When he first saw us at the entrance (I will tell you something amazing) he stopped and looked sharply at us, demanding
to know what talk this was, what sort of competition we were having. But we remained silent, for we remembered what we had said 735
and we felt ashamed. Then, pointing to a young boy who knew
nothing of praise or self-importance, he said to us: 'Let no one aspire to the councils of heaven until he has learnt the vanity of titles 740
and thoroughly suppressed all love of fame, just as this child here
seeks no praise. Only thus does the path to heaven lie open.
Sooner will clouds be able to dwell in the salt sea and fish to haunt
the fields and trees to bloom suspended in the plains of the air.' 745

"I shudder to remember how my pious mother vainly asked,
when Jesus should reside in the heavenly halls of his Father, raised
up amid the angels, that my brother and I should be granted the
signal honor of sitting next to him, one clasping his right hand, 750
the other clinging to his left. At once he seemed angry, not at her

dextram alter iuxta amplexus, laevae alter inhaerens.
Extemplo gravis ille obtutuque asper acerbo
non matrem (quid enim mater pietate merebat?),
755 sed nos, qui vano ignaram summisimus astu,
corripuit meritos verbis haud mollibus urgens.
Usque deum premere elatos longeque superbos
averti, quos famae agitat, laudumque cupido.
      'Ipse ideo haud impar genitori cum sit, et illa
760 quae pater aeque eadem possit, tamen ora canentum
saepe sibi laudes genitorem vertit in ipsum,
nil se audere hominem supra confessus, ab alto
ni pater omnipotens vires aspiret Olympo.
Iccirco gravibus morbis quencunque levasset,
765 plerunque edixit ne factum proderet usquam.
Quove suas tegeret vires, cum tabida posset
hulcera corporibus solo depellere nutu,
aegros saepe tamen medicas legabat ad undas,
ut vitium exuerent omne auxiliaris aquae vi.
770 Quid referam quot eum populi, quot moenibus urbes
optavere sibi et voluere imponere regem,
mittentes trabeam sceptrumque sacramque tiaram?
Ipsi etiam comites hortatu instare frequentes,
armatus Syriae regnandam invaderet oram;
775 mox fore continuo, ut sua sub iuga mitteret armis
quodcunque Oceanus terrarum anfractibus ambit,
immensumque novis frenaret legibus orbem.
Cum vero hortantes urgerent, protinus ipse
occuluit sese montesque aufugit in altos.
780   'Immanes tamen invidia et crudelibus isti
insurgunt odiis poenasque uno ore reposcunt,
uniusque petunt caput omnes. Scis quibus illum
huc furiis traxere, quibus clamoribus omnem
implerunt trepidi captam velut hostibus urbem.

(for what blame could her piety merit?), but at us for duping her into this manipulative piece of vanity. And so he attacked us, deservedly, with no kind words. Ever thus does God abase self-important men. He spurns the proud and all those who are driven by love of fame and praise.

"He himself is by no means inferior to his Father and so can do all that his Father can. Yet when people sing his praises, he turns that praise upon his Father, confessing that he dares attempt nothing more than human, unless he be inspirited with strength from his Almighty Father in high heaven. For that reason, whenever he cured people of grievous illness, he mostly instructed them not to say what he had done. To conceal his powers, although he might, merely with a nod of his head, have banished the running sores from some body, still he would often send the sick to curative springs, so that all infirmity could be removed through the power of the waters. Why should I tell you how many peoples, how many walled cities chose him for their king, sending him their scepters and their sacred crown? His companions often urged him to take up arms, to invade and rule the shores of Syria. They assured him that, using force, he could soon place under his yoke whatever lands Ocean holds within its circling waters, and bridle the measureless orb with new laws. But when they pressed him with these exhortations, he would immediately flee and hide himself in the high mountains.

"But now, through envy and cruel hatred, these vile men rise up against him, and with one voice they all cry out for the head of one man. You know the rage that has brought these men to drag him to you, how in their fear they have filled the city with clamor, as though it had been captured by an enemy. In obedience to his Father's commands, the one person who surely deserves all things

785 Ipse patris mandata obiens tulit omnia certus
digna, indigna pati, nam se quaerentibus ultro
obtulit, et noctis cum munere posset opacae
defendi, bis se manifestum prodidit ipse.
Vidi illos tamen ad capti procumbere vocem
790 attonitos terramque gravi consternere casu.

'Nec vero sacris aut templo demit honorem
nec gentis leges veterumve edicta refigit,
quanvis visceribus monet et lustralibus extis
parcendum posthac, nec iam ultra caede litandum.
795 Verum alios longe ritus moremque sacrorum
indicat obscura verborum ambage latere,
legiferique aperit voces animumque magistri,
quodque magis mirere, sciunt et scire fatentur
aereas vatem venturum lucis ad auras,
800 unus qui nobis coeli invia claustra recludat,
e tenebrisque pios vehat alta ad sidera manes.
Id patribus promissum; omnes id voluere vates;
hunc animis certi expectant. Miseri quibus atris
non datur in tenebris praesentem agnoscere lucem
805 et mediis largi sitiunt in fluminis undis.
Nam quem non moveant, nisi prorsum aversa voluntas,
tanta viri virtus, tot facta ingentia, talis
oris honos? Ipse ut vidique hausique loquentem
et dulcem toto iactantem corpore amorem,
810 fortunas, patriam, genitricem, cuncta reliqui.
Id socii fecere. Neque hunc me deinde secutum
poenituit. Verum quantum ingens saepe favilla
surgit ab exigua semperque fit acrior ignis,
huius amor tantum visus mihi crescere in horas
815 et mage cor dulci semper flammescere cura.
Quique adiere semel, validis compagibus haerent.

has steadfastly suffered all things. For he has surrendered himself 785
willingly to those who pursued him, and though he could have escaped into the darkness of the night, he twice gave himself up to
them. Yet I have seen these same men fall prostrate at their captive's voice, striking the ground with a heavy fall. 790

"In truth he does not dishonor the rites of the temple or undo
either the laws of his race or the edicts of his forefathers, although
he teaches that hereafter we should forbear from offering the or-
gans of animals in atonement and from shedding blood in sacrifice. But he does show that very different rites and customs hide 795
under the obscurity of sacred words. He elucidates the words and
the meaning of our lawgiving teacher. And even more astonishing,
they know and openly admit that a prophet will emerge into the
light of day, who alone can open to us the impregnable gates of
heaven and lead the souls of the pious up to the stars. This was 800
promised to our ancestors. Our prophets predicted it and the
present generation awaits it. Pitiful are they who are so steeped in
darkness that they cannot see the light, who thirst beside an abundant stream. For who except someone of wayward will would not 805
be moved by this man's great virtue, his miraculous deeds and the
nobility of his countenance? When I myself first saw him and imbibed his words, when he sent forth sweet love from his entire
body, I abandoned my wealth, my country, my parents and everything else. The other disciples did the same thing. Nor do I have 810
any regrets in following him. Often has a fire grown from a little
spark, and it grows ever stronger! My love of him seems to me to
grow with each hour and my heart is ever aflame with tender care
for him. Whoever has seen him only once is joined to him by un- 815
breakable bonds.

'Nec nos aut donis aut verbis fallere crede
pollicitis blandis illectos. Omnia nobis
aspera promittit, cunctos diversa manere
820 scilicet exilia extorres passimque vagantes.
Promissis nec vana fides, adeo usque malorum
pullulat ex alia atque alia densissima silva.
Unius ferro tantum caput excipit; unum
(quisquis is est) placida clausurum lumina morte,
825 ast alios caedes omnis instare cruentas.
Nostra iubet nos interea contemnere opesque
partiri atque inopi miserorum impendere turbae
quos circunveniunt, morbique algorque famesque
pauperiemque pati rebusque assuescere egenis.
830 Multi nos ideo viderunt saepe per agros
aut silice in nuda proiectos ducere somnos
aut gravidas fessos rerum decerpere aristas,
indomitisque famem solari frugibus, undamque
alta haurire cavis pronos ad flumina palmis,
835 aut si quos usquam tellus dabat arida fontis.
Non mihi perpetuam si centum pectore aheno
sufficiant vocem linguae, percurrere possem
quantas quoque modo erumnas quantosque labores
hoc ducente animis durantes hausimus aequis.
840 Nam licet interdum penuria adaxit edendi
exhaustos rerumque inopes quas flagitat usus,
regum opibus tamen usque animos aequavimus altos
et mens in parvis aderat ditissima cuique.
'Nec minus ingentem huc comitum adventare novorum
845 cernere semper erat numerum, matresque virosque,
omnibus idem animus quibus et mens certa sequendi.
Haud secus ac bellum si cui rex maximus urbi
indixit, iamque arma ciet iamque agmina cogit,
cladem orae exitiumque ferens populisque ruinas,

"Nor should you imagine that he deceived us with words and gifts or seduced us with fine promises. Rather he assured us that everything would be hard, that our lot was to be scattered in exile and endless wandering. And that has proved to be the case. Dense   820 forests of evil arise, one after another. Only one will he exempt from the sword—whoever he may be—to die a peaceful death. But the rest of us can expect to die violently. Meanwhile Jesus bids   825 us hold what is ours in contempt, sharing our wealth and giving it to the indigent flock of poor people, galled by disease and hunger and cold, while we expose ourselves to disease, cold, hunger and poverty and accustom ourselves to want. Many people have seen us stretched out and sleeping in the fields or on some bare rock.   830 They have seen us wearily plucking stalks, satisfying our hunger with wild fruits, drinking with cupped hands the water of springs or any other stream that the dry earth yielded. Even if I had a   835 hundred tongues and a heart of brass, still I could not relate how many sorrows and labors we bore with equanimity, guided by him. For though we have suffered great hunger, exhaustion and poverty,   840 still, in our exalted souls, we felt as rich as kings, despite our humble circumstances.

"And a large number of new disciples could be seen joining us every day, men and women, all bent heart and soul on following   845 him. It was as if some great king had declared war on a city, brandishing arms and marshalling troops to bring slaughter and death to the land and ruin to the people: not only do the sworn troops

850 non tantum iurata manus lectaeque cohortes
incedunt, sed praeterea quos dirus habendi
duxit amor, varia cupidos ditescere praeda,
agglomerant multi atque iniussi castra sequuntur.
Non sat erant lataeque viae campique patentes
855 tot populis, iret quacunque, sequentibus ultro.
Saepe heros sese ingenti subducere turbae
et montes petere et desertos quaerere saltus.

'Atque equidem memini, cum propter stagna profectus
ferret iter passimque manus praetexeret ingens
860 littora et urgeret supra densissima morem,
proripuit sese ac cymbam, quae forte parata,
insiliit, subitoque iubens praecidere funem
teli intra iactum liquidum processit in aequor.
Constitit hinc, terramque aspectans plenaque circum
865 littora, divinis affari vocibus orsus,
iustitiaeque aperire viam et vestigia recti.
Hic illic stabant arrectis auribus omnes
interclusi undis, inhiabantque agmine longo
attoniti, miraque animos dulcedine capti.
870 Ipse loquebatur; circum sedata silebant
aequora, ubique modo spirantibus incita flabris,
frondiferaeque domus avium sine murmure circum
stabant immotae procurvo in littore silvae.
Sed non interea longaevae parcere matres
875 vocibus; illum omnes mirari insueta loquentem,
felicemque uteri matrem, felicia matris
hubera clamabant, quae talem enixa tulisset,
et teneris immulsisset[3] plena hubera labris.
'Nanque docebat humi foede in tenebrisque volutas
880 ad coelum mortale genus sustollere mentes
et lucem aspicere et vanis desuescere curis;
tum pacem hortari: "Placidam super omnia mites

and selected cohorts join in, but there are also men who follow the   850
camp unbidden, attracted by a love of gain, hoping to enrich
themselves on the spoils of war. So it was that neither the broad
roads nor the open fields sufficed for all the multitudes who eagerly followed wherever he might lead them. Often the hero re-   855
treated from the great crowd of his followers, seeking the mountains and deserted groves.

"I remember once, as he set out along the shallows to embark
on a voyage, a large number lined the shore and urged him on
with unusual zeal. But he hastened away, jumping into a skiff that   860
happened to be on hand. He ordered the rope to be cut quickly
and made his way through the clear waters, a spear-cast from
shore. He remained there, looking at the land and the shore full of
people. Then he began to speak with divine utterance, revealing   865
the path of justice and the way of right. On all sides people stood
in rapt attention, separated from him by the water, a multitude lis-
tening in gaping amazement, their hearts captivated by his marvelous sweetness. As he spoke, the sea, which just now had been agitated by the winds, became silent and calm. And the leafy glades,   870
home to birds, stood without murmur or motion along the curving strand. But the aged mothers did not refrain from speech.
Marveling at his wondrous words, they declared his mother   875
blessed in her womb. They blessed the breasts of the mother who
had borne such a child and had offered her breasts to his tender
lips.

"Indeed, he used to instruct the human race to lift its mind,
trapped in darkness, from the filthy earth to heaven, to look into   880
the light and cease from the pursuit of vanities. Then he would
urge peace upon them, saying, 'Above all, men, be gentle and

pacem optate viri, tumidosque remittite flatus,
demissique animis, nil vanae laudis egentes,
885 mortales contemnite opes, contemnite honores,
et duris vitam assueti parvoque beati,
pauperiem tolerate. Brevis quaecunque voluptas
ista adeo atque diu nihil est mortalibus aegris.
Vobis haud propriae hic sedes, concessaque longum
890 regna manent meliora, graves ubi solverit artus
mors anima, vos stelligera pater optimus aula
protinus excipiet laetos melioribus oris,
pax ubi tranquilla et cunctarum opulentia rerum
et secura quies, nunquam peritura voluptas.
895 Et dubitet tanta quisquam mercede laborem
ferre brevem terrisque sequi me sponte relictis?
Ad veras emergere opes, emergere honores
tendite, quos nulli casus, nulla auferat aetas.
Este pii; inter vos mentem exercete benignam,
900 inque vicem placati animis miserescite vestri.
Tum longe prohibete iras, odiisque ferendo
parcite, rumoresque vagos contemnite vulgi.
Nulli fas ideo accepto pro vulnere vulnus
reddere, praestiterit vero pulsantibus ultro
905 sese offerre, genisque ictum expectare secundum.
Vana alii certent armis pro laude nocensque
ferrum acuant pulchramque petant per vulnera mortem.
At tu mortales nullo discrimine amare
disce omnes pacemque inglorius hostibus opta,
910 nec tibi ventosae sint tanti murmura famae.
Omnibus in primis sit mens interrita leti,
nullaque vos animis duros vis avocet aequo.
Terrenos artus homines moribundaque membra
interdum extinxisse queant et perdere ferro;
915 tuta anima ipsa manet durae haud obnoxia morti.

choose the tranquillity of peace; put aside all pride and boastful-
ness. With humble hearts and no desire for empty praise, hold
honors in contempt. Accustom your souls to hardship. Be happy   885
with little and accept poverty, for brief are the pleasures of this
world, and nothing remains for long among weary mortals. Where
you now live is not your true home. A better kingdom awaits you,
granted as of old, when death shall free your soul from the weight
of your body. Then will the Supreme Father accept you rejoicing   890
into his starry hall, a better place. There reign serene peace and an
abundance of all things, rest and security and never-ending joy.
And who would hesitate to labor briefly for so great a reward, to   895
leave the earth and follow me? Make haste to come into your true
wealth and honors, which no vicissitude or passing of years can
ever diminish. Be pious and kind to one another. At peace in your
souls, take pity on one another. Keep anger far from you and re-   900
spond to hatred with patience. Hold in contempt the fickle voices
of the crowd. It is not right for any man to repay one blow with
another. Rather should he offer himself willingly to his attackers
and expect a second blow on his cheek. Let others take up arms in   905
pursuit of empty glory. Let others sharpen their lethal swords and
seek a glorious death through wounds in battle. Rather you should
learn to love all men without difference, and choose to live in
peace and anonymity with your enemies, paying no heed to the
murmurs of empty fame. Most important of all is that each man   910
be able to look on death without fear. Let no force seduce your
disciplined souls from the path of justice. For the swords of men
may sometimes extinguish and destroy the earthly body and the
mortal parts of a man. But the soul, unharmed, is not susceptible
to harsh death. For the Almighty Father is watching over you from   915

Et vos omnipotens coelo pater aspicit alto
avertitque malis, cuius sine numine vestrum
haud hominum quisquam valeat divellere crinem.
Summissos vos hunc unum fas usque vereri;
920   huic o rite preces, huic digna piacula ferte,
cui mare, cui tellus campisque patentibus aer
obsequitur, nitidique tremit plaga lucida coeli.
Huic procumbite humi, prostrati huic pandite vota,
vos⁴ siquidem aeternis etiam post funera poenis
925   ipse potest sontes sub tetro urgere barathro.
Nec timor admissos cuiquam sit adire leones
seclaque pictarum saevissima pantherarum.
Ite mei obiectu protecti nominis; ite
adversum intrepidi. Mansuescent protinus ursi
930   vestraque parcentes allambent vulnera lingua.
Quin humiles victus animis secludite curas.
Observate genus pecudum, genus altivolantum:
nullae illis artes, nulla illis cura futuri.
Non tamen aut tegimen, victus aut copia defit.
935   Omnia dives alit rerum sator, omnia curat.
Ille etiam iniusso tellurem gramine vestit,
floribus appingens sata versicoloribus arva,
arboribusque comas atque umbras montibus addit.
    '"Fraudes insidiaeque absint ac foeda libido,
940   neve modum supra mensis gaudete paratis,
desidiasque animis atque ocia pellite vestris.
Nec vetitos thalamos inconcessumque cubile
affectate, sitisque alieni desinat auri.
Quisque suis opibus contenti vivite, et ultro
945   spes interdictas et inania ponite vota.
Neve autem scelerum facies nunc persequar omnis,
quid dicam quibus est cordi fraus atque libido
dira iuvat, ficto simulant tamen ore latentes

high heaven and will protect you from evil. Without his consent, there is no man who can harm a hair on your head. You must obe- diently fear God alone. Direct your prayers and due offerings to 920 him who rules the sea, the earth and the open fields of air. Even the shining plains of heaven honor him. So bow down on the ground before him and offer up your prayers, seeing that he has the power to afflict you even after death, if you are guilty, with eternal punishment in the dark pit of hell. Let no man fear to ap- 925 proach ravening lions or the savage breed of spotted panthers. Rather go forth protected by the warrant of my name. Go forth without fear. Bears will prove tame and mercifully lick your wounds. Verily, do not trouble your souls with the necessities of 930 life. Observe the fishes and the birds; they have no crafts and no thought for the future. Yet they do not want for shelter or abun- dance of food. The creator of the universe nourishes and cares for 935 all things. He clothes the earth with grass unbidden and spangles the seeded fields with flowers of every hue. He gives leaves to the trees and shadows to the mountains.

"'Keep treachery and deceit at bay and low desires, nor take im- moderate pleasure in feasting. Reject laziness and indolence in 940 your souls. Lust not after illicit couplings or forbidden loves and suppress all thirst for the gold of others. Let each man live happily in his own wealth and willingly set aside forbidden hopes and vain wishes. Not to catalogue all the forms of sin, what should I say of 945 those who, though false of heart and slave to base desire, yet imi-

virtutem subeuntque dolis et crimina obumbrant?
950 Ne, iubeo, ne talem animis assuescite pestem.
Nil adeo latet, ipsa dies quin detegat ultro.
Praeterea cohibete oculos; ne quaerite vestris
vulnera sponte animis. Fandi hinc compescite amorem;
saepe olim incautos non lingua coercita mersit.
955 Discite iamque ideo posthac haud falsa profari,
iamque novos purgati animis inducite mores.
Si qua tamen veteris culpae vestigia restant,
diluite et sacris contagia vincite lymphis.
Ipse ego fons veluti liquidam purissimus undam
960 sufficiam. Properate ad aquas; haurite liquentem
matres atque viri sitientes protinus amnem.
Ferte pedem huc omnes. Nec opus potantibus auro
argentove: mei fontis patet omnibus unda.
Sic leti vitate vias; ita sidera aditur
965 sidereasque domos, mutari nescia regna.
Haec mihi praedixit genitor, quae voce monerem
veridica; sunt fonte mihi verba omnia ab illo."

    'Talia dicta dabat, coeli super omnia regem
placandum non visceribus, non sanguine caeso,
970 sed votis precibusque, iubens exposcere pacem.
Et modus orandi quisnam foret ipse canebat:
"Omnipotens genitor, sedes cui lucidus aether,
sic nomen laudesque tuae celebrentur ubique,
et promissa orbi incipiant procedere lustra,
975 cum tua non minus in terris gens iussa facessat
mortalis, quam coelicolae tibi in aethere parent.
Nos divina hodie coelo dape reffice ab alto.
Parce dehinc bonus, ut nostris ignoscimus ipsi
hostibus, ac nullis adversis obiice inermes
980 tentando, prohibe a nobis sed cuncta pericla."

tate virtue with fair-seeming and conceal their crimes through deceit? I bid you not to accustom your souls to such a pestilence. For nothing can hide; indeed, time itself will bring it to light. Then control your gaze. Do not go looking for things to wound your souls. And suppress your love of chatter. Often has an unchecked tongue brought trouble to incautious men. Learn then to speak no untruth. Having purified your souls, learn new habits. And if some trace of your former sins remains, wipe that pestilence away and vanquish it with holy water. Like a pure spring I shall provide a clear stream. Hasten to its waters. Drink the draughts, all you men and women who thirst. Come hither, everyone. You need no gold or silver coin to drink. The waters of my stream are open to all. In this way will you avoid the paths of death and reach heaven and the starry realms that know no change. For so was I taught by my Father that I might teach it with the voice of truth, and all my words are from his source.'

"So he spoke, ordering us not to propitiate the king of heaven with entrails and spilt blood, but with prayers, and bidding us to pray for peace. He himself told us how to pray to him: 'Almighty Father, enthroned in the brilliant sky, may your name and your praises be sung everywhere, and may the promised ages begin to descend upon the earth, when the race of mortals does thy will, no less than the angelic orders of heaven. Feed us today our divine meal from heaven above. Kindly pardon us even as we forgive our enemies, and do not expose us, defenseless, to temptation, but protect us from all dangers.'

950
955
960
965
970
975
980

'Addidit et ventura canens, fore cum vagus olim
sol claram speciem concreto lumine tectus
exuat, et subito stellanti nocte perempta
sufficiat nullam luna orbi argentea lucem,
985 sanguineis faciem maculis perfusa nigrantem,
praecipitentque polo passim turbata labanti
sidera, quae lapsu certo spatiove feruntur.
Visque ea, quae coeli irrequietos conciet orbes,
desinat, incerto rapiantur ut omnia motu,
990 atque prope avulso absiliat de cardine mundus,
dum terras veluti rapidum per inania fulmen
ipse iterum petat, et multis cum millibus idem
adveniens hominum vitas, et crimina quaerat.
Ut res promisso simul ac succenderit igni
995 flammarum totum tempestas sparsa per orbem,
continuo tellure nova coeloque recenti
defunctas animas vita in sua corpora rursus
evocet ad blandum lumen populosque sepulcris
eliciat, secumque pios educat ad astra,
1000 quos pater a prima praevidit origine rerum
mente suos fore et aethereo transcripsit Olympo.
Ibunt aligeri iuvenes coelumque profundum
horrifico sonitu implebunt atque aere recurvo
quattuor a ventis excibunt undique gentes.
1005 'Iudicis ad solium properabitur aethere toto.
Ipse alte effultus, montisque in vertice summo
arbiter effulgens circunferet ora tremenda,
secernetque pios, dextraque in parte locabit.
Laeva autem coget sontes, quae plurima turba.
1010 Qualis post hyemem exactam, cum gramine molli

"Foretelling the future, he spoke of a time when the wandering sun, covered in murky light, will throw off its brilliance. And the silvery moon, suddenly stricken from the starry night, will offer no more light, its blackened face covered in blood-red stains. And the 985 stars, jarred out of that determined course that guides them now, will fall headlong through the foundering firmament. Then that force that moves the ever-restless orbs of heaven will cease and all things will be thrown into chaos. The universe will nearly become 990 unhinged and fly off through the emptiness of space, until he himself comes back to earth, like a bolt of lightning through the empty air. Then will he descend and inquire of the millions about their lives and misdeeds. And as soon as a fire-storm has spread through the whole world and consumed the universe with its promised flames, then immediately on the new earth and in the 995 new heavens he will summon all souls back to their bodies, back to life and to the sweet light of day. From their graves he will call forth the multitudes. Up into heaven he will lead the pious, whom, from the beginning of the world, God foresaw as one day 1000 being his, and so he inscribed them in his celestial book. Winged angels will fill the depths of heaven with a terrifying noise. And with the sounding of a curved trumpet, all the races will come forward from the four quarters of the earth.

"Throughout heaven, all will rush before his throne. Seated 1005 atop a lofty mountain, he will shine forth, a judge, and cast his terrible glance all around him. He will separate out the souls of the just and place them on his right. But the majority, who are sinners, he will place upon his left: as when, at winter's end, the soft grass of the fertile fields calls forth the cattle from the newly-opened sta- 1010

pascua laeta vocant stabulis armenta reclusis,
ipse greges pastor nitidos missurus in agros
sortitur; placidas primo legit ille bidentes
dinumerans, olidasque iubet procul esse capellas.
1015 Cernere erit liquidas longe fulgere per auras
corpora clara hominum, quibus atrae obnoxia morti
abluet omnipotens pater, aeternumque manebunt
amplius haud rerum subiecti casibus ullis.
Nemo illam ante diem speret cum corpore sedes
1020 aetheris, exceptis paucis quos ipse sepulcro
exurgens secum superis deus invehet oris.
Solae animae interea tali statione fruentur.
Contra autem sontes tenebris ac nocte prementur
aeterna, et meritas pendent per secula poenas.
1025   'Omnia quae sera nuper mihi nocte canebat,
cum caput, ipsius in gremio moerore gravatum,
una eadem accumbens sponda, admotusque loquenti
saepe reclinarem, moesti solamen amoris.
Quid repetam quae saepe vagi Iordanis ad undas
1030 ediderit? Quae Iudaeae sub montibus altis
nunc caecis vera involvens ambagibus ultro,
nunc manifesta palam claro sermone loquutus,
dum populi circunsistunt stipantque frequentes?
Nunc se principium rerum finemque canebat;
1035 nunc veri fontem atque hominum lucemque viamque.
Nos fortunatam prognatam hoc tempore prolem!
Nos felix tellus, nos secula laeta tulere!
Nobis divinam vocem divina loquentis
verba haurire dei propius saepe obtigit unis.
1040 Scilicet hinc lustris veniet labentibus aetas,
cum seri optabunt eadem vidisse nepotes.'
Talia Ioannes cunctis mirantibus ore
perstabat memorans, cum protinus ecce tumultu

bles, and the pastor divides his flock and sends them into the bright fields: he first counts and selects the gentle sheep and keeps the rank-smelling goats far off. Even so, from afar through the clear air it will be possible to see the shining bodies of men. The Almighty Father will cleanse their mortal bodies, exposed to dark death, so that they remain eternally beyond the reach of chance or change. Before that day, let no one expect that his body will go to heaven, except for a few whom God himself at his Resurrection will take from their tombs and carry up with him. In the meantime, only the souls will enjoy that station. As for the guilty, they will be oppressed by eternal darkness and night, and they will pay the penalty they deserve.

"All this he told me late one night, when my sorrow-burdened head lay upon his lap as we reclined upon the same couch. Often I drew near to him as he spoke, finding some solace for my sad love. Why should I repeat what he often taught beside the waves of the wandering Jordan or on the hill-tops of Judea? Sometimes he would cloak his words in obscure ambiguities; sometimes he would declare them openly in clear language, while all the people came and crowded around him. He would say now that he was the beginning and the end of all things, now the fountain of truth, the light and path of men. How fortunate we are to be born at this time, into a fecund earth and a happy age, for it fell to us alone to hear directly the divine voice of God, speaking of things divine. Surely hereafter, when many years have passed, generations to come will wish to have seen what we have seen."

Such were the words that John spoke, to universal admiration. He was continuing to relate these things when all at once an impi-

ingenti Solymum irrumpit manus impia, et urbis
1045   rectorem appellant poenasque uno ore reposcunt.
Diffugiunt ambo, et magnam stat adire parentem,
ignaramque diu tantarum fallere rerum.

ous crowd of citizens rushed noisily in before Pilate and cried out
unanimously for punishment. John and Joseph fled. They decided   1045
to go his illustrious mother, Mary, but to keep her long in ignorance of all that was taking place.

LIBER V

Insonti vero Romanus parcere capto
toto corde petens, huc mentem dividit atque huc.
Fama viri virtusque animo egregiique recursat
oris honos, nec iam obscurum genus esse deorum.
5   Omnia respondent auditis. Denique ad ipsos
conversus Solymos fremitu tectum omne replentes,
'Ite,' ait, 'et posito mox huc certamine adeste.
Sit qui pro cunctis numero delectus ab omni
fando aliquis doceat, quo tandem is crimine morte
10 mulctandus, quod tantum obstet scelus, ordine pandat
insonti. Simul haec, simul illi abiere frementes
Christo animis certi nunquam desistere vivo.

    Parte alia, regem qui foede prodidit hosti,
mutatus scelus agnoscit periurus Iudas.
15 Ah miser, infectum quam vellet posse reverti!
Nulla quies animo; saevire in pectore dirae
ultrices caecasque ob noxam sumere poenas,
nec capit insanos curarum pectore fluctus.
Hinc secum aera manu sceleris causam attulit amens,
20 quae Solymi magno dederant in munere pacta,
atque sacerdotum sacrata ad limina venit
vociferans: 'Vestrum hoc argentum, haec munera vestra,
accipite! En scelerum pretium exitiale repono.
Heu heu, quid demens volvi mihi? Quo scelus ingens
25 inductus pretio admisi? Vera dei ille
progenies verusque deus—nunc denique cerno;
discussaeque abeunt tenebrae et mihi reddita mens est.'
Sic fatus, simul argentum coniecit in ipsos.
Olli autem flentem risere ac sera videntem.

BOOK V

With all his heart the Roman governor wanted to spare his innocent captive, and his thoughts went in many directions. In his mind he kept returning to Christ's renown and virtue and fine appearance and he was no longer in doubt about the man's divine origins. Everything he had observed corresponded with what Joseph and John had just told him. Finally he turned to the citizens of 5 Solomon's city, who filled the hall with their raucous cries. "Go now and come back when this quarrel has been settled," he said. "Choose someone from this great throng to speak for all the rest and explain to me in detail for what crime this man is to be found guilty and punished with death." At once the crowd went away 10 murmuring, determined never to relinquish their anger as long as Christ lived.

In another part of the city, the faithless Judas, who basely betrayed his king to the enemy, now recognized his crime and repented. How he would have wished to undo what he had done! He had no peace of mind, haunted as he was by vengeful furies 15 ready to exact savage punishment for his deed. He couldn't bear the anguish that flooded his heart with madness. Grasping the coins that had tempted him to commit his crime, his reward from the citizens of Jerusalem, Judas shouted at the sacred doors of the 20 priests. "Here is your silver! Here is your reward! Take it! I give back to you the deadly wages of sin. What was I thinking in my madness? What price could have induced me to commit such a crime? He is the true Son of God, the true God—I finally see it. 25 The clouds have vanished and now my sanity returns." So speaking, he threw the pieces of silver at them. But they only mocked his tears and his belated recognition of the truth, and so he bitterly departed.

30   Infelix abit. Hinc amens caecusque furore
multa putat; curae ingeminant, saevitque sub imo
corde dolor, coelique piget convexa tueri.
Tum secum huc illuc flammantia lumina torquens:
'Hem, quid agam infelix? Quaenam quae secula porro
35   sera adeo tantum scelus unquam oblita silebunt?
Accedamne iterum supplex crimenque fatebor,
atque ausim veniam sceleri sperare nefando?
Quo vero aspiciam vultu, quove alloquar ore
quem semel indignum decepimus inque merentem?
40   Hinc igitur longe fugiam, quantum ire licebit,
ignotusque aliis agitabo in finibus aevum?
Hinc me praecipites me me hinc auferte procellae,
quo fugit usque dies a nobis luce peracta!
At quis erit tutus tandem locus? Omnia praesens
45   aspicit ac terras deus undique fulmine terret.
Et me conscia mens atque addita cura sequetur,
sive iter arripiam pedibus seu puppe per undas.
Quos? Quibus? At moror, et ludunt insomnia mentem.
Vos precor o mihi vos magnae nunc hiscite terrae.
50   Quid dubito? Nunc te tangunt scelera impia, Iuda
infelix! Tunc debueras, tunc ista decebant,
cum revocare pedem, cum fas occurrere pesti.
Nunc morere atque nefas tu tantum ulciscere dextra
sponte tua lucemque volens hominesque relinque!'
55   Talia iactabat certus iam abrumpere vitam
invisam et saevum leto finire dolorem,
curarum hanc unam metam ratus atque laborum.
Fluctuat atque sibi semper tellure videtur
absumi aut rapido de coelo afflarier igni.
60   Usque adeo ante oculos capti obversatur imago.

Maddened and blind with rage, his mind was racing. As his 30
cares redoubled, sorrow raged deep in his heart. He hated to look
upon the vault of heaven. His eyes flashed all about and he asked
himself, "What age to come will be so remote that it will forget
and fall silent about so great a crime? Should I go back, a suppli- 35
ant, and confess my crime? Dare I hope to be forgiven for this terrible offense? How can I look at, how can I address this man
whom I have deceived, this man who so little deserved it? Perhaps
I should flee from here, as far as I can go, living in obscurity in 40
some other land. Winds, carry me hence to where the sun flees
when day is done! But what place will be safe? God is present everywhere and sees everything; he can strike any land with his
dread thunder. But care and a guilty conscience will follow me 45
wherever I go, whether I run away or sail the seas. And whom
shall I run to? From whom should I flee? But I am wasting time.
Idle dreams delude my mind. I implore you, great earth, open and
swallow me up. Why do I wait? Now your impious deeds are
coming home to you, unhappy Judas! You should have had such 50
thoughts long before this. That was the time to step back and
fight this pestilence. Now die and avenge this great infamy with
your own hand! Of your own will, leave the company of men and
the light of day!"

Such were his thoughts as he decided to end his hateful life and 55
all its raging pain. He saw no other way to stop the anguish and
anxiety. But still he hesitated. He seemed to be swallowed up by
the earth, to be struck down by the violent fire of heaven. Before
his eyes was the ever-present image of the captive. His face grew 60

Pallor in ore, acies circunlita sanguine et artus
algentes tremit, instantis vestigia leti,
et nox multa cava faciem circunvolat umbra.
Omnia nigrescunt tenebris caliginis atrae.
65   Demens, qui potius veniam sperare fatendo
non ausus, neque enim precibus non flectitur ullis
rex superum et iustae bonus obliviscitur irae.
    Ergo ille inceptis perstans et sedibus haerens
isdem abiit silvaeque tremens successit opacae,
70   regia quae propter frondebat plurima tecta,
atque ibi, dum trepidat, qua tandem morte quiescat
incertus — latebrasne animae scrutetur acuto
fortiter et pectus procumbens induat ense,
an se praecipiti iaciat de culmine saltu —
75   ipsae quae attonitum mortisque cupidine captum
ducebant semper furiae infensaeque praeibant,
informem prona nectentes arbore nodum
ostendere viam. Collo nanque inde pependit,
ut meritus, laqueoque infami extrema sequutus
80   spiramenta animae eliso gutture rupit,
et totos subito pendens extabuit artus.
    Nondum picta novo coeli plaga mane rubebat,
iamque sacerdotes concursu cuncta replentes
vestibulum iuxta astabant longisque fremebant
85   porticibus. Nempe antiquo de more licebat
ulli luce sacra pollutum insistere limen.
Tandem Romulides iuvenum stipante caterva
fascibus egreditur patriis ostroque superbus
et solio ante fores sedit sublimis eburno.
90   Consedere patres pariter iuxta ordine et ipsi
atque diu siluere. Orsus dux denique fatur:
'Dicite quo tandem demitti crimine morti
poscitis egregium iuvenem. Quaesivimus ipsi

pale, his eyes were bloodshot and his body trembled in pain—
signs of impending death—as the ever-gathering shadows of night
shrouded his face. Insane, he dared not hope for pardon through
confession, though the King of Angels is always swayed by prayers   65
and of his goodness forgets his righteous anger.

Sticking to his plan and his usual haunts, the trembling Judas
went to the dark, dense woods that grew beside the royal palace.
Because of his fear, he was uncertain which form of death to   70
choose. Should he bravely fall upon his sword and let it probe the
hiding place of his soul? Or should he fling himself headlong from
a cliff? But the Furies, who constantly goaded and cruelly pursued
this frightened and suicidal man, finally revealed to him the path   75
of death by fixing a shameful noose to a sloping tree. He hanged
himself with that infamous noose, as he deserved. As it broke his
neck, he wheezed out his last breath, and his hanging body in-   80
stantly shriveled up.

The field of heaven was not yet painted anew with red dawn,
and the priests stood in a solid mass outside the entrance to the
palace, quarreling under the porticoes. For by ancient custom no   85
man on a holy day was permitted to cross an unsanctified threshold. Finally Pilate came forward, followed by a crowd of young
men. He was resplendent in his purple robes and Roman symbols
of office, and sat before the entrance, raised up on an ivory throne.
The fathers likewise sat down in order and were long silent.
Finally the ruler began to speak. "Tell me then for what crime you   90
want this fine young man to be executed. I myself inquired into

et genus et vitam; nil dignum morte repertum,
95   sed potius factis fama illum ingentibus effert.
Ut propius vinctum vidi audivique loquentem,
ut stupui! Ut visus mihi nil mortale sonare,
cuncta deo similis vultum vocemque oculosque!
Aut certe deus ille, dei aut certissima proles.
100 Cedite. Ne regem vestrum ignorate volentes.'
     His dictis cunctis penitus dolor ossibus arsit
ingens. Infremuere omnes gemitumque dedere.
Tum senior surgit fandi doctissimus Annas
in medio et dictis exorsus talibus infit.
105 'Si tibi non aliis per se manifesta pateret
res signis, Romane, vel hinc dignoscere promptum
cuique foret, teque in primis dux multa moveri
convenit, huc cum tot collectos undique cives
convenisse vides unius crimina contra.
110 Hic auctor fandi multos sermone fefellit,
et facie (ne cede dolis) mentitur honesta
virtutem. Scelerum tegit alto in pectore amorem.
Nonne vides, haec relligio quo se nova vertat,
orgia quo, coetusque et nocturni comitatus?
115 Seditione potens Iudaeas suscitat urbes,
ausus se passim terrarum dicere regem
progeniemque patris summi, cui sidera parent.
Atque ideo veluti deus ultro crimina fassis
dat veniam poenaeque metum post funera solvit,
120 quod scelus haud aliter poterit quam morte piare;
sic veteres sanxere. Sed et vetera ipse retractans
iura, novas figit simulato numine leges,
instituitque novos ritus, nova sacra per urbes,
quae servent seri ventura in secla nepotes.
125   'Quin ipsas haud obscura, pro! voce minatur
deiecturum aras, seque igni templa daturum,

his life and ancestry and have found nothing worthy of death. Rather fame exalts him for his great deeds. How I marveled when I first encountered the captive and heard him speak! He seemed to utter nothing mortal. His face, his voice, his eyes—in these he was like a god! If not a god himself, he is most certainly the son of a God. Yield to him. Do not obstinately refuse to avow your king."

But no sooner had he spoken than his listeners felt an enormous sense of grievance burning deep within their bones. They all raged and groaned. Then the aged Annas, the most eloquent among them, stood up in their midst and began to speak: "Roman, if this matter is not clear to you from other signs, it should be self-evident to everyone—and this concerns you especially as ruler—from the fact that so many citizens have hastened here to oppose one man's crime. This glib orator has deceived many with his speech and with an honest-looking face that feigns virtue. But do not be deceived. In his heart he has a deep love of crime. Don't you see the purpose of this new religion, of its secret rites and meetings and nocturnal covens? Gaining strength by sedition, he awakens all the cities of Judaea, daring to call himself everywhere the king of the world and the Son of the Supreme Father, whom even the stars obey. And as though he were God, he presumes to pardon those who have confessed their sin, releasing them from punishment after death. Such a crime cannot be answered by anything other than execution. For so our forefathers commanded. Abolishing old rights on his own authority, he decrees new laws on the basis of his pretended divinity and establishes new rites and new sacraments among the cities, for our distant offspring to preserve.

"And what is more, in no uncertain terms he threatens to overturn the altars and set fire to the temples that our forefathers built

95

100

105

110

115

120

125

templa olim impensis tantorum structa laborum.
Et iam iam volet ipsum etiam restinguere solem
sideraque obsesso verbis deducere coelo.
130 Haud scelus ille tamen fallaci pectore quivit
dissimulare diu, neque enim scelerata subire
tecta horret, nec se vetitis conventibus aufert
admonitus, sociique epulis capiuntur opimis.
Quin etiam, interdum si qua tota impius urbe
135 inventus fama ante alios ob crimina notus,
continuo paribus gaudens adit impiger illum,
nec requies donec sibi conciliarit amicum.
Tantus amor scelerum, tantum illi fallere cordi.
Tum festis, cum fas nihil exercere diebus,
140 ipse tamen pellit morbos aegrisque medetur.
Quid memorem, ut socii vetitis impune per aedes
vescantur dapibus, cereremque et pocula tractent
haud prius ablutis manibus sine more, sine ullis
legibus immundi, contactuque omnia foedent?
145 Scilicet omnipotens placitos tot secula ritus
retractet pater et mentem sententia vertat.
Quae nova tempestas? Eane inconstantia coelo?
Dede neci! Ne thuricremas, quibus imminet, aras
destruat, et posthac non ausit talia quisquam.
150 Dede neci! Poenas sceleri impius hauriat aequas.
A sacris prohibe infandos altaribus ignes.'
Dixerat, atque omnes eadem simul ore fremebant.
  Romulus at dictis nequicquam flectitur ullis.
Nec nova primum audit nunc crimina. Cuncta nefando
155 scit fabricata odio, dum Christi gloria et ingens
sacrilegos stimulis virtus exercet amaris,
atque ait: 'Haec coram fama est vos saepius illi
obiecisse, quibus semper sermone paratus
restitit, et vera victor ratione refellit.

with such toil. Surely the time will come when with his spells he
will want to restrain the sun in its course and draw down the stars
from a vanquished heaven. But his lying heart could hardly con- 130
ceal his crimes for long, since he scarcely scruples to enter sinful
homes and, though warned, he does not avoid forbidden con-
gresses, while his disciples revel in lavish feasts. If anywhere in this
city someone stands out for villainy, Jesus runs to him at once, like 135
to like, and doesn't rest until he has won the man's friendship.
Such is the love of sin and deceit that lives in his heart. And then
on holy days, when no labor is to be performed, he cures diseases
and tends to the sick. And do I need to mention that, in many 140
homes, his disciples eat forbidden meals without penalty, that they
take bread and wine without having washed their hands according
to custom? Unrestrained by any law, they basely defile everything
they touch. As though the Almighty Father would retract the sacred rites that have pleased him for so long! As though he had 145
changed his mind! What new age is being born? It this incon-
stancy the fault of heaven? Put him to death! Don't let him destroy the incense-filled altars, as he has threatened to do, and let
no one after him dare to do the same! Kill him! Let him receive 150
his just punishment. Let no impious fires touch the sacred altars."
So he spoke, and all the rest roared their approval.

But the Roman was unmoved by any of these words. For this
was not the first time he had heard such accusations; he knew that
they were all fabrications created by the unspeakable hatred of 155
Christ's impious enemies, on whom his glory and great virtue
worked like harsh goads. So Pilate said, "It is well known that you
have often made such accusations, which he has always readily re-
futed and victoriously repelled with right reason. He himself does

160 Nec se progeniem superi negat ipse parentis,
    quem vos promissum coelo divinitus olim
    venturum tandem auxilio mortalibus aegris
    non latet, ut veteres genitoris molliat iras
    concilians generi vestro, culpamque parentum
165 ipse sua virtute luat. Sic ferre priorum
    accepi monimenta, patres id prodere vestros,
    et rebus probat ipse. Adeo circum oppida lustrans
    arrexit totam monstris ingentibus oram,
    quae non ullae artes hominum, non ulla potest vis.
170 Quin etiam in lucem quosdam revocavit ab umbris,
    quis penitus iam mors totos immissa per artus
    solverat haerentes animae de corpore nexus.
    Quare agite o odiis miseri desuescite iniquis!
    Ne frustra pugnate, deum sed discite vestrum.'
175   Dixerat. At magis atque magis violentia gliscit
    omnibus. Ingenti clamore insistere et una
    infreni saevire humerisque abscindere amictum.
    Nec secus increvere animis ardentibus irae
    quam cum Athesimve Padumve undis laeta arva parantem
180 diluere agricolae subiti compescere tendunt
    aggeris obiectu, praeceps magis aestuat amnis
    insultans, victorque altas ruit agmine moles.
       Forte autem rex et soboles hoc tempore regum
    Herodes studio sacrorum advenerat urbem.
185 Munere Romulidum pars huic amissa paterni
    reddita erat regni, Galilaeaeque oppida habebat.
    Quem postquam accepit rector Romanus adesse,
    solveret ingrato quo sese munere tandem,
    transmisit Galilaeum illi vinctum Galilaeo,
190 atque ipsum iussit vitamque et crimina, si qua,
    quaerere pro meritisque viro decernere poenas.
    Tum vero audito Christi rex nomine laetus

not deny that he is the Son of his Father, that, heaven-sent, he has   160
come to you at last, as promised, to help ailing mortals and to rec-
oncile your people with his Father's long-standing anger, even as
he wipes away the sins of your ancestors with his own virtues. I
understand that your ancient scripture predicts his coming, that   165
your forefathers foretold it, and his deeds prove it. And so, passing
through the surrounding cities, he aroused the whole land with his
great miracles, which no force or skill of man could perform. Indeed, he has even recalled to life those whose souls death fully sev-   170
ered from their bodies. Therefore desist, O miserable men, from
this wicked hatred! Do not oppose him in vain, but recognize him
as your god."

So he spoke. But the crowd became ever more violent. Stead-   175
fast in fury, they raged without restraint and tore their cloaks from
their backs. Their incensed souls were like the Adige or Po as it
prepares to inundate a wide expanse of fields. Though the farmers
hasten to contain it by building earthworks, the river swells even   180
more, overleaping the bulwark and victoriously overturning the
lofty piles.

It happened at this time that Herod, the king and son of kings,
reached the city, eager to perform the Passover rites. Through a
gift of the Romans, part of his lost kingdom was restored to him   185
and he held sway over the cities of Galilee. Hearing that he had
arrived, the Roman governor sought to free himself from a thank-
less task. He remanded the bound Galilean to the illustrious Galilean. Then he bade Herod inquire into Jesus's life and crimes, if   190
any there were, and so pronounce a just penalty. When Herod
heard Christ's name, he was delighted and ordered him to be

duci intro iubet, ingenti correptus amore
compellare virum ac propius vera ora tueri.
195 Quem dehinc aggreditur vario sermone, sed ille
nil contra atque oculos nusquam avertebat Olympo.
Ergo illum nil supra hominem miratus, et ultro
irridens iterum iubet ad praetoria duci,
et rursum haud laeto Romano redditur insons.
200   Hic me deficiunt animi, mens labitur aegra.
Horresco meminisse, dei quae vera propago
pertulerit mala factus homo deus, auctor Olympi,
quem mare, quem tellus vacuique patentia tractus
atria nec capit immensi plaga lucida coeli.
205 Aura tuo omnipotens vires mihi reffice lapsu,
aura polo demissa, tuo hic me numine firma.
Haec animi victus quoties evolvere tento,
omnia me circum nigrescunt. Pallida cerno
astra caputque atra roseum ferrugine solem
210 occulere et moestum in lachrymas se solvere coelum.
Tantane te pietas miserantem incommoda nostra,
tantus adegit amor, coeli o lux clara sereni,
vera dei ut soboles, verus deus aethere missus
tam gravia haec velles perpessuque aspera ferre,
215 divinumque caput terrena mole gravatus
subiiceres tot sponte malis? Haec praemia ferres,
nostra tua bonus ut deleres crimina morte?
Nos dulces vetita decerpsimus arbore foetus,
tu trunco infando pendens crudele luisti
220 supplicium, o nimium nostros miserate labores.
Tu, quanvis deus atque dei indubitata propago,
heu! nunc haec hominum, nunc cogeris illa subire
arbitria in vinclis et iudicis ora vereri,
qui toti advenies olim datus arbiter orbi.
225   Pontius ut vinctum sua rursum ad limina reddi

brought in. The king desired greatly to speak with him and see him face to face. He began to raise various points. But Christ made no answer, his gaze fixed on heaven. The king found nothing super-human to marvel at in the man, so despite his innocence he mocked him and ordered him taken back to the praetorium, much to the governor's displeasure. 195

Here my spirit sinks and my mind grows unsteady and infirm. I shudder to recall the evils that the true Son of God, himself God, suffered in human form, this creator of heaven, whose immensity could be contained neither by sea, nor earth, nor the spacious halls and shining shores of heaven. Almighty Breath of Heaven, descend and, with your spirit, support my flagging strength. For as often as I try to express these things, everything around me becomes dark. I see the stars grow pale and the sun cover its radiant face in black clouds and the weeping skies dissolve in tears. Clear light of heaven, was your piety and your loving compassion so strong that it made you pity our sad lot, that it led you, true God and heaven-sent Son of God, to suffer these harsh and heavy chastisements, that it led you, weighed down with the burden of the flesh, willingly to subject yourself to great pains and burden your divine person with earthly travails? Was this the recompense of your goodness, that you should wipe away our crimes with your death? We were the ones who plucked the sweet fruit from the forbidden tree, while you hung from that unspeakable trunk and paid the cruel price, you who pitied our travails too greatly. Though surely God and the Son of God, you are compelled to submit to the arbitrary will of vicious men and fear the countenance of a judge, you who one day will come as the judge of all the world. 200 205 210 215 220

When he saw the captive being brought back in bondage to the palace, Pilate understood that he could not escape passing judg- 225

conspicit, arbitrio nec se subducere tristi
posse videt, saevis curarum tunditur undis,
iamque his iamque illis¹ iterumque iterumque retentat
crudeles animos et parcere nescia corda
230 irritus ac studio frustra adversatur² inani.
Quam magis ille animis tendit sermone mederi,
nunc supplex placidusque, minis nunc asper acerbis,
tam magis accensis crudescunt cordibus irae.
Tandem ait: 'Haec redeunt (vestrorum antiqua parentum
235 vana superstitio) certis cum sacra diebus,
unum ego de multis inclusis carcere suevi
reddere et ex arctis impune emittere vinclis.
Hunc igitur vobis ipsum solvine iubetis
insontem? Nam quem potius dimittere possim?
240 Et iam poenarum satis ac feritatis abunde est.
Aut solvo aut porro vos hinc abducite, et atrae,
ut libet, immeritum sine me demittite morti.'
Non tulit et medium sermonem abrupit acerbans
crimina falsa cohors et poenas ingravat ore.
245   Forte illis Barabas populo patribusque diebus
invisus, quo non scelere usquam immanior alter,
iandudum in vinclis poenam expectabat acerbam.
Nulla fugae spes prorsus, ei via nulla salutis.
Huic igitur praeses vellent ne, an parcere Christo
250 scitatur, sperans ita tandem evadere posse.
Illi autem victique odiis caecique furore
exolvi Barabam poscunt veniamque precantur
uni omnes, Christumque absumi funere tendunt,
atque obstant summa studiis rectoris opum vi.
255 Ille autem loris caedi virgisque salignis
divinum mandat (visu lachrymabile) corpus.
'Fors,' ait, 'innocui potero hac extinxe cruoris

ment, and suddenly he felt great anguish. With one argument after another, he repeatedly tried to restrain their cruel spirit and
unforgiving heart, but to no avail, and he vainly opposed them
with fruitless efforts. The more he tried to reason with them, now   230
in calm and pleading tones, now in sharp and threatening ones,
the more he angered their insensate souls. Finally he said, "According to the vain and ancient superstition of your forefathers at
the high holidays, I have been in the habit of liberating one of the   235
many men who are imprisoned, of freeing him from his tight
bonds. Will you not bid me free this innocent man to you? For
whom should I rather release? Already there has been more than
enough punishment and savagery. Either I release him, or you go   240
on and lead him hence and, as you wish, condemn this undeserv-
ing man to a harsh death without my aid." But the mob wouldn't
hear of it and cut the speech short, exaggerating Christ's trumped-
up crimes and demanding harsher punishment.

It happened in those days that Barabbas, a greater criminal   245
than any other and a man hated by the people and their leaders,
had long languished in chains and awaited harsh punishment. He
had no hope of escape, no path to safety. The governor asked
whether they wanted to spare him or Christ. In this way he hoped
to avoid having to pass judgment himself. But they were overcome   250
with hatred and blind fury. Unanimously calling for Barabbas to
be pardoned and freed and for Christ to be put to death, they vehemently opposed the governor's wishes. And so he turned over
the divine body to be cut with ropes and harsh branches—a pitiable sight. "Perhaps in this way," he thought, "I can quench their   255
thirst for innocent blood. His worst enemy will pity him. And

arte sitim; sic immitis miserebitur hostis,
et lacerum totos cernentes comminus artus,
260   ipsi ultro satiati animos a morte reducent.'
     Iam largo undabat foedatum sanguine corpus,
perfusique artus tabo, liventia crura,[3]
collaque brachiaque et detectae verbere costae
atque eiectabat crassum roseo ore cruorem.
265   Talem in conspectu populi statuere: cruentos
nudum humeros pectusque ambasque a poplite plantas,
nam medium texto velabat carbasus albo.
Palluit aspectu coelum; conterrita fugit
cornibus obtusis sub terram argentea luna,
270   nimbosoque diu latitans evanuit ore,
et pariter visa astra polo cecidisse sereno.
Non tamen hostiles explevit sanguine poenas,
sed magis atque magis crudescunt corda precando,
quae non ullae artes, quae vis non mitigat ulla.
275   Immerito letum intendunt extremaque poscunt
supplicia infensi; resonant clamoribus alta
atria. Certatim se cuncti hortantur in iras.
Eumenides missique inferna e nocte ministri
tartarei, tenues animae, sine corpore vitae ·
280   circumeunt stimulosque acuunt ardentibus acres
et lucem eripiunt miseris agitantque furentes.
     Romanum interea monet ipsa exterrita visis
per somnum coniux, iuvenis ne sanguine sese
polluat, abstineat capto; portenta minari
285   magna deum in somnis. 'Is erat, is candidus ille
agnus,' ait '(nunquam ludunt me somnia vana)
quem circunfusique canes sudibusque petebant
pastorum globus omnis. Eum mox omnia ademptum
pascuaque et notis flebant cum saltibus agri.
290   At pater altitonans manifesta percitus ira

when they see with their own eyes that his entire body has been
savaged, they will be sated and cease to call for his death." 260

Already bloodstains bathed his entire body, its gore covering his
bruised shins, his neck, his arms and his ribs, which stood revealed under the lash. He spat blood from his red lips. Thus they
placed him in full sight of the people: his bloody shoulders were 265
naked, like his chest and legs below the knee; a white cloth covered his mid-section. Heaven paled at the sight. The silvery moon,
with blunted horns, fled beneath the earth and for a long time hid
itself in a cloud, and stars could be seen falling from the serene 270
heaven. But even with his blood, he had not fulfilled the sentence
demanded by his enemies. Rather their hearts grew ever more
cruel. No art, no force, could mitigate them. Determined to put
an innocent man to death, they heartlessly demanded the utmost
punishment. The lofty halls rang with their cries. Each of them, 275
as though in competition, goaded the others to ever greater anger.
The Furies and the ministers of hell, sent up from nether night,
thin souls without living bodies, circled about and sharpened their
goads against the incensed multitude, depriving them of reason 280
and driving them to fury.

In the meantime, the wife of Pilate told him of a terrifying
dream. She bade him not to pollute himself with the young man's
blood, nor to have anything to do with him, since God had made
dire threats to her in the dream. "This very man (for my dreams 285
never deceive me) appeared to me as a white lamb, beset by
hounds and shepherds wielding rods. And the flocks and the very
fields soon wept for the captured victim in the familiar woods. But
then, far-thundering God, stirred up by evident anger, raged from 290

desuper auctores caedis saevibat in ipsos.
Turbatum extemplo visum ruere undique coelum,
et campos late ac silvas quatere horrida grando.
Tum subito audita ex alto voxque acta per auras:
295 "Parce deo, Romane, hominum compesce furorem."
Credo equidem hunc (non te fallit) genus esse deorum.
Parce manus scelerare, pio, vir, parce cruori.
Ipsi haec coelicolae placidi portenta refutent,
Iudaeosque petant solos generique minentur.'
300   Talibus auditis Solymos animo acrior urget
Romulides certus vesano obstare furori.
Iamque minis agit et dictis haud amplius arcet
mollibus insanos et non toleranda frementes.
Iamque videbatur demptis dimittere vinclis
305 velle virum et tantis se tandem solvere curis.
Sensit atrox Erebo umbrarum regnator in imo,
aeternam servans memori sub pectore curam.
Ingemuit, vincique animo indignatus amaro est.
Protinus horriferum latebrosa ab sede Timorem
310 evocat atrum, ingens et ineluctabile monstrum.
Tristior haud ulla est umbrosis pestis in oris
scilicet atque hominum egregiis magis aemula coeptis.
Frigus ei comes et deiecto Ignavia vultu.
Extemplo hanc superas torpentem ascendere ad auras
315 imperat, intonsi qua molli vertice surgunt
Phoenicum montes, Solymorumque alta subire
moenia, ut Ausonii flectat ducis aspera corda
deiiciens subigatque metu desistere coepto.
Iussa facit; sibi nigrantis accommodat alas
320 nocturnarum avium, inque atros se colligit artus.

above against the authors of this outrage. At once heaven seemed
to come falling down around me, and the wide fields and woods
were struck by harsh hail. Then suddenly a voice was heard in
heaven. 'O Roman, spare this god and quell the anger of men.' For   295
I do believe (and it has not escaped your notice either) that he is
of the race of gods. Cease to defile your hands, husband, with his
holy blood. May the angels themselves show us favor by checking
these portents, and menace the Jews and their progeny alone."

At that the scion of Romulus was all the more resolved to urge   300
the citizens to quell their crazed fury. And now he resorted to
threats, no longer using mild words to dissuade these madmen,
who were shouting insufferable things. He seemed to want to release the man from his chains and free himself at last of these   305
troubles. In the depths of Erebus, the terrible lord of the shades
sensed this, for he was always mindful of that consuming care; he
groaned and grew wrathful at the bitter thought of defeat. Presently he called horrific Fear from its lair, a huge, dark, irresistible
monster. In all the realms of shade no pestilence was more terrible   310
or more envious of the great deeds of men. His companions were
Cold and Indolence with downturned face. At once he ordered
this torpid being to ascend to the upper air, where the wooded
Phoenician mountains rise with their gentle slopes. He was to en-   315
ter the city's walls and, bending the Roman's determined heart
with fear, compel him to abandon his intention. The creature did
as bidden, assuming the black wings of the birds of night, and
gathered itself into the form of their dark bodies. After this filthy   320

Iamque emensa viae tractus obscoena volucris
purpurei crebra ante oculos se praesidis ecce
fertque refertque volans circum importuna sonansque
nunc pectus, nunc ora nigris everberat alis,
325   immisitque gelu et praecordia frigore vinxit.
     Diriguit visu subito atque exalbuit ille,
surrectaeque comae steterunt, gelidusque per ossa
horror iit. Genua aegra labant; vox faucibus haesit.
Quem, simul ac cives sensere insueta timentem
330   pallentemque genas et toto corpore versum,
his subito arrepto clamantes tempore dictis
aggressi: 'Iste ausus vulgo se fingere regem.
Aspirat sceptris regisque affectat honores.
Quem, si forte neci mavis subducere nec te
335   crimina tanta movent, Iudaeas protinus urbes
seditione potens Romanis legibus omnemque
artibus avertet Syriam ditione Quiritum.
Res igitur tibi si curae Romana decusque
Caesaris, hanc superis pestem citus aufer ab oris,
340   hauriat ut meritas haud uno crimine poenas,
ne gentem repant contagia dira per omnem.'
Talia perstabant uno omnes ore frementes.
Dux vero expertus genus intractabile, regis
palluit ad nomen (praecordia ad intima saevit
345   subdita pestis enim) nec iam superantibus obstat
amplius, et sese victus cedensque remittit,
haud ultra potis insano pugnare furori.
     Ceu cum rostratae sese opposuere triremi
protinus adversi mediis in fluctibus Euri,
350   luctatur primum celsa de puppe magister
hortaturque viros validis insurgere tonsis;
demum, ubi se niti contra intolerabile coelum
incassum videt ac ventos superare furentis,

thing flew across immense tracts of land, he reached the noble
governor. Flying back and forth before his eyes, it struck now his
face, now his chest with its black wings, filling him with a dread
chill.   325

At the sight of it Pilate stiffened and turned white. His hair
stood up and a cold fear seeped into his bones. His knees stiffened
and his voice stuck in his throat. As soon as the citizens saw that
he was strangely afraid, that his cheeks were pale and that his
whole body was in turmoil, at once they assailed him with these   330
words: "This man dared to pass himself off to the people as their
king. He wants the scepter and claims the honors of a king. If you
don't put him to death, if such great and seditious crimes don't
move you, soon by his arts he will cause all the cities of Judaea and 335
Syria to revolt against the laws and authority of Rome. If you care
for Rome and for the honor of Caesar, purge the air of this pestilence. Make him suffer the punishment he deserves, and for more
than one crime, lest this dire contagion infect the entire populace." 340
Thus they insisted with one voice. The governor, knowing that
they were an intractable race, grew apprehensive at the word king
(for hidden pestilence raged within his heart). No longer opposing 345
them, he saw he was vanquished and gave up, no longer able to
fight against their crazed fury.

As when on the high seas Eurus rages against the beaked prow
of a bireme, at first the pilot struggles from atop the deck, urging 350
his men to row against the wind. But when he sees that it is vain
to oppose the unbearable assault of heaven and the unconquerable

vertit iter, quocunque vocat fortuna per aequor
355 multivium atque auris parens subremigat aeger.
Haud tamen abstinuit verbis vocive pepercit.
'Verum vincor,' ait, 'nec habet vestra ira regressum.
In me nulla mora est: moriatur crimine falso
damnatus. Vos triste manet, speroque propinquum
360 supplicium. Vos sacrilego serique nepotes,
o miseri, meritas pendetis sanguine poenas.'
Sic effatus, aquam plena iubet ocius urna
afferri, abstergensque manus haec addidit ore:
'Ut nunc his manibus maculae absunt, sic mihi nullum
365 hac in caede nefas, meque omni crimine solvo.'
Dixit, et exurgens solio intra tecta recessit.
Illi autem: 'Deus haec nobis gnatisque reservet
instauretque graves poenas, quascunque meremur.'
    Haec dum porticibus populo spectante geruntur
370 vestibulum ante ipsum, famuli ducis aedibus intus
armati illudunt capto irridentque silentem,
quodque illum populi regem optavere per urbes,
purpureis ornant tunicis ostroque rubenti
atque alte effultum sublimi sede locarunt.
375 Pro capitis crinali auro regumque corona
sentibus obnubunt flaventia tempora acutis.
Pro sceptro datur insigni fluvialis arundo.
Tum populo laeti portis bipatentibus omni
ostendunt plausu magno regemque salutant.
380 Haud aliter ludo pueri cum ex omnibus unum
delegere ducem, sociis qui sponte subactis
imperitet, laeto cuncti stant agmine circum
condensi assurguntque omnes regisque superbi
iussa obeunt ludicra, ingens it ad aethera clamor.
385 Tali intus famuli indulgent manus effera ludo.
Dehinc iuveni vestis obtentu lumina inumbrant,

276

winds, he finally turns wherever chance takes him along the many
tracts of the sea and wearily rows in obedience to the winds. But   355
Pontius Pilate hardly remained silent or held his tongue. "Truly I
am defeated," he said, "and there is no restraining your anger. I
will not delay you. Let him die, condemned on a trumped-up
charge. As for you, a dreary punishment awaits you, and I hope it
comes soon. You and your descendants, wretched men, will pay   360
for this with your sacrilegious blood!" So speaking he ordered that
an urn be brought to him full of water. Washing his hands, he
said, "As the dirt is now removed from my hands, even so have I
no guilt in this act of violence, and I absolve myself of all crime."
So he spoke. Rising from his throne, he returned within the pal-   365
ace. But they answered, "Let God hold this in store for us and for
our children, and let him punish us as severely as we deserve."

While all of this was happening at the entrance to the palace,
before the very vestibule and in full sight of the people, inside the
building armed servants of the governor mocked their silent cap-   370
tive. Because the people had chosen him as king, the servants
wrapped him in a costly purple robe and set him upon a lofty
throne. In place of a golden diadem and kingly crown, they cov-   375
ered his blond temples with sharp thorns. And rather than a noble
scepter, he was given a reed from the river. Then they merrily
threw open the doors, showed him to the entire populace, who applauded loudly and hailed him as their king. As when jesting boys
choose one of their number to be king and to lord it over his sub-   380
missive playmates, they all crowd round him laughing and with
loud clamor obey the foolish commands of their proud monarch:
even such was the sport of these shameless servants. Then they   385
blindfolded the young man and struck his divine head with their

divinumque caput palmis et arundine pulsant.
Hic digitis vellit concretam sanguine barbam;
ille oculos in sidereos spuit improbus ore
390 immundo et pulchrum deformat pulvere corpus.
Nec mora nec requies: versantque agitantque ferentem
omnia, nec verbis ullis indigna querentem,
nec dare permittunt iam lumina fessa sopori.
O dolor, heu! species inhonesta, indignaque visu!
395 Non silvis avibus frondes, non montibus antra
quadrupedum generi desunt, ubi condere sese
in noctem atque suos possint educere foetus.
At rerum auctori, coeli cui regia servit,
omnibus in terris defit locus, omnibus oris,
400 quo caput acclinet fessusque in morte quiescat.
    Tum vero Solymi victores cuncta parare
supplicia atque omnes poenarum exquirere formas,
perferat ut saevos crudeli morte dolores.
Iamque illum erecto properant distendere ligno
405 affixum et lenta paulatim perdere morte.
Nec mora, diffindunt malos. Sonat acta securis,
altaque quadrifidis fabricatur roboribus crux,
tormenti genus. Hac olim scelera impia reges
urgebant poena sontesque hac morte necabant,
410 difficiles miserorum obitus longique dolores.
Tum neque honos erat, infami neque gloria trunco;
at nunc numen habet sanctum et venerabile lignum
suppliciter cuncti colimus sacrisque minores
argento atque auro contectum imponimus aris
415 et laetum ex illo memores celebramus honorem.
Illa etiam coelo fulgebit lampadis instar
aethereae et totum lustrabit lumine mundum,
cum dabit exitio una dies animalia cuncta
interitumque feret rebus mortalibus ignis.

hands and rods. One man plucked his beard, stiff with blood, while another spat from his filthy mouth into Jesus' celestial eyes and sullied his noble body with dirt. Without rest or pause they 390 spun him about and shook him. But he bore all of it and said nothing in protest, though they would not even allow his weary eyes to close in sleep. How painful, how base and unworthy a spectacle! Woodland birds have trees and four-legged creatures 395 have mountain caves where they can hide at night and raise their young. But the creator of the world and lord of the kingdom of heaven found no place on earth to lay his head or lie down wearily in death. 400

But now the victorious men of Jerusalem prepared every kind of torment and sought every manner of punishment to draw out the sharp pain of his cruel death. Now they rushed to stretch him upon an upright timber and to destroy him gradually with a slow death. Without delay they split the wood of an apple tree; the 405 noise of the ax resounded as the lofty cross was shaped from four-fold timber, a form of torture. This was the penalty kings once imposed for crimes against piety; the guilty used to suffer intense pain and a lingering and wretched death by this means. Then the 410 infamous cross carried no respect or glory; but now the cross has divine power. And those of us who were born to a later age bow reverently before this venerable and saintly wood, which we place, gilded with silver and gold, upon our sacred altars. Since that time, we have celebrated its noble honor. And it will shine in 415 heaven like an ethereal lamp, illuminating the entire world with its light, on the day that will bring death to all living things, when fire will consume all mortality.

420   Vix terris lux alma aderat, cum iam undique tota
urbe ruit studio visendi accita iuventus,
implenturque viae, concursuque omnia fervent.
Et iam purpureos habitus insignia ludicra
exutum, vinctumque manus clamore trahebant
425   dirum ad supplicium magna sectante caterva.
Per medios longis raptatus funibus ibat
semianimisque artusque tremens plagisque cruentus
nocturnis, humeroque trabem duplicem ipse gerebat
praecisis gravidam nodis ac robore iniquo,
430   qua super infando mortales linqueret auras
supplicio et duros finiret morte labores.
    Armati circunsistunt, clypeataque iuxta
agmina densentur; collucent spicula longe
spiculaque et rubris capitum cava tegmina cristis,
435   aereaque alterno conspirant cornua cantu.
Pars pedes insequitur; pars sese lucidus altis
fert in equis; resonant colles clamore propinqui.
Multi autem, quorum melior sententia, flebant,
praecipuae matresque piae mitesque puellae,
440   cernentes nudis pedibus per scrupea saxa
tendere et offendi crebro ad salebrosa viarum,
dum monte adverso protrudit robur iniquum,
ad quas suspirans heros sic ore loquutus:
'Ne vero, ne me matres indigna ferentem
445   flete piae. Vobis potius deflete propinquum
exitium et vestris hinc debita praemia natis.'
Sic fatus linquit non aequis passibus urbem.
    Interea superum rex tanto in cardine rerum
verticis aetherei sublimem evasit ad arcem,
450   mortalis nati letum ut crudele videret
ipse sui spectator. Eum gens incola coeli
aligeri stipant cunei et comitantur euntem.

But that life-giving light was hardly present in the land now   420
when from all over the city youths were sent for and rushed up in
their desire to watch. The roads were filled with great commotion.
They clamorously removed the royal robes, his mock regalia and,
binding his hands, they bore him toward dreadful torment, followed by a large crowd. He was dragged through the throng with   425
long ropes, half-conscious, his limbs trembling and bleeding from
the wounds of the night before. With strength unequal to the
task, he carried on his shoulder a twofold timber, gnarled and
heavy. On this he was to breathe his last amid unspeakable agony,   430
bringing an end to his harsh labors with death.

Columns of armed men with shields surrounded and closed in
on him, their shafts and red-crested helmets shining from afar,
while the brazen trumpets sounded one after the other. Next came   435
the infantry and the dazzling cavalry, filling the surrounding hills
with their clamor. But many wiser people wept, especially pious
mothers and sensitive maidens who saw Jesus struggling barefoot
over the sharp stones, often bruising his feet upon the rough path   440
as he carried the treacherous timber up the steep hill. With a sigh
the hero addressed them thus: "Dear mothers, do not weep for me
that I should bear these indignities. Rather weep for your own imminent death and for the recompense that will be exacted from   445
your children." Thus speaking he stumbled beyond the city's walls.

Meanwhile, at this critical moment, the King of Angels fled to
the utmost citadel of heaven in order to see and witness in person
the cruel death of his mortal Son. The winged denizens of heaven   450
assembled and followed him in martial array. At the very summit

Est templum gemmis interlucentibus auro
e solido factum sublimi in vertice Olympi,
455   tectum immane, ingens, superi penetrale parentis,
sidera despiciens subter labentia mundi.
In medio clivus duro ex adamante tumescit,
paulatim exacuens instar fastigia pinus;
multiplices circum sedes subterque supraque
460   dispositae gradibusque novem super aethera surgunt.
Conveniunt huc coelicolae, regemque canendo
ingressi thiasis lustrant; se sedibus inde
omnes composuere suis, tumulumque corusci
ter late circum terna cinxere corona
465   secreti ordinibus certis; neque enim omnibus aequa
conditio viresque pares eademque potestas;
verum, aliis alii ut praestant, ita rite locantur
munere quisque suo contenti ac sorte beati.
In medio pater omnipotens solio aureus alto
470   sceptra tenet, lateque acie circum omnia lustrat
totus collucens, totus circum igne corusco
scintillans radiisque procul vibrantibus ardens.
Mox autem infaustis Iudaeae lumina tantum
defixit terris, tristemque ante omnia collem
475   spectabat. Gens moesta simul spectabat Olympi
collem infelicem, sacram egredientibus urbem
qui prior occurrit, humanis ossibus albus.
Auctores scelerum poenas ibi morte luebant
informi; circum pendebant corpora passim
480   arboribus truncis incocto lurida tabo.
      Huc simul atque emensus iter miserabilis heros
pervenit sensitque sibi crudele parari
supplicium atque trabem vidit iam stare nefandam,
deiectos oculos porro huc iactabat et illuc,
485   omnia collustrans, comitum si forte suorum,

of heaven stands a temple of solid gold and sparkling gems, a great
and massive structure, the inmost dwelling of the Supreme Father,   455
that looks down upon the stars of heaven that glide beneath it.
From its center arose a sloping surface of adamantine stone, gradually coming to a point, like a pine tree. Its many seats were set in a
circle above and below, rising above the heavens in nine rows. Here   460
the angels convened, hymning their lord and dancing solemnly
around him; then they assumed their assigned seats. Flashing
brightly, they encircled the hill in thrice three rows that were divided into separate ranks — for they were not all equal in condition, strength or power. Rather each was arrayed according to his   465
rank, and all were content and blessed in their lot. In their midst
the Almighty Father, a golden radiance on a lofty throne, held
the scepter and cast his gaze on all things near and far, scattering   470
his brilliant light in every direction. But then, together with the
mournful race of angels, he fixed his gaze upon the sad lands of
Judaea, and especially on the sad hill that first appeared as one left   475
the city, conspicuous with human bones. Here criminals paid the
penalty of an ugly death. All around it ghastly corpses, hanging
from tree-trunks, baked and putrefied in the sun.   480

As soon as the pitiable hero had reached the end of his trek and
saw the cruel suffering that awaited him — the unspeakable cross
was already standing — his downcast eyes glanced in all directions,
hoping to see one of his disciples amid the ranks of his enemies.   485

si quem forte acies inimicas cerneret inter.
Fidum in conspectu nullum; videt agmina tantum
saeva virum campique armis fulgentibus ardent.
Cari deseruere omnes diversa petentes,
490 non aliter quam cum coelo seu tactus ab alto
pastor, sive ferae insidiis in valle peremptus,
continuo sparguntur oves diversa per arva
incustoditae; resonant balatibus agri.
    Iamque trabem infandam scandens pendensque per auras
495 horruit atque deum veluti se oblitus, acerbi
pertimuit dirum leti genus; aestuat intus,
atque animum in curas labefactum dividit acres,
tristia multa agitans animo, totosque per artus
pallentes mixto fluit ater sanguine sudor,
500 et patriam crebro reminiscitur aetheris aulam.
Tum coelum aspectans haec imo pectore fatur:
'Heu, quianam extremis genitor me summe periclis
deseris? Aut gnati quo iam tibi cura recessit?'
    Audiit has summus voces pater; audiit omnis
505 coelestum chorus. Ipse (alta secum omnia mente
versabat genitor, nutu haud oblitus agi rem
nempe suo) stetit immotus seseque repressit.
At circunfusos coetus, gentem aetheris alti
aligeram, iniussos potis est vis sistere nulla.
510 Omnibus exarsit subito dolor; omnibus ingens
aestuat ira. Volunt nato succurrere herili
et prohibere nefas duroque resistere ferro.
Bella cient; arma ingeminant arma acrius omnes.
Hic puer, haud volucri extremus de gente, recurvo
515 aere vocare acies quo non magis utilis alter,
ascensu superat celeri ardua culmina praepes,
tum super axe sedens roseique in vertice coeli,
signa canit belli. Latus dissultat Olympus

But he could find no faithful friend. All he saw were rank upon rank of cruel men, as the fields blazed with gleaming arms. All his friends had deserted him, fleeing in all directions: as when a shepherd is struck by lightning or waylaid unawares by some beast in a   490 vale, at once the flocks, unguarded, run in every direction through the fields and fill them with their bleatings.

Now he had mounted the unspeakable timber and, as he hung suspended, he shuddered. He seemed to forget that he was divine and, dreading this frightful and bitter kind of death, he was in tur-   495 moil within. His wavering heart was rent with sharp cares, as sweat, mixed with blood and filth, covered his entire body, now grown pale. Frequently he recalled his Father's house in heaven   500 and gazing up, he spoke thus from the depths of his heart. "Father, why have you abandoned me in this utmost peril? Do you no longer care for your Son?"

His Supreme Father heard, as did the chorus of angels. Weighing all these things in his heart and knowing that they were   505 done by his decree, the Father checked himself and remained unmoved. But there was no force able to contain the winged angels who surrounded him and were convulsed and overwhelmed by sudden pain and anger. They wished to come to the aid of his Son   510 and heir, to end this outrage and resist the violence. And so they declared war, all fiercely echoing 'To arms! To arms!' At this a boy, hardly the least among the winged race and most skilled at sounding the curved trumpet and marshalling their battalions, flew   515 headlong in swift ascent. Seated above the universe at the summit of golden heaven, he sounded the call to war. In all directions, the breadth of heaven shook with the noise, and the stars trembled

undique, et insolito tremuerunt sidera motu.
520 Audiit et sonitum, si quem procul orbe remoto
distinet incedens humili luna humida gressu.
Audivere, quibus generis custodia nostri
in terris olim sorti data, vastaque tellus
protinus ingenti tremuit concussa fragore.
525 Tum quos rex superum varias legarat in oras,
aereos relegunt tractus mandataque linquunt
imperfecta fugaque poli super ardua tendunt.
Ac velut in pastus celsa quae sede columbae
exierant varios, cum tempestate repente
530 urgenti caeco misceri murmure coelum
incipit et nigrae cinxerunt aethera nubes,
continuo linquunt arva undique et ardua pennis
tecta petunt celeresque cavis se turribus abdunt.
     Iam passim ingentis properatur vertice Olympi,
535 et toto ancipitis ferri coelo ingruit horror,
aeratique sonant currus, gemitusque rotarum
audiri sonitusque armorum desuper ingens.
Tam vastos motus axis miratur uterque,
miranturque ignes coelique volubilis orbes,
540 cum tenues animae, cum sint sine corpore vitae,
sensibus a nostris quibus est natura remota.
Saepe autem, seu mortales mittuntur ad oras
sive opus in fratres olim capere arma rebelles,
corporis afficti sibi quisque accommodat alas
545 aereosque artus, simulacrumque aptat habendo,
spiritus ut queat humanos admittere visus.
Ergo illi rapido circundant turbine densa
corpora sub nostros etiam venientia sensus,
circundantque humeris desueta micantibus arma
550 aetheris aerisono subito de poste refixa
coelicolum exuvias, belli monimenta nefandi,

with an unfamiliar motion. The sound was heard even by him whom the moon, moist on her low-lying path, imprisons in her 520 distant orb. It was heard as well by those who were appointed once to protect our race here below; the entire earth trembled, struck by this great blow. They whom the King of Angels had sent into various regions returned now to the fields of air. Their charges 525 abandoned, they hastened up to the height of heaven. They were like doves that have scattered from their high nests in search of food: when the skies darken with a sudden storm and the heav- 530 ens, shorn of light, tremble as black clouds fill the sky, at once the birds leave the fields and hasten for cover in lofty eaves and hollow towers.

Now there was a great rush to the summit of Olympus, and the dread of open war loomed all over heaven. Brazen chariots re- 535 sounded everywhere and you could hear the groan of wheels and the clamor of arms above. Both poles of heaven, with the stars and orbiting planets, marveled at the vast commotion, although the nature of these rarefied and disembodied beings is far remote from 540 our senses. Often, however, when they are sent to mortal lands or if they ever must take up arms against their rebellious brethren, the angels put on the wings and airy forms of an assumed body, and, adjusting their form, become visible to human sight. Thus 545 they surround their solid bodies with a swift whirlwind, and so come within the range of even our senses. About their gleaming shoulders they place unwonted arms that they have stripped from the airy gates of heaven, angelic trophies and monuments of that 550 dreadful war that once they bore against their maddened kinsmen.

quod socios olim contra gessere furentes.
Hic bonus armatur iaculis hastamque trabalem
crispat agens; rapit ille faces; rapit ille sagittas
555   suspenditque humeris lunatum ardentibus arcum,
atque alius palmas insertat caestibus ambas;
pars tereti funda dextram implicat. Omnibus ensis
aureus in morem vagina pendet eburna.
Infrenant alii coeli per coerula currus;
560   caetera pars pictis librare celerrima pennis
corpora: non eadem vis omnibus ipsa volandi.
Mobilitate vigent[4] varia: pars remigat alis
binis alternante humero; pars ordine ad auras
tollunt se triplici pennatis undique plantis.
565   Haud unam in faciem, sed nec color omnibus idem.
Nanque hos punicea cernas effulgere pluma
flammipedes, igni assimiles rutilantia terga,
herbarum hos speciem viridesque referre smaragdos,
terga illis croceo lucent circunlita luto;
570   centum aliis alii pinxere coloribus alas.
Qualis ubi exactos post aestus arbore ab omni
exornat pomis se versicoloribus annus,
et caput Autumnus circunfert pulcher honestum.
Et iam pennipotens liquidis exercitus ibat
575   tractibus, ac volucri cingebant agmine coelum,
millia quot nunquam nascentum ab origine rerum
visa hominum in terris coiisse, ter agmina terna,
terque duces terni. Toto dux vertice supra est,
nuper Iapygii Gargani e vertice vectus
580   armipotens, veteris quem quondam gloria pugnae
sublimem longeque alios super extulit omnis.
In medio ibat ovans, galea cristisque superbis
aureus et longe gemmis lucentibus ardens,
nunc etiam spolia edomiti fulvamque draconis

One good creature arms himself with lances and takes a wooden
shaft in hand, while another picks up a torch and still another,
equipped with arrows, attaches a curved bow to his gleaming
shoulders. Others put on pugilists' gloves or the smoothed sling,   555
while each angel, according to custom, wears a golden sword
sheathed in ivory. While some ride chariots through the serene
heavens, others remain aloft on wings of many colors. For all are   560
not equally skilled in flight. Varied are their means of movement:
some row through the air on paired wings beating in alternation.
Others rise through the air on three sets of wings, for their feet are
winged as well. Nor do all the angels have the same appearance or   565
coloration. Some you see gleaming with brilliant plumage and
flaming feet and backs that glow like fire. Some are the color of
grass, like emeralds, while the backs of others gleam with saffron.
A hundred more have wings of different hues, as when at sum-   570
mer's end, the year adorns itself with motley apples on every tree,
and lovely Autumn raises its noble head.

Already the winged army had passed through the clear tracts of
air, flooding the sky with their pennoned phalanxes. Never in the   575
lands of men had so many thousands been seen together since the
creation of the world: thrice three battalions with thrice three generals. Taller by a head than the rest was a leader but recently borne
up from the summit of Monte Gargano, exalted over all the rest
by the glory of his earlier battle. As he passed through their midst   580
he exulted, his helmet gleaming with lofty crests and shining jewels. Now he displayed as his trophy the skin of the vanquished

585 pellem ostentabat spiris ingentibus, ipsumque
     innixus tergo pedibusque hastaque premebat.
     Arma procul radiant; umbo vomit aureus ignes,
     stellantique procul micat ensis iaspide fulgens.
         Ventum erat ad coeli portas. Hic omnibus irae
590 incaluere magis, belli ut monimenta prioris
     sunt oculis oblata. Vident nam turribus altis
     pendentes currus suspensaque postibus aera,
     spiculaque et clypeos, victis de fratribus arma
     olim, immane nefas! coelo crudeliter orsis,
595 dum frustra aspirant sceptris felicis Olympi
     immemores victique animis et vana tumentes,
     quos ipsi contra steterant meliora sequuti,
     aethereque expulerant certamine debellatos.
     Quam pugnam in foribus quondam caelarat ahenis
600 artificum manus atque operoso impresserat auro.
     Cernere erat liquidas coeli pendere per auras
     hinc acies atque hinc acies certamen adortas,
     nunc huc, nunc illuc ultro citroque volare,
     aetheraque in medio venientibus obscurari
605 missilibus, iam iam certari comminus armis,
     miscerique acies et iam, quis spicula deerant,
     crinibus implicuere manus hostilibus uncas,
     suspensosque comis circum per inane rotabant.
     Iamque hos paulatim concedere, desuper illos
610 urgere aspicias, donec toto aethere versi
     palantesque fugae simul hostes terga dedere,
     praecipiti assimiles nimbo atque procacibus Austris.
     Nam pater omnipotens armatus fulmine dextram
     deturbabat agens flammisque sequacibus arce
615 siderea; excussos Erebi domus atra recepit.
         Pugnae igitur superi admoniti veterisque trophaei
     aetheris ardebant fractis erumpere portis.

dragon, with its huge coiling tail: the dragon itself he trampled un- 585
derfoot and harrowed with a spear. His armor gleamed into the
distance. The golden boss of his shield vomited fire while the
sword shone from far off, spangled with jasper.

They reached the gates of heaven. All of them seethed with
mounting anger as reminders of previous campaigns came into
view: chariots hanging from tall towers and from the gates the 590
swords, shafts and shields, the weapons of those vanquished
brothers who once had cruelly taken up arms in heaven—a grievous sin. Heedlessly and in vain they had striven for the dominion
of happy Olympus, their minds vanquished and abased by their 595
vain aspirations. In this they had been opposed by those who, following a better course, routed them in battle in mid-air. Artisans
soon carved the record of this battle onto brass doors, skillfully
wrought with gold. Forwards and backwards, hither and yon, you 600
could see troops suspended in the clear air of heaven and roused
into conflict, as the sky darkened with oncoming missiles and
troops clashed in hand to hand combat. Those who lacked spears 605
hooked their enemies' hair in their hands and spun them round in
the air. Little by little you could see one side yielding as the other
pressed the attack from above. Finally routed throughout heaven,
the exhausted enemy could be seen turning and openly taking to 610
flight, like swift storm clouds or the fierce west winds. For the Almighty Father, armed with the thunderbolt, had driven them from
heaven, pursuing them with flames. The dark house of Erebus received those who had been driven out. 615

Thus reminded of that battle and of the ancient trophies, the
angels yearned to burst forth and fight, breaking down the gates of

Iamque adeo evassent omnes terrisque potiti
sontem incendissent oram, iamque urbibus igni
620 correptis, Iudaea nocens, commissa luisses,
ni pater altitonans stellanti nixus Olympo
(motus enim tanto subito flagrante tumultu)
coepta redargueret verbisque inhiberet acerbis
bellum importunum, cunctis haud mollia mandans.
625 Nam circunspiciens, sibi centum astare ministras
virgineas volucrum humana sub imagine formas
hinc atque hinc videt et nutum observare paratas.
Quarum quae placido mitis Clementia vultu est,
eligitur numero ex omni, cui talia mandet:
630 'Vade,' ait, 'et volucri per coelum labere curru.
Fratribus haec fer dicta tuis. Non aetheris illis,
non illis vasti commissas orbis habenas,
ut ferro iniussas meditantes edere pugnas
omne ausint miscere meo sine numine coelum
635 terramque et tantos animis accendere motus.
Considant, positisque adsint huc ocius armis.'
      Dixerat. Illa viam raptim secat alite curru
et patris ingentes passim denuntiat iras,
ni redeant positisque quiescant protinus armis.
640 Addunt se comites Pietas Paxque aurea; it una
Spesque Fidesque piique parens placidissima Amoris.
Omnibus in manibus rami canentis olivae.
Quaque egere viam, videas procul ilicet arma
proiicere et studiis cunctos mitescere versis.
645 Iamque in conspectu positis exercitus armis
regis adest, dicto parentes. Sede locarunt
ordine sese quisque sua pariterque quierunt.
      Hic tum nimbipotens genitor circuntulit ora
ter torquens illustre caput, ter cardine moto
650 terribilem increpuit sonitum; dein farier infit:

heaven. Even now they would all have escaped and overrun Judaea, setting fire to the guilty land. Already, guilty Judaea, you would have paid for your crimes, your cities consumed by fire. But 620 the far thundering Father, sitting in starry Olympus, was moved by this great and sudden tumult. He opposed the angels' purpose and, with bitter words, he checked this importunate conflict, commanding them in stern terms. As he looked around he saw on every side a hundred angelic ministrants, in the virginal form of human women, ready to obey his command. He chose one of them 625 from all their number, the temperate Clementia, of peaceful countenance, whom he bade thus: "Glide through the skies upon a swift chariot. Bear these words to your brethren. These angels 630 have not been vouchsafed control of the air or the vast earth so that they might plot unbidden to unleash war and without my consent throw all of heaven into turmoil. Let them retreat and 635 come hither, having laid down their arms."

So he spoke. Swiftly she departed in a winged chariot, and spread everywhere the word that their Father would be greatly angered if they did not return forthwith and peacefully lay down their arms. Piety and golden-haired Peace went with her. Hope 640 went as well, with Faith and the kindly mother of holy Love. Each of them carried an olive branch in her hand. Wherever they passed, you could see the troops at once laid down their arms and grow gentle, their zeal confounded. Once they had relinquished their weapons, the army appeared before their king, obedient to 645 his words. Each angel assumed his assigned seat in silence.

Then the father of the clouds thrice turned round his noble head and thrice, as the earth's axis moved, a terrifying sound went forth. Then he began to speak. "Heavenly ones, why this mad 650

'Quae superi vetitum contra haec insania ferri?
Quo ruitis? Quia ne auxilio subsistere nostro
non queat ille, meae aut sint fractae denique vires?
Ne saevite animis atque hanc deponite curam,
655 quandoquidem haud fert haec nostro sine numine natus —
scitis enim — ut moriens crimen commune refellat.
Sic generi humano clausum stat pandere Olympum.
Illum ideo duros volui exercere labores
atque agere in terris extrema per omnia vitam,
660 finibus exactum cunctis, inopem, omnium egentem.
Iamque ad supremum ventum. Manet exitus illum
hic hodie gravis insontem, irrevocabile letum,
et morti caput ipse sua sponte obvius offert.
Nunc autem subito visu horruit et timor illi
665 confusam eripuit leti ipso in limine mentem.
Quippe, deum velut exutus, mortalis, inermis
restitit et telis mansit violabile corpus.
Nil aliter vis divinos valuisset in artus
ulla hominum, et cunctis foret impenetrabilis armis.
670 Non adeo vires, non parva potentia nostra,
ut nequeam, si versa retro sententia, natum
eripere in medio versantem turbine leti,
contra illum insurgant omnes, ab origine rerum
quidquid ubique hominum natum extinctumque per aevum.
675 Non ita me experta est Babylon, ubi ad astra gigantes
tentavere vias educta turre sub auras,
et poterant magnos manibus divellere montes;
nunc etiam fumant praefractae fulmine turres.
Ut nimborum acies tempestatumque quiescant,
680 quae vastum rapiant convulsum a cardine mundum,
ipse manu terras quaterem; coelum omne cierem
diluvio cuncta involvens. Meme ignibus atris
nunc nunc accinctum teloque tricuspide dextram

warfare in violation of my orders? Whither do you hasten? Do
you think that my Son cannot rely upon my help? Or have I at
last become powerless? That is madness! Set aside this care and
anger. You know that my Son does not bear these afflictions without my consent, that he will die so that he may atone for the com-   655
mon crime of men. Thus it is resolved to open up heaven, now
closed to humankind. For this have I wished him to carry out such
cruel labors, to spend his life on earth in all manner of hardship,
to be chased from all borders, needy and destitute. But now he has   660
reached the end. Today this grievous and irreversible death awaits
him, innocent though he is. Though he willingly submits to his
execution, now he is terrified by this spectacle, as fear seizes his
confused mind at the very threshold of death. Indeed, as if throw-   665
ing off his divinity, he has become mortal and unarmed, his body
rendered vulnerable to the lance. In no other way could any force
of man have power against his godly form, which would be impervious to all arms. My strength and power are not so slight that, if I   670
changed my mind, I could not rescue my son from his present
danger of death, though all the men who ever lived and died since
the beginning of the world should rise up against him. The Babylonians did not find me weak when they tried, like giants, to reach   675
heaven with their towers, though they could level great mountains
with their hands. Even now those towers lie smoldering, lightning-
struck. And though the troops of clouds and storms were still,
which could seize the vast world and unhinge it from its moorings,
I myself could shake the world with my hand; I could rouse all   680
heaven and engulf the universe in flood waters. Even now the race

armatum mortale genus saevire videret,
685   hunc difflare globum, haec passim metere agmina ferro.
At sinite; adveniet (neque enim mora longior) urbi
tempus ei, frustra hunc cum magno optaverit emptum
haud tetigisse, genus cui ducitur aethere ab alto.'
Sic ait, et moto tremefecit vertice mundum,
690   Terrifico quatiens tonitru coelestia templa.
     Continuo superum furor acer et ira quievit.
Prosequitur tantum votis chorus omnis amicis,
atque deum e summo taciti miserantur Olympo.
Sicut ubi inclusi septis vacuo aequore campi
695   pro laude ac decore accensi certamina miscent
inter se aequatis iuvenes duo comminus armis;
hinc spectat procul atque hinc circunfusa iuventus.
Tum si forte alter minus ac minus utilis, ore
palluit aut terra cecidit deceptus iniqua,
700   consurgant fidi aequales studiisque sequantur.
Quam vellent, nisi pacta vetent, succurrere amico!
Stant aegri et casum longe execrantur acerbum.
     Haud secus indefensus, inermis restitit heros.
Illum nudum humeros, nudum omne a vertice corpus,
705   directum longo malo applicuere furentes.
Nuda dehinc tendunt transverso brachia ligno,
diversaque ambas affigunt cuspide palmas
hinc atque hinc; mucrone pedes terebrantur eodem
confixi. Largum manat de stipite flumen.
710   Instant vi multa. Ferro ardua robora adacto
dant gemitum; reboat diro stridore supinus
mons circum ingeminans, ictusque resultat imago.
Tum supra caput et nomen patriamque necisque
inscripsere notis variis in stipite causam.
715   Dextra autem laevaque duos gemina arbore fixos
addiderant socios, quos ob commissa merentes

of men could see me rage, armed with the thunderbolt and girt
with dark flames, as I unleashed a ball of fire and mowed down
their ranks everywhere. But be patient. Before long the time will 685
come when this city will be willing to pay a high price never to
have touched him whose ancestry is from high heaven." Thus he
spoke, and made the world tremble at his nod, shaking the heavenly temples with a terrifying blast of thunder. 690

At once the angels' rage and anger subsided. With gentle vows,
the entire chorus obeyed, pitying the Son of God in silence from
the summit of heaven. It was as if two youths were enclosed in a
ring on an empty field, vying for glory and honor. As they fight 695
hand to hand with equal might, all the other youths gather round,
looking now at one side and now at the other. If one of them happens to be less skilful and shows fear or trips on the uneven
ground, his faithful friends jump up, eager to help him. How they 700
would like to succor their friend, but the rules forbid it! They
stand about helplessly and curse from afar his bad luck.

So stood the hero, defenseless and unarmed. His crazed tormentors stretched him lengthwise across the tall timber, his shoulders and upper body bare. Then they stretched out his arms on 705
the cross, piercing his hands with nails and driving a spike through
both feet. A stream of blood shot forth. They pressed on with all
their might. The tall wooden boards groaned as the nails were
driven in. The mountain slopes echoed and amplified the dire 710
sound. Above his head, at the summit of the cross, they wrote in
several languages his name, his country and the reason for his
death. On his left and right they placed two other men who, be- 715
cause of their crimes, had received a just penalty under the law.

leges supplicium ad iustum poenamque vocabant.
Verum ipsum amborum in medio longe altius arbos
extulerat, veluti scelerum exhortator et auctor,
720 aut furtis foret ante alios immanior omnes.
    Infelix Solyma, infelix Iudaea propago!
Ultro infesta piis, non ipsis vatibus aequa!
Haec digna hospitia, has sedesque torosque parasti
coelicolum regi? Hos socios, hunc addis honorem,
725 qui mortale genus propter delapsus Olympo
sponte sub humana lustravit imagine terras?
Hic genus ipse tuum Phariis eduxit ab oris
et pedibus salsas dans ire impune per undas,
marmoreum tibi stravit iter pontumque diremit.
730 Idem etiam te coelesti dape pavit euntem
per deserta tuos miseratus vasta labores.
Huius ope hausisti dulcem de caute liquorem,
cum procul et fontes et liquida flumina abessent.
Hic te posthabitis aliis longe omnibus unam
735 gentibus elegit, meritis quam ad sidera ferret
muneribusque suis sublimi aequaret Olympo.
Promeritum his cumulas donis? Haec digna rependis?
Non vatum voces, non te miracula rerum
ulla movent, aut non praesentia numina sentis?
740 Cui unquam scelerum auctori tam dira parasti
supplicia, aut usquam quis tam crudeliter hosti
acceptus tales luit alter corpore poenas?
    Iamque trabi applicitus tergo alte haerebat. In illum
versi omnes observabant, quae funere in ipso
745 signa daret, quae spes aut quae fiducia victo.
Ille autem tacitus iandudum cuncta ferebat
immotusque. Decor roseo nondum omnis ab ore
cessit, adhuc oculis divinum est cernere honorem;
tantum respersusque genas pallentiaque ora

But his cross, set between theirs, rose far higher, as though he were an author and instigator of crimes, indeed, the most monstrous outlaw of all.   720

Miserable Jerusalem, miserable race of Judaea! Cruel to the pious and unjust even to your own prophets! Is this the welcome, is this the resting place that you have shown the King of Angels? Are these the companions and is this the respect that you have bestowed on him who willingly descended from heaven for the sake of men, and who walked the earth in human form? He led your   725 people out of the land of the Pharaoh. He made you to wander unharmed across the salt sea. Dividing the waters, he set before you a smooth path. Indeed, as you journeyed on, he fed you with manna from heaven, for he pitied your travails in the vast desert.   730 And through his bounty, you drank the sweet water of the rock, when all rivers and fresh-water streams were far off. He chose you before all the other peoples of the world, intending to lead you into heaven through his merits, and with his gifts to raise you up   735 into lofty heaven. Are these the gifts with which you requite him, are these the honors with which you repay him? Are you unmoved by the words of the prophets and by his many miracles? Can you not feel his divinity near at hand? Has there ever been a criminal for whom you have prepared such tortures? Indeed, has anyone   740 else, when captured by an enemy, endured such cruel and painful penalties?

Now he was hanging on high, his back against the cross. All eyes turned to him, watching to see what signs, what hope, what   745 faith he would show at the moment of his death and defeat. For a long time he bore everything in silence, without moving. The beauty had not yet left his noble face. You could still see the divine nobility of his eyes, but his cheeks and pale countenance were

750 humectat cruor et mixto cum pulvere sudor
plurimus, infectique rubent in sanguine dentes.
Qualis, qui modo coerulea perfusus in unda
Lucifer astrifero radios spargebat Olympo,
si mundi species violetur clara sereni,
755 et subita incipiat coelum pallescere nube,
nondum omne occuluit iubar obtusaque nitescit
pulcher adhuc facie et nimbo tralucet in atro.
    Interea matris, quam magnam nuper ad urbem
traxerat incertus rumor, certissimus aures
760 nuntius implevit natum extra moenia duci,
ad mortemque rapi captum insidiisque subactum.
Palluit infelix mediisque in vocibus artus
diriguit, licet haec patris sciat omnia certo
consilio fieri atque ipsius numine nati;
765 altius ingenti tamen exuperante dolore
cuncta oblita ruit. Resonant plangoribus aedes
foemineis. Frustra lachrymantem et acerba gementem
solantur fidae comites, iamque illa per urbem
atque huc atque illuc errat tristemque requirit
770 indefessa locum; nunc hic, nunc haesitat illic
vestigans oculis atque auribus omnia captans,
sicubi concursum voces aut hauriat ullas.
Ac veluti pastu rediens ubi vespere cerva
montibus ex altis ad nota cubilia, foetus
775 iandudum teneri memor, omnem sanguine circum
sparsum cernit humum, catulos nec conspicit usquam;
continuo lustrans oculis nemus omne peragrat
cum gemitu; tum si qua lupi, si qua illa leonis
raptoris signa in triviis conspexerit, illac
780 insequitur tota observans vestigia silva,
perque viam passim linquit pede signa bisulco.
Haud aliter, simul atque iugo prospexit in alto

dampened by a profusion of blood and sweat. Even his teeth were   750
red with blood. He was like the morning star that just now was
scattering its rays across the starry heavens: if the clear and serene
sky pales and is blemished by some sudden clouds, its light is not   755
yet entirely obscured, but still glows beautifully, though weaker
than before, as it shines through the dark downpour.

Meanwhile his mother had recently come to the city, drawn by
a vague rumor. But now she received an indisputable report that
her son had been led beyond the walls, that he had been captured   760
through treachery and sentenced to death. The unhappy woman
went pale. Her limbs stiffened as she heard the news. She knew
that all of this was according to the unalterable design of the Father and the will of the Son, yet she forgot all of that and rushed
off, overcome by her deep sorrow. The houses resounded with fe-   765
male lamentation. In vain did her faithful companions try to console her tears and bitter sobbing. Now she wandered everywhere
through the city, seeking without rest to know the sad place of execution, pausing now here, now there, seizing on every sight and   770
sound, wherever she might hear the voices of a crowd. As when a
doe, returning at evening from the mountaintops to her familiar
resting-place, mindful of feeding her tender young, finds the   775
ground all about spattered with blood, but her fawns nowhere to
be seen; running at once through the entire wood, she groans as
she scans it with her eyes. If she sees some sign of a wolf or rapa-
cious lion in her path, she follows it through the woods, her cloven   780
hoof leaving a track behind her. Just so, as soon as Mary looked up

collis oliviferi, late qui maximus urbi
incubat, ingentem concursum et lucida circum
785   spiculaque clypeosque et fulgentes equitatus,
per medios ruit et cursum extra moenia torquet.
Illam porticibus spectant altisque fenestris
effusae matres, longe et miserantur euntem.
Iamque hos iamque ruens cursu praevertitur illos,
790   ungula crebra licet volucrum proculcet equorum.
Addunt se flenti comites, pariterque sequuntur
fidus Ioannes cum matre atque innuba Martha
et soror et Salome et coniux aegra Cleophae;
cunctae atro pariter velatae tempora amictu.
795   Ecce autem videt infando iam proxima monti
erectamque trabem et scalas defixaque signa.
Quanvis nescit adhuc quae sint ea robora porro,
horruit illa tamen metuens et pectus honestum
terque quaterque manu tundens pectusque caputque,
800   'Hei mihi, nescio quid moles atque illa minatur
machina,' triste inquit. 'Gentis scio acerba furentis
circunfusa odia, et genus undique Iudaeorum,
iandudum nobis infensum, exposcere poenas.
Hoc erat, hoc tota insomnis quod nocte videbar
805   cernere signum, olim Isacidae quo summa notarunt
limina quisque suum, fuso agni rite per aedes
sanguine post longa exilia indignosque labores
Niliacis moniti furtim decedere terris.'
Haec memorans simul ibat. Eam sine more ruentem
810   rumpentemque aditus per tela, per agmina densa,
reiiciunt clypeorum obiectu et longius arcent.
Iam magis atque magis non vani signa timoris
clarescunt, propiusque in vertice conspicitur crux,
ingens, infabricata et iniquis aspera nodis.

at the crest of the olive-rich hill that brooded over the city and saw
a large mob and the gleam of spears and cavalry, she hastened   785
through the city and beyond the gate. Watching her from their
porticos and high windows, mothers pitied her from afar. As she
ran, she passed now one group of people and then another, even
though the hooves of the swift horses jostled her. Her companions   790
joined the weeping woman, and likewise the faithful John; his
mother and the virgin Martha, her sister and Salome and the sick
wife of Cleophas followed after her. All of their heads were covered in dark veils.

Suddenly, nearing the infamous hill, she saw the raised cross,   795
the ladders, and the sign fixed to the cross. Though she did not yet
know the purpose of the timbers, still she trembled with fear.
Thrice and four times she struck her noble head and breast. "Alas,
that cross, those implements" she said sadly, "portend nothing
good. I know the bitter hatred of that raving people surrounds us,   800
and that the Jews have long been hostile to us and have demanded
that we be punished. This was the sign that I seemed to see last
night when I could not sleep: the sign by which each of the sons
of Isaac marked his lintel, when the blood of the lamb had been   805
duly shed in each house and, after long exile and base labors, they
were bidden to pass stealthily from the land of Nile." So speaking,
she continued on her way. As she came rushing on, giving no
thought to propriety, forcing her way through the spears and
dense ranks, the soldiers pushed her back with their shields and   810
kept her at a distance. The proof of her fears, hardly unfounded,
came ever more clearly into view. At the summit she could see the
Cross, huge, gnarled and rough-hewn.

815   Ut vero informi mulctatum funere natum
affixumque trabi media iam in morte teneri
aspexit coram infelix, ut vidit ahena
cuspide traiectas palmas palmasque pedesque,
vulnificisque genas foedataque tempora sertis,
820 squalentem ut barbam, turpatum ut sanguine crinem,
deiectosque oculos dura iam in morte natantes,
inque humerum lapsos vultus morientiaque ora,
Alpino stetit ut cautes in vertice surgens,
quam neque concutiunt venti neque saeva trisulco
825 fulmine vis coeli, assiduus neque diluit imber —
hispida, cana gelu longoque immobilis aevo.
Ipsi illam montes, ipsa illam flumina longe
videre ingentem fessae miserata dolorem,
eque sacro aereae lachrymarunt vertice cedri.
830 Filius at postquam pinu conspexit ab alta
dilectam genitricem, animi miseratus in illa,
ut potuit, subito morientia lumina fixit
semianimis dulcemque oculis respondit amorem.
    Mox sic exanguem visu victamque dolore
835 affari extremum curasque avertere dictis:
'Hactenus, o mulier, stetimus. Non te tamen aegram
tantus edat tacite dolor. Haud sine mente parentis
haec ferimus, solo qui temperat omnia nutu.
Hic tibi pro nato' (admotum nam forte parenti
840 vidit Ioannem lachrymantem et multa gementem)
'semper erit.' Iuvenem mox idem affatur amicum:
'Haec tibi erit genitrix. Oro tutare relictam
tu saltem et matris serva communis amorem.'
His dictis lachrymas perculsis mentibus hostes
845 non ipsi tenuere; ferae ingemuere cohortes.
    Hic demum matri rediit vox faucibus aegrae,
ingentemque dedit gemitum. Tum robora largo

When the poor woman saw her son face to face, punished with   815
shameful death and nailed to the cross half dead, when she saw his
hands and feet pierced by brazen nails and his cheeks and his temples bloodied by thorns, his beard filthy and his hair rank with
gore, when she saw his downcast eyes already swooning in cruel   820
death and his dying face slumped onto his shoulder, she stood like
a cliff on an Alpine mountain top—craggy, white with frost, immutable through long ages—which neither the winds nor the blast
of three-pronged lightning can shake, nor the driving rain. Far off   825
the very mountains and streams were moved to pity as they saw
the weary woman's great sorrow. From their sacred hill the lofty
cedars wept for her. But as soon as her son, from atop the crucifix,
saw his beloved mother, he pitied her, fixing upon her his half-   830
dead gaze and reciprocating, as best he could, his mother's sweet
love.

Then he spoke to her for the last time, seeking to dispel the
cares of his mother, ashen and overcome by sorrow. "I have been   835
steadfast thus far, O woman. But let not this great sorrow silently
consume you. Hardly have I suffered these things without the
consent of my Father, who rules the universe by his nod." At this
he saw John, weeping and sighing profusely, as he stood beside his
mother. "He will always be as a son to you." Then he spoke to the   840
young man, his friend. "She will be your mother. I ask you to
watch over her who survives me, and preserve the love of our common mother." Stricken by these words, even his enemies could not
withhold their tears. The hardened soldiers groaned.   845

Finally, his grieving mother found her voice again as she let out
a deep sigh. Heartbroken, she bathed the wooden cross with her

tristis inexpletum lachrymans lavit humida fletu,
et tales amplexa trabem dabat ore querelas:
850 'Nam quem te miserae matri, pulcherrime rerum
nate, refers? Talin voluisti occumbere leto?
Nec tibi noster amor subiit, ne funera adires
talia, ne culpam alterius hac morte piares,
et letale dares miserae sub pectore vulnus?
855 Heu, quem te nate aspicio? Tuane illa serena
luce magis facies aspectu grata? Tui ne
illi oculi? Quae tam scelerata insania tantum
ausa nefas? Heu, quam nato mutatus ab illo,
cui nuper manus impubis omnisque iuventus
860 occurrit festam venienti laeta per urbem,
perque viam ut regi velamina picturata
arboreasque solo frondis et olentia serta
sub pedibus stravere, deum omnes voce fatentes?
His exornatum gemmis, hoc murice cerno?
865 At non certe olim praepes demissus Olympo
nuntius haec pavidae dederat promissa puellae!
Sic una ante alias felix ego, sic ego coeli
incedo regina? Mea est haec gloria magna,
hic meus altus honos? Quo reges munera opima
870 obtulerunt mihi post partus? Quo carmina laeta
coelestes cecinere chori, si me ista manebat
sors tamen, et vitam cladem hanc visura trahebam?
Felices illae, natos quibus impius hausit
insontes regis furor ipso in limine vitae,
875 dum tibi vana timens funus molitur acerbum.
Ut cuperem te diluvio cecidisse sub illo!
Hos, hos horribili monitu trepidantia corda
terrificans senior luctus sperare iubebat
et cecinit fore, cum pectus mihi figeret ensis.
880 Nunc alte mucro, nunc alte vulnus adactum.

tears. Embracing it and weeping uncontrollably, she lamented: "Is it thus that you return to your miserable mother, fairest of creatures? Did you wish to meet such a death? Was your love for me 850 not strong enough that you should seek such a death, that you should wish to redeem the sins of others even as you dealt me a mortal wound? Alas, who is this person I see, my son? Is that really your noble face, more pleasing to me than light itself? Are 855 those really your eyes? What wicked insanity would dare perform such an outrage? Oh, how changed from that son who so recently was greeted on your arrival in the jubilant city by crowds of youths! Before your feet, as before a king's, they laid painted car- 860 pets and strewed the ground with fronds, even as they all acclaimed you a god! Do I see you now adorned with such royal purple and jewels? Surely these were not the promises given by the heaven-sent messenger to a frightened girl. Is it thus that I am 865 more fortunate than all other women? Is it thus that I go in majesty as Queen of Heaven? This is my great glory, this is my high honor? Why did the kings bestow splendid gifts upon me at your birth? Why did the celestial choirs sing hymns to me if this was 870 the fate that awaited me? Why did I live long enough to witness such slaughter? Happy were those mothers whose children, all innocent, were taken through the king's rage at the threshold of life, when with baseless fear he plotted to compass your death! How I 875 wish you had fallen under that deluge! Such, such were the struggles that the old man bade me expect, terrifying my fearful soul with horrid admonition, and predicting a time when a sword would pierce my heart. Now the sword has struck home, leaving a great wound. Look upon me, at least, you who walk this way! 880

Saltem huc ferte oculos, vos o quicunque tenetis
hac iter, et comitem dulci me reddite nato,
quando nulla mihi superant solatia vitae,
atque meo maior nusquam dolor. Addite meme
885 huic etiam, si qua est pietas, et figite trunco.
Aut vos o montesque feri, quaeque ardua cerno
me supra frondere cacumina, parcite quaeso
vos saltem. Vos, o nostro exaturata dolore
respicite, et miserae tandem succurrite matri.
890 Nunc, nunc praecipiti casu convulsa repente
in me unam ruite et tantos finite labores.'
Hos virgo atque alios dabat ore miserrima fletus,
nec comites possunt flentem illam abducere fidae,
    Attamen armati morienti illudere pergunt,
895 (estque hosti duro in bello multo optimus hostis);
crudeli quassant risu caput. Undique circum
insultant tolluntque has laeti ad sidera voces.
'En, qui se coelo missum superique parentis
progeniem iactat, temploque urbique minatus,
900 seque deum fictor fandi mentirier audet.
I sequere, illiusque pius nunc numen adora!
Qui multos leti eripuit de faucibus olim,
non potis ipse sibi tali in discrimine adesse.
Falsus abest illi longe, nec talia curat
905 nunc genitor. Sane infami nunc liber ab orno
desiliat, si numen habet; vincla omnia rumpat.
His quoque nos signis missum credemus Olympo!'
Talia iactabant mediaque in morte dolore
semianimem hoc etiam cumulabant. Cuncta ferebat
910 ille animi invictus. Saevis clementius aequo
hostibus orabat veniam patremque rogabat
parceret ignaris rerum caecisque furore.

Make me a companion to my dear son, since I have no solace left
in life and no sorrow has ever been greater than mine. Join me to
him and, for pity's sake, nail me to a cross. You wild mountains,   885
you tree-clad peaks that rise up above me, may you at least show
me mercy! Look at me, you who have glutted yourself upon my
sorrow, come and at last help a mournful mother! Now, now, tear
yourselves asunder and come down in an avalanche upon me, end   890
my unbearable sufferings!" The wretched mother uttered these
and other lamentations, and her faithful companions could not
lead the weeping woman away.

   But the soldiers continued to mock the dying man (for enemy
treats enemy well only in hard war) and they struck his head with   895
a cruel laugh. They jeered him on all sides, laughingly raising their
voices to the stars. "Behold the man who boasted that he had been
sent down from heaven, who said he was the Son of God, who
menaced the temple and the city and dared to lie that he was a
god! Go follow him and pray piously to his divinity! He who once   900
saved many from death cannot save himself in this gravest danger.
The Father he falsely claimed is now far away and no longer cares
for him. But let him jump down from the tree if he is a god, and   905
burst all his bonds! With such signs even we will believe that he
was heaven-sent!" Thus they boasted, and as he was dying they
afflicted his half-dead body with this additional torment. But he
bore all with an unvanquished soul. More clement than was just,
he asked pardon for his tormentors and bade his Father forgive   910
them in their ignorance, blinded by rage.

At vero inter se adversis decernere dictis
auditi, poenas qui iuxta ob furta luebant
915   supplicio aequali iuvenes gemina arbore fixi.
Alter enim furiis longisque doloribus actus
ipse etiam verbis morientem heroa superbis
stringebat miser ac tales dabat ore loquelas:
'I nunc, et templi multa constructa virum vi
920   demolire adyta et post tris rursum erige luces.
Nunc, tibi si genus e summo traheretur Olympo,
eque deo genitore fores, ut te ipse ferebas,
his te nos pariterque malis prohibere liceret.
Verum, omnes quando iactasti vana per urbes,
925   nobiscum moriere, dei mentita propago.'
     Non tulit haec alter, dextra qui in parte propinquus
iam morti pendebat, et haec extrema profatus:
'Infelix, quae tanta animo dementia sedit?
Nos ambo merito luimus peccata. Sed insons
930   proditur hic odiis. Quin nos commissa fatentes
aequius hic fuerat veniam pacemque precari.'
Sic ait. Hinc divum conversus lumina in ipsum
talibus orabat: 'superi tu certa parentis
progenies (nam celsa manent te sidera), ab alto
935   respice me et dexter morienti protinus adsis!'
Annuit, et verbis deus est dignatus amicis:
'Tu partem laudis capies, tu gaudia mecum.
Quae me cunque hodie, una eadem te regna beatum
accipient,' ait. 'Astra alacri iam concipe mente.'
940   Vix ea, nam vitae labentis fine sub ipso,
dum luctante anima fessos mors exuat artus,
aestuat. It toto semper de corpore sudor
largior, et siccas torret sitis arida fauces.
Tum vix attollens oculos iam morte gravatos
945   exiguum sitiens laticem suprema poposcit

Now the youths who were crucified on either side of him and who were enduring like punishment for their thefts were heard to disagree about him. One of them, driven by rage and extremity of 915 pain, insolently railed at the dying hero with these words: "Go now and tear down the temple, built by many men, and build it up again in three days! If you were truly born of heaven, if you were 920 truly the son of God, as you yourself have said, then you could free yourself, and us while you're at it, from these evils. But since you have boasted vainly through all the land, now die with us, false son of God!" 925

The other man could not bear this. Hanging at Christ's right hand side and already near death, his last words were these: "Miserable man, what madness has lodged itself in your soul? We have both been punished deservedly. But this innocent man has been betrayed by hatred. Rather it would be more fitting for us, having 930 confessed our sins, to pray for peace and pardon." So he spoke. Then turning his glance upon the divine one himself, he spoke thus, "O you who are truly the Son of God (for the stars above await you) look down upon me and be propitious to me as I die." The god agreed and bestowed upon him these kind words. "You 935 shall have your share of praise and joy with me. Whatever realms will receive me this day will receive you also into beatitude. Be of good hope that you will reach the stars."

He could barely say these words, for his life was slipping away, 940 and he grew feverish as death freed his struggling soul from its exhausted body. Sweat covered his entire body and an arid thirst burned in his parched throat. Then, scarcely lifting his eyes, heavy with death, he asked, as a final favor, for something to drink. At 945

munera. Vix tandem corrupti pocula Bacchi
inficiunt, felle et tristi perfusa veneno,
ingratosque haustu succos, inamabile virus
arenti admorunt morientis arundine linguae,
950 quae, simul extremo libans tenus attigit ore,
respuit, atque diu labris insedit amaror.
    Interea magno lis est exorta tumultu,
dum tunicam, nato genitrix quam neverat olim,
partiri inter se famuli certamine tendunt
955 exuviasque petunt; sed erat haud sutilis ipsa
vestis et in partis ideo non apta secari.
Sorte trahunt igitur concordes: sic fore quondam
praedixere sacri corda haud improvida vates.
    Iamque fere medium cursu traiecerat orbem,
960 cum subito, ecce, polo tenebris caput occulit ortis
sol pallens, medioque die (trepidabile visu)
omnibus incubuit nox orta nigerrima terris,
et clausus latuit densis in nubibus aether,
prospectum eripiens oculis mortalibus omnem.
965 Hic credam, nisi coelo absint gemitusque dolorque,
aeternum genitorem alto ingemuisse dolore,
sidereosque oculos terra avertisse nefanda.
Signa quidem dedit, et luctum testatus ab alto est.
Emicuere ignes; diffulsit conscius aether,
970 concussuque tonat vasto domus ardua Olympi,
et caeca immensum percurrunt murmura coelum.
Dissiluisse putes divulsi moenia mundi.
Sub pedibus mugit tellus; sola vasta moventur;
tecta labant; nutant succussae vertice turres.
975 Obstupuere humiles subita formidine gentes
et positae extremis terrarum partibus urbes.
Causa latet, cunctis magnum ac mirabile visum,

last they grudgingly mixed a cup of rancid wine with gall and bitter poison and syrups noxious to the taste, but no sooner had they dipped a reed in it and raised it to the mouth of the dying man   950
than he spat it out. For a long time a bitter taste remained on his lips.

Meanwhile an altercation arose with great tumult, as servants fought over the cloak that Mary once had woven for him. They would have divided it up, but it was not sewn together and could   955
not be easily taken apart. So they agreed to play at dice for it. The sacred prophets in their provident hearts had once predicted this would occur.

Already the career of the sun had passed the mid-point of the earth, when suddenly it hid its wan head and darkness consumed the heavens. At noontide (a thing terrible to behold) darkest night   960
brooded over all the earth, and the heavens were concealed behind dense clouds, stealing all vision from mortal eyes. But for the fact that heaven knows neither tears nor sorrow, I might believe that   965
the Eternal Father was groaning with deep sadness, averting his sidereal eyes from the sinful earth. Indeed, he gave a sign and declared his sorrow from on high. The fires of heaven flashed and the aether in complicity grew dark. The lofty palace of Olympus thundered with a great roar and blind rumblings raced throughout   970
the vastness of heaven. You would have thought that the walls of the universe had been shaken and were tumbling down. The earth groaned underfoot and an earthquake ensued, as houses fell and towers tumbled, shaken from their heights. Seized with fear, the peoples in the lands below were dumbstruck. Even the most distant   975
tant cities were shaken. The cause lay hidden, but it seemed to everyone to be a great and prodigious event. Astonished populations

et populi aeternas mundo timuere tenebras
attoniti, dum stare vident caligine coelum.
980   Ipsam autem propior Solymorum perculit urbem
ac trepidas stravit mentes pavor. Undique clamor
tollitur in coelum; sceleris mens conscia cuique est.
Templa adeunt subito castae longo ordine matres;
incedunt mixti pueri intactaeque puellae,
985 perque aras pacem exquirunt, quas thure vaporant
suppliciter, sacrisque adolent altaria donis.
Ecce aliud coelo signum praesentius alto
dat pater altitonans et templum saevit in ipsum.
Velum latum, ingens, quod vulgi lumina sacris
990 arcet inaccessis, in partis finditur ambas,
et templi ruptae crepuere immane columnae.
Iamque deus rumpens cum voce novissima verba
ingenti, horrendumque sonans: 'en cuncta peracta!
Hanc insontem animam tecum pater accipe,' dixit,
995 supremamque auram ponens caput expiravit.

feared that eternal darkness would overwhelm the world as they watched the sky being consumed by shadow.

Closer at hand, fear struck the citizens of Jerusalem, prostrat- 980
ing their trembling minds. Everywhere the cries of the people rose to heaven, as each person remembered his own role in the crime. At once chaste matrons hastened to the temple in long lines, walking with their sons and virgin daughters. They prayed for peace at all the altars, burning incense in supplication, and the altars 985
smoked with holy offerings. Suddenly from high heaven, the deep-thundering Father gave another, clearer sign, as he struck the temple itself. The broad and massive screen, which hid the secret rites from vulgar eyes, was rent in two, and the temple's pillars shat- 990
tered with a tremendous cracking sound. Bursting forth with a great cry, the Son of God spoke his last, terrifying words: "All is accomplished! Now, Father, gather to yourself this guiltless soul." At which his head fell and he breathed his last. 995

LIBER VI

Iamque nigrescenti properabat vesper Olympo.
Corpora adhuc stabant inhumata infletaque cano
vertice, stipitibusque etiam nunc fixa manebant.
Talia Iosephus veniens Arimathide ab ora
5   non tulit egregiusque animi praestansque iuventa
et bellis assuetus, agri ditissimus idem
atque auri. Is Christi miratus maxima facta
addiderat comitem modo se, quocunque vocaret.
Ergo dum silvis alii formidine turpi,
10 speluncisque vagi passim conduntur in altis,
protinus ipse, animi intrepidus fretusque iuventa,
aggreditur gentis rectorem, ac talia fatur:
'Optime Romulidum, te cari in caede magistri,
quem gens nostra odiis leto mulctavit iniquis,
15 fama pias servasse manus caecumque furorem
adversus totis nequicquam viribus isse.
Scis falsa exceptum sub proditione, quod illis
obstaret coram, scelera urgens impia verbis.
Quod potes, exanimum terrae succedere corpus
20 da saltem, sociis casus solamen acerbi.
Ipse novo condam, mihi quod de more paravi,
funera mecum animo dum verso incerta, sepulcro.'
    Pontius haec contra. 'Ut potius concedere vivum
nunc corpus cuperem! Vos veri conscia testor
25 numina, tentavi versans mecum omnia, si qua
insontem morti excipere ac dimittere possem.
Et nobis pietas colitur sanctique penates.
Sed nihil invita tandem profecimus urbe;

BOOK VI

Now evening swept across the darkening heavens. Still nailed to
their crosses, the bodies remained unburied and unmourned atop
the white hill. This was intolerable to Joseph of Arimathea, noble
of soul and remarkably youthful, a veteran of wars and a man rich 5
in land and gold. Having marveled at the acts of Christ, he had recently become a disciple and followed wherever the master led.
And so, while the others, stricken with abject terror, hid themselves in forests and deep caves, Joseph went fearlessly and in the 10
vigor of his youth to see Pilate, whom he thus addressed: "Noblest
of the sons of Romulus, it is well known that your hands were
guiltless in the death of our dear master, whom our race unjustly
and odiously executed, and that you tried with all your might,
though in vain, to oppose their blind rage. You know that he was 15
captured through false betrayal, because he openly opposed them
and assailed their impious crimes. But here is something that is in
your power to grant: let me place his lifeless body in the earth, a
solace to his disciples in this sad event. I myself will bury him in a 20
new grave that, according to custom, I had prepared for myself,
conscious as I was of the uncertainties of life and death."

Pontius responded thus: "How I should have preferred to surrender him to you alive! I call the gods to witness, for they know
the truth, that I tried everything I could to save this innocent man 25
from death and to set him free. I too honor piety and my household gods. But because the citizens would not allow it, I could do

crudelis vicit gentis furor. Ite, sepulcro
30 muneribusque pii exanimum decorate supremis.'
　　Dixerat. Ille gradus montis contendit in altos,
cui sese comitem iungit Nicodemus, et ipse
multum animo cari concussus funere amici.
Iamque propinquabant paribus vestigia curis
35 figentes, unde infaustus de colle videri
iam poterat locus. Ecce autem fulgentia circum
arma vident, cinctumque armato milite clivum.
Nam, ne luce sacra pendentia corpora truncis
solennem funestarent laetae urbis honorem,
40 primorum missu armati venere ministri,
semineces qui stipitibus de more refixos
hoc ipso iniecta tumularent vertice arena.
Stabant, supplicium meritum qui hinc inde luebant
semianimes, et adhuc spirantes funere in ipso
45 optabant duros leto finire labores
et montem implebant lachrymosis vocibus omnem.
Protinus hinc atque hinc longis hastilibus instant
armati franguntque viris tabentia crura
et miseris mortem properant trabibusque refigunt;
50 deinde cava infodiunt proiecta cadavera terra.
　　At simul exanimem, qui nostra ob crimina poenas
pendebat, videre, manum abstinuere, nec ultra
sunt passi saevire in cassum lumine corpus;
mirati properos obitus collapsaque membra
55 tam cito et ora modis iam tum pallentia miris.
Quidam etiam vidisse ferunt pendere per auras
coelivagos iuvenes feralia robora circum
plaudentes alis niveaque in veste coruscos
divinum multo stillantem e vulnere rorem
60 suscipere et superas pateris perferre sub auras.
Hic ausus solus lato cui lancea ferro

nothing. Their cruel fury carried the day. Go then, and piously give the dead man the honor of a tomb and the final offerings." 30

So he spoke. Now Joseph hastened up the steep hill. He was accompanied by Nicodemus, himself greatly affected by the death of his dear friend. As they struggled along with equal concern, they looked up and saw the ill-omened place, surrounded by sol- 35 diers armed with gleaming weaponry. For this was a holy day and the leading citizens had sent guards to take down the mutilated corpses, still hanging and scarcely breathing, lest they cast a pall over the festive mood of the city. Then they were to bury them on 40 that very hill-top, covering them with sand. The two men who paid the just penalty for their crimes were still breathing, even near death. They prayed for death to end their torments and they 45 filled the entire mount with their tearful wailing. With long shafts, the soldiers assailed the two men, breaking their weakened legs and hastening their death. After that they pulled them down from the cross and threw their cadavers into the hollowed earth. 50

But as soon as they saw the corpse of Jesus, who died for our sins, they did not touch him, nor did they rage any further against his lifeless body. Rather they marveled at his swift death, at his body's having fallen so quickly, and at his face, which was so strangely pale. Some even claimed to have seen angels, in splendid 55 white robes, floating in the air about the cruel cross. As they beat their wings, they caught in chalices the holy blood that poured from his many wounds and they carried it back to heaven. Only 60

Longinus sanctos violare ignobilis artus;
irruit et longa transverberat abiete costas.
Intepuit ferrum; sanctum ebibit hasta cruorem.
65   Vulnere quo perhibent bicoloris fluminis instar
et purum laticem et rorem exiliisse rubentem.
Diluta est humus; erubuerunt gramina circum.
    Huc sese in medios Arimathes urbis alumnus
infert conscenditque trabem atque exangue magistri
70   detrahit, et densis procul aufert corpus ab armis,
veste tegens, modo quam tales mercatus in usus.
Huc volucres pueri coelique effusa iuventus
ferte pedem; aeterni largum date veris honorem.
Pallentem violam calathis diffundite plenis
75   narcissique comas ac moerentes hyacinthos
et florum nimbo divinum involvite corpus.
    Ecce autem late reboant plangore propinqui
foemineo montes; responsant flebile saltus.
Omnia flere putes sola lamentabile letum.
80   Ipsa sedet vivo genitrix moestissima saxo,
aegro corde, comis passis totoque cruentum
heu! natum complexa sinu, miserabile corpus,
atque oculos fovet ore patensque in pectore vulnus.
Nec iam ullos gemitus, nec iam ullos amplius edit
85   singultus, magno sed enim exanimata dolore
frigida, muta silet, gelidoque simillima saxo.
Circunstant aliae tunsae omnes pectora palmis.
Pars calidis corpusque lavant et vulnera lymphis;
textilibus membra involvunt pars squalida donis.
90   Haec siccat fuso rorantia genua capillo
vulneribus super accumbens haerensque cruentis;
oscula dat manibus pedibusque rigentibus illa.
Indulgent omnes lachrymis tristique ululatu
cuncta replent. Vix inde viri divellere possunt,

the ignoble Longinus dared to violate the holy body with his broad
iron-tipped lance. He ran up and struck Christ's ribs with his
wooden shaft. The iron point grew warm as it bathed in the holy
blood. It is said that a stream, like a river of two colors, issued   65
forth, formed of red blood and clear water. At once the ground
was moistened and the grass grew red.

Stepping into their midst, the man from Arimathea now
climbed the cross and brought down the lifeless body of his master. He wrapped the body in a cloth that he had just bought for
this purpose and then he bore it away, far from the press of arms.   70
Hasten hither, winged youths, angels descended from heaven!
Give him the abundant honor of eternal springtime! In laden baskets bring garlands of pale violet, of shaggy narcissus and weeping   75
hyacinth, and deck his divine body in a halo of flowers!

And now the neighboring hills resounded afar with the lamentation of women, and the woods reechoed with their plaintive cry.
You would think that all lands bewailed this sad death. His inconsolable mother sat upon a rough stone outcropping. Her heart   80
ached and her hair was unkempt as she held across her lap the
pitiable remains of her mutilated son. She kissed his eyes and the
open wound in his chest. And now she no longer moaned or
sighed: almost lifeless in sorrow, she remained as silent as a cold   85
stone. Around her, other women beat their breasts with their
hands. Some washed his body and his wounds with warm water.
Others brought clothes to cover his defiled body. One woman
dried his bloodstained knees with her hair, bending over him and   90
embracing them, while another kissed his stiffening hands and
feet. As they all gave way to weeping, the place was filled with
their lamentations. The men could hardly remove them, but

95 ipsi etiam guttis humentes grandibus ora.
  Tum corpus miseras solati exangue sepulcro
  condunt marmoreo atque affati extrema recedunt
  et magnam comites genitricem in tecta reportant.
   At Solymos penitus nondum omnis cura reliquit
100 sollicitos, sed adhuc timor acer corda premebat.
  Saepe etenim audierant sociis moerentibus hostem
  sese olim superas rediturum lucis ad auras
  promisisse, palamque sacros id prodere vates.
  Id veriti armatos subito misere viros, qui
105 noctes atque dies servarent flebile bustum,
  ne forte auferret furto quis nocte sepultum
  et totam impleret falsis rumoribus urbem,
  defunctum vita rediisse ad luminis oras
  vitalesque auras haurire atque aethere vesci.
110 Aura veni afflanti patris omnipotentis ab ore,
  aura potens coeli numen superumque voluptas:
  quicquid adhuc superat mihi dira e caede dolorum
  mente fuga laetosque animi nunc reffice sensus
  et placidos per membra riga mihi numine motus.
115 Sit fas laetitiae sentire in pectore lapsus,
  laetitiae, qua gens fruitur felicis Olympi,
  larga ubi latifluo passim torrente redundant
  gaudia, nec fines novit diffusa voluptas.
  Vertitur hic rerum facies; hic gaudia nostra
120 incipiunt. Longe in melius versa omnia cerno.
   Iam deus, ut sacros vates et sancta piorum
  concilia educens tenebris inferret Olympo,
  corporeis liber vinclis concesserat imos
  spiritus ad manes, animarum regna silentum,
125 per caecos aditus et praecipites anfractus,
  solis inaccessos radiis, loca nocte perenni
  obsita, terrificam caecae formidinis aulam.

looked on, their eyes heavy with tears. Consoling the weeping   95
women, they buried the bloodless body in a marble tomb and,
having said a few final words, they withdrew. Then the companions of the noble mother brought her back to her dwelling-place.

But the citizens of Jerusalem were still oppressed by cares, and
fear had not yet left their hearts. For they had often heard that   100
their foe promised his grieving disciples that he would return to
the light of day, and that this was clearly foretold by the prophets.
Out of fear of this, the citizens sent armed troops to guard the
tomb night and day. They feared that someone might steal the   105
corpse and fill the city with false rumors that he had returned
from the dead, that he was breathing the life-giving air of heaven.

O mighty breath of heaven! Come to me, come, wafted from
the Almighty Father's mouth, delight of the angelic orders! Banish   110
from my mind whatever sorrows remain from this dire slaughter.
Restore the happiness to my soul and fill my body with divine
peace. May I be permitted to feel joy in my heart, that joy known   115
to the angels in blissful heaven, where happiness flows everywhere
in a wide stream and expansive delight knows no bounds! Here
the face of nature is changed. Here our joy begins. I see all things
changed to something far better!   120

Now God intended to lead the sacred prophets and the holy
councils of pious men out of darkness and into heaven. A spirit
freed from the shackles of the body, he withdrew to the nether
spirits, the kingdoms of silent souls. He journeyed over sightless
paths and steep cliffs untouched by the sun, realms covered in per-   125
petual night, a baleful dwelling of blind fear. Here the night-
wandering brethren spent their days, ruling those realms unreach-

Hic stabulant vivisque tenent impervia regna
noctivagi fratres, superi quos ira parentis
130 coelo immane nefas animis excussit adortos,
Tartareisque genus miserabile mersit in antris,
quando illos tenuit regnandi tanta cupido.
Nunc miseros poenis manes — miseri magis ipsi —
exercent vinctosque tenent nigrantibus oris.
135 Interiora habitant barathrum irremeabile clausae
crudeles animae ad superos dum vita manebat.
Nunc merita expendunt vasta fornace sepultae
supplicia undantemque ferunt caligine fumum.
Ignis ibi aeternus, semper nova flamma renascens.
140 Innocuae circum sedes secretaque longe
atria circuitu longo. Hic incendia nulla,
nulli obsunt penitus flammis ultricibus ignes,
umbrarum sed iners requies penitusque silentis
mundi temperies. Secretae his sedibus aevum
145 insontes degunt animae, quibus haud sua damno
admissa, at primi scelus exitiale parentis
detinet hic clausas, nostrae nil lucis egentes,
poenarum prorsum expertes, nisi luce carerent
iucunda, qua gens gaudet stellantis Olympi.
150 Hic patres sanctum genus antiquissima proles,
qui vitam vinclo nullo, non legibus ullis
compositam incultos primi degere per agros
inter oves, patrio tantum se more tenentes,
iustitiae memores ultro rectumque colentes.
155 Hic vatesque pii, qui quondam numine pleni
ventura intrepide magnas cecinere per urbes,
quique dedere orbi leges divina reperta,
quosque datis olim iuvit parere volentes,
matronae atque viri vitaeque in limine rapti.
160 Omnibus unus amor coelique arrecta cupido.

able by living men. In his anger, the Heavenly Father had flung
them down from heaven for plotting unspeakable outrage, and he   130
condemned their miserable race to dwell in these Tartarean caves,
if they so greatly desired to rule. Now they were even more miserable than the miserable ghosts they punished and held captive in
this dark land. Trapped in the deepest recesses, the pit whence
none returns to the upper world, were those souls who knew only   135
cruelty while yet they were alive. Now they paid the penalty they
deserved by being buried in a vast furnace and suffering the constant billows of black smoke. There stood an eternal fire, its flame
constantly reborn.

But elsewhere were dwellings for the innocent, not uncomfort-   140
able, and hidden halls arrayed in a great circuit. Here one encountered no fires with punitive flames, but rather the motionless peace
of the shades and the stillness of a silent world. Here blameless
souls, admitted through no fault of their own, sat out their days.   145
It was the mortal sin of their first parents that kept them here.
They were not deprived of our light and they had no part of pain,
though they lacked that happy light enjoyed by the angels of starry
heaven. Here were the patriarchs, oldest of the chosen race, who   150
first lived chaste lives as shepherds in the fields, without restraint
or law. Ruled only by paternal custom, they were just by nature
and cultivated righteousness. Here as well were the pious prophets
who once, inspired by God, sang fearlessly of things to come   155
throughout the great cities of the world, giving laws and divine
revelations. And there were those who were pleased to obey the
laws willingly and those souls, male and female, who had been
snatched away at the very threshold of life. All of them were
united in their love and desire of heaven. And remembering what   160

325

Et iam promissi memores, tum forte per umbras
secla recensebant tacitis volventia lustris
ducebantque animis finem adventare malorum.
    Atque haec inter se laeti sermone serebant:
165 'En tandem volvenda dies, en imminet illa,
cum lucem liceat supera et convexa tueri.
Hanc claro pater omnipotens manifestus Olympo
ostendit nobis divino numine plenis.
Nos aliis subito mortalibus ore canentes
170 optandam votis venienti liquimus aevo.
Iam iam aderit lux nostra, dei indubitata propago:
ille erat, ille! feri sub imagine saepe leonis
ostensus nobis oculos caligine pressis,
unus pro multis qui sese proderet ultro
175 morti defensosque daret nos hoste subacto.
Vicit, io! tandem leo magni a sanguine Iudae
Davidae genus! O passim gaudete, beati
mortales, gaudete animae iam corpore functae!
Iam vos astra vocant; nunc, quae tot clauditur annos,
180 ianua siderei nobis aperitur Olympi!
Iamque erit, ut, nostris promissum vocibus olim,
laetitia exiliant montes collesque resultent,
pampineis vincti formosa cacumina sertis,
quales creber agris aries oviumque minores
185 subsiliunt foetus mollique in gramine ludunt,
balatus matrum dum per iuga longa sequuntur.
Ipsi iam fontes, ipsa et vaga flumina passim
melle fluant, niveo passim vaga flumina lacte,
lacte mero, et dulci distillent nectare rupes!'
190   Talia perstabant memorantes; cuncta fremebant
intus laetitia ingenti plausuque secundo.
Sicut ubi cives longa obsidione tenentur
urbem intra et vallum portarumque obiice tuti,

had been promised, they happened just then to be sitting in the shadows, counting the silent passage of the centuries and thinking that the end of their travails was at hand.

And with joy they conversed thus with one another: "Truly that day has come round, that day is nigh, when we shall be per- 165
mitted to see the light again and look upon the vault of heaven. The Almighty Father foretold to us that day, filling us with his divine spirit as he himself appeared in the clear heavens. We sang to other men about this glorious day, leaving it as a dream for coming ages. Soon, soon our light will come in the form of the true Son 170
of God. Often, when our eyes were plunged in darkness, he revealed himself as a wild lion, he who, for the sake of all, would willingly die to defend us and vanquish our enemies. And now the 175
lion of Judah of the race of David has prevailed! Oh blessed mortals, rejoice! Rejoice, you whose spirits are already freed from your bodies. The stars call to you. The gates of starry heaven, closed these many years, stand open! And now it shall come to pass, as 180
was promised through our voices long ago, that the mountains leap for joy and the hills dance, with their lovely, vine-covered peaks! May they be like a ram in the fields or lambs that constantly skip and disport themselves in the meadows, as they follow 185
the bleatings of their mother along the hilltops! Soon all the streams and all the meandering rivers will flow with honey and snow-white milk, with pure milk, and the rocks will exude sweet nectar!"

Such was their constant discourse and everything around them 190
seemed to second these words with great joy and inward approval. They were like citizens whom a long siege has confined within a city's walls, protected by fortifications, while the enemy is heard

dum circum sonat atque in muros arietat hostis,
195 tum si forte acies procul auxiliaribus armis
adventare vident socias e turribus altis,
consurgant animosque alacres spe ad sidera tollant.
    Ecce autem foribus succedens maximus ultor
haud cunctatus adest divina luce coruscus!
200 Porta ingens adversa manet centum aerea vastis
vectibus, aeterni postes. Hanc nulla neque igni
vincere vis valeat, neque duri robore ferri.
Constitit hic deus ac dextra stridentia claustra
impulit, intremuit quo late exterrita tellus
205 impulsu; vaga contremuerunt sidera mundi,
regiaque umbrosis immugiit atra cavernis.
Ad sonitum horrifico adventu de vallibus imis
lucifugi raptim trepido adsunt agmine fratres,
humana facie crurum tenus, inde dracones.
210 Tum rudere insuetum dirumque e faucibus ignem
efflare atque domum piceo omnem involvere fumo.
Continuo patuere fores; procul ecce repente
sponte sua absiliunt convulsi a cardine postes.
Apparet confusa intus domus altaque circum
215 atria; rarescunt tenebrae et nox caeca recessit.
Nam deus haud secus obscuris conspectus in antris,
perstringens oculos divina luce refulget
quam cum gemma ignes splendore imitata corusco
in noctem thalamis lucet regalibus atrasque
220 exuperat tenebras, largo et loca lumine vestit
purpurea circum perfundens omnia luce.
    Ut vero in mediis divum penetralibus hostes
videre et faciem invisam agnovere per umbras,
ardentem radiis ac mira luce coruscam,
225 protinus aspectu subito terrentur et imas
coniiciunt sese in latebras linguaque remulcent

328

everywhere, pounding the battlements: if perchance from the lofty
towers they see some allied troops afar off, approaching with arms   195
to aid them, they rise to their feet and, buoyant with hope, let
forth a shout that reaches all the way to heaven.

Behold! Their supreme avenger, beaming with divine radiance,
stood even now at the gates. In his path was an enormous portal
and posterns of eternal brass, fortified with a hundred bolts. The   200
portal was so strong that not even fire or the hardness of iron
could overcome it. Here stood the Son of God and he pushed
open the screeching door with his right hand. Frightened, the
ground shook in all directions at the impact, and the wandering
stars of heaven trembled, and the drear palace groaned in its shad-   205
owy caverns. At the noise, the brethren who flee the light, that
timid crew, suddenly appeared from their deepest vales in a terrifying onrush, human down to their waist and dragons below. They
began to roar strangely, breathing a baleful fire from their gullets   210
and filling the palace with black smoke. At once the doors swung
open and fell over of their own accord, violently wrenched from
their jambs. Now the interior, with its lofty halls, was dimly revealed. The shadows grew thinner and blind night receded. For   215
even so did the Son of God, seen amid the darkness of caves,
blind their eyes with his divine radiance, like a jewel whose splendor rivals fire, a jewel that shines at night in royal chambers and,
vanquishing the darkness, decks everything with its golden glow.   220

When the enemies of God saw that he had reached the innermost parts of their palace, and recognized, amid the shades, his
hated face, radiant with divine light, they were immediately struck
with terror and ran for cover to the deepest lairs of hell, licking   225
their tails, which lay across their bellies. Prostrate on the floor of

commissas utero caudas stratique tremendum
nequicquam umbrosis in spelaeis ulularunt,
quales quae celsis habitantes Alpibus Euros
230   semiferae gentes semper patiuntur et imbres,
Romanas si forte procul fulgentibus armis
ora exertantes antris videre phalangas,
fumosa extemplo palantes tecta relinquant,
dispersique iugis, si qua altius exit in auras,
235   rupe sedent longeque duces mirantur euntes.

     At casti circum manes fulgore repente
lustrati passas tendunt ad sidera palmas,
laetitiaque fremunt subita lachrymasque dedere,
nec saturare queunt animos oculosque tuendo.
240   Tum laeto ultorem propius clamore salutant
una omnes: 'Ut te coeli lux clara sereni
optatum aspicimus, nec nos spes nostra fefellit,
qui revehis mundo primo concessa parenti
munera et humanum genus omne in pristina reddis,
245   ignotasque vias aperis ad sidera coeli!
Venisti; aethereae facies tua lampadis instar
diffulsit, tandemque oculis lux reddita nostris.

     Sed quibus exhaustum erumnis quantisque procellis
iactatum accipimus? (Nigras ea fama sub oras
250   detulit.) Indigno quis sanctum vulnere corpus
foedavit? Quaenam hasta tuo intepuisse cruore,
quod ferrum tulit? An tantum mortalibus ullis
in terris licuit scelus? O quae clausa remotis
aequora littoribus terrarum cingitis orbem,
255   quae vos, quae tenuere morae? Quibus abdita claustris,
leto opifex tam crudeli cum vester obiret?
Vos tum diluvio mortalia cuncta decebat
obruere et terras penitus delere nocentes!
Nosne per haec superi soboles certissima regis

330

the shadowy caves, they let out in vain a tremendous bellowing. They were like the half-savage inhabitants of the lofty Alps, who constantly endure wind and rain; if they chance to stick their 230 heads out of their caves and see far off the Roman phalanxes approach their land with gleaming arms, at once they quit their smoke-filled homes and scatter along the peaks. Seated atop the highest cliff they can find, they marvel to see far off the approaching generals. 235

But the chaste spirits, purified by the splendid light, held up their hands to heaven and sang out and wept with sudden joy. They could not fill their hearts or their eyes enough with looking on him. Then with a joyous noise all of them together hailed their avenger. "Oh, clear light of serene heaven, how gladly we look 240 upon you, whose coming we have yearned for, and not in vain! You restore to the world those gifts promised to our first father. You return the human race to its former goodness, opening up unknown paths to the stars of heaven. You have come, you face glow- 245 ing like the lofty lamp of the sun. Finally the light has been restored to our eyes!

"But we have heard—since news of it reached even to the nether world—of the great cares that tormented you and the great storms that buffeted you. Who has defiled your sacred body with an undeserved wound? What spear or sword could bear to grow 250 hot with your blood? How could any human on earth commit such a crime? Oh, you waters that circle the earth, girt by distant shores, why did you delay? In what caves were you hiding when 255 your Maker suffered so cruel a death? Then should you have flooded all mortal things! Then should you have completely destroyed the offending earth! True son of heaven's king, is it so that we have been saved by these wounds of yours? No! The prize was

260 vulnera servamur? Non, o non praemia tanti,
non tanti ipsa salus erat olim nostra! Tua ingens
haec pietas. Adeon tibi curae incommoda nostra,
o hominum dulcis requies superumque voluptas?
Nos patris aversi nostro irritavimus iras
265 crimine; tu diras solvisti sanguine poenas.'
      Talia per campos iactabant undique inanes.
Tum laeti obscuro pariter se carcere promunt
ultoremque deum supera ad convexa sequuntur,
sedibus ut placidum degant stellantibus aevum
270 felices animae. Gens iam defuncta periclis
humanis, secura operum, secreta laborum!
Primus it ipse hominum generis pater ante, nec ora
conscius antiquae noxae audet tollere coelo;
primores procerum inde alii, non vana futuri
275 pectora, quis nivea velantur tempora vitta.
Ingemuere illi, quos ob commissa cremandos
sorbet in abruptum fundoque exercet in imo
Tartarus eructansque incendia dira caminus,
unde animis miseris nullo patet exitus aevo.
280 Praecipue rex ipse aulae illaetabilis alto
cum sociis moerens ducit suspiria corde,
et fortunatis sedem, quam liquerat ipse,
invidet aetheream, furiis immanibus actus.
      Illi iter ad coeli debentia regna tenebant
285 aera per tenerum laeti regemque canebant,
felices animae, quibus est in secula vitae
iam nunc parta quies praeclusaque ianua leti.
Applaudunt volucres purum tranantibus aurae.
Subsidunt Euri; fugere ex aethere nimbi,
290 arridetque procul clari liquidissima mundi
tempestas; coelo arrident rutila astra sereno.

not worth the price. Our salvation was not worth your wounds. 260
Your piety is great. Is it possible that our tribulations should concern you so, sweet solace of men and delight of heaven? By our
crime, we incited the anger of our Father and alienated him, while
you, with your blood, paid the harsh price." 265

Such were the words spoken by the shades throughout the underworld. Then they joyously went forth from their dark prison,
following their divine avenger up to the vaulted heaven. There, on
starry thrones, these happy souls would spend their peaceful eternity, freed from human perils, freed from toil and labor. First went 270
the father of the human race. But he, ashamed of his ancient sin,
dared not raise his face to heaven. Then followed other leaders of
their race, souls who did not prophesy in vain, their temples girt
with snowy chaplets. But others groaned whose sins condemned 275
them to be consumed by fire. They were swallowed up and shoved
into the pit of hell by the Tartarean furnace that belched forth
baleful fires, from which, eternally, there was no escape. Especially
the king of that joyless realm sighed and pined in the depths of his 280
heart; together with his companions, he envied the blessed the
ethereal abode that he himself had left, driven by tremendous fury.

Meanwhile the others happily journeyed through the thin air to
their well-earned abode in heaven. Having won a life of eternal 285
peace, having shut the doors of death, these happy souls now
hymned their king. The wandering breezes hailed them as they
swam through the air. The winds subsided and the clouds vanished, and far off the purer climate of the resplendent sky smiled
upon them. The stars smiled in the serenity of heaven and dawn 290

Assurgit matutinis aurora volucrum
cantibus; assurgit rubefacta vesper ab aethra.
    Atque ea dum longe vastum per inane geruntur,
295   iam lux Eois properabat tertia ab oris,
et pater omnipotens, nato immortalia membra
illustrans, penitus divinum afflavit honorem,
quodque fuit mortale modo et violabile corpus,
immortale dedit. Non tanta luce sereno
300   sidera clara polo, non aureus ipse nitet sol.
Ceu qui per noctem imposito cinere obrutus ignis
delitet et nusquam tecto se lumine prodit,
si quis eum flabris exsuscitet arida circum
nutrimenta serens, subitis ad tecta favillis
305   emicet et totas lustret splendoribus aedes.
Talis, ubi turpe irrepsit senium, unicus ales,
congessitque sibi ramis felicibus altum
summo in colle rogum posuitque in morte senectam,
continuo novus exoritur nitidusque iuventa
310   effulget cristis et versicoloribus alis.
Innumerae circum volucres mirantur euntem;
ille suos adit Aethiopas Indosque revisit.
    Iamque adeo in terris hominum miranda paventes
terruerant animos visa. Umbris orbe fugatis
315   sole recens orto, moestissima Magdalene,
amissi desiderio perfixa magistri,
cum sociis ibant prima sub luce ferentes
in gremiis molles patriae felicis odores,
myrrhamque et costum spicaeque unguenta Cilissae,
320   supremum tumulo munus, varioque serebant
multa inter sese tristes sermone per agros:
'Nos miseras, quas non secum lachrymabilis heros
duxerit ad letum! Vigiles quis fallere nobis
custodes dabit, aut quis grandia saxa sepulcro

arose, accompanied by the angelic matins. Then evening rose, covering the reddish sky.

And while this was taking place far off in the vast fields of air, already the third day was rising out of the East and the Almighty   295
Father, glorifying the immortal body of his Son, filled him entirely with divine breath. And what had just now been a mortal body, subject to harm, was made immortal. The brightest stars on the clearest evening, the golden sun itself, shine not with such brilliance. He was like a dim fire that hides at night, covered with   300
ashes, never betraying itself because its flame is hidden; but if someone should blow on it and feed it dry tinder, at once it flares up to the roof in swift sparks, lighting up the entire house with its splendor. He was like that nonesuch of a bird that, at the on-   305
set of ignoble old age, goes to a hilltop and builds itself a lofty pyre of fertile fronds. Putting its old age to death, it immediately rises up reborn. Blazing with youth, it gleams forth crested and adorned with dazzling wings, and all the other birds marvel as it   310
passes. Then it flies off to its Ethiopian home and revisits the Indies.

Meanwhile, upon the earth, the recent miracles terrified the timid souls of men. The darkness was driven from the world, and a new sun had arisen. The inconsolable Magdalene, filled with   315
longing for her lost master, went with her companions at daybreak carrying in their skirts the sweet incense of their fertile fatherland, myrrh and spikenard and the unguents of sweet-smelling Cilicia, as a final offering at the tomb. And they sadly talked of many   320
things as they passed through the fields. "Alas for us! Our lamented master did not take us with him to his death. Who will help us to elude the guards? And who will roll away the huge

325 evolvet clauso, ut saltem fungamur inani
munere deserto solventes debita busto?'
Talia fundentes, tumulum venere sub ipsum,
iactantesque oculos faciles huc plurima et illuc,
milite conspiciunt collem et custode vacare,
330 claustraque mirantur secum patefacta sepulcri.
Accedunt. At ubi tumulum conspexit inanem,
naribus unde ingens fluctus se evolvit odorum,
hoste putans clam sublatum, pulcherrima virgo
flebat, inornatum vellensque a vertice crinem,
335 et nemora et montes gemitu silvasque replebat.
Cui iuvenis subito effulgens in vestibus albis
aligerum genus et coeli de gente, 'Quid,' inquit,
'quaeritis o matres? Longo iam parcite luctu
atque animis moestum tandem revocate timorem.
340 Laetitiam certa iam spe praesumite vestram,
quandoquidem, quem vos adeo lugetis ademptum
funestaeque trabi fixum, ut scelus omne piaret
vestraque sponte sua deleret crimina morte,
unus pro cunctis, Erebi iam rege subacto
345 manibus ex imis has rursum lucis in oras
victor iit, superaque etiam nunc vescitur aura
corporis ablutus, quaecunque obnoxia morti.'
Haec ait, et nubi volucer se immiscuit atrae.
Ipsa etiam res ecce oculis oblata repente
350 firmavit dubiumque animum tenebrasque resolvit.
Nanque morae impatiens atque acri saucia amore
dum virgo sedet ac miratur inane sepulcrum
artificumque manus, videt ipso in marmore fictum
littus arenosum, porrectum in littore piscem,
355 fluctivomum, ingentem, nant aequore qualia in alto
mole nova ignaros nautas terrentia cete.
Monstrum turpe, atrum, spaciosi bellua ponti,

stones that seal the tomb, so that, at the very least, we can offer   325
this small gift, as custom prescribes, at his deserted tomb?" So
speaking, they came to the tomb itself. As their nimble eyes darted
in all directions, they saw that the hill was free of soldiers and
guards. To their astonishment, the doors to the tomb stood open.   330

They entered. But when the beautiful virgin saw the empty
tomb, from which a huge wave of incense rose into her nostrils,
she wept, imagining that Jesus' enemies had removed his body by
stealth. Pulling at her disheveled hair, she filled the woods and
mountains and dales with her cries. Suddenly a youth of the   335
winged race of angels, splendid in his white robes, said: "What do
you ask of the angels, O women? Do not weep, and banish fear
and lamentation from your souls. Confident in hope, be happy,
since he whom you mourn as lost, who was nailed to the woeful   340
cross to atone for the sins of all and who wished to expiate your
sins through his own death, has once more returned victorious
from the depths into the realms of light. For the sake of all the   345
dead, he single-handedly defeated the lord of hell. Even now, freed
from his body and from all that partakes of death, he breathes the
air of heaven." So he spoke and then hid himself in a dark cloud.

Now this sudden apparition strengthened Mary's foundering
faith and scattered all darkness from her mind. For as the young   350
woman sat there, transfixed by love and impatient of delay, she
marveled at the empty sepulcher and the skill of the artists who
had fashioned it. Carved in the very marble was a sandy beach and
a fish stretched out across it. This creature, spitting up sea water,
was as huge as the whales that swim the deep, terrifying ignorant   355
mariners with their monstrous size. As the black, foul beast of the
broad sea spouted water from its mouth, the prophet Jonah could

cuius ab undivomo vates imperditus ore,
redditus aereas rursum veniebat ad auras.

360 Tum secum: 'Superi nunc, o nunc visa secundent
praesentes. Veterum agnosco non vana futuri
signa,' inquit, 'nempe, ut monstri deformis in atro
tris vates latuit luces, tris gutture noctes
ingluviem passus vastaeque voraginis antrum,

365 sic heros multum ad superos defletus amicis
inclususque cavo saxo terraque sepultus
delituit, saepe ut (memini) praedixerat ipse,
ad coelum rediit saxumque reliquit inane.'
Talia versanti subito sub imagine falsa

370 ignoti agricolae sese deus obtulit ipse
et tumulum iuxta astabat. Mox farier orsum
virgo amens animi agnovit, conversaque luce
respicit ecce nova illustrem radiisque coruscum.

      Corruit ac genua amplexans, satis ora tueri

375 clara nequit, corpusque oculis obit omne volutis,
et moestum aspectu dulci saturavit amorem.
Continuo tristi penitus de pectore moeror
omnis abit rediitque decor suus ilicet ori
marmoreo. Sed adhuc turgentibus humida gemmis

380 lumina inornatique fluunt per colla capilli.
Sic ubi rore madens pluvio rosa languida honestum
demisit caput atque comam largo imbre gravatam,
tum si purpureo sol lumine vestiat arva
et redeat madido facies innubila coelo,

385 protinus attollens sese rursum illa resurgat
puniceique sinus divinum pandat honorem:
talis erat posito virgo pulcherrima luctu.
Ardet amans ipsum affari regemque deumque
et coram solitas haurire ac promere voces;

be seen once more emerging unharmed into the upper air. Mary said to herself: "Oh angels, be present and confirm what I have now seen! The ancient prophet's portents were not in vain. For even as the prophet hid three days and three nights in the black belly of that hideous monster, suffering the onrush of water in the whirling cave of its mouth, even so did Jesus hide in a hollow grave, buried in the earth and lamented by his friends. And yet, as I often remembering him predicting, he has returned to heaven, leaving an empty grave." Such were her thoughts when suddenly Jesus appeared in the guise of a unknown farmer. He stood beside the tomb, and as soon as he began to speak, the virgin turned to him, beside herself, for she recognized him. She looked upon him in his splendor and radiance, covered with an unearthly light.

She ran to him and clasped his knees. But she could not get her fill of gazing on his glorious face, and as her eyes surveyed his entire body, she satisfied her sorrowing love in his sweet regard. At once all sadness departed from the depths of her heart and the native beauty returned to her serene face. But her eyes were still wet with tears and her unkempt hair spilled over her neck. She was like a dew-covered rose that hangs its fair head and leaves heavy with rain. If perchance the sun favors the fields with its lovely light and the clouds disperse in the rainy sky, suddenly the rose lifts itself up and returns to life, unfolding the divine beauty of its empurpled bosom. Such was the lovely virgin, once she had laid aside her lamentation. She longed to speak to the king and god himself, to exchange well-known words with him face to face. But

390   dum trepidat quae prima haerens exordia sumat,
     mortales visus adopertus nube reliquit.
       Fama Palaestinas subito haec impleverat urbes.
     Iamque sacerdotes trepidare et quaerere, si qua
     multiplici vulgi sermoni occurrere possint
395   rumoremque astu premere atque extinguere famam.
     Custodes busti in primis, qui cuncta canebant,
     muneribus superant subiguntque haud vera profari,
     sublatum furto intempesta nocte cadaver.
     Sed non ulla datur verum exuperare facultas,
400   quoque magis tendunt serpentem sistere famam,
     amplius hoc volat illa omnemque exuscitat oram.
     Sunt etiam qui se ore canant vidisse patentes
     sponte sua tumulos multosque exisse sepulcris,
     quorum iampridem tellus acceperat ossa.
405   Interea socii, quos in diversa paventes
     iandudum terror longe disiecerat omnes,
     tabescunt moesti. Coelo cecidisse videtur
     omnibus extinctum aeterna caligine solem,
     et penitus mundo iucundum lumen ademptum.
410   Tandem conveniunt et adhuc loca nota frequentant
     tectaque, quae vivo sibi quondam rege fuissent
     dulcia, sed casu nunc desolata recenti.
     Dux nusquam; miseris nusquam datur illa tueri
     ora illosve oculos aspectu luce serena
415   iucundos magis aut coelo radiantibus astris,
     et cunctis nomen dulce obversatur ad aures.
     Aegrescunt moesti; squalent circum omnia luctu.
     Haud secus atque olim exemit cum subere pastor
     cerea dona cavo vacuumque alveare reliquit:
420   tunc etiam, fumus quas longe dispulit ater,
     hinc illinc glomerantur apes et inania frustra
     tecta adeunt denso volitantes agmine circum,

while she hesitated, wondering how to begin, he wrapped himself   390
in a cloud and concealed himself from mortal sight.

At once the news of what had occurred spread through the cities of Palestine. The priests were aghast and sought a way to silence the incessant chatter of the people. They meant to suppress
this rumor by guile and so to extinguish it. First they bribed into   395
silence the guards at the tomb, who were revealing everything.
Then they compelled the guards to lie and say that his cadaver
had been purloined at night. But there was no way to get around
the truth. The more they tried to stop the spreading rumor, the   400
more it went around, rousing all the land. Indeed, some said that,
with their own eyes, they saw graves open wide of their own will,
that many who had long been buried in the earth rose and walked
out of their tombs.

Meanwhile Jesus's disciples, whom terror had long since dis-   405
persed in all directions, were filled with mourning. All of them felt
as if the sun, its ancient splendor past, had fallen from the sky, as
if all the sweet light had been rent from the world. Finally they returned to the houses they knew. While yet their king lived, these   410
had been places of joy. But now, after the recent event, they stood
desolate and their leader was nowhere to be found. Nowhere could
his disconsolate disciples look on his face. No more could they see
those eyes more lovely than gentle daylight or the light of the   415
heavenly stars, and his sweet name was ringing in all their ears. In
their mourning, the disciples languished. Everything seemed squalid
with lamentation. As when a shepherd has taken the waxen honey
from a hollow cork-tree, leaving the hive empty, the bees, who
were driven off by black smoke, gather from all directions. In vain   420
they approach their empty hive, flying around it in a dense swarm,

direptosque favos aegrae populataque passim
mella vident, nequicquam hyemi congesta futurae.
425   Ecce viros autem tali moerore sepultos
attonitae miris matres rumoribus implent:
vidisse aligeros coeli de gente ministros;
regem ipsum vidisse novo fulgore micantem,
et vacuum porro tumulum vestesque relictas.
430 Protinus ergo alii montis petere ardua cursu
contendunt rapido festini, ubi inane sepulcrum,
ast aliis incredibile ac mirabile visum,
et primo ancipites delusos credere matrum
effigie pavitantum oculos et imagine falsa,
435 ut nobis saepe in somnis spectare videmur
absentum vultus simulacraque luce carentum,
donec sera illis sub luce in tecta coactis
ingrediens sese ostendit manifestius heros,
voce habituque deum confessus, imagine nota,
440 divinum toto iaciens de corpore lumen.
    Hinc Thomas aberat Didymus, vicina pererrans
oppida, quo metus impulerat duce nuper adempto.
Isque ubi dein rediens est sacrae redditus urbi
acceptusque domo, socios videt ecce recenti
445 attonitos casu ac caeco terrore silentis,
quales aut templum, domini aut ubi divitis aedes
marmoreas petiit ruptis de nubibus ignis
terrificisque locum implevit splendoribus omnem,
stant intus pavidi cives; quatit omnibus horror
450 pectora; vix longo post tempore corda residunt.
Obstupuit visu ignarus causamque requirit,
et socios dictis Didymus demulcet amicis,
quem senior Petrus amplexus lachrymisque profusis
menti caniciem humectans sic denique fatur:
455 'Vidimus (o iam nos felices!), vidimus ipsum,

saddened to find all the combs gone and all the honey stolen
which they had gathered in vain for the coming winter.

Now the awestruck women brought the wondrous news to the   425
men, still buried in their great sadness. They told of seeing angelic
ministers of heavenly descent. They told of seeing the king himself, shining in weird glory, his grave empty and his clothes scattered. At once several of them ran to the steep mountain, where   430
the grave stood empty. But to others this seemed incredible, miraculous. At first they imagined that the uncertain eyes of the frightened women had been deluded by a mirage, as when in dreams we
seem to see the faces of those who are absent and the forms of   435
those who have died. Until one evening, when they had all gathered within the house, their hero entered and manifested himself
in complete clarity. By his wonted voice and form and dress, he revealed himself a god, casting divine light from his entire body.   440

It happened that Thomas, called the Twin, was absent. He was
wandering through nearby towns, driven by fear at the recent
death of his teacher. Returning to the sacred city and welcomed
once more into the house, he found that his friends were awestruck by what had just happened and dumbfounded with blind
fear. It was as if the sky had opened up and lightning struck some   445
temple or the marble home of some rich lord, filling everything
with a terrifying splendor, as all the frightened citizens stand still
within: every heart pounds with fear, and even much later the
beating has scarcely subsided. Not knowing what had happened,   450
Thomas was amazed and asked the cause, calming his friends with
kind words. The aged Peter embraced him and wept profusely, his
white beard moistening with tears, and he said: "We saw him! We
saw him, as we used to see him in the past! The King of Angels   455

ut soliti, regem spirantem aurasque trahentem
coelicolum regem, qui nos modo morte reliquit!'
Haec ait, exultansque animo coelum usque tuetur.
Ille autem (neque enim narranti talia credit)
460   'Ipsene rursus,' ait, 'coeli hoc spirabile lumen
aspicit? An potius simulacri apparuit umbra
atque oculos fallax vestros elusit imago?'
    'Immo," ait, 'illum ipsum divino illa ipsa gerentem
vulnera et antiquam servantem corpore formam
465   vidimus ac veros manibus tractavimus artus.
Vidi oculis, vidi ipse meis et vulnera novi!
Vesper erat clausaeque fores clausaeque fenestrae.
Nos intus pavidi latitare et corpora victu
curare ac positis moesti discumbere mensis.
470   Ecce autem tecti in mediis penetralibus ipse
improvisus adest et inobservabilis heros
effulget, clausis ingressus limina portis —
improvisus adest inopinaque gaudia portat.
Continuo ad lucem visum tectum omne cremari.
475   Nos trepidare animis subitoque horrescere visu
attoniti. Verum ille metus vanumque timorem
increpitans, vetuit trepidos exurgere mensis.
"Ipse ego sum; pacem unanimes agitate metusque
solvite," tentandosque dabat simul omnibus artus,
480   vulneraque, insigni quae corpore quina gerebat;
quin etiam parcis nobiscum accumbere mensis,
non fugiens, solito est coram de more loquutus,
ceu mortalis adhuc quae verba novissima nuper
ad mortem properans nobis memoranda reliquit.
485   Tum demum liquidis abiens se immiscuit auris.'
Haec senior, sociique eadem simul ore canebant.
    Necdum finis erat verbis, cum protinus ecce
cum clamore ruit Cleophas, fidissimus unus

was breathing again, who but recently died and left us!" As he
spoke, he gazed up at heaven with an exultant heart. But Thomas
did not believe and he asked, "Does he really look once again   460
upon this light of heaven that we breathe? Or was it rather the
shadow of a dream, some false image that deceived your eyes?"

"Truly," Peter replied, "we have seen his divine body as it used
to be, but bearing the wounds of his crucifixion. With our hands
we touched his actual body. With my own eyes I saw him and rec-   465
ognized his wounds. It was evening and the doors and windows
were shut. We were frightened and hid within the house. We fed
our bodies, reclining sadly at the meal that had been set. Sud-   470
denly, in the inmost part of the house, Jesus himself unexpectedly
appeared, crossing the threshold unobserved through the closed
door and bringing us unlooked-for joy. At once the whole place
seemed to be on fire with his light. We trembled in our souls and
felt a thrill of fear at the sight of him. But he chid us for our vain   475
trepidation and forbade us to rise from the table. 'I am he. Be at
peace, all of you, and do not be afraid!' And he offered us his body
to examine, with its five wounds. Indeed, he sat with us to the   480
modest meal. Without fleeing, he spoke to us in his accustomed
way. And as though he were still mortal, still hastening to his
death, he repeated what he had recently spoken in life. And then
he disappeared into thin air." So Peter spoke, and his companions   485
confirmed this account.

They had not yet finished speaking when Cleophas, the most
faithful of those whom Jesus had added to the twelve disciples,

e multis quos bis senis subiunxerat heros,
490 atque haec dicta dabat: 'Vos, o iam solvite luctu!
Vivit adhuc socii leti iam lege solutus!
Vivit adhuc! Vidi his oculis, vidi ipse, deique
auribus his hausi vocem consuetaque verba!
Audiit hic etiam mecum viditque loquentem'
495 (atque manu nutuque propinquum Amaona signat.)
'Nam modo forte animis moesti dum incedimus ambo,
qua se demissi incipiunt subducere montes,
extulit aereas Emaus ubi turribus arces,
advena in ignota nobiscum veste profectus,
500 externosque gerens habitus comes additur ultro.
Taedia dumque viae vario sermone levaret,
interdum eruptis roramus fletibus ora,
et gemitus imis dolor exprimit ossibus ardens,
ille aegros dictis solari et quaerere causas
505 crebra resurgentis luctus. Nos ordine cuncta
pandimus, atque ducis letum crudele profamur,
quo moriente simul perierunt gaudia nostra,
ut factis verbisque animos spe arrexerit ingens
ingenti, sed dehinc nos morte fefellerit omnes.
510   'Non tulit ulterius contraque haec reddidit ille:
"Non pudet, o semper caecos et lucis egentes?
Nonne ducis vestri quondam crudelia vates
funera praedixere omnes, casusque nefandos
tot veterum monimenta docent, haud credita vobis?
515 Sponte sua leto caput obvius obtulit ipse,
unus pro multis, patrias quo flecteret iras,
atque iter ipse suo signaret ad astra cruore.
Haud ita vos ille erudiit. Nam saepe futura
haec eadem de se longe ante retexit amicis.
520 Atque equidem memini, nuper media urbe canebat,

346

rushed clamorously in. "Leave off your lamentations!" he cried.   490
"He lives, friends, freed from the grip of death! I saw him with my
own eyes and heard him with my own ears, speaking as he was always wont to do." He pointed to Amaon, who stood beside him.   495
"He heard and saw him too. Just now we were walking sadly near
where the mountains join the plain, where the windy citadel of
Emaus rises up with its towers. A wayfarer set out with us, though
in his foreign garb we could not recognize him. With his varied   500
conversation he lightened the tedium of the journey. At times
tears bedewed our faces and a sigh would rise up from deep within
us. With his words he comforted us in our pain and asked the
cause of our recurring sadness. We told him everything that had   505
happened, including the cruel execution of our teacher, whose
death ended all our joy and how, through word and deed, this
great man had awakened great hopes in our hearts, but how all of
these expectations were disappointed by his death.

"Finally he seemed to lose patience and answered with these   510
words: 'Oh you blind men, deprived of light, are you not
ashamed? Haven't all the prophets predicted the cruel death of
your master? Didn't the records of old times, which you hardly believed, foretell this disgraceful end? Of his own volition he exposed himself to death for the sake of all, sparing us his Father's   515
vengeance. By his own blood he marked for us the path to heaven.
This is not the way he taught you. For he often told his disciples
that these events would come to pass. Indeed I remember that, in
the midst of the city, he was just recently speaking, but concealed   520

obscura sed verborum rem ambage tegebat.
Nunc autem manifesta patent, nunc omnia aperta,
nube palam ablata, nec spes fovistis inanes.
  '"En rex, qui positas conseverat ordine vites,
525 praetendens sepem insidiis hominumque ferarumque,
omnibus immissis incassum ex urbe ministris,
quos leto dedit insontes manus effera agrestum.
Demum infelices natum ipsum misit in agros.
Nam pater omnipotens, post tot fera funera vatum,
530 ipse suum iussit natum descendere Olympo.
Ecce Palaestini, furiis immanibus acti,
natum etiam hauserunt crudeli funere herilem.
Haud impune tamen: rex urbe ultricibus armis
iam iam aderit, flammisque feros agitabit agrestes,
535 et pangenda aliis credet vineta colonis."
  'Sic fatus, coepit voces ex ordine vatum
obscuras veterumque evolvere facta parentum,
cuncta docens letum Christo crudele minari,
quo mortale genus tenebris educeret atris.
540 Ut clara antiquis portendi haec omnia signis
monstrabat ratione, oculis caligine abacta!
Ut nostros mira inflexit dulcedine sensus!
Ut resoluta novo ardebant praecordia amore!
Qualiter aut aeris rigor acri solvitur aestu,
545 aut glacies concreta novo sub sole liquescit.
Non illum tamen immemores agnovimus ante
quam ventum ad sedem parvamque subivimus urbem.
Nanque iter ulterius fingentem seque ferentem
longe alias sedes petere, ambo oravimus, isdem
550 nobiscum haud asper tectis succederet hospes.
Id quoque praecipiti suadebat vesper Olympo,
iam piceo terras infuscans noctis amictu.
Paruit, et mensas comitum est dignatus egenas.

his meaning in dark riddles. Now all stands revealed. All clouds
have been dispersed and you have not hoped in vain.

"'Consider that king who planted all his vines in a row and
built a fence against the wiles of men and beasts. From the city he   525
sent thither all his ministers, but in vain. They were unjustly slain
by an enraged mob of peasants. And so he finally sent his own son
into the ill-omened fields. Even so did the Almighty Father, after
the death of so many of his prophets, send down his own Son
from heaven. Behold how the people of Palestine, driven by insane   530
rage, consumed that Son and heir in a cruel death. But not with
impunity. For the Lord will soon return to the city with avenging
arms and will harass the husbandmen with his flames, and he will
give over his vineyards to be planted by other farmers.'   535

"Thus speaking he began to interpret the obscure words of the
prophets and the deeds of our ancestors. He taught that all things
portended that Christ would suffer a cruel death, so that he might
lead the race of men out of darkness. How clearly he showed that
all these events were forewarned in ancient prophecies, and thus   540
he drove the darkness from our eyes. How sweetly he enthralled
our senses! How resolutely our hearts burned with a new love, like
hard bronze melting away in the fire, or compacted ice in the
morning sun! But in our confusion, we did not recognize him un-   545
til we reached our resting place. He claimed that he had further to
go, that he was seeking a distant land. But we both besought him
to join us and to be our welcome guest under the same roof. He   550
was also persuaded by the advent of evening, which descended
from heaven and covered the earth in the dark mantle of night.
And so he willingly joined us in our humble meal. As soon as he

Ut primum fruges tostas cerealia liba
555 attigit et solito fregit de more, repente
nox abiit, tandemque oculis lux addita nostris.
Agnosco, et supplex manifestum numen adoro.
Sed subito volucres abiens ceu fumus in auras
respuit humanos visus sensusque refugit.'

560   Talia narrabat Cleophas, quae, credita cunctis,
vera negat Thomas et coeptis perstat in isdem.
'Haec mihi (dicam iterum) nemo persuaserit unquam,
illum ipsum his oculis clara nisi luce videndum
hausero et his manibus nisi vulnera contrectaro.'

565 Sic fatur. Simul ecce deus cum lumine largo
improvisus adest iterum sociosque revisit.
Et clausae mansere fores, mansere fenestrae.
Non aliter vitri, quod tectis summovet auras,
lumine sol penetrat splendentes aureus orbes,

570 insertim radios iaciens in opaca domorum,
nec tamen ulla viae apparent vestigia adacta
luce, sed illaeso saepe itque reditque metallo.
Sternunt sese omnes terrae genibusque salutant.
Ut vero Didymus manifesto in lumine vidit

575 vulnera monstrantem et se nomine compellantem,
horruit et prono confestim corruit ore,
multaque se incusans animo sic denique fatur.
'Vera mihi facies, verus deus, omnia novi.
Haud equidem (fateor) vivum te credere quibam

580 post obitus coeli hoc iterum spirabile lumen,
has auras haurire. Animo tua dicta labanti
exciderant penitus, modo quae suprema dedisti.
Demens, qui te obita non posse huc morte reverti
crediderim, cum quarta alios iam luce sepultos

585 ad superas coeli nuper revocaveris oras,
et memini atque aderam. Sed me mens laeva tenebat.

touched the baked wheat cakes and broke bread according to custom, suddenly night departed and our eyes could see. I recognized   555
him and in suppliant fashion adored his now manifest divinity.
But he disappeared at once like smoke in the wandering breeze, rejecting human sight and fleeing from our senses." Thus spoke
Cleophas.

    Though all believed him, only Thomas denied the truth of his   560
words and could not be swayed from that opinion. "To repeat," he
said, "no one will ever persuade me of such things, until I clearly
see Him with my own eyes and touch His wounds with my own
hands." So he spoke. And behold, at once, unexpectedly, the god
reappeared to his disciples in an abundance of light. Yet the   565
doors and the windows remained closed: as when the golden sun
passes through the shining orbs of glass that keep the wind from
the house, casting its rays into the dark interior, it leaves no trace   570
of the light's path as it passes and repasses without breaking
the metal frame. All of them prostrated themselves and greeted
him on their knees. When he saw Christ manifest, revealing his
wounds and calling him by name, Thomas was awestruck and   575
suddenly prostrated himself as well. Full of self-reproach, he spoke
thus: "You are the true face of God and truly God! Now I see! I
confess I could hardly believe that after your death you could be
alive, could breathe again the air and see the light of day. Your final   580
words quickly left my inconstant heart. Even when you called others forth into the fields of heaven four days after their burial, even
then, foolishly, I could not believe that you would return, though I   585
remember your miracle, though I was there. But my wayward

Forsan at[1] haec tamen haud vestro sine numine tanta
(credo equidem) venit dementia. Forsitan olim
proderit hic seris haesisse nepotibus unum,
590   et manibus voluisse prius contingere corpus,
ne facies aut vana oculos eluderet umbra.'
     Talibus orantem deus et lux ipsa reliquit
nunc hos, nunc adiens alios et pectora firmans.
Nec prius evasit mundi mortalibus oris
595   quam quater exoriens dena sol luce rediret.
Forte igitur Petrus et socii vada salsa secabant
remigiis lembum subigentes, dum sibi victum
arte parant solita piscesque in gurgite captant.
Et iam per totam vano quam longa labore
600   defessi noctem frustra madefacta legebant
retia, cum iuvenem egregium videre liquentis
fluctifrago tractus e littore prospectantem.
Nec primo agnovere deum divinaque membra,
quandoquidem se mortali celaverat ore.
605   Ipse dehinc tali compellans voce natantes
'Dextram,' ait, 'affectate, viri. Huc appellite puppim.
Hac dabitur vanum non effudisse laborem.'
Nec mora, praeceptis parent dextraque per undas
detorquent alacres cursum nodosaque lina
610   proiiciunt; moti sonuit plaga coerula ponti.
     Iamque senex tacito sociis Petrus innuit ore
auxilioque vocat nutuque manuque silentes,
significans praedam innumeram. Vix retia cuncti
plena trahunt; capti saliunt per vincula pisces.
615   Sensit Ioannes hic numen et 'Heus!' prior inquit,
'o socii, non fallor, adest deus, ille magister,
ille quidem! Agnosco divinos oris honores.
Laetitiam ut iactat vultuque oculisque decoris!'
Quod simul accepit Petrus, haud cunctatus, ab ipsa

mind deceived me. It may be that this great madness has not come without your divine influence, as I believe it did. Perhaps someday it will profit our distant descendants to know that one man hesitated to believe until he had touched your body with his own hands, lest his eyes be deceived by some empty shadow."   590

God and the light itself left Thomas after he had spoken, passing now to one man, now to another, fortifying their hearts. And Christ did not leave the world's mortal shores before the sun had risen and set forty times. Sometime later it happened that Peter   595
and the other disciples were rowing a boat upon the salt sea, obtaining food for themselves by their accustomed trade of catching fish. And now, wearied from having spent the whole long night toiling in vain, they were pulling in their damp nets when they saw   600
a resplendent youth looking out across the clear waves from the breakwater of the shore. At first they did not recognize the Son of God or his divine body, for he had concealed himself in mortal form. But he called to the men in the boat with words like these: 605
"Keep to your right, men. Steer the boat here. You will not labor in vain." They obeyed his words at once and eagerly altered their course, tossing their knotted ropes, which made a splashing sound upon the blue surface of the restless sea.   610

Now the aged Peter silently nodded to his companions and, by his expression and the gestures of his hands, he sought the assistance of his silent friends, indicating a big catch. All of them together could hardly pull up the full nets. The captive fish were jumping through the netting. John first sensed the presence of divinity. "O friends," he said, "I am not mistaken: God, our divine   615
teacher, is here with us. I recognize the divine nobility of his countenance. What joy shines forth in his face and his fine eyes!" As soon as Peter heard, he jumped from the ship and threw himself

620   desiliit rate et aequoreas se iecit in undas,
      quo regem salsos per fluctus primus adiret,
      quanvis multa timens gliscentibus aequore ventis.
      Caetera deinde manus terrae advertuntur, et omnes
      remivaga siccum cupidi tenuere carina.
625   Tum victu ut vires revocent, cerealia mensis
      dona onerant iussi, vivosque in littore pisces
      una omnes torrere parant, succensaque pruna
      suggeritur circum. Teter petit aethera nidor.
         Ut compressa fames, surgit rex optimus ipse,
630   confessusque deum, sociis ita denique fatur:
      'Pacem optate, viri; pacem laudate quieti.
      Salvete aeternum, socii, aeternumque valete.
      Este mei memores; ego claro poscor Olympo.
      Iamque adeo duris animos aptate ferendo
635   omnia, nec propius saevos adiisse tyrannos
      sit timor atque duces affari et vera monere.
      Non vos maiestas soliorum aut sceptra superba
      terrificent regum, lucis nil huius egentes.
      Haud longe tum quaerendum, quae tempora fandi,
640   quis modus aptus. Ego praesens adero omnibus, ora
      vestra regens. Dabitur verborum copia cuique,
      nec coelo vires vos et solamen ab alto
      deficient. Cum sol decimo iubar aureus ortu
      extulerit, pater afflabit coelestibus auris,
645   diffusumque animis numen divinitus addet,
      praeside quo freti, reges rerumque potentes
      nil veriti, nostrum vulgabitis undique nomen.
      Tum sanctum sese genus aurea tollet ad astra,
      densus agens veluti laxis se palmes habenis
650   luxuriat, foliisque simul foetuque gravescit.
      Denique, cum suprema dies illuxerit orbi,
      omniaque eliciam patefactis ossa sepulcris,

into the sea, wanting to be the first to swim through the salt waves   620
and reach the king, even though he feared the winds that now
stirred the waters. The rest directed their boat toward the shore
and eagerly reached dry land in their oar-driven skiff. To regain
their strength with a meal, they were bidden to heap loaves of   625
bread on the tables and they prepared to grill over charcoal, all together, the fish they had hauled to shore. The strong smell reached
to heavens.

Once they had satisfied their hunger, their great king rose and
avowed his divinity, speaking thus to his fellows: "Choose peace,   630
men. Praise it in the serenity of your hearts. And so forever,
friends, be well and farewell! Remember me. For now I am called
back to bright heaven. Prepare your souls for hardship by enduring everything. Have no fear in approaching tyrants or addressing   635
powerful men and teaching truth. Nor should you be frightened
by the majesty of thrones or the proud scepters of kings, since you
yourselves have no need of this world. You need not spend a long
time seeking the right moment and the right manner in which to
speak. I shall be there with you, guiding your words. Each man   640
will be given eloquence enough. Nor will the strength and solace
of heaven desert you. When the golden Sun raises its glowing lan-
tern on the tenth day, my Father will breathe down upon you a
heavenly wind, filling your souls with divine spirit. Relying on   645
that, you will not fear kings or powerful men, but will proclaim
our name everywhere. Then a saintly race will raise itself up to the
golden stars, rising untrammeled like a thick vine, laden with fruit
and leaves. And when the final day shines upon the earth, I will   650
call forth all the bones from their open graves, and they whom the

atque iterum in lucem emergent, quos terra tegebat,
hanc vallem, densa hos implebunt agmina colles,
655　matres atque viri, vixque hausta luce perempti;
ipse ego iura dabo mediaque in valle sedebo
quaesitor, vitas populorum et crimina pendens.
Vos etiam mecum, bis senis sedibus ipsi
sublimes, mortale genus censebitis una,
660　bis senaeque tribus gentis tum vestra subibunt
arbitria, et vestros mirabitur orbis honores.
　　'Interea, Petre, te (nulli pietate secundum
novi etenim) his rerum summam clavumque tenentem
praeficimus cunctis, ultro qui nostra sequuti
665　imperia. Hoc te praecipuo insignimus honore.
Tu regere et populis parcens dare iura memento.
Summa tibi in gentes iam nunc concessa potestas.
Iamque pios tege pace; voca sub signa rebelles.
Quencunque in terris scelus exitiale perosus
670　admonitum frustra iusta devoveris ira,
colloquio absterrens hominum coetuque piorum,
idem erit invisus coelo. Non ille beatis
sedibus aspiret, nisi tu placabilis idem
dignatus venia meliorem in pristina reddas.
675　Iamque adeo tibi concessum mortalibus aegris
claudere siderei portas ac pandere coeli.'
　　Talia mandabat, terras hominesque relinquens.
Sic natis moriturus oves et ovilia pastor
commendans caris, furta insidiasque luporum
680　edocet et pecori contraria pascua monstrat.
Sic sociis aevo iam fessus nauta biremem
credit inexpertosque docet varias maris oras
et brevia et syrtes et navifragas sirenas.
　　His animadversis totius lucida circum
685　palmiferi nubes collis capita ardua texit,

earth has concealed will emerge once more into the light, and their multitude will fill the valleys and the hills, women and men and those who lived but briefly after birth. On that day I will lay down 655 the law and, in the midst of a vale, like a judge I will weigh the lives and transgressions of all the people. And you, raised up on twelve seats, will join me in judging the human race. The twelve tribes will submit to your judgment and the world will marvel at 660 your glory.

"And since you, Peter, stand second to none in piety, I have placed you as paramount, as keeper of the keys for all who follow our teachings; I set you above the rest; I grant you this special honor. Rule the people gently, even as you lay down the law. To 665 you is now given supreme power over the nations. Protect the pious with peace and recall to your standard those who have revolted. Whomsoever you have warned in vain upon the earth, in your hatred of his mortal sin, whomsoever your just anger has excommunicated from the society of men and the company of the 670 pious, he will be despised by heaven as well. Let him not aspire to beatitude unless your indulgence deigns to forgive him and restore him, a better man, to his earlier lot. For you have the power to shut or throw open the doors of heaven to toiling men." 675

With these commands, he left behind humanity and the earth. Even so does an aged shepherd commend his sheep and sheepfolds to his dear sons, warning them of the thefts and cunning of wolves and the fields that are harmful to the flocks. Even so 680 does the mariner, weary with age, commend his ship to his companions; and as they are inexperienced, he teaches them about the various regions of the sea, its shallows, sandbanks and shipwrecking sirens.

With these instructions given, a bright cloud covered the steep bluffs of the palm-rich hill, and the curving shores glowed with 685

et curva aethereis fulserunt littora flammis.
Interea totum exercent nova gaudia coelum.
Alituum coelestum acies sanctique volucres
dant manibus plausus et multicoloribus alis,
690   instaurantque choros; fremitu aetheris atria fervent.
Pars pendent speculis et propugnacula laeti
coeli summa tenent et moenia celsa coronant.
Obvia pars portis parat ire patentibus, et se
quisque auris credunt ac pennis aethera obumbrant.
695   Hi plectro indulgent fidibusque; his tibia cantus
dat bifores; alii cava cornua flatibus implent,
raucisonasque tubas et ahenea cymbala iactant.
Atque ubi ter patris ad solium pernice chorea
indulsere choris, ter ludo lucida regna
700   lustravere polique e vertice decurrere.
Non aliter sunt ingressi volucri agmine contra,
concentu vario et multisono modulatu,
quam, prolapsa Remi cum nondum urbs alta iaceret,
Tarpeiaeque arces starent, lateque subactis
705   iura daret populis rerum pulcherrima Roma,
consul victor, ovans pugnatis undique bellis,
intrabat rediens Capitoliaque alta subibat.
    Talis nubivago tendebat ad aethera gressu
vera dei soboles. Ut vero flectere quiret,
710   iratus quoties genitor mortale pararet
exercere genus meritis ob crimina poenis,
omnia fert secum caedis monimenta nefandae,
in primis duplicemque trabem infandamque columnam,
brachia cui vinctus tulit aspera verbera, et acres
715   virgarum fasces infectaque sanguine lora
hastamque et calamo pendentia pocula levi.
Tris deinde ingentes et acuta cuspide vectes
cernere erat, quibus effossus palmasque pedesque,

flames from above. Throughout heaven a new joy was felt. The
angelic host, with their wings of many hues, rose up in applause.
As they joined in choruses, the halls of heaven resounded with 690
their happy noise. Part hung down from the watch-towers, joyously holding on to the utmost battlements of heaven and crowning its lofty walls. From the opposite direction, others prepared to
pass through the open doors, entrusting themselves to the air and
darkening the skies with their wings. Some struck the lyre with a
quill, while others played the reed-pipe with twin holes. Others 695
blew on hollow horns and raucous trumpets, or clashed brazen
cymbals. In swift choirs, they thrice sang hymns before the throne
of God and thrice traversed the shimmering realms in joy, swiftly
descending from the heavenly heights. These choirs came together 700
swiftly, joining in a concert of many parts. It was exactly so when
the city of Remus was not yet laid low and the Tarpeian Rock
stood proud and Rome, most beautiful of all things, gave laws to
the nations it had conquered abroad: a victorious consul, celebrat- 705
ing a triumph after wars had been fought on all sides, returned to
the city and ascended the lofty Capitol.

Even so did God's true son hasten toward heaven with an airy
step. But to mitigate the anger of his Father, whenever, in his
wrath, he was about to punish humanity for its transgressions, Je- 710
sus carried with him all the implements of his shameful execution,
above all the cross and the infamous post to which his arms had
been bound when he was harshly lashed and beaten with rods and
bloodstained whips. There was also a spear and a cup hanging 715
from a smooth reed. Then came three spikes, large and sharp, that
had pierced his hands and feet, and the crown of prickly thorns.

sertaque nexilibus vepribus conserta rigebant.
720 Illic et longo Romani signa senatus
hastili suspensa cavoque latentia cornu
lumina, quod superas abies tollebat ad auras,
quamque manu rex pro sceptro gestavit arundo,
omnia quae pueri coelestes ante gerebant,
725 singula quisque, polique arcem per inane petebant.
Suspexere viri attoniti acieque sequentes
alituum nubem ac regem videre per auras
tollentemque manus coelique serena secantem,
cum subito rutila haec venit vox reddita ab aethra:
730 'Ne trepidate. Quid haeretis supera alta tuentes?
Cum genitore deus regnandum accepit Olympum.'
    Nec mora, carminibus coeli domus ardua longe
auditur resonare modisque per astra canoris.
Contra etiam plausere atque haec alterna canebant
735 laeta viri, coelumque oculis animisque petebant.
'Omnes o plausu gentes linguisque favete
atque deum canite ascensu supera alta tenentem!
Quadrupedum volucrumque genus mutaeque natantes
exultent, tractus terrarum ubicunque patentes!
740 Ipsi dent montes, ipsa et dent flumina vocem
laeta suam et scatebris volventes flumina fontes,
quodque ambit longis terras anfractibus aequor.
Cuncta suum agnoscant auctorem et carmina dicant,
semper ut idem ingens regnarit, originis expers,
745 cum genitore deo deus, omnia numine complens;
ut nullis mox principiis aut semine nullo
omnia condiderit, coelum terrasque fretumque
quaeque vago passim subsunt animantia coelo;
ut terras ponto discluserit, aethera terris;
750 luciferis coeli lustraverit atria flammis,
tellurisque sinum variis appinxerit herbis,

Hanging from a long spear were the emblems of the Roman Senate and lamps hidden in a hollow horn, raised aloft on a pine-   720
wood spear. Finally the stalk that he, as king, had carried in place
of a scepter. Each of these objects was carried by a different celestial youth, as they rose through the air to the heavenly palace. The   725
disciples looked on in astonishment and followed the droves of
angels with their eyes. They watched the king lift his hands as
he rose through the air, swimming through the serene fields of
heaven. Suddenly a voice came down from the gleaming heights of
heaven: "Be not afraid. Why do you stand there looking up at   730
high heaven? Together with his Father, our God has received
heaven as his realm."

Without delay, heaven's lofty homes rang far and wide with
singing, while tuneful harmonies rose into the stars. The disciples
applauded and sang in joyous responsion, longing for heaven with
their eyes and souls. "Join us, all you nations, with tongues of   735
praise; hymn the god who has ascended to his heavenly kingdom.
Let the birds, the beasts and the voiceless swimmers of the deep
exult, and the expanses of earth spreading in all directions. Let the   740
very mountains and rivers find voice, and the undulous streams at
freshet, and great Ocean who engirds the world in his broad meanders. May all of nature know its Creator and sing how he has
reigned, eternal and uncreated, God and God the Father, enfolding all things in his divine power; how, in due course, he created   745
everything without origin or seed, heaven and earth, the sea and
all the souls who inhabit the lands beneath the wandering heavens; how has he divided the earth from the sea and the air from
the earth, and lighted the halls of heaven with his dazzling flames,
and spangled the lap of earth with flowers of every hue; and pro-   750
vided food from crop and nourishing drink from the vine. You

sufficiatque satis fruges et vitibus almum
humorem. Tu cuncta moves; tibi maximus aether,
quique super latices concrescunt aethere, parent.
755 Nubila te ventique timent; te vesper et ortus
observant obeuntque tuo sua munera nutu,
et tibi monstriferi obsequitur plaga coerula ponti.
Tu manibus validis terrarum pondera libras,
atque gravem vacuo suspendis in aere molem,
760 rerum elementa locans aeterno foedere, ut omnia
concordi in medium tendant nitentia motu.
Tu liquidas per inane vias is nubibus actus,
aurarumque sedens veheris pernicibus alis.
Non tibi tempus equis fugit irrevocabile adactis;
765 semper idem ante tuos oculos praesensque moratur,
quodque est quodque fuit, simul et quod deinde sequetur.
Ipse etiam parens tibi coeli in vertice fixus
sol stetit. Ipsa etiam surgens in cornua luna
atque suos penitus requierunt sidera cursus.
770 Te mandante suam vim saepe innoxius ignis
dedidicit; pueri in mediis fornacibus astant
illaesi, iactantque tuas ad sidera laudes.
Tu mare navigerum concreta dividis unda
et populis medios das ire impune per aestus.
775 Tu rapidos flectis ripis mirantibus amnes.
Tu largam tactis e cautibus elicis undam,
idem largifluos fontis et flumina sistens.
Ipsa tuo tremit aspectu conterrita tellus,
quosque procul tangis fumant ad sidera montes.
780 Assurgunt reges pavidi, tibi sceptra, tibi arma
deponunt longeque tremunt et numen adorant.
     'Tu surdis aures, oculos tu lumine captis,
et vocem mutis et vires sufficis aegris.
Tu revocas in vitam obita iam morte sepultos

move everything and hold sway over the sky and the rains that form in heaven. The clouds and winds fear you. Evening and morning dance attendance upon you and carry out their assigned 755 tasks at your pleasure; so too the blue expanses of the sea, rich in beasts. With your powerful hands you balance the weight of the earth, suspending its ponderous mass in the emptiness of space and binding nature together in eternal compact, as all things strive 760 in concordant motion toward a common center. Floating on clouds, you rise through clear paths of air, drawn along by the swift, winged breezes. Irretrievable time, with its rushing horses, does not flee from you. Ever and always constant in your eyes re- 765 main what is, what was, and what is yet to be. In obedience to you, the very sun stood fixed at its summit. The very courses of the stars and the newborn moon were suspended too. Fire, at your command, made harmless, forgot its wonted strength, as youths 770 stood unscathed in the fiery furnace and shouted your praises to the stars. You split open the ship-bearing sea, turning the waves into solid mass, that men might walk unharmed amid the surge. You bend rushing rivers while the banks look on in wonder. From 775 rocks your touch brings forth abundant streams, even as you dry up fountains and rivers. The earth trembles at the sight of you and the mountains, at your touch, shoot smoke far up into the stars. Frightened monarchs rise up and yield to you their scepters and their arms, trembling far off and praying to your divinity. 780

"You give ears to the deaf and eyes to the blind and voice to the mute and strength to the weak. You recall to life those who are

785 et rursum potes amissos accendere sensus.
    Non te vis crudi perterruit horrida leti;
    non Erebi confusa domus, loca foeta timoris.
    Te manes tremuere. Plagae regnator opacae
    umbrarum passim populantem immitia regna
790 non tulit atque imis trepidus se condidit antris,
    prostrataeque metu procul Eumenides latitarunt,
    dum superas praeda ingenti vehereris ad arces,
    nunc ubi iam victor regnas superumque beato
    concilio imperitas, provisaque tempora longe
795 disponens, reparas fugientia secula mundo,
    nec requiesse sinis solis volventia lustra.
    Salve opifex rerum vastique salutifer orbis!
    Aspice nos propius, propius genus aspice nostrum!
    Morte tua patet aetherei cui ianua Olympi,
800 et veteres tandem pater obliviscitur iras.'
      Talia littorea laeti sub rupe canebant
    undeni proceres omnisque effusa iuventus.
    Non tamen exuerant vanum inter tanta timorem
    gaudia, nondum animos firmati numinis aura
805 aetherea, sed adhuc latebras cavaque antra petebant.
    Sicut ubi accipiter celsa de sede columbam
    sustulit apprensam, quam rostro evisceret unco,
    diffugiunt aliae huc illuc; mox turribus imis
    condunt se celeres et inania murmura miscent.
810 Haud illi secus attoniti post funera regis
    inclusi tecto stabant, promissa magistri
    coelo expectantes, venturum numen ab alto.
      Iamque aderat promissa dies, deciesque tenebras
    flammifera sol exoriens face ab orbe fugarat,
815 cum pater omnipotens coeli regione serena,
    sidera purpureo reficit qua purior aether
    lumine, coelicolum in medio media arce sederet,

dead and buried and you reignite their lost senses. The horrid 785
might of death could not affright you, nor the dusky house of
Erebus, fecund in fear. The ghosts trembled before you. The ruler
of that dark land could not bear to see you empty his baleful realm
of all its shades, and so he timidly hid himself in the deepest caverns. Far off the prostrate Furies took cover until you had as- 790
cended to heaven with all your spoils. Now that you reign there in
triumph, now that you rule the blessed council of angels, you dis-
pose times yet far off with your providence, you restore the fleeting
ages of the world and suffer the revolutions of the sun never to be 795
stilled. Hail, Creator of the world, who bring health to the entire
universe! Look on us with favor, look on our generations! Your
death has opened for us the doors of heaven, and your Father has
finally forgotten his ancient anger." 800

So the eleven men sang joyously beside the sea, joined by all the
youth of the land. Yet even in this joy they had not shed their vain
fears. For their souls had not yet been strengthened by the breath
of the heavenly Spirit, and so they still sought hiding places
among the hollow caves. As when a hawk from his lofty lair holds 805
a dove he has seized and eviscerated with his hooked beak, all the
other doves flee this way and that, hiding in the tall towers, cooing
in vain; even so, at the death of their king, did the disciples remain 810
shut up in doors, waiting for what the master had promised them,
the Divine Spirit that would descend from high heaven.

Now the promised hour approached. On the tenth day the
glowing sun, with its fire, drove the darkness from the earth. The
Almighty Father sat enthroned in the serenity of heaven, where 815
the purer air makes the stars burn brighter. In his palace, amid the

tempora dispensans secretaque foedera mundo.
Cui se tum exutus moribundos filius artus,
820   diffulgens radiis ac mira luce coruscus,
obtulit et magno genitorem affatus amore est.
'O pater et sociis tandem succurrere nostris
tempus,' ait, 'quos amisso duce protinus omnes
acer agit timor huc illuc atque omnia terrent
825   imbelles, quoniam mortali corpore creti.
Discute terrorem hunc animis et pectora firma,
ne casus nequeant alacres procurrere in omnes.
Illis me propter Solyme Iudaeaque passim
insidias infensa odiis molitur iniquis;
830   Tu tamen hos olim fore, qui praestantibus ausis
per gentes canerent nostrum indelebile nomen,
quacunque Oceano terrarum clauditur orbis,
et populos nova conversos ad sacra vocarent,
pollicitus, genitor, tibi nec sententia nutat.
835   Hos (quando coeli demum non abnuis arcem)
ipse ego saepe tua fretus pietate labantes
firmavi implevique animis, siquidem affore Olympi
promisi auxilium subito et tutamen ab arce,
quo freti reges regumque minacia iussa
840   contemnant alacresque ruant in funera leti
sponte sua verae pro relligionis amore.'
    Sic fatus, palmas ferro ostentabat acuto
traiectosque pedes et hians in pectore vulnus
sertaque et hamatos vepres quos hostia gessit.
845   Annuit oranti, delibansque oscula nato
reddidit haec pater aeterno devinctus amore:
'Iam concessa petis. Dabitur tibi nate quod optas.
Promissa (ne tende manus) afflabimus aura
quos vis, atque viros nostro flammabimus igni,
850   ut pro te blandae proiecto lucis amore

angels, God dispensed the seasons and struck the secret covenants of the world. He the radiant Son, having shed his mortal frame and glittering with wondrous light, addressed his Father with great love: "O Father, it is time to aid my disciples at last. On the death of their master, fear has driven them in all directions. Everything frightens their timid souls, born to mortal bodies. Shake this fear from their minds and strengthen their hearts, that they might be able gladly to encounter whatever may come. On my account Jerusalem and all Judaea, hatefully and unfairly, set traps for them. Father, you promised that one day they would be the ones who with great daring would sing my undying name to the nations, wherever the globe is encircled by Ocean, and would call converted peoples to new rites; nor has your intention changed. Since you do not deny them a place in heaven, often did I invoke your piety to strengthen their wavering hearts and fill them with courage. I promised that help would soon arrive from heaven. With that assurance they could look with contempt upon the threats of kings and rush eagerly to their deaths for love of the true religion."

So speaking, he showed his wounded hands and his pierced feet. He revealed the gaping wound in his chest and the crown of hooked thorns that he had worn as a sacrificial victim. And his Father granted his wish. Vanquished by eternal love, he kissed his Son and said: "What you ask has already been granted. What you hope for will be yours. You needn't hold out your hands in supplication. As you wished, I will inspire those men and inflame them with my fire. So shall they set aside their love of dear life and, for

820

825

830

835

840

845

850

non ferrum aut flammas metuant morsusve ferarum
aut crinita rotis circum laniantibus haustra.
Quique reformidant nunc omnes aeris auras,
obiicient certis alacres se sponte periclis
855   pugnando et claras animas de corpore reddent
contemptu necis et vera virtute superbi.
Non illos aestus, non illos frigora sistent,
letiferum aut campos cum sidus findit hiulcos,
coerulea aut glacie cum nectit flumina bruma,
860   verum ultra Gangem auditi, Bactra ultima supra,
Ismara Bistoniasque plagas Seresque[2] remotos
Gadibus et virides penetrabunt voce Britannos.
Implebunt terras monitis et cuncta novantes
templa, pererrato statuent tibi maxima mundo;
865   ad tua mutatae properabunt nomina gentes,
divisae penitus toto orbe per aequora gentes,
seclaque conversis procedent aurea rebus.
Quae tibi saepe ego pollicitus, scisque omnia mecum.
   'Nec tantum tua, nate, piis haec vulnera Olympum
870   nunc pandi meruere, nigra quos nocte premebat
insontes primi scelus exitiale parentis,
verum alios mox atque alios per secula coelo
efficient dignos, sua quos commissa piacla
sidereis procul arcebant a sedibus olim.
875   Tanta tuae merces, ea vis, ea gratia mortis.
Atque adeo, quodcunque homines ab origine rerum
admisere, aliis quidquid peccabitur annis,
huc coeat; satis illa tui pars parva superque
omnia diluere prorsusque abolere cruoris.
880   Quin etiam mox tempus erit, cum scilicet olim
ter centum prope lustra peregerit aethereus sol,
tum veri, Graium obliti mendacia, vates
funera per gentes referent tua carmine verso,

your sake, they will fear neither sword nor flames, neither the jaws of beasts nor the bone-crushing implements of torture. Though they now fear all the winds of heaven, they will go forth eagerly and willingly to meet perils and oppose them. They will win ac- 855 claim for their souls through contempt for death, and they will be proud in the possession of true courage. Neither heat nor cold will stop them, nor that pestilent star that cracks open the parched fields, nor the chill of winter that blocks rivers with blue ice. Truly they will be heard beyond the Ganges and farthest Bactria, in 860 Ismara and the Bistonian fields, and China, far distant from Cadiz, and their words will reach all the way to the green British isles. They will fill the earth with their teachings. Wandering the world, they will raise to you the greatest temples, making them new. Converted peoples will hasten to your name, races separated 865 by oceans, a world away. And a golden age will dawn over an al-tered world. These things I have often promised and you know that all things are in my power.

"For these wounds of yours, son, have gained heaven not only for those pious souls who, though innocent, were oppressed by black night on account of the mortal sin of their first father: soon, 870 in the centuries to come, they will make many more worthy of heaven, those whose sins once kept them far from the heavenly realm. Such is the recompense, such the force and grace of your death. Whatever men have done since the beginning of the world, 875 whatever sins they may commit in future years, though all be rolled in one, yet that little part of your blood is enough and more than enough to cleanse everything and wipe it away. Indeed the time will come when the ethereal sun has completed the course of 880 fifteen centuries hence and poets, having forgotten the lies of the Greeks, will tell the nations of your death in song. All cities will

atque tuis omnes resonabunt laudibus urbes,
885 praesertim laetam Italiae felicis ad oram,
Addua ubi vagus et muscoso Serius amne,
purior electro tortoque simillimus angui,
qua rex fluviorum, Eridanus, se turbidus infert,
moenia turrigerae stringens male tuta Cremonae,
890 ut sibi iam tectis vix temperet unda caducis.
Illic tum, nivei velut inter nubila cygni,
omnibus in ripis pueri innuptaeque puellae
carmina casta canent mixtique in gramine molli
laudibus incipient certatim assuescere nostris,
895 et teneri prima coetus te voce sonabunt.
Haec tibi certa manent, haec vis movet ordine nulla.'
Sic fatus, dulcem nato inspiravit amorem.
    Interea scelus infandum pellacis Iudae
multa execrantes, socii se ad iussa parabant
900 munera, diversas sortiti protinus oras
quas peterent moresque novos, nova sacra docerent.
Quove autem patribus bis senis caetera, ut ante,
pareret pubes, numerum sanctumque senatum
quod superest supplent, sociisque ex omnibus unus
905 sortitu gaudes tanto praelatus honore,
Matthia, obscurum genus et sine luce propago.
Tum cuncti inter se moesti sic ore precari:
'Si nunc, si nobis aurai coelitus almae
halitus omnipotens patefacto aspiret Olympo,
910 quandoquidem toties nobis deus omnibus illum
auxilio fore pollicitus! Sane omnia vera
praedixit; defit veris hoc hactenus unum.'
Talia suspensi secum aegra mente serebant.
    Ecce autem coeli ruere ardua visa repente,
915 et superum tonat ingenti domus alta fragore.
Suspiciunt: nova lux oculis diffulsit, et ingens

resound with your praise, especially those by the happy shores of
Italy the Blessed, in the regions of the wandering Addua and   885
Serio, whose mossy banks are brighter than amber and as sinuous
as a snake. There flows the turbid Po, monarch of rivers, wrapping
itself around the insecure walls of turreted Cremona so that its
waters scarce keep themselves back from the ruinous houses.
There, like snow-white swans among the clouds, youths and maid-   890
ens will sing chaste songs along the banks. Together upon the soft
grass, they will grow accustomed to sing your praise in antiphon,
and choirs of the young will sing of you with their children's
voices. Such is what awaits you and no force can change that." So   895
speaking, he breathed sweet love into his Son.

Meanwhile the disciples reviled the heinous acts of traitorous
Judas and were girding themselves for their appointed tasks, each
having been assigned a part of the earth to visit and to teach new   900
customs and sacraments. And in order that young people might
obey the twelve apostles as before, they supplied their number and
sainted senate with the one missing member. Of all the followers,
Matthew, you alone rejoice in having been allotted this great
honor, though your race and family were not illustrious. Then the   905
disciples began to pray in sadness: "If only heaven would open for
us now, and the all-powerful breath of the divine life-giving spirit
would descend upon us to help us, as Jesus so often promised it
would! Everything else he predicted has come true. Only this is   910
yet wanting." Such was their uneasy discourse and they were sick
at heart.

But just then the heights of heaven seemed to come crashing
suddenly down! And the angelic mansion thundered with a tremendous noise. As they looked up, a strange light shone in their   915

visus ab aethereo descendere vertice nimbus
lucis inardescens maculis, tectumque per omne
diversi rumpunt radii. Tum innoxius ignis
920   omnibus extemplo supra caput astitit ingens
et circum rutilis incanduit aura favillis,
stricturis veluti crebrae crepitantibus olim
dissiliunt scintillae, acres dum incudibus ictus
alternant Chalybes, robustaque brachia tollunt
925   candentem curva versantes forcipe massam.
Nam pater omnipotens superaque aequaevus ab arce
filius aspirant una omnipotentibus auris
infunduntque viris numen. 'Deus ecce repente,
ecce deus!' Cunctis divinitus algida corda
930   incipiunt afflata calescere. Numine tacti
implentur propiore viri, sacrumque furorem
concepere, deumque imis hausere medullis.

    Nec mora, nec requies. Ter scintillantibus igneis
terrifico radiis fulgore, ter alitis aurae
935   turbine correpti, blando flammantur amore,
ignescuntque animis atque exultantia cunctis
exercent acres stimulis praecordia motus.
Diffugiunt animis terrores. Mira loquuntur,
mira canunt. Eadem variis (mirabile dictu)
940   gentibus accipitur vox haud obscura, sibique
quisque videbatur patrias haurire loquelas,
multi ut tunc ierant variis huc partibus orbis
sacrorum studio visendaeque urbis amore,
solennem quae luce illa celebrabat honorem,
945   quinquaginta actis post orgia prima diebus,
orgia cum mensis epulandum apponimus agnum.
Hic sua verba audit tellure Libystide[3] cretus,
hic Galli sua, Romulidae Parthique Scythaeque,
necnon subiecti glaciali sidere Thraces,

372

eyes and a huge nimbus descended from the airy summit, its dazzling sparks and scattered rays bursting forth throughout the
house. At once a huge fire stood over the head of each person
present, though it did not harm them. And the air around them   920
was ignited with deep red flames. These resembled the multitudi-
nous sparks that leap up from hissing iron as the Chalybians, in
alternation, strike their anvils, their strong arms turning over the
glowing mass with curved pincers. For the Almighty Father and   925
his coeval Son breathed down from high heaven a powerful
breath, infusing the men with their Spirit. "Behold, behold! Suddenly God is here!" Their cold hearts began to warm as they were
inspired. They were touched and filled with the heavenly Spirit   930
close at hand. A divine madness seized them and they received
God into the very marrow of their bones.

    There was neither pause given nor respite. Caught thrice in a
whirlwind of winged air and thrice in the terrifying glow of the
gleaming fire, they were aflame with sweet love. Their spirits were   935
ignited and powerful passions shook their hearts, which rejoiced
in every goad. All terror left them and they began to speak and
sing extraordinary things. The same utterance, hardly obscure, was   940
miraculously received by the different races, and each man seemed
to hear his mother tongue. For just then many had come from distant parts of the world because of their religious zeal and desire to
see the holy city: on that day it was celebrating a solemn rite, fifty
days having passed since the first feast where lamb was set upon   945
the table. Libyans heard their language, the Gauls theirs, and so
too the Parthians and the Scythians, the Thracians always under a

950 Afrique Cretesque Phrygumque e gente profecti,
atque Indi atque Arabes et arenivagi Garamantes.
Mirantur cuncti circum, mirantur et ipsi.
Nanque hominem velut exuti moribundaque membra,
mente domos coeli peragrant atque aethera apertum
955 intenti et superum taciti sermone fruuntur.
    Iamque canunt ventura. Animis deus expulit atram
lustrans corda intus nubem, quae corpora circum
caligatque hebetatque humanas humida mentes.
Quosque modo durae mortis formidine turpi
960 speluncis atris terrebant omnia clausos,
liberius nunc luce palam atque licentius audent,
terrorum expertes. Nec iam mortalia curant.
Non ferrum aut flammas metuunt morsusve ferarum,
sed regem vulgo testantur, morte peremptum
965 immerita, genus aethereo deducere Olympo.
Iamque pudet metuisse omnes, animosaque leti
spes magis atque magis viget acris numinis haustu.
Haud secus ac crebris cum rimis terra dehiscit,
cum sitit omnis ager, tum quae morientia languent
970 gramina, coeruleus si coelo venerit imber,
continuo attollant rursus capita, arvaque ponant
squalorem, redeatque decor suus omnibus agris.
    Ergo abeunt varias longe lateque per oras
diversi, laudesque canunt atque inclyta vulgo
975 facta ducis, iamque (ut vates cecinere futurum
antiqui) illorum vox fines exit in omnes.
Audiit et si quem medio ardens aethere iniquo
sidere desertis plaga dividit invia terris,
quique orbem extremo circunsonat aequore pontus.
980 Continuo ponunt leges moremque sacrorum
urbibus. Infectum genti lustralibus undis
eluitur scelus et veteris contagia culpae,

wintry star; the Africans, Cretans and Phrygians; the Indians, the   950
Arabs, and the Garamantes who ply the desert sands. All around
people marveled and so did the disciples. For as though freed from
their humanity and from their mortal bodies, in their minds they
keenly traversed the heavenly mansions and the expanse of heaven,
hearing in silence the discourse of the angels.   955

As they sang of things to come, God purified their hearts, driving from their souls the dark cloud that obscures moist bodies and
wearies the human mind. Those who just now had been shut up
in dark caves and frightened by everything because of their base
fear of a harsh death, went forth without inhibition or restraint   960
into the open light, free of their terrors. They had no care of mortal things. They feared neither swords, nor flames, nor the mouths
of beasts, but gave testimony to the people that their king, who
had met an undeserved death, was the Son of God. And all were   965
ashamed to have ever been afraid. Their bold longing for death
grew ever greater, as they imbibed the invigorating spirit. As when
the parched earth lies split and cracked and all the fields are thirsting and the grass droops and dies, if dark rains should come from
the skies, at once fountains rise up again, the fields throw off their   970
squalor and glory returns to every meadow.

And so the disciples departed to varied and distant shores.
They sang their Lord's praises and spread the news of his miracles.
As the ancient prophets had foretold, their voices went out into all   975
lands. Their words were heard even by the inhabitants of the sun-
scorched and ill-omened desert, divided from the rest of the
world, and by the inhabitants of lands where Ocean circles the
earth with its terminal stream. Soon the disciples laid down laws
and religious observances in the cities. The baneful crime of the   980
people was washed away in the waters of baptism and with it the

relligioque novas nova passim exsuscitat aras.
Protinus hinc populos Christi de nomine dicunt
985 Christiadas. Toto surgit gens aurea mundo,
seclorumque oritur longe pulcherrimus ordo.

SI QUID HIC FACTUM DICTUMVE CONTRA SANCTORUM PATRUM
SCITA, INFECTUM INDICTUMVE ESTO. QUISQUIS ES, AUTOR TE AD-
MONITUM VULT SE NON LAUDIS ERGO OPUS ADEO PERICULOSUM
CUPIDE AGGRESSUM, VERUM EI HONESTIS PROPOSITIS PRAEMIIS A
DUOBUS SUMMIS PONTIFICIBUS DEMANDATUM SCITO, LEONE X
PRIUS, MOX CLEMENTE VII, AMBOBUS EX ETRUSCORUM MEDYCUM
CLARISSIMA FAMILIA, CUIUS LIBERALITATI ATQUE INDUSTRIAE
HAEC AETAS LITTERAS AC BONAS ARTIS, QUAE PLANE EXTINCTAE
ERANT, EXCITATAS ATQUE REVIVESCENTES DEBET. ID VOLEBAM
NESCIUS NE ESSES CAUTUM EST, UT IN ALIIS, NE QUIS HOC POEMA
AUTORE INSCIO INVITOVE DE CAETERO IMPRIMERE NEVE VENALE
HABERE IMPUNE USPIAM AUDEAT.[4]

pestilence of original sin. The new religion called forth new altars everywhere, and from that time onward the people were called Christians after the name of Christ. A golden race now rose up 985 throughout the world and the most beautiful age of all was just beginning.

IF THERE BE SOMETHING HERE DONE OR SAID CONTRARY TO THE DECREES OF THE HOLY FATHERS, LET IT BE UNDONE AND UNSAID. WHOEVER YOU ARE, THE AUTHOR WISHES YOU TO BE INFORMED THAT HE DID NOT UNDERTAKE A WORK SO DANGEROUS IN THE DESIRE FOR PRAISE, BUT BE AWARE THAT IT WAS COMMISSIONED WITH AN OFFER OF HONORABLE REWARDS FROM TWO POPES, FIRST LEO X, THEN CLEMENT VII, BOTH FROM THE DISTIN- GUISHED FAMILY OF THE TUSCAN MEDICI, TO WHOSE LIBERALITY AND ENERGY THIS AGE OWES THE REVIVAL AND REBIRTH OF LITERATURE AND HUMANITIES, WHICH HAD QUITE DIED OUT. I WANTED YOU, WHOEVER YOU ARE, TO BE PUT ON NOTICE, FUR- THERMORE, THAT NO ONE HENCEFORTH SHOULD EVER DARE TO PRINT OR SELL THIS POEM WITH IMPUNITY WITHOUT THE AU- THOR'S KNOWLEDGE AND APPROVAL.

Note on the Text and Translation

The Latin text of the *Christiad* in this volume is based on a fresh collation of what is thought to the definitive 1550 edition of the work, prepared under Vida's personal supervision.[1] The *editio princeps* published in Cremona in 1535 has also been recollated and its few variants indicated in the Notes to the Text.

The present edition also includes a first collation of a manuscript believed by Mario A. Di Cesare to be the dedication copy: Florence, Biblioteca Nazionale Centrale, Conv. soppr. C 8, 1177 (**F**).[2] Careful corrections were made to F by a second hand (**F²**), which may well be Vida's own hand or that of an amanuensis working with his archetype. The existence of this manuscript was noted in the *Iter Italicum* of P. O. Kristeller, vol. 1 (Leiden—London: E. J. Brill, 1963), p. 150a (catalogue excerpt). In his bibliographical study, *Bibliotheca Vidiana*, p. 243, Di Cesare advanced the claim that this codex was the dedication copy presented to Clement VII in 1532. There is no incontrovertible proof in the manuscript itself that it was indeed the dedication copy aside from the fact that it explicitly names Clement VII (†25 September 1534) as dedicatee, whereas the printed editions do not; but Medici ownership of the codex is certainly possible given its provenance.[3]

In any case, collation discloses what is certainly a redaction of the text previous to that found in the first printed edition of 1535. The variants of this redaction have been recorded in a separate section following the Notes to the Text. A large number of the variants distinguishing this redaction from that of the *princeps* seem to have been occasioned by Vida's initial uncertainty about the metrical value of Hebrew names. His study of the early Christian poets (see Notes to the Translation) would have offered some guidance on this point. On at least one occasion (4.26), a revision seems aimed at avoiding theological error.

To improve readability, capitalization and punctuation have been modernized. The orthography of the 1550 edition has been followed, except that *j* has been changed to *i*, and *v* has been written for vocalic *u*.

379

Enclitic *-ne*, *-que*, and *-nam*, usually written as separate words in the 1550 edition, have been coalesced with the words preceding them, and fusions such as *siquis*, *siquid* and the like have been separated. The spellings used in *F*, 1535, and 1550 are nearly identical, and are likely to reflect Vida's own preferences; F^2 evinces a taste in orthography that most closely approximates that found in the 1535 edition.

The Latin text was prepared by James Hankins, who collated *F in situ*; J. H. would like to thank Dr. John Gagné, who kindly collated the 1535 and 1550 editions from copies in the Houghton Library (Harvard University). J. H. has, however, rechecked all the variants identified by Dr. Gagne and in the edition of Drake and Forbes (see Bibliography).[4] The vast majority of the source notes were compiled by Mr. Justin Stover, who traced most of the sources and echoes in the Bible as well as in classical Latin and early Christian sources. Other material in the notes was supplied by James Hankins and by the translator. The Notes to the Translation are greatly indebted to A. S. Pease's commentary on Book IV of the *Aeneid*, which noted numerous parallels between the *Aeneid* and Vida's masterpiece, and to a review-article of Richard Bruère; both works are cited in the Bibliography. Richard Tarrant, who read the book for the press, also noted a large number of sources and parallels which have been gratefully incorporated.

J. H.

In writing this prose translation I have tried as best I could to achieve a tone that did justice to the grand manner that Vida uses throughout. Though I thought it expedient to avoid expressions that were jarringly contemporary, I have also largely avoided formulations that felt patently archaic. Rather I have tried to capture that mirage of linguistic timelessness that Vida, because he was writing in Latin, was able to achieve throughout his poem with remarkable success.

One of the issues that confronts a translator of metrical poetry, and especially of pre-modern narrative verse, is the degree of fidelity owed to the specifics of the original. Often indeed will Vida use expressions, or repeat names, simply for reasons of meter or of filling out a line of verse. To this end, he is not above saying the same thing in several different ways. When the reward for this pleonasm is a fluent hexametric line in Latin, the reader may be able to tolerate the padding. But when the same sentiment is rendered into English prose, all that is left is the cloying redundancy, which on more than one occasion I have found it preferable to excise.

For reasons of meter as well, Vida shifts indiscriminately between primary and secondary tenses, that is, between present and past, sometimes within a single line. Once again, this is tolerable given the formal conventions of Latin verse and the satisfactions of the hexametric line. But to attempt the same thing in modern English prose would be intolerable. For that reason, in the narrative portions of the poem, as opposed to speeches by the characters, I have chosen to preserve the past tense throughout.

Though I have occasionally followed Vida in using expressions like "hero" to refer to Christ, and "Olympus" to refer to Heaven, since I believe they are important to the classicizing strain of Christianity that the poet favored, I have nevertheless used them selectively rather than consistently, where it felt right to do so. Whether to translate *deus* as 'God', 'a god', or 'the god' also presented difficult choices; though Vida was certainly an orthodox Christian monotheist, he was also writing in a classicizing idiom which tolerated the suggestion of the polytheistic. Here too my renderings have not been consistent but vary with the context. As regards English versions of Vida's Latin renderings of Hebrew place names — pre-eminently in his description of the tribes of Israel in Book II — I am happy to acknowledge that I have thoroughly co-opted the forms that Gertrude C. Drake and Clarence A. Forbes used in their 1978 translation of the poem.

J. G.

NOTES

1. Di Cesare, *Vida's Christiad*, 32.

2. As there is no published description, the following one may be of use: Cart., s. XVI 2/4, 170 + II leaves, 200 x 145 (written area 150 x 100), 18 long lines per page. Full leather gold-stamped binding (Roman?). Written in a fine italic hand, brown ink, no decoration. The text of the

Christiad occupies folios 1r-170r. There are no other Latin manuscripts of the *Christiad* in Kristeller's *Iter*, which refers to or describes perhaps a third of Renaissance literary and philosophical manuscripts.

3. Piero Scapecchi of the Biblioteca Nazionale in Florence kindly pointed out to J. H. that the manuscript had come into the Nazionale from the monastery of Camaldoli, which is known to have possessed an incunable of Leo X, via the former *custode* (1512–32) of the Vatican Library, Romolo Mammacino; see P. Scapecchi, *Gli incunaboli della Biblioteca Comunale "Rilliana" di Poppi e del monastero di Camaldoli* (Florence: Regione Toscana, 2004), p. 75, no. 251.

4. Drake and Forbes also collated the 1535 and 1550 editions but not F. They reproduced exactly the spelling, capitalization and (often misleading) punctuation of the 1550 edition. I have not thought it worthwhile to list the few typographical errors found in their edition.

Notes to the Text

৯৫৫৯

LIBER PRIMUS

1. *Title:* Marci Hieronymi Vidae Cremonensis Christiados libri sex F 1535, 1550; F *continues* ad Clementem VII ponticem maximum

2. procerae F: procera 1535, 1550

3. Veh F, 1535

4. *Corrected to* ostia *from* hostia *by* F²

5. bacis F, 1535, 1550: *corrected to* baccis *in the errata of* 1550

6. olim F, 1535, 1551; *the emendation is R. Tarrant's.*

7. dracone F, 1535

LIBER II

1. quocunque F

2. Sichelechidaque F, 1535, 1550: *corrected in the errata of* 1550

3. Isacharis F

4. Remetiaque 1550

5. Cedaris F

6. nomina *before correction in* F

7. Ascrota F

8. Hemon F

9. orbi F

10. *added s.s.* F²

11. alio F, 1535

LIBER III

1. effusa F

2. *Emended:* ipsa F, 1535, 1550

3. *Corrected:* imitatur *F, 1535, 1550*

4. bacis *1535, 1550:* baccis *F and in the errata of 1550*

5. tanto *F*

6. Heoos *1535, 1550:* Eoos *F and corrected in the errata of 1550.*

LIBER IV

1. ipso *1550; see also earlier redaction*

2. effluxisse *1535*

3. immulxisset *1535*

4. *Corrected:* vox *F, 1535, 1550*

LIBER V

1. aliis *1535*

2. adversatus *F*

3. colla *F, 1535, 1550: the emendation is J. Hankins's; for* liventia crura *see Ovid,* Amores *2.2.47.*

4. viget *1550*

LIBER VI

1. et *F*

2. *Corrected:* Serasque *F, 1535, 1550*

3. Libysside *1550*

4. Si quid . . . uspiam audeat (cautum est . . . audeat *omitted in 1550*): Si quippiam in hisce dictum factumve contra sanctorum patrum traditiones, indictum infectumque esto; autor insuper te, quisquis es, admonitum vult se non laudis aut gloriae cupiditate temere aggressum esse quicquid, hoc est negotii perdifficile sane ac valde periculosum, verum ei a duobus summis pontificibus, Leone X prius, mox Clemente septimo demandatum scito *F*

Variants of the First Redaction

For this redaction see Note on the Text and Translation. A few unique readings of *F* have been treated as variants of the definitive text rather than elements of the earlier redaction; for these consult the Notes to the Text. All variants of *F* here are in italics.

1.3. e superi qui sede parentis] *superum qui sedibus ultra*

1.11. mihi te duce] *duce te mihi*

1.48. luendum] *luenda*

1.83. hominem] *hominum*

1.97. hospitis adventu *non distulit omnia egenis*

1.98. *partiri,* cuique suum *male reddere parta*

1.118. Bethanae] *Bethanaeam*

1.146. horrentia fingunt] *affingere sueti* (before correction)

1.182. obiice] *obice* (corrected by F²)

1.214. vera] *facta*

1.268. taciti] *cuncti*

1.557. porro] *longe*

1.621. cyparissis] *cupressis*

1.664. pro meritis] *iratus*

1.665a. *funeris expertes animae letoque carentes* (additional line)

1.670. serpens] *flexum*

1.681. quos *pater Abramus humeris extantibus omnes*

1.693. *Hic pauci extinctis cunctis* mortalibus ibant

1.742. mitissime] *placidissime*

1.743. quaenam] *nam quae*

1.817. illis] *aliis* (compare 5.228)

385

1.821. *Pro sue signantur* Veneris mala gaudia foedae

1.886. omnia quae mecum *praescisti ab origine rerum*

1.891. Omnes *proiecto te propter* lucis amore

1.909. invicti] *victi*

1.943. ingens] *ipse*

2.15. omnes] *cuncti et*

2.73. Unus non *fugere evaluit tuus Iscara alumnus*

2.74. Iscarius] *insidias*

2.239. mox] *cito*

2.296. intacta] *in sede*

2.314. *his superum regem* prosit regionibus ortum

2.315. illo] *isto*

2.323. arces] *urbes*

2.334. sacra] *ob sacra*

2.343. *maliferamque Adulan humilique in valle Raphoean*

2.344. *Selis ubi, et Lyde,* ventosaque Iamnia et Hippa

2.346. quaeque *fluentisono perfunditur aequore Ioppe*

2.351. Deseritur *Nepse, miratur et Emaus agros*

2.352. *civibus ipsa suos vacuos siluisse profectis*

2.352a. *miraturque suos Aegypti proximo regnis* (additional line)

2.375. decerpse] *quem ferre*

2.378. cupiere] *optavere*

2.412. viros] *illos*

2.413. ducem] *virum*

2.427. *Arctipus haud Labanae numero, nec cessit Azibae*

2.428. hos iuxta *Zabulone sati gens accola ponti*

2.429. littoreas *seram in noctem soliti urere myrtos*

2.434. aerias] *superas*

2.444. Samarea penates] *cultore relicta est*

2.445. deseruit] *Samaria*

2.451. et quos *Genasare piscosis alluit* undis

2.463. *atque opibus quondam nulli Mageda*

2.468. Rubene creati] *gens orta Rubene*

2.486. *Esebaque immitis quondam impia regna Seonis*

2.493. Isacidum] *Abrami*

2.498. quarta regem] *regem quarta*

2.499. Bethane obstupuit] *mirata est Bethane*

2.567. menstrua luna] *caetera et astra*

2.580. omnes] *hunc iam*

2.670. haec] *ea*

2.795. scelus id] *crimen*

2.897. discussisque] *sublatisque*

2.920. devenerat] *pervenerat*

3.84. et rabiem *infensae* compressi gentis *iniquam*

3.112. Principio *generis* pater *olim Abramus* auctor

3.114. generi] *genti*

3.115. Isacon *ille* dedit; *dedit Isacus inde Iacobum*

3.116. bis senos *hic* mox proceres, *gens a quibus* omnis

3.117. gens secta] *disscerpta* (sic)

3.122. Davides] *rex Davides*

3.141. nymphas] *matres*

3.237. implicuit] *implevit*

3.286. Accedo *et supplex rogo* per connubia *nostra*

3.321. discedere] *se pandere*

3.454. consilia, antiquis *deus omnia vatibus ista*

3.455. obscuris vera involvens *ostenderat olim*

3.576. *nigra modo fuerant, nunc aurea stramina cernas.*

3.602. Haec subito exisset *coepi quoque quaerere ab ipsis*

3.613. hominum genus] *genus hominum*

3.645. Idem etiam, quod *siderea rex arce futurus*

3.707. sponte admissa] *crimina sponte*

3.858. resupini infantis] *pueri ridentis*

3.1009. errabunda ducis *vestigia quaque sequutus,*

4.26. complexus circum penitus *diffusus ubique*

4.90. coniugis hortatu, *draco quam deceperat astu*

4.161. Zacchariae *infoecunda seni parit, obsitaque aevo*

4.196. eluet] *auferet*

4.247. deprenderit] *invenerit*

4.278. socii] *comitis*

4.287. *liquerat extinctum sol* impositumque sepulcro

4.305. aut corrupti] *corrupti aut*

4.370. Sic ait. *Hinc* tali genitorem voce precatur

4.420. Iam nunc] *Tam cito*

4.483. adunco] *obunco*

4.558. *Senos cuique legens, numerum* tamen ipse dolebat

4.559. exiguum *neque tam paucos* satis esse ferebat

4.576. hanc unam *restare viam rata nempe* salutis

4.644. confessus] *manifestans*

4.705. Samaritidos orae] *sitientia rura*

4.706. *Samariae antiquis Sicharae sub* moenibus urbis

4.935. Omnia] *Omnes*

4.999. pios] *illos*

4.1001. suos] *pios*

5.43. quo fugit usque dies *properantibus impiger horis*

5.46. *Et curae ultrices, mens consciaque usque sequuntur*

5.47. *seu quis iter carpat* pedibus seu puppe per undas

5.57. ratus atque] *requiemque*

5.98. oculosque] *animumque*

5.152. Dixerat, atque *eadem cuncti* simul ore *ferebant*

5.230. adversatur] *adversatus*

5.267. *velabat tenui nam carbasus inguine texto*

5.391. *Non* mora, *non* requies [etc.]

5.691. acer] *omnis*

5.740. Cui *scelerum autori olim* tam dira parasti

5.770. haesitat] *haeret et*

5.793. et soror et Salome *Cleophaeque aegerrima coniux*

5.836. stetimus] *potui*

5.854. et letale] *aeternumque*

6.4. *Non tulit Arimathes veniens Iosephus ab ora*

6.5. *Nephtalides animi egregius,* praestansque iuventa

6.26. possem] *quirem*

6.68. *Infert huc sese medium Iosephus in agmen*

6.69. *conscenditque trabem corpusque* exangue magistri

6.70. detrahit, et *mediis aufert animosus ab armis*

6.177. *veridici Davidis genus, o passim gaudete*

6.249. ea] *cito*

6.256. *tam crudeli opifex cum funere* vester obiret?

6.291. rutila] *nitida*

6.321. tristes] *vario*

6.441. *Didymus inde aberat Thomas* vicina pererrans

6.452. *Didymus et socios dictis* demulcet amicis

6.486. sociique] *cunctique*

6.498. extulit aereas *ubi turribus Emaus* arces

6.499. advena *cum* ignota *nobis in* veste profectus

6.574. *Didymus ut vero* manifesto in lumine vidit

6.587. at] *et*

6.618. Laetitiam *en vultu ut iactet* oculisque decoris!

6.655. matres atque viri *vitaeque in limine rapti*

6.661. arbitria] *imperia*

6.724. pueri] *iuvenes*

6.744. semper ut *extitere expers ortusque obitusque*

6.905. *Matthias tanto potitur* praelatus honore,

6.906. *Matthias, genus obscurum* sine luce propago

6.929. algida] *aspera*

Notes to the Translation

BOOK I

1.1–7. The opening sentence is structured as a counterpart to the opening seven lines of the *Aeneid*, ending with a clear echo of that opening (*manesque pios inferret Olympo* ~ *Aen.* 1.6 *inferretque deos Latio*). With lines 1–2, compare the opening of Lucretius's *De rerum natura* (1.2–4): *Alma Venus, caeli subter labentia signa / quae mare nauigerum, quae terras frugiferentis / concelebras.*

1.1. Compare Prudentius, *Apotheosis* 153: *qui mare qui terras qui lucida sidera fecit.* With *numine comples* compare Juvencus, *Evangelia* 3.272 *(lumine comples)* and Ennodius, *Carmina* 2.90.6 *(numine comples)*. Compare also *Aeneid* 6.724–6; *Eclogues* 4.51.

1.2. For *spiritus alme* see, for example, Dracontius, *De laudibus Dei* 2.152, Venantius Fortunatus, *Carmina* 5.5.13, and Arator, *Historia apostolica* 1.226 and 2.580. The same invocation occurs in many medieval and Renaissance hymns. For *mihi munere* in the same metrical position see Statius, *Silvae* 3.1.62 and Paulinus of Nola, *Carmina* 15.32. For the line-ending *munere regem* see Venantius Fortunatus, *Carmina* 6.2.11.

1.3. Twice-born: Compare Commodian, *Instructiones* 1.12.1.

1.6. With *tenebris et carcere* compare *Aeneid* 6.733.

1.10. With *terruit orbem* compare Ovid, *Metamorphoses* 1.724, 14.812, and Paulinus of Nola, *Carmina* 31.127.

1.11. With *te duce* compare *Eclogues* 4.11.

1.12. For *ore loqui* beginning a line see Ovid, *Heroides* 12.67. For *attollere coelo* at line end, see [ps.] Vergil, *Aetna* 224.

1.13. For *summique parentis* see Paulinus of Nola, *Carmina* 18.138. With *evolvere causas* compare Boethius, *De consolatione philosophiae* 4.m6.1 and *Aeneid* 1.8–9.

1.15. With *finisque laborum* compare *Aeneid* 1.241.

1.19. With *fama trahebat* compare Ovid, *Tristia* 3.6.13.

1.20. Compare *Aeneid* 4.173.

1.25. Viso: A mountain in the Cottian Alps and the source of the Po. This passage was probably inspired by Ariosto's *Orlando Furioso* 37.92.1–5 and appears to have inspired Tasso's *Gerusalemme Liberata* 9.46. Compare *Aeneid* 10.708.

1.26. Compare *Georgics* 4.372, *Aeneid* 8.63 and Lucan, *Bellum civile* 4.588.

1.29. With *auxiliaribus undis* compare Ovid, *Metamorphoses* 1.275.

1.30. With *se capit alveo* compare *Aeneid* 9.32 (*se condidit alveo*).

1.32–89. These lines follow Matthew 16:21–8, Mark 8:31–9:1 and Luke 9:18–27.

1.38. With *ventum ad supremum* compare *Aeneid* 12.803.

1.40. With *pii manes* compare Statius, *Silvae* 5.3.284.

1.44. For *non inscius ipse* see Paulinus of Pella, *Eucharisticos* 471; for *inscius ipse* alone see Lucretius, *De rerum natura* 3.878 and *Aeneid* 10.249.

1.46. For *morte . . . piabo* compare Statius, *Thebaid* 9.60 (*ego morte piabo*).

1.50. With *caede abluta* compare *Aeneid* 9.818 (*abluta caede*).

1.54–5. Compare *Aeneid* 3.167: *hae nobis propriae sedes.*

1.55. With *aetheris alti* compare *Aeneid* 12.181 and Boethius, *De consolatione philosophiae* 4.m5.6.

1.56. The phrase *lucida templa* is Lucretian (*De rerum natura* 1.1014 and 2.1039). For *florentia regna* at the end of a line, see [ps.] Cyprianus Gallus, *De resurrectione mortuorum* 190. Compare [ps.] Vergil, *Ciris* 464.

1.57. Compare Statius, *Silvae* 3.5.85. With *requies optata* compare Avitus, *Carmina* 4.549.

1.58. Compare *Aeneid* 7.122: *hic domus, haec patria est.*

1.59. *Angustum iter* (narrow path) is a classical reworking of Matthew 7:13.

1.60. With *lumina moestis*, compare Ovid, *Metamorphoses* 6.304.

1.62. On the opening *tum senior Petrus* compare *Aeneid* 11.122: *tum . . . senior Drances*. On the whole line, see *Aeneid* 2.534: *nec uoci iraeque pepercit*. Compare also 5.356, below.

1.64. In the *Aeneid*, Aeneas is eleven times addressed as *nate dea*. The application of this phrase to Christ *(nate deo)* was already anticipated by Prudentius (*Apotheosis* 1.418). See Pease, *Aeneidos*, 456 (*ad* 4.560).

1.68. Compare Juvencus, *Evangelia* 4.164: *ni soli rerum Domino, qui sidera torquet*. Compare also *Aeneid* 9.93.

1.69. For *instat agendum* at line-end see Venantius Fortunatus, *Carmina* 8.2.1.

1.70. With *ingratusque salutis* compare *Aeneid* 10.666.

1.71. Compare *Aeneid* 4.319.

1.74. Compare Statius, *Achilleid* 2.42.

1.80. With *tempus eget* compare *Aeneid* 2.522. With *iussis haud mollibus* compare *Aeneid* 9.804 and *Georgics* 3.41.

1.82. This line is copied directly from Cicero's translation of *Iliad* 2.299 at *De divinatione* 2.30.

1.84–87. A version of Matthew 5:11–12.

1.85. For *nomina vestra* at line-end see Sedulius, *Carmen paschale* 4.161.

1.88–9. Compare *Aeneid* 5.348–9.

1.94. Zacchaeus: This episode, to line 99, is derived from Luke 19:1–10.

1.95. Compare Ovid, *Metamorphoses* 6.585 and Paulinus of Nola, *Carmina* app. 2.2 (*per fas nefasque cogere*).

1.96. For *luce recepta* at line-end see Lucan, *Pharsalia* 9.940 and Dracontius, *De laudibus Dei* 1.644.

1.102. Lazarus: This episode, to line 299, derives from John 11:41–44, but is embellished with details from Jacopo da Varagine's 13th-century *Golden Legend*.

1.103. With *dives opum* compare Vergil, *Georgics* 2.468. For the phrase *a sanguine regum* at line-end compare Propertius, *Elegies* 3.9.1, where it occurs in an epithet to his patron Maecenas.

1.107. Compare Vergil, *Aeneid* 6.127.

1.113. This line is closely modeled on Lucretius, *De rerum natura* 3.67: *et quasi iam leti portas cunctarier ante.*

1.114. Compare *Aeneid* 6.455.

1.121. Compare Juvencus, *Evangelia* 2.265.

1.123. Compare *Aeneid* 8.201.

1.125. Compare Statius, *Thebaid* 540–1.

1.126. Compare *Aeneid* 4.630.

1.135–8. The language is drawn from *Aeneid* 7.513–5 and 11.474–5.

1.135. Compare *Aeneid* 7.519.

1.138. Compare Cicero, *De consulatu suo* 25 (in *De divinatione* 1.18): *aut cum se gravido tremefecit corpore tellus.*

1.139–46. Compare Milton, *Paradise Lost*, 2.622–27:

> Perverse, all monstrous, all prodigious things,
> Abominable, inutterable, and worse
> Than fables yet have feigned or fear conceived,
> Gorgons, and Hydras, and Chimeras dire.

1.140. *Lucifugus* (a Lucilian coinage) was used by Vergil, *Georgics* 4.242.

1.141. Compare *Aeneid* 3.427.

1.143–6: Compare the list of monsters in *Aeneid* 6.286–9. See also Sannazaro, *De partu virginis* 1.393 ff.

1.147–9. Compare *Aeneid* 10.565–7.

1.147. Compare *Aeneid* 6.287 and 7.783–4.

1.148. Compare [ps.] Vergil, *Maecenas* 2.25 and Valerius Flaccus, *Argonauticon* 1.558.

1.152. Compare Tibullus, *Elegies* 1.3.69.

1.155. Compare Statius, *Thebaid* 1.56.

1.165. See Ovid, *Metamorphoses* 1.330 for the rare word *tricuspidus*.

1.169. Compare Varro, fr. 10 (*apud* Quintilian, *Institutiones* 1.5.18): *Tum te flagranti deiectum fulmine, Phaethon.*

1.184. Compare Statius, *Thebaid* 11.349.

1.222. Compare *Aeneid* 8.443 and 11.335.

1.223. Compare *Aeneid* 8.441.

1.224. *Vix ea fatus (erat)* is a common Vergilian phrase; compare 2.549, 2.785, 3.916, 4.975. With *iussa facessunt* compare *Aeneid* 4.295. With this whole line compare Ennius, *Annales* fr. 57 (*apud* Nonius 306.23): *haec ecfatus, ibique latrones dicta facessunt*.

1.225. Compare Dracontius, *Orestes* 482, 498 and 714.

1.226. Compare Ovid, *Fasti* 4.267: *longo tremuit cum murmure tellus*.

1.227. Compare Ovid, *Metamorphoses* 10.349 (*crinitas angue sorores*).

1.229. Compare Cyprianus Gallus, *Heptateuchos: Genesis* 381. On the hexameter line-ending *per auras*, with bibliography, see Pease, *Aeneidos*, 241.

1.230. Compare Ovid, *Metamorphoses* 15.366.

1.231. Compare Columella, *De re rustica* 10.288.

1.234. Compare *Aeneid* 1.231.

1.235. Compare Boethius, *De consolatione philosophiae* 2.m6.1.

1.236. Compare Statius, *Thebaid* 2.375.

1.237. Compare Martial, *Epigrams* 6.3.2 (*vera deum suboles*). Both Martial and Vida have Vergil's 'messianic' Fourth Eclogue in mind (4.49: *cara deum suboles*). For *moenibus instat* see Silius Italicus, *Punica* 12.487.

1.241. The identity of Mary Magdalene is a matter of some dispute. Here, in accordance with one tradition, she is taken to be the sister of Martha and Lazarus. Compare this line with Arator, *Historia apostolica* 2.40.

1.249. Compare Lucretius, *De rerum natura* 4.924.

1.252. Compare Lucan, *Bellum civile* 2.4 and Arator, *Historia apostolica* 2.1117.

1.260. This line is Vergilian, modeled closely on *Aeneid* 12.608. Compare 3.159.

1.261. Compare *Aeneid* 10.267.

1.263. With this line and the next, compare *Aeneid* 2.63–4: *uisendi studio . . . iuuentus / circumfusa ruit*. *Omnia complent* is a Lucretian line-ending (*De rerum natura* 4.1017 and 5.1066).

1.264. Compare Claudian, *Carmina* 15.425.

1.265–6. Compare *Aeneid* 1.93, where a prayer is also introduced.

1.272. Compare *Aeneid* 3.90.

1.273–4. Compare *Aeneid* 3.259–60.

1.275. Compare *Aeneid* 8.70.

1.276. *Summe parens* begins a hexameter in Corippus, *Iohannis* 4.270. Compare Lucan, *Bellum civile* 4.110 and *Ilias Latina* 89.

1.282. Compare Statius, *Thebaid* 1.533. The line-ending *claustra sepulcri* occurs in a similar context in the Christian poets Paulinus of Perigueux (*De vita Martini* 1.310) and Paulinus of Nola (*Carmina* app. 3.22.1).

1.284. Compare Claudian, *Carmina* 18.38.

1.285. Compare Ovid, *Metamorphoses* 11.108 and Claudian, *Carmina minora* 27.67.

1.294. Compare *Aeneid* 8.60.

1.297–8. Compare Paulinus of Nola, *Carmina* 18.139 (*laeta piorum / turba*).

1.299. Compare Paulinus of Nola, *Carmina* 21.521.

1.300. The account of Simon the Pharisee and the young woman in the next paragraph is drawn from Luke 7:36–50.

1.301. Compare Lucan, *Bellum civile* 3.475.

1.310. Compare *Aeneid* 10.137–8.

1.320. The application of the epithet *praedives* to God is well attested in Christian poets (see, for example, Prudentius, *Peristephanon* 2.172 and Cyprianus Gallus, *Heptateuchos: Iudices* 399).

1.322. Compare Avitus, *Carmina* 3.36.

1.324. Misguiding passion: Compare Paulinus of Nola, *Carmina* 21.520. Compare also *Aeneid* 6.276.

1.330. Compare *Aeneid* 12.699.

1.333. Compare *Aeneid* 4.532, 8.19 and 12.486.

1.334. Compare *Aeneid* 6.353.

1.339–40. Compare Ovid, *Metamorphoses* 12.197.

1.343. *Pabula amoris* is Lucretian (compare *De rerum natura* 4.1063).

1.345. Compare Ovid, *Metamorphoses* 7.17 and Petronius, *Satyricon* 127.3.

1.355. Compare *Aeneid* 10.314.

1.357. Compare *Aeneid* 3.607.

1.359. See Luke 7:38 and 7.44 for *lachrymis rigabat*. Compare also *Aeneid* 9.251.

1.361–4. Compare Ovid, *Metamorphoses* 10.398–400.

1.372. Erinnys: One of the Furies or Erinyes of Greek mythology, avengers of crimes, especially crimes against kin. Vida does not specify which of the three Furies he intends.

1.376. O patriarch, etc.: Noah. Jerusalem in the Vulgate is first mentioned as the city ruled by Melchizedek, whom the Ordinary Gloss on the Bible (*Patrologia cursus completus, series latina*, ed. J.-P. Migne [Paris, 1844–91], vol. 113, col. 120) identifies as Shem, son of Noah.

1.376. Compare *Aeneid* 7.409.

1.377. *Pater vitisator* comes from the tragedian Accius (fr. trag. 241, *apud* Macrobius, *Saturnalia* 6.5.11). Compare *Aeneid* 7.177–9.

1.381. Jebusites: A Canaanite tribe that, before being conquered by King David, occupied the site of what would later become Jerusalem. See the Ordinary Gloss on the Bible (*Patrologia*, ed. Migne, vol. 113, p. 138).

1.389. Compare Silius Italicus, *Punica* 15.694.

1.391. Compare *Aeneid* 5.266.

1.398. Compare *Aeneid* 5.94.

1.400–35. These lines describe Christ's triumphal entry into Jerusalem. See Luke 12:29–40, John 12:12–18, Matthew 21:1–11, and Mark 11:1–10. Vida's account follows most closely that of John.

1.402. Compare Prudentius, *Dittochaeon* 10 and Sidonius Apollinaris, *Carmina* 15.198.

1.408–9. Compare Silius Italicus, *Punica* 15.636–7. Compare 2.10.

1.409. Compare [ps.] Tertullian, *Carmen adversus Marcionem* 3.267.

1.410. Compare Silius Italicus, *Punica* 4.751.

1.411. Compare Ovid, *Metamorphoses* 11.574–5.

1.416. Compare Ovid, *Ars amatoria* 1.217.

1.419. Compare Lucretius, *De rerum natura* 3.913.

1.424. Compare Statius, *Thebaid* 3.593 and Silius Italicus, *Punica* 2.417. Both these hearken back to *Aeneid* 4.665. Compare on 1.229.

1.425. Compare *Aeneid* 4.68–9.

1.430. Compare Corripus, *Panegyricus* 1.391.

1.432–3. Compare *Aeneid* 1.747.

1.434. Compare *Aeneid* 7.277.

1.444. Compare *Georgics* 1.272.

1.445. Based on John 5.2.

1.454. See note on 1.229.

1.458. The epithet *pater superum* comes from *Aeneid* 6.780. For the line-ending *misit Olympo* see Venantius Fortunatus, *Carmina* 1.11.9.

1.479. Compare *Aeneid* 4.132.

1.484. Compare Claudian, *Carmina* 7.33 and *Carmina minora* 31.21.

1.492. For *crimen aquae* see Ovid, *Tristia* 3.10.42.

1.496. Compare Juvenal, *Satires* 6.96.

1.497. Compare *Georgics* 1.272. Compare 1.444.

1.500. Compare Horace, *Satires* 2.6.93 and Ovid, *Metamorphoses* 11.139.

1.510. Compare *Aeneid* 2.475 and Horace, *Carmina* 3.11.20.

1.511–537. These lines describe the expulsion of the the money-changers from the Temple. See John 2.13–18, Matthew 21.12–13, Mark 11.15–17 and Luke 19.45–6. Vida follows most closely John's account.

1.522. Compare Lucretius, *De rerum natura* 1.273.

1.533. Compare *Aeneid* 6.620.

1.534. For *volentem* see *Aeneid* 5.712 and 8.133.

1.537. With *numen adorat* compare Ovid, *Metamorphoses* 11.539.

1.540. Compare Valerius Flaccus, *Argonautica* 4.254.

1.543. Compare Manilius, *Astronomica* 1.503.

1.550. Compare Ovid, *Fasti* 4.453 and *Aeneid* 7.395.

1.556. This line recalls the language of *Canticle of Canticles* 1:16.

1.562–81. These lines relate Christ's prediction of the destruction of the temple. See John 2:20.

1.564. Compare *Aeneid* 6.19.

1.565. Compare *Aeneid* 5.449.

1.567–9. These lines paraphrase Matthew 23:34–9.

1.576. Compare Ovid, *Metamorphoses* 13.394 and [ps.] Vergil, *Culex* 28 and 306.

1.578. Compare Lucretius, *De rerum natura* 5.1202.

1.579. Compare Lucretius, *De rerum natura* 5.1081.

1.579–80. A distant land . . . another city: Italy and Rome.

1.580. See Augustine, *Epistula* 171a 2.

1.581. With *terminus esto* compare Statius, *Silvae* 2.6.55.

1.582 and following. This ekphrastic passage — or literary description of a work of visual art — is modeled on, among other sources, Vergil's description of the murals in Dido's palace in *Aeneid* 1.453–493.

1.609–11. Compare Ovid, *Metamorphoses* 1.13–14.

1.637. Compare *Georgics* 3.385.

1.643–4. Compare Lucretius 1.20 (a famous passage in the Renaissance).

1.686. Compare *Aeneid* 1.40–1.

1.694. Enclosed in a wooden boat: In the Latin the allusion to Vergil's description of the Greeks inside the Trojan Horse (*inclusi ligno*) is clearer.

1.725. The story of the woman taken in adultery derives from John 8:1–11. The reasons for Vida's identifying her with Susanna are unclear. Vida probably chose the name to evoke the story of Susanna, wife of Joachim, who was accused by two elders of adultery after she rejected their advances (Daniel 13). The similarities between the two accounts are striking and Vida heightens the comparison by emphasizing the role of the Jewish elders in the woman's condemnation.

1.728–9. Compare *Aeneid* 2.403–4.

1.744. Compare *Aeneid* 10.627.

1.761. Compare *Aeneid* 3.395 and 10.113.

1.799. Compare Ovid, *Ars amatoria* 2.371, where Menelaus forgives Helen.

1.830. Compare *Aeneid* 8.280.

1.834. Mount Tabor is in Lower Galilee, near the eastern end of the Jezreel Valley. Among other distinctions, it is the supposed site of the Transfiguration of Christ. See Matthew 17:1–8, Mark 9:2–8 and Luke 9:28–36.

1.840. Compare Silius Italicus, *Punica* 6.466.

1.854. Compare *Aeneid* 2.619.

1.872 and following. The most obvious precedent for this prophecy by a father to a son is the prophecy of Anchises to Aeneas in the latter half of Book Six of the *Aeneid*. That passage was itself inspired in part by the prophecy of Tiresias to Odysseus in the *Odyssey*, 10.539–40. See also below, 6.847–96, for a similar passage.

1.880–2. Compare God's prophecy of Judas here with Vergil's depiction of Queen Dido (*Aeneid* 1.712).

1.894. A reference to the famous remark of Tertullian (*Apologeticus* 50) that "the blood of martyrs is the seed of the church."

1.905–906. Beyond the furthest barriers of Ocean: A reference to the European missions in the New World.

1.917. One above all: The pope. An ingratiating notion, given that the *Christiad* was commissioned by Leo X and dedicated to Clement VII.

1.925. Incursions of barbarians: Doubtless Vida is alluding to the Sack of Rome in 1527 by mercenaries in the pay of Charles V, as well as to the invasions of Rome by barbarians in the late ancient world.

1.932. Compare *Aeneid* 12.247.

1.938–9. Compare *Aeneid* 1.403–5. Here Vida applies Vergil's language describing Venus revealing herself as a goddess with Christ's transfiguration. For *per auras* see note on 1.229, above.

1.948. Flanked by two prophets: The allusions are to Ezekiel and Moses, respectively.

1.956. For *oscula libat* see *Aeneid* 1.256. Compare 3.188 and 6.845, below. For *per auras* see note on 1.229, above.

1.957. Compare *Aeneid* 8.581.

BOOK II

2.1–20. The opening of this book is based on Luke 11:47–8 and John 12:19.

2.7. Compare *Aeneid* 8.15.

2.8. Compare, for example, *Georgics* 4.441 and Juvencus, *Evangelia* 3.675. *Fama volat* is typically Vergilian (see *Aeneid* 7.392 and 8.554).

2.10. Compare 1.409, above.

2.18. Compare Ovid, *Metamorphoses* 13.709 and Statius, *Silvae* 1.4.121.

2.19. Compare *Aeneid* 4.42.

2.21. Compare *Georgics* 4.188 (*mussantque oras et limina circum*).

2.22–3. Compare *Aeneid* 2.268–9 and 3.511 (*inrigat artus*).

2.23. Compare Silius Italicus, *Punica* 4.724.

2.30. Perhaps a reference to the famous phenomenon of the spring return of the quails in vast swarms to Nettuno, described in Biondo Flavio, *Italy Illuminated* 3.7, ed. J. White in this I Tatti series, volume 1, pp. 127–28. Biondo reports that as many as 100,000 might be caught by fowlers in a single day. For the phrase *vere tepenti* see Ovid, *Ars amatoria* 3.185.

2.40. Compare *Aeneid* 12.665.

2.44. Compare *Aeneid* 4.190.

2.54. As when a rumor spreads: Reminiscent of the fall of Troy as narrated in *Aeneid* 2.

2.73–118. Judas's demonic possession is mentioned in Luke 22:3 and John 18:2.

2.73–4. Compare *Aeneid* 1.712.

2.85. The line is an adaptation of *Aeneid* 11.766.

2.89. Compare *Aeneid* 11.849.

2.91. Gaetulian lions dwelt in the land of the Gaetuli, a bellicose Libyan tribe. Such a lion is mentioned in *Aeneid* 5.352 and in Horace's *Odes* 1.23 at line 10.

2.106. Compare *Aeneid* 4.232 and 4.272.

2.112. Compare *Aeneid* 4.570 and 10.664.

2.113–4. Compare *Aeneid* 1.355 and 1.660.

2.114. Compare Statius, *Thebaid* 11.234.

2.124. Compare *Aeneid* 6.721.

2.132. Compare [ps.] Vergil, *Dirae* 101.

2.133–150. These lines follow John 11:54–7.

2.140. Compare Lucretius, *De rerum natura* 4.227 and 6.935; *Aeneid* 5.458 and 12.553; *Georgics* 3.110; and compare 4.519, below. For *in pectora cunctis* compare Paulinus of Nola, *Carmina* 18.115 and context. Compare *Aeneid* 2.228.

2.142. This line almost repeats *Aeneid* 6.160.

2.143. Compare *Aeneid* 6.709.

2.145. Young man: Lazarus. The plot to kill Lazarus is mentioned in John 12:10–11.

2.151–252. The debate between Caiaphas and Nicodemus is based on John 7:50–2. Many of the details of the speeches, however, could have been drawn from the *Gospel of Nicodemus*, c. 5.

2.153. Compare *Aeneid* 2.35.

2.159. Compare *Aeneid* 2.96 and Ovid, *Metamorphoses* 15.762–3.

2.166. Compare *Aeneid* 11.232.

2.168. Compare Prudentius, *Apotheosis* 793: *verus, verus deus ille.*

NOTES TO THE TRANSLATION ·

2.170. Compare *Aeneid* 2.184.

2.172. Compare Lucretius, *De rerum natura* 3.726.

2.192. Compare Silius Italicus, *Punica* 10.267 and 15.780.

2.199. Vida adapts a line quoted by Cicero about the rage of Achilles (*Tusculan Disputations* 3.9.18): *Corque meum penitus turgescit tristibus iris.*

2.204. Compare Ovid, *Metamorphoses* 15.612 and *Aeneid* 2.53.

2.206–7. Compare *Aeneid* 7.464–66.

2.210–13. Compare Milton, *Paradise Lost* 6.586–92.

2.213. Compare *Aeneid* 9.356.

2.216. Compare *Aeneid* 11.241.

2.220. Compare *Aeneid* 4.359.

2.249. Compare *Aeneid* 5.815.

2.251. Compare *Aeneid* 12.296.

2.253–72. The betrayal of Jesus by Judas is recounted in Matthew 26:14–16, Mark 14:10–11 and Luke 22:4–6.

2.254. Compare *Aeneid* 11.132.

2.255. Compare *Aeneid* 3.60.

2.262. Compare *Aeneid* 7.448–9; and compare 5.33, below.

2.272. Compare *Aeneid* 6.900, where Aeneas leaves behind the underworld and returns to his companions.

2.285. Compare Silius Italicus, *Punica* 10.31.

2.292. Compare Lucretius, *De rerum natura* 1.728 and *Aeneid* 4.132.

2.307. Compare Lucretius, *De rerum natura* 3.451.

2.312. Vida takes this line almost directly from Catullus (*Carmina* 68.43).

2.324. Compare Silius Italicus, *Punica* 15.425.

2.332–529. The locus classicus for the following catalogue of Hebrew tribes and descendants of the sons of Isaac is Homer's catalogue of ships from Book II of the *Iliad*. Many of the details of the individual tribes are based on Jacob's benediction of his sons, the patriarchs of the twelve tribes, in Genesis 49.

2.356 and following. See Genesis 19. The young wife is the wife of Lot, who is turned into a pillar of salt for having witnessed the destruction of Sodom, against a divine command.

2.361. Compare *Aeneid* 10.275.

2.363. Compare *Georgics* 4.411 (*obducunt sentibus herbae*).

2.365. Compare Juvencus, *Evangelia* 1.183.

2.368. Compare Statius, *Thebaid* 2.39.

2.386. Compare *Georgics* 2.184.

2.388. Compare Ovid, *Metamorphoses* 15.710.

2.394. A prophet: Elijah, who is supposed to have lived in a cave on Mount Carmel. See 2 Kings 2:11.

2.396. Compare *Aeneid* 3.704.

2.408–9. Compare Vergil, *Georgics* 2.404.

2.412. Vida's association of the Anti-Christ with the tribe of Dan derives from, among other sources, Revelation 7:1–8.

2.416. Compare *Georgics* 1.505, and compare 1.195, below.

2.422. Compare *Aeneid* 7.793.

2.431. See John 2.

2.449. Samaria was renamed Sebaste, Greek for Augusta, by Herod the Great (37–4 BCE).

2.478. The line is closely modeled on *Aeneid* 6.776.

2.489–93. See Joshua 3:15–16.

2.492. Compare *Aeneid* 4.489.

2.498. Its king: Lazarus, whose resuscitation Vida described in Book I.

2.507. Compare *Georgics* 1.301.

2.515–18. God caused the sun to stand still during the war between the Israelites and the Amorites: see Joshua 10:12.

2.518. One youth: Saul of Tarsus, later Saint Paul. For *puer altior ibat* see *Aeneid* 8.162–3: *altior ibat / Anchises.*

2.530–606. The narrative here follows Matthew 26:17–21, Mark 14:12–7, and Luke 22:7–14, Luke providing Vida with the most detail.

2.549. With *mandata . . . facessunt* compare *Aeneid* 4.295. Compare 1.224, 2.785, 3.916, and 4.975, below.

2.560. Compare Horace, *Satires* 2.7.85.

2.567. Compare *Georgics* 1.353.

2.589. Compare Lucretius, *De rerum natura* 2.35.

2.595. Compare Paulinus of Nola, *Carmina* 14.104.

2.598. Compare Silius Italicus, *Punica* 1.684.

2.607–642. Simon's song, essentially an elaborated Passover Haggadah, depicts the events described in the book of Exodus (cc. 12–17) and Genesis (c. 14). Vida, however, specifically chooses events which Christians would recognize as traditional symbols or types of the Eucharist, in order to set the stage for the Last Supper that follows.

2.619. Compare *Eclogues* 8.97.

2.632–3. Compare *Aeneid* 1.210.

2.639–42. Builder: Melchizedek. Compare Genesis 14:18–20.

2.639. The epithet is modeled on that given by Vergil to King Evander, *Romanae conditor arcis* (*Aeneid* 8.313).

2.643. Compare *Aeneid* 4.359.

2.648. For the phrase *regifico luxu* see *Aeneid* 6.604–5.

2.651–662. These lines describe the Last Supper, and particularly the institution of the Eucharist. Although Vida is following the biblical narrative (see Matthew 26:26–9, Mark 14:22–5, Luke 22:19–20 and 1 Corinthians 11:23–26), he also has the the Eucharistic prayer (or Canon) of the liturgy in mind.

2.657. Compare Paulinus of Nola, *Carmina* 26.59, where Paulinus is discussing the Eucharist.

2.667–9. A poetic statement of the doctrine of transubstantiation.

2.671–713. These lines describe Christ washing the feet of the disciples and his final discourse with the apostles, as found in John 13:4–35.

2.672–5. Vida combines here elements from *Aeneid* 7.463 and 12.417.

2.700. Compare *Aeneid* 1.683–4.

2.708. Compare *Aeneid* 11.386.

2.709. Compare *Aeneid* 11.336–9, where the phrase *frigida . . . dextera* is applied to the coward Drances. Compare on 1.62.

2.710. Compare Ovid, *Fasti* 2.793 and *Metamorphoses* 6.551.

2.714–24. Christ's prophecy of Peter's denial follows Matthew 26:31–5, Mark 14:27–30, Luke 22:33–4, and John 13:36–8. Vida follow's John's chronology, where the exchange with Peter occurs before they leave the city.

2.725–30. Peter's rejoinder is found in Mark 14:31.

2.731–64. These lines recount Christ's agony in the garden of Gethsemani on the Mount of Olives, as found in Matthew 26:36–46, Mark 14:26–42, and Luke 22:39–46. Vida's account follows most closely that of Luke.

2.738. Compare *Aeneid* 9.326.

2.740. Compare Ennodius, *Dictiones* 28.23.

2.753. Compare *Aeneid* 4.15.

2.754. Compare *Aeneid* 11.133 (*pace sequestra*).

2.756. Compare *Aeneid* 12.16.

2.757–64. The bloody sweat and the consoling angel are mentioned only by Luke (22:43–4).

2.757. Compare *Aeneid* 4.332.

2.758. Compare *Aeneid* 9.812 (*toto corpore sudor*).

2.765–874. Christ's capture in the garden is described in Matthew 26:47–56, Mark 14:43–50, Luke 22:47–54 and John 18:2–12.

2.765. Compare *Aeneid* 2.164 (*scelerumque inventor Ulixes*).

2.770. This line Vida takes from Ennius, *Annales* 11.363 (*apud* Priscian 9.38): *Tum clipei resonunt et ferri stridit acumen*.

2.785. Compare 1.224, 2.549, above, and 3.916 and 4.975, below.

2.791. Compare *Aeneid* 2.265 (*somno vinoque*), 6.520 (*somno . . . gravatum*), and 9.316–7.

2.802. Compare *Aeneid* 4.121.

2.803. Compare *Aeneid* 4.131.

2.810. Compare *Aeneid* 2.236.

2.812–843. Malchus's name is found only in John (18:10).

2.820. Compare *Aeneid* 11.390 (*ventosa lingua*).

2.833. Compare *Aeneid* 10.682.

2.843. Compare *Aeneid* 10.30.

2.846. Molossian hound: Mentioned by Vergil in *Georgics* 3.404–408. A famously fearsome hound named for the Molossians, an ancient Greek tribe that lived in Epirus.

2.866. Compare *Aeneid* 4.123.

8.869–70. This detail is based on a curious anecdote in Mark 14:51–52.

2.874. Compare *Aeneid* 5.150.

2.875–918. Vida's depiction of Caiaphas's interrogation of Christ is based on Matthew 25:57–66, Mark 14:53–65, and Luke 22:66–71.

2.917. Compare *Aeneid* 2.585–6.

2.918–63. Peter's three denials of Christ are found in Matthew 26:69–75, Mark 14:66–72, Luke 22:55–62 and John 18:17–8, 25–7.

2.918–9. These lines are modeled on *Aeneid* 6.475–6.

2.922. Compare *Aeneid* 4.300.

2.964–1001. Christ's first encounter with Pilate is described in Matthew 27:1–14, Luke 23:1–7 and John 18:29–38.

2.970. The highly sympathetic portrait of Pilate drawn here and throughout the rest of the *Christiad* reflects the influence of the Christian apocryphal literature on Pilate, the most important of which was the *Acts of Pilate*, a medieval forgery also known as the *Gospel of Nicodemus*.

2.976–7. Compare *Aeneid* 11.120–1.

BOOK III

3.1. Compare *Aeneid* 4.174 and 7.549.

3.12–3. Compare *Aeneid* 4.407 and 9.373.

3.15–7. Compare *Aeneid* 2.318–21.

3.20. The phrase *quo res nostra loco* varies *Aeneid* 2.322, *quo res summa loco?*

3.47. Compare *Aeneid* 2.22.

3.49. Compare *Aeneid* 4.407.

3.57. Compare *Aeneid* 4.51.

3.81. Compare *Aeneid* 9.429.

3.83–4. These lines are modeled on *Aeneid* 5.801–2.

3.86. A variation on *Aeneid* 1.517, *quae fortuna viris.*

3.88. Compare *Aeneid* 7.273 (*si quid veri mens augurat*).

3.96. Compare *Aeneid* 9.205.

3.105. The Marian narrative in Book III is closely related to a Franciscan text of the late thirteenth century, the *Meditationes vitae Christi* attributed dubiously to St. Bonaventure. Its most famous representation in art is found in Giotto's Arena Chapel in Padua.

3.121. A variation on *Aeneid* 1.641.

3.128. For the phrase *mare velivolum* see *Aeneid* 1.224 and context.

3.132. Compare *Aeneid* 2.325 and context.

3.145. *Virgo pulcherrima*, Vida's favorite epithet for Mary, comes from a well-known medieval hymn, and is also sanctioned by Ovid (*Metamorphoses* 12.190).

3.151. For *per auras* see note on 1.229, above.

3.155. Compare on 1.229.

3.178. Compare on 3.145.

3.179–80. Compare *Aeneid* 12.68–9.

3.184. Compare *Aeneid* 1.496–7 and 1.503.

3.185. Compare *Aeneid* 7.593.

3.186. Compare *Aeneid* 4.361.

3.187–8. Compare [ps.] Vergil, *Moretum* 107: *lacrimantia lumina tergit*. For *oscula libat* see *Aeneid* 1.256. Compare 1.956 and 6.845.

3.190. The ecstatic dance of Saint Anne is modeled on the Cumaean Sibyl in *Aeneid* 6.98f.

3.195. Compare *Aeneid* 11.220–1.

3.220–2. Compare *Aeneid* 4.18–19.

3.220. Compare *Aeneid* 9.136–7.

3.267–72. Compare *Aeneid* 1.591–3.

3.279. Compare *Aeneid* 2.777.

2.283. Compare on 3.145.

3.285. Compare *Aeneid* 4.30. Compare 3.704.

3.294–395. Mary's speech is based on the events in Luke 1:26–38.

3.297. Compare *Aeneid* 4.314.

3.301. Compare *Aeneid* 3.521.

3.302. Compare *Aeneid* 4.6 and 7.148.

3.303–12. Ancient prophets: Above all, Vida has Isaiah 7:14 in mind: "Therefore the Lord himself shall give you a sign. Behold a virgin shall conceive, and bear a son, and his name shall be called Emmanuel."

3.303. Compare *Aeneid* 3.102.

3.309. For *mirabile dictu* in the same position, see, for example, *Aeneid* 4.182.

3.310. This line varies *Aeneid* 7.660, *sub luminis edidit oras*.

3.312. This is a paraphrase of a line from Vergil's 'messianic' fourth Eclogue (l. 9). Thus in these lines Vida combines both Hebrew and pagan prophecies of the Incarnation.

3.335. The angel's speech echoes Jupiter's prophecy in *Aeneid* 1.278–9.

3.338. Compare *Aeneid* 1.75 (*faciat te prole parentem*).

3.342. The name "Jesus" is derived from Hebrew words meaning "Jehovah rescues."

3.353. Compare *Aeneid* 4.27.

3.362. St Elizabeth was the mother of John the Baptist.

3.375–84. An elaboration of *Aeneid* 5.87–9.

3.385–7. These lines refer to the famous passage in the sixth book of the *Aeneid* (726–7): *Spiritus intus alit, totamque infusa per artus / Mens agitat molem et magno se corpore miscet.*

3.395–445. These lines follow Matthew 1:19–24.

3.395–6. Compare *Aeneid* 8.391–2.

3.414. Compare *Aeneid* 11.488–9.

3.421–5. Three boys: Shadrach, Meshach and Abednego. See Daniel 3 and compare 6.770–1, below.

3.443. The phrase *coniugio adjungens stabili* is based on the Vergilian *coniubio iungam stabili* (*Aeneid* 1.73 and 4.126).

3.455. Compare *Aeneid* 6.100.

3.457–58. Horned prophet: Moses. The notion that Moses had horns after his descent from Mt. Sinai is based on the Vulgate translation of *Exodus* 34:29–30. On Mt. Sinai, Moses heard a voice from a bush that burned but was not consumed, which was interpreted by Christians as a type of Mary's virginity. See Exodus 3:2–4.

3.458–9. Compare *Aeneid* 2.683–4.

3.460–4. Fleece: The fleece of Gideon, a traditional image of Mary's virginity. Asking God for a sign of victory, the judge Gideon left a fleece outside his tent to see if the fleece would remain dry while the ground around it became wet with dew. See Judges 6:36–40.

3.465–498. The visitation of Mary to her cousin Elizabeth is described in Luke 1:39–45.

3.478. For *mirabile dictu* in the same position, see, for example, *Aeneid* 4.182.

3.480–2. Compare *Aeneid* 8.405.

3.486–7. Compare *Aeneid* 9.20.

3.500–504. Praises: The reference is to Mary's canticle, called the *Magnificat*, which these lines summarize (Luke 1:46–55).

3.512. Your Ausonian land: Ausonia is a Vergilian name for Italy. That there were rumors of Christ's coming in Italy is an allusion to Vergil's Fourth Eclogue, commonly seen as a pagan prophecy of Christ.

3.520. Compare *Aeneid* 4.358.

3.526. See note on 3.145, above.

3.527–8. Compare *Aeneid* 6.883.

3.534. An echo of Vergil's Fourth Eclogue.

3.537. Compare *Georgics* 1.508: *curvae rigidum falces conflantur in ensem.* While employing (and reversing) the language of Vergil, Vida paraphrases Isaiah 2:4: *conflabunt gladios suos in vomeres et lanceas suas in falces.* Compare Micah 4:3.

3.541–646. The account of Christ's birth follows closely that of Luke (2:1–21).

3.542. Compare *Aeneid* 10.100.

3.562. An echo of *Aeneid* 3.709, where Aeneas is speaking of his father.

3.569–70. Compare *Aeneid* 8.409–13.

3.589. The simile is inspired by *Aeneid* 9.668–71. For "hollow clouds" see Lucretius *De rerum natura* 6.272; Vergil *Aeneid* 1.516, 5.810, 10.636, 11.593, and Sannazaro, *De partu virginis* 3.389.

3.609. For *per auras* see note on 1.229, above.

3.645. See Pliny the Elder, *Natural History* 35.165, where Pliny says that the priests of Cybele use broken pieces of Samian pottery to perform their ritual castrations.

3.646. Christ: *Kristos* means "anointed" in Greek.

3.647–738. The account of the purification of Mary in the temple follows Luke 2:22–35.

3.652. For *torquatos . . . columbas* ("doves with colored necks") see Propertius, *Elegies* 4.5.65.

3.657–9. Compare *Aeneid* 3.20–1.

3.685. Simeon the Righteous, mentioned in Luke 2:25–35. The line combines two Vergilian phrases, *nomen aui referens* from *Aeneid* 5.564 and *obsitus annis* (in Vergil *aeuo*) from *Aeneid* 8.307.

3.686. Compare *Aeneid* 2.426–7.

3.704. Compare *Aeneid* 11.41 and 4.30. Compare 3.285.

3.705. Blessed be thou *(macte virtute):* an archaic idiom in Vergil; see *Aeneid* 9.641.

3.712. Simeon's prayer is often called the *Nunc dimittis*, from its opening words in the Vulgate; see Luke 2:29–35.

3.715. For the phrase *in tenebris lux* see John 1:5.

3.725. Possibly an echo of the opening of Lucan, *Bellum civile*, book 7, describing the day of the battle of Pharsalus.

3.730. Compare *Aeneid* 9.445.

3.739–99. The visit of the Magi, Vida's three kings, is described in Matthew 2:1–12.

3.749. Fiery lamp: The pillar of fire, which guided the Israelites by night as they escaped from Egypt. See Exodus 13:21–2.

3.764. Compare *Aeneid* 1.379.

3.765. Compare *Aeneid* 8.19.

3.780. Compare *Aeneid* 4.136.

3.785. Compare *Aeneid* 10.272–3.

3.786. Compare *Aeneid* 8.366.

3.794. Compare *Aeneid* 4.135.

3.800–95. The slaughter of innocents by King Herod and the flight of Joseph, Mary, and Jesus into Egypt is described in Matthew 2:13–23.

3.829. The passage recalls the invocation to Venus at the beginning of Lucretius' *De rerum natura* (quoted above on 1.1). Compare *Aeneid* 2.728 *(omnes terrent aurae).*

3.839–40. Compare *Aeneid* 7.33–4.

3.850. For *per auras* see note on 1.229, above.

3.871. Pelusium was a city along the eastern end of the Nile Delta, while Memphis was on the west bank near modern Cairo.

3.876–7. Compare *Aeneid* 7.518.

3.895–918. These lines are an extended gloss on Luke 2:40 and 51–2.

3.896. Compare *Aeneid* 2.506.

3.899–902. Compare *Aeneid* 1.372–4.

3.901. Compare *Aeneid* 4.334.

3.910–1. Compare *Aeneid* 7.11–4.

3.913. Compare *Georgics* 1.369.

3.916. Compare 1.224, 2.549, 2.785, and 4.975.

3.917. Vida is cleverly inverting *Aen.* 1.716: *falsi impleuit genitoris amorem* (Cupid in the guise of Ascanius satisfies the love of his pretended father, Aeneas).

3.918. Compare *Georgics* 4.418 (*habilis membris venit vigor*).

3.919–68. The boy Jesus in the temple conversing with the elders is described in Luke (2:41–50).

3.956–7. Compare *Aeneid* 1.709–14.

3.980–1002. The wedding at Cana, where Jesus turned water into wine, is described in John 2:1–12.

3.1020. Compare *Aeneid* 2.1.

BOOK IV

4.4. Saint John's rapture resembles those in other famous works of Renaissance literature, such as the rapture of the holy man at the end of Pietro Bembo's *Gli Asolani*, or Bembo's own rapture at the end of Baldassar Castiglione's *Il Cortegiano*. For *mortalia linquens*, see [ps.] Damasus, *Epigrammata* 66.9.

4.8. Compare Ennodius, *Carmina* 2.150.6.

4.9. Compare Paulinus of Nola, *Carmina* 19.722 and Commodian, *Instructiones* 2.27.4.

4.11. The queen of birds: the Eagle, the traditional image of Saint John. The four creatures seen by Ezekiel were often identified with the Four Evangelists, and the eagle with John in particular. See Ezekiel 1:10 and Apocalypse 4:7. For *per auras* see note on 1.229. above.

4.17. Compare *Aeneid* 6.520.

4.18. Compare Paulinus of Nola, *Carmina* 26.21.

4.19. Compare *Aeneid* 1.521.

4.20–58. The beginning of John's discourse, though hearkening back to Genesis, looks most of all to the prologue of his gospel (John 1:1–18). The ensuing account of the creation of the universe and of mankind owes almost as much to Hesiod, Lucretius and Ovid as to the Bible.

4.20. Though the phrase *sator rerum* heakens back to Silius Italicus (*Punica* 4.430), it enjoyed a rich Christian usage. See, for example, Paulinus of Nola, *Carmina* app. 3.205 and Venantius Fortunatus, *Carmina* app. 2.

4.22–4. Compare Statius, *Silvae* 2.1.41–2.

4.26. Compare Ovid, *Metamorphoses* 3.647.

4.28. Compare Ovid, *Metamorphoses* 9.678.

4.31. Compare *Aeneid* 6.732.

4.36. Compare Ovid, *Metamorphoses* 1.257 and Lucretius, *De rerum natura* 5.473. Compare 1.1 and note, above.

4.38. Compare Lucretius, *De rerum natura* 5.1052.

4.39. The phrase *deus unus uterque est* is lifted from Hilary of Poiters's *De Trinitate* (e.g. 5.10, 8.36 and 11.1).

4.41. Compare Lucretius, *De rerum natura* 4.1216.

4.44. Compare Dracontius, *De laudibus Dei* 1.600.

4.46. Lucretius, *De rerum natura* 3.365.

4.58–79. The fall of Satan and his angels is described in John's Apocalypse (12:7–9).

4.61. Compare Paulinus of Nola, *Carmina* 19.315.

4.66. Compare *Aeneid* 12.925.

4.67. Compare Ovid *Heroides* 15.167.

4.69. Compare Statius, *Thebaid* 5.568.

4.75. This line is modeled on *Aeneid* 2.244.

4.80–145. In these lines, Saint John summarizes the Old Testament from Genesis through the Prophets.

4.80. Compare Manilius, *Astronomica* 1.386.

4.84. Compare Lucretius, *De rerum natura* 2.78.

4.86. Compare Lucretius, *De rerum natura* 1.163. and *Georgics* 4.223.

4.99. This line is closely modeled on Catullus, *Carmina* 64.397: *sed postquam tellus scelere est imbuta nefando*.

4.100–5. These lines follow *Aeneid* 6.273–7.

4.100. Compare Paulinus of Nola, *Carmina* 21.519–20.

4.101–2. Compare *Georgics* 1.145–6.

4.105. Compare *Georgics* 2.295 and Lucretius, *De rerum natura* 3.948.

4.116. Compare *Aeneid* 12.836 (*morem ritusque sacrorum*).

4.129. Compare *Aeneid* 5.616.

4.133. Compare Propertius, *Elegies* 1.5.25.

4.134. Compare *Eclogues* 4.12.

4.141. *Moenia mundi* is typically Lucretian, used at line-end ten times in the *De rerum natura*.

4.143. Compare *Aeneid* 4.569.

4.146–203. Saint John's account of the career of John the Baptist follows his Gospel (1:19–28), with some additional details drawn from Matthew 3:1–12, Mark 1:1–8 and Luke 1:5–25 and 3:1–20.

4.146. Compare *Aeneid* 4.249.

4.171. Compare *Aeneid* 2.98.

4.196–8. These lines echo Vergil's 'messianic' Fourth Eclogue (especially ll. 9–13).

4.200. Vida adopts the language of *Aeneid* 2.781–2, describing the river Tiber, to characterize the river Jordan.

4.204–240. The baptism of Christ is described in John's Gospel (1:29–34), as well as in Matthew 3:3–17, Mark 1:9–11 and Luke 3:21–3.

4.205. Compare Ennodius, *Carmina* 1.7.7.

4.206. Compare *Aeneid* 4.415.

4.208. Compare *Aeneid* 6.822: *ferent ea facta minores*. Though most editions rightly read *minores*, one manuscript of the *Aeneid* as well as a quotation of this line in Macrobius's *Saturnalia* (4.6.18) reads *nepotes*.

4.210. Compare *Aeneid* 6.685.

4.232. Compare *Aeneid* 6.46.

4.233. Compare Ovid, *Heroides* 7.113 and *Metamorphoses* 15.114.

4.241–274. The calling of the twelve Apostles is found in John 1:35–51, Mark 3:13–9 and Luke 6:13–6.

4.242. Compare Cyprianus Gallus, *Heptateuchos: Exodus* 755.

4.246–8. Compare *Aeneid* 8.441 and 12.427.

4.250. Compare Lucretius, *De rerum natura* 3.332.

4.251. Bethsaide: A city to the east of the Jordan River.

4.258. Compare *Aeneid* 5.158.

4.262. Compare Matthew 4:20.

4.270. Compare *Georgics* 3.366.

4.274. This line is modeled on *Aeneid* 2.264.

4.280. Compare *Aeneid* 12.25.

4.282. Compare *Aeneid* 6.512.

4.286. The king of Bethany: Lazarus. With this line compare *Aeneid* 6.356.

4.290. Compare Propertius, *Elegies* 2.5.11.

4.302–307. Compare the description of disease in Lucretius, *De rerum natura* 487–94.

4.304. Compare Cyprianus Gallus, *Heptateuchos: Iudices* 171.

4.314. Compare Paulinus of Perigueux, *De vita Martini* 6.268.

4.315–42. This episode is found only in Luke 7:11–17.

4.323. Compare *Aeneid* 3.491.

4.324. Compare Lucretius, *De rerum natura* 5.1114.

4.325–8. Compare the similes in *Aeneid* 9.435–7 and 11.67–9.

4.327. Compare Ovid, *Metamorphoses* 13.746.

4.335. Compare Ovid, *Metamorphoses* 14.389.

4.336. Compare *Aeneid* 10.324.

4.337. Compare Livy, *Ab urbe condita* 6.3.4: *parcere lamentis . . . iussit.*

4.343–8. The raising of the daughter of Iarus (Jairus) is described in Matthew 9:23–6, Mark 5:37–43 and Luke 8:51–56.

4.347–8. Compare *Aeneid* 11.338 and 6.815–6.

4.349–50. The reference is to the wedding at Cana (John 2:1–12), already described by Vida at 3.980–1002. The opening *Quid repetam* comes from *Aeneid* 10.36.

4.351. Compare Ovid, *Metamorphoses* 11.503.

4.352–88. The feeding of the five thousand is related in Matthew 14:15–21, Mark 6:35–44, Luke 9:12–17 and John 6:3–14.

4.368. Compare Silius Italicus, *Punica* 16.287.

4.370. Compare Juvencus, *Evangelia* 4.386: *tali genitorem uoce precatur.*

4.371. Compare Corippus, *Iohannes* 4.270.

4.372. Compare Ovid, *Epistulae ex Ponto* 2.1.13 and context.

4.381. Compare *Aeneid* 1.194.

3.389–98. The cursing of the fig tree is described in Matthew 21:19–22 and Mark 11:12–14.

4.398. Compare Ovid, *Metamorphoses* 8.51. For *per auras* see note on 1.229, above.

4.399–426. Saint John's account of Christ calming the sea is based on Matthew 8:23–7, Mark 4:36–41 and Luke 8:23–5.

4.399–401. Compare *Aeneid* 3.285.

4.410. Compare *Aeneid* 2.685.

4.419–20. Compare *Aeneid* 8.395–6. The phrase *timor omnis abesto* comes from *Aeneid* 11.14. Vida follows Juvencus in putting these words into Christ's mouth during the storm at sea (*Evangelia* 3.107).

4.427–48. The miraculous discovery of the silver coin in the fish is described in Matthew 17:23–26.

4.443. Compare *Aeneid* 1.606 and 10.597. For *vetito . . . concubitu* see Ovid, *Metamorphoses* 10.353.

4.446. Sacred ritual: Vida may mean to refer to the Ten Days of Repentance between Rosh Hashanah and Yom Kippur.

4.449–531. Christ's casting the demon into a herd of swine is recounted in Matthew 8:28–34, Mark 5:1–20 and Luke 8:26–39.

4.473. Compare *Aeneid* 4.551 (*degere more ferae*).

4.476. Compare *Ilias latina* 476 and Paulinus of Perigueux, *De vita Martini* 1.204.

4.485. This line is modeled on *Aeneid* 11.497.

4.493. Compare *Aeneid* 5.514, 7.471 and 12.780.

4.494. Compare *Aeneid* 2.680.

4.498. Compare Lucretius, *De rerum natura* 5.263 and 6.609, as well as Ovid, *Metamorphoses* 15.266 and context.

4.499. Lago di Piediluco: Lit. the lake of [the river] Velino. Vida is alluding to the roar of the Cascata delle Marmore, the famous man-made waterfalls near Terni in Umbria that flow from the Lago di Piediluco. See Pliny the Elder, *Natural History* 3.13.108–9. Flooding from the Velino river was a constant concern of the Renaissance popes, and only ten years after the publication of the *Christiad* Pope Paul III commissioned the architect Antonio San Gallo to build another channel to contain the waters.

4.501. Compare *Eclogues* 8.58.

4.504. Compare Propertius, *Elegies* 4.1.5.

4.506. Compare *Aeneid* 9.504.

4.508. Compare *Aeneid* 2.491.

4.515. Compare *Aeneid* 6.140.

4.519. Compare Lucretius, *De rerum natura* 4.227 and 6.935; *Aeneid* 5.458 and 12.553; and *Georgics* 3.110. Compare 2.140, above.

4.526. Vida copies this line from Lucilius, *Satires* 3.113 (*apud* Nonius 38.26).

4.530. Compare 1.424, above.

4.532–37. The mission of the apostles is described in Matthew 10:1–42, Mark 6:7–13 and Luke 9:1–6.

4:538–64. This incident is found in Matthew 17:14–18, Mark 9:14–27 and Luke 9:37–43.

4.540. Compare *Georgics* 3.538 and Paulinus of Nola, *Carmina* 15.201.

4.546. Compare Paulinus of Perigueux, *De vita Martini* 2.117.

4.548. Compare Ovid, *Heroides* 17.37.

4.550. Compare *Aeneid* 4.489 and Sannazaro, *De partu Virginis* 2.22 (*sistunt vaga flumina cursus*).

4.555. The light of men: Compare Matthew 5:14 and context.

4.558–61. The mission of the Seventy is described in Luke 10.

4.572–582. The woman healed by touching Christ's garment is described in Matthew 9:20–2, Mark 5:24–34 and Luke 8:42–8.

4.574. Compare Cyprianus Gallus, *Heptateuchos: Genesis* 1091.

4.599–601. The death of John the Baptist is related in Matthew 14:1–12.

4.604. Erebus: Satan, since Erebus, in classical mythology, was equated with the kingdom of Hades. The encounter between Jesus and Satan, which Vida describes in lines 604–655, is found in Matthew 4:1–11, Mark 1:12–3 and Luke 4:1–13.

4.614. Tartarus, like Erebus, is another classical name for the underworld.

4.618–9. Compare Seneca, *Troades* 461: *magni certa progenies patris.*

4.621. Compare *Aeneid* 7.109.

4.632–6. Compare *Aeneid* 7.586–90 and *Georgics* 4.262.

4.633. Compare *Aeneid* 1.721.

4.646–51. Compare *Aeneid* 11.492–6.

4.647. Compare Martial, *Epigrams* 12.38.5.

4.651. Compare *Aeneid* 3.202–3.

4.662. Compare *Aeneid* 1.574 and 10.108.

4.670. Compare Lucretius, *De rerum natura* 6.879.

4.676. Compare *Aeneid* 11.347.

4.678. Matthew: The evangelist and apostle Matthew, who had been a tax collector. For *dives agri* see Ovid, *Metamorphoses* 5.130.

4.679. Zachaeus: Another tax-collector. See Luke 19:1–10.

4.690–703. The finding of the lost sheep is recounted in Luke 15:1–7 and briefly in Matthew 18:12, though Vida draws many of the details from the parable of the prodigal son in Luke 15:11–24.

4.702. This line is modeled on Lucretius, *De rerum natura* 3.895: *nec dulces occurrent oscula nati.*

4.704–15. Christ's meeting with the Samarian woman at the well is described in John 4:7–10. Sychar, known in the Old Testament as Shechem, was an Israelite city belonging to the tribe of Manasseh.

4.711. At his command: Alluding to how Moses brought forth water from a rock in the wilderness by asking God to command it (Exodus 17).

4.716–32. This episode is found in Matthew 19:13–5, Mark 10:13–6 and Luke 18:15–7.

4.716. Compare *Aeneid* 5.556.

4.719. Compare Statius, *Thebaid* 4.128.

4.731. Compare Ovid, *Metamorphoses* 11.525 and Statius, *Achilleid* 1.512.

4.733–46. This dispute is related in Matthew 18:1–6, Mark 9:33–7 and Luke 9:46–8.

4.733. For *mira loquar* see Ovid, *Metamorphoses* 7.549.

4.738. Compare Ovid, *Heroides* 1.109.

4.744–6. These lines are closely based on Lucretius, *De rerum natura* 5.128–30.

4.747–58. My pious mother: Salome, the wife of Zebedee, the mother of James and John. Her request to Christ is related in Matthew 20:20–3 and Mark 10:35–41.

4.757. Compare 1 Peter 5:5: *Deus superbis resistit.*

4.777. Compare Boethius, *De consolatione philosophiae* 3.m2.2–4: *immensum / legibus orbem prouida seruet / stringatque.*

4.783–4. Compare Silius Italicus, *Punica* 16.472.

4.786. Compare *Aeneid* 12.811.

4.791. Compare Ovid, *Metamorphoses* 13.16.

4.793. Compare *Aeneid* 8.183.

4.797. Our lawgiving teacher: I.e., Moses. Jesus offers a new interpretation of Jewish law.

4.804–6. Compare John 1:5.

4.805. Compare Ovid, *Metamorphoses* 9.761.

4.806. Compare *Aeneid* 12.647.

4.808. Compare *Aeneid* 4.359.

4.809. Compare Lucretius, *De rerum natura* 4.1054.

4.816. Compare Manilius, *Astronomica* 4.828.

4.821–2. Compare *Georgics* 2.17.

4.823. Only one: Saint John himself, who is traditionally understood to have died of old age on Mount Patmos, unlike the other Apostles who were violently martyred.

4.829. Compare Horace, *Carmina* 3.2.1. and *Aeneid* 8.365.

4.834. This line is based on Propertius, *Elegies* 1.20.43.

4.842. Compare *Georgics* 4.132.

4.852. Compare Lucretius, *De rerum natura* 5.1249.

4.858–967. Christ preached from a boat on several occasions, most notably in Luke 5:3. The discourse he delivers here seems to be Vida's combination of several speeches, most notably the Sermon on the Mount (Matthew 5:1–8:1 and Luke 6:20–49).

4.865. Compare Lucan, *Bellum civile* 2.241.

4.867. Compare *Aeneid* 2.303.

4.871. Compare Lucretius, *De rerum natura* 6.428.

4.883. Compare *Aeneid* 11.346.

4.885. Compare *Aeneid* 8.364.

4.888. Compare *Aeneid* 10.861.

4.890–1. Compare *Aeneid* 4.384.

4.895–6. Compare *Georgics* 2.433.

4.903. Compare Cyprianus Gallus, *Heptateuchos: Exodus* 848.

4.907. Compare *Aeneid* 11.647 and *Georgics* 4.218.

4.927. Compare Ovid, *Metamorphoses* 3.669.

4.932. The phrase *genus altivolantum* comes from Ennius (*Annales* 1.81, apud Cicero, *De divinatione* 1.107).

4.937. Compare 6:310 and note.

4.946. Compare *Georgics* 1.506.

4.957. Compare *Eclogues* 4.12.

4.972–80. These lines paraphrase the Lord's prayer, as found in Matthew 6:9–13 and Luke 11:1–4.

4.975. Compare 1.224, 2.549, 2.785, and 3.916, above.

4.981–1028. These lines recount Christ's description of the end of the world and the Last Judgment, usually known as the Synoptic Apocalypse. See Matthew 24:1–44, Mark 13:1–37, and Luke 21:5–36. It is appropriate the Saint John conclude his speech to Pilate with this episode, as he was traditionally regarded as the author of the last book of the Christian Bible, the Apocalypse. Later (l. 1025, below) John claims to have heard these prophecies from Christ himself, whereas in Revelation the prophecies are said to have been delivered to John by an angel.

4.983. This line comes from Cicero, *De consulatu suo* (apud *De divinatione* 1.18).

4.1008. Compare Juvencus, *Evangelia* 4.263, also describing the Judgment.

4.1015. For *per auras* see note on 1.229, above.

4.1022. Only the souls: I.e., before the second coming of Christ, only souls will be in heaven with Christ; afterwards souls will receive glorified bodies.

4.1034. The beginning and the end, etc.: Compare Apocalypse 1:8 and John 14:6.

BOOK V

5.1. The opening of this book looks to Vergil's famous mandate to the Roman (*Aeneid* 6.851–3).

5.2. Compare *Aeneid* 4.285: *nunc huc . . . nunc illuc dividit.*

5.4. Compare *Aeneid* 4.12.

5.13–81. The despair of Judas is described in Matthew 27:1–10. Compare Acts 1:16–20.

5.13. Compare Silius Italicus, *Punica* 17.137.

5.15. Compare Ovid, *Metamorphoses* 10.661 and *Aeneid* 6.436–7.

5.16–53. Compare Vergil's depiction of Queen Dido's madness (*Aeneid* 4.529–64).

5.18. Compare *Aeneid* 7.466.

5.19. Compare Statius, *Thebaid* 8.627.

5.26–7. Compare *Aeneid* 12.669.

5.31–2. Compare *Aeneid* 7.466 and 12.666–7.

5.33. Compare *Aeneid* 7.448–9 and *Georgics* 3.433. Compare 2.262, above.

5.34. Compare Terence, *Hecyra* 444.

5.47. Compare Ovid, *Metamorphoses* 5.653.

5.48. Compare Silius Italicus, *Punica* 10.357.

5.49. Vida copies *magnae nunc hiscite terrae* from an anonymous verse quoted by Quintilian (*Institutiones* 9.2.26).

5.55–6. These lines imitate *Aeneid* 4.631: *invisam quaerens quam primum abrumpere lucem.*

5.62. Compare Lucretius, *De rerum natura* 3.530.

5.64. Vida seems to have in mind the fragments of the obscure poet Furius Antias, as quoted by Aulus Gellius (*Attic Nights* 18.11.4): *sanguine diluitur tellus, cava terra lutescit / omnia noctescunt tenebris caliginis atrae.*

5.77. Compare *Aeneid* 12.603.

5.79. Compare *Aeneid* 9.204.

5.80. Compare *Aeneid* 9.580.

5.82–182. These lines follow Matthew 27:1–4, Luke 23:1–7 and John 18:29–38, with some details drawn from the *Acts of Pilate*, c. 4.

5.86. The line is modeled on *Aeneid* 6.563.

5.87. Compare *Aeneid* 1.497.

5.99. The epithet given Aeneas by Vergil, *deum certissima proles* (*Aeneid* 6.322), was already applied to Christ by Juvencus (*Evangelia* 2.55). Compare 6.259.

5.103. Annas was a Jewish high priest from AD 36–7. Compare this line with *Aeneid* 11.122 and 11.338, both in reference to the coward Drances.

5.115. Compare *Aeneid* 11.340, where the phrase *seditione potens* is applied to Drances.

5.117. Compare *Aeneid* 10.176.

5.122. Vida is here adapting a verse from Cicero (*De consulato suo*, quoted in *De divinatione* 1.19.14): *tum species ex aere vetus venerata que Nattae / concidit elapsae que vetusto numine leges.*

5.133. Vida here alludes to a line from the fragmentary *Satires* of the early Roman poet Lucilius (20.404, *apud* Nonius 51.3): *illi praeciso atque epulis capiuntur opimis.*

5.138. Compare Arator, *Historia apostolica* 2.999.

5.144. Compare *Aeneid* 3.227.

5.151. Compare *Aeneid* 1.525.

5.152. Compare *Aeneid* 1.559, 5.385 and 11.132.

5.155–6. Compare *Aeneid* 11.336–7.

5.164. Compare Statius, *Silvae* 3.3.45.

5.167. Vida here echoes a line from Lucilius (*Satires* 30.946, apud Nonius 335.30): *quem sumptum facis in lustris, circum oppida lustrans.*

5.175–6. Compare *Aeneid* 12.9.

5.179. Adige: A river in Northern Italy that flows from the Alps into the Adriatic Sea.

5.187–99. Jesus before Herod is recounted in Mark 15:1–5 and Luke 23:8–12.

5.193–4. Compare *Aeneid* 8.163–4.

5.204. Compare Statius, *Thebaid* 1.25.

5.205. Breath of Heaven: i.e., Holy Spirit.

5.213. This line echoes Vergil's 'messianic' Fourth Eclogue (l. 5).

5.225–54. These lines follow Matthew 27:15–26, Mark 15:6–15, Luke 23:13–25 and John 18:38–40.

5.231. Compare Claudian, *Carmina minora* 30.138.

5.233. Compare *Aeneid* 7.788.

5.248. Compare Lucan, *Bellum civile* 10.538–9.

5.254. Compare *Aeneid* 4.132.

5.255–281. Vida follows John 19:1–3 here. Compare Matthew 27:26 and Mark 15 :16–20.

5.258. Compare *Aeneid* 2.645.

5.267. Compare *Aeneid* 8.33–4.

5.272. Compare *Aeneid* 7.766.

5.284–299. Pilate's wife's dream is found in Matthew 27:19.

5.294. For *per auras* see note on 1.229, above. Compare Ovid, *Metamorphoses* 2.587.

5.295. Vida's "divine voice" consciously employs the language of Vergil's famous mandate to the Romans (*Aeneid* 6:851–3): *Romane, memento . . . parcere subiectis et debellare superbos;* see 5.1, above.

5.296. Compare *Aeneid* 4.12.

5.297. Compare *Aeneid* 3.41–2.

5.300–68. Vida follows the account in John 19:4–16.

5.301. Compare *Aeneid* 4.91.

5.305. Compare Paulinus of Nola, *Carmina* 18.308.

5.309. Fear: *Timor*, the personification of fear, is probably based on the Greek *Phobos*, son of Ares and Aphrodite. The god is mentioned in *Aeneid* 8.556–7, among other passages.

5.310–30. Much of Vida's description of Pilate's fear is drawn from *Aeneid* 12.843–68.

5.323–4. Compare *Aeneid* 12.866.

5.327–8. Compare *Aeneid* 4.280, 12.868 and 12.905.

5.349. Eurus: The personification of the west wind, son of Eos, the dawn.

5.350–4. Compare Lucan, *Bellum civile* 1.501–2 and 5.645–6.

5.356. Compare *Aeneid* 2.534. Compare 1.62, above.

5.357–66. Compare *Aeneid* 7.591. Vida seems to be drawing a parallel between Pilate, whom these lines describe, and Vergil's indecisive King Latinus.

5.359–61. Compare *Aeneid* 7.595–7.

5.362–8. Compare Matthew 27:24–5.

5.375–400. The crowning with thorns is described in Matthew 27:29, Mark 15:17 and John 19:2.

5.384. Compare *Aeneid* 12.268 and 12.409.

5.390. Compare *Aeneid* 10.844.

5.395–400. An elaboration of Matthew 8:20.

5.400–480. The carrying of the cross is described in Matthew 27:31–3, Mark 15:20–2, Luke 23:26–33 and John 19:17. Vida draws many of his details from Luke's account.

5.412. Compare *Aeneid* 12.767.

5.416–7. Compare *Aeneid* 3.637.

5.417. This line is taken from Cicero's *De consulatu suo* (quoted in his *De divinatione* 1.17.12): *et totum conlustrat lumine mundum.*

5.420. Life-giving light: *Lux alma*, the title and incipit of a famous hymn of St. Bernard of Clairvaux, used in the office for the Feast of the Transfiguration. The phrase is also found in Vergil, *Aeneid* 3.311.

5.424. Compare Juvencus, *Evangelia* 4.588–9.

5.429. Compare *Georgics* 1.164.

5.432–3. Compare *Aeneid* 7.793–4.

5.435. Compare *Aeneid* 7.615.

5.438. Compare *Aeneid* 2.35.

5.479–80. Compare *Aeneid* 8.197.

5.485. Compare *Aeneid* 3.651.

5.488. Compare *Aeneid* 11.602.

5.494. For *per auras* see note on 1.229, above.

5.498. Compare Statius, *Thebaid* 9.44.

5.499. Compare *Ilias Latina* 746: *mixtusque fluit cum sanguine sudor.*

5.500. Compare *Aeneid* 10.782.

5.501. Compare Claudian, *In Rufinum* 2.205.

5.502–3. The first of the "Seven Last Words of Christ," a frequent object of meditation and devotion in Vida's time: "My God, My God, why hast thou forsaken me?" (Mark 15:34 and Matthew 27:46).

5.503. Compare *Aeneid* 2.595.

5.513. Compare *Aeneid* 1.541.

5.514. Hardly the least among the winged race: The angel Gabriel.

5.535. Compare *Aeneid* 2.301.

5.545. Compare *Aeneid* 12.88.

5.451. Compare *Aeneid* 10.443.

5.553. Compare Statius, *Thebaid* 4.5–6.

5.562. Compare *Aeneid* 4.175.

5.570. Compare *Aeneid* 7.191.

5.575. Compare Milton, *Paradise Lost* 1.573–587.

5.577. A leader: St. Michael. For the dragon see Revelation 12:7–10. Monte Gargano on the coast of southeastern Italy boasts the site of the oldest shrine to St. Michael in Western Europe, Monte Sant'Angelo sul Gargano.

5.580. His earlier battle: The reference is to Michael's role in putting down the revolt of Lucifer; the detail of the snakeskin trophy (584–6) recalls the allegorical account in Revelation 12:7–10, where Satan takes the form of a dragon defeated by Michael and the other angels.

5.587. Compare *Aeneid* 10.271.

5.601. For *per auras* see note on 1.229, above.

5.605. Compare *Aeneid* 12.890.

5.621. This line comes from Cicero, *De consulatu suo* (quoted in his *De divinatione* 1.19 and 2.45).

5.622. Compare *Aeneid* 11.225.

5.658. Compare *Aeneid* 8.378.

5.673. Compare Paulinus of Nola, *Carmina* 29.14.

5.675. The Babylonians: Referring to the Tower of Babel in Genesis 11:1–9.

5.686–8. Compare *Aeneid* 10.503–4. With 686 compare Juvenal, *Satires* 2.167.

5.690. This line is closely modeled on Lucretius, *De rerum natura* 6.388.

5.695. Compare Silius Italicus, *Punica* 9.330.

5.697. Compare Claudian, *Carmina maiora* 12.425.

5.712. Compare *Georgics* 4.50.

5.727–33. Referring to episodes described in Exodus 16 and 17.

5.739. Compare *Aeneid* 5.466.

5.751. Compare *Aeneid* 5.470.

5.766–7. Compare *Aeneid* 12.607.

5.772. Compare *Aeneid* 4.359.

5.781. Compare Ovid, *Metamorphoses* 7.113.

5.786. Compare *Aeneid* 4.674.

5.789. Compare *Aeneid* 12.533–4.

5.793. The sick wife of Cleophas: Mary of Clopas or Cleophas, one of several Marys in the New Testament, is mentioned explicitly only in John 19:25.

5.805. See Exodus 12:13: "And the blood shall be to you for a token upon the houses where ye are: and when I see the blood, I will pass over you, and the plague shall not be upon you to destroy you, when I smite the land of Egypt."

5.833. Compare *Aeneid* 6.473–4.

5.835. Compare *Aeneid* 4.394.

5.842–3. The second of the Last Words: "When Jesus therefore had seen his mother and the disciple standing by whom he loved, he saith to his mother: Woman, behold thy son. After that, he saith to the disciple: Behold thy mother." (John 19:26–7).

5.843. Compare *Aeneid* 10.850.

5.846–93. A humanistic version of the *planctus Mariae* genre; the analogous iconic type in the visual arts is the *mater dolorosa*. There is probably also some influence of the well-known medieval sequence *Stabat mater*, a text frequently set to music from the thirteenth century onwards. The lament of Euryalus' mother in book 9 of the *Aeneid* is also present as a model.

5.850–1. Compare *Aeneid* 9.490–1.

5.862. Compare [ps.] Vergil, *Copa* 35.

5.867–8. Compare *Aeneid* 1.46.

5.880. Compare *Aeneid* 10.850.

5.881–4. These lines are meant to recall a famous passage of the Lamentations of Jeremiah (1:12): *O vos omnes qui transitis per viam: attendite et videte si est dolor sicut dolor meus.* The text was part of the office of Matins for Holy Saturday, and was often set to music in the fifteenth and sixteenth centuries; it was (and is) also commonly used as a text to accompany statues of the Mater dolorosa.

5.889. Compare Ovid, *Fasti* 6.517.

5.902. Compare Claudian, *Carmina maiora* 8.58.

5.910–3. The third of the Last Words: "Father, forgive them, they know not what they do" (Luke 23:34).

5.910 Compare Lucretius, *De rerum natura* 3.313.

5.913–39. The fourth of the Last Words: "This day thou shalt be with me in Paradise" (Luke 23:39–43).

5.919. Compare *Aeneid* 4.381 and Lucretius, *De rerum natura* 1.728.

5.928. Compare *Aeneid* 5.465.

5.942. Compare Ovid, *Metamorphoses* 5.487.

5.943. Compare Petronius, *Carmina* 39.7: *illic inter aquas urit sitis arida fauces.*

5.944–6. The fifth of the Last Words: "I thirst" (John 19:28).

5.944. Compare Ovid, *Metamorphoses* 4.145.

5.952–7. The soldiers casting lots for Christ's garment are described in Matthew 27:35–6, Mark 15:24, Luke 23:34 and John 19:23–4.

5.953. Compare *Aeneid* 10.818.

5.958. Sacred prophets: i.e., David. See Psalm 22:18.

5.959–79. The earthquake is mentioned in Matthew 27:51. The darkness covering the land is found in Matthew 27:45, Mark 15:33 and Luke 23:44–5.

5.975. An echo of *Georgics* 1.330–1.

5.980–91. The rending of the veil of the temple is described in Matthew 27:51, Mark 15:38 and Luke 23:45.

5.985. Compare *Aeneid* 4.56.

5.993. The sixth of the Last Words: "It is finished" (John 19:30).

5.994. The seventh and final of the Last Words: "Into thy hands, O Lord, I commend my spirit" (Luke 23:46).

BOOK VI

6.1–30. These lines follow the narrative of Matthew 27:57–8, Mark 15:43–45, Luke 23:50–2, and John 19.38.

6.1. Compare Catullus, *Carmina* 62.1, *Aeneid* 1.369 and 2.280, and *Georgics* 6.82.

6.9. Compare *Aeneid* 2.399–400.

6.11. Compare *Aeneid* 5.430.

6.12. *Ac talia fatur* is a very common Vergilian line-ending.

6.20. Compare Claudian, *In Eutropium* 1.26.

6.23–4. Compare *Aeneid* 11.111.

6.27. This line is modeled on Columella, *De re rustica* 10.279: *casta fides nobis colitur sanctique penates.*

6.30. Compare *Aeneid* 11.25.

6.32–3. Compare *Aeneid* 5.868–9.

6.32. That Nicodemus accompanied Joseph of Arimathea is attested only by John 19:39.

6.35. Compare *Aeneid* 8.605.

6.37. Compare Statius, *Thebaid* 1.851.

6.37. Compare Lucan, *Bellum civile* 6.544.

6.38–67. This passage accurately follows John 19:31–37, which occurs, however, before Joseph's request to Pilate. Vida reworked the sequence of the biblical narrative presumably to allow for Joseph's dramatic entrance in line 68.

6.53. Compare *Aeneid* 8.153 and Paulinus Nolanus, *Carmina* 31.577.

6.55. Compare Lucretius, *De rerum natura* 1.112 and *Aeneid* 10.822 and *Georgics* 1.822.

6.56. For *per auras* see note on 1.229, above.

6.61. Compare Ovid, *Metamorphoses* 3.53 and Statius, *Thebaid* 7.552.

6.62. Compare Sedulius, *Carmen paschale* 1.216.

6.63. Compare *Aeneid* 2.16.

6.64. Compare Silius Italicus, *Punica* 12.264 and Statius, *Thebaid* 9.283.

6.68–98. These lines are based on John 19:39–42, Luke 23:53–6, Mark 15:46–7, and Matthew 27:59–61.

6.71. Compare *Aeneid* 9.488.

6.72. Compare *Aeneid* 7.812.

6.74–6. These lines combine images and phrases from Columella, *De re rustica* 10.94–100 and Manilius, *Astronomica* 256–60.

6.80–86. A literary version of the well-known genre scene in the visual arts known as the *Pietà*, of which Michelangelo's version is only the best-known.

6.81. The first half of this line is copied directly from Ennius's *Annales* (10.349, *apud* Nonius 370.19).

6.82. Compare *Aeneid* 11.59.

6.83. Compare *Aeneid* 11.40.

6.86. Compare Ovid, *Metamorphoses* 13.540.

6.88. Compare Ovid, *Metamorphoses* 13.531 and Statius, *Thebaid* 1.527.

6.89. Compare Lucretius, *De rerum natura* 2.35 and *Aeneid* 3.485.

6.92. Compare Ovid, *Metamorphoses* 2.863.

6.98–109. The detail noted here is found only in the Gospel of Matthew (37:62–6).

6.108. The phrase *luminis oras* is from Ennius (*Annales* 1.110 and 2.131) and was afterwards very common in Latin epic, Classical and Christian. See, for example, a line from Juvencus, also describing the Resurrection (*Evangelia* 4.761): *Christum remeasse in luminis oras.*

6.111. This and other of Vida's invocations may have suggested to Milton such passages as the invocation to light at the beginning of *Paradise Lost,* Book III.

6.121–291. These lines describe Christ's descent into hell, traditionally called the Harrowing of Hell. This ancient teaching, that Christ, after his Crucifixion, went down down to hell to free the souls of the just, Adam foremost among them, is derived from 1 Peter 3:19–20 and 4:6, as well as Ephesians 4:8–10 and Isaiah 24:21–22, among canonical sources, and the *Acts of Pilate,* cc. 17–27, among apocryphal. See note on 2.970, above. For lines 140 and following compare Dante's description of the souls in Limbo in *Inferno* 4.51–63.

6.131–2. Compare *Georgics* 1.36–7.

6.133–8. Many of the phrases used to describe hell in these lines come from long and well-established Christian usage, such as *barathrum, ignis aeternus,* and *flammae ultrices.* Compare *Aeneid* 6.739–40, where Vergil describes the punishments of the underworld. The adjective *irremeabile* recalls the *ripam inremeabilis undae* of *Aeneid* 6.425, describing the waters of the Styx.

6.136. The phrase *dum vita manebat* is Vergilian (see *Aeneid* 5.724, 6.608 and 6.661).

6.137. Compare *Aeneid* 8.446.

6.146. Compare *Aeneid* 6.511.

6.147. Compare Statius, *Thebaid* 4.486 and context.

6.149. Compare Claudian, *Carmina minora* 31.21 and *Carmina maiora* 7.33.

6.151. Compare *Aeneid* 2.159.

6.157. Compare Lucretius, *De rerum natura* 6.7.

6.159. Compare *Aeneid* 6.427–8.

6.160. Compare *Aeneid* 5.138.

6.164. This line is based on *Aeneid* 6.160. Compare Silius Italicus, *Punica* 15.283.

6.166. Compare *Aeneid* 4.451.

6.171. Compare Paulinus of Nola, *Carmina* 23.209. The description of Christ as "our light" hearkens back to the prologue of John's Gospel (1:1–9).

6.176–7. An allusion to Revelation 5:5: "And one of the elders saith unto me, Weep not: behold, the Lion of the tribe of Juda, the Root of David, hath prevailed to open the book, and to loose the seven seals thereof."

6.180. Compare Silius Italicus, *Punica* 12.665.

6.182. Compare *Aeneid* 8.305.

6.187–9. Compare the description of Paradise in Lactantius, *Divine Institutes* 7.24.7:

Terra uero aperiet fecunditatem suam et uberrimas fruges sua sponte generabit, rupes montium melle sudabunt, per riuos uina decurrent et flumina lacte inundabunt.

"The earth will display its fertility and will spontaneously produce the richest fruits, the rocks of the mountains will drip with honey. Through the streams will course wine and the rivers will flow with milk."

6.190. Compare *Aeneid* 2.650.

6.195. Compare Ovid, *Metamorphoses* 6.424.

6.198–9. Compare *Aeneid* 2.526 and 2.469–70.

6.198. Compare *Aeneid* 8.201.

6.204. Compare *Aeneid* 3.673.

6.212–5. Compare *Aeneid* 2.480–7.

6.213. Compare Cyprianus Gallus, *Heptateuchos: Iudices* 650.

6.220–1. Compare *Aeneid* 6.640–1.

6.221. Compare Lucretius, *De rerum natura* 2.148.

6.222–4. Compare *Aeneid* 2.507–8.

6.226–7. Compare *Aeneid* 11.812–3.

6.228. For *ululerunt* see *Aeneid* 4.168.

6.232. For *ora exertantes* compare Livy 7.10.5.

6.239. Compare *Aeneid* 8.265–6.

6.240. Compare *Aeneid* 3.524 and Ovid, *Metamorphoses* 15.731.

6.242. Compare *Aeneid* 6.691.

6.246. Compare *Aeneid* 3.637.

6.253. Compare Ennodius, *Carmina* 2.90.5.

6.255. Compare *Aeneid* 2.282 and Lucan, *Bellum civile* 10.445.

6.259. See note on 5.99, above.

6.262. Compare Statius, *Thebaid* 2.462 and 10.711.

6.275. Compare *Aeneid* 6.665 and Ovid, *Metamorphoses* 5.110.

6.285. Compare *Aeneid* 7.698.

6.287. Compare Ovid, *Metamorphoses* 1.662.

6.288. For *volucres . . . auras* see *Aeneid* 5.503 and 11.795. Compare 6.558, below.

6.291. Compare Arator, *Historia apostolica* 1.519.

6.292–3. Compare *Aeneid* 8.456.

6.293. Compare Cyprianus Gallus, *Heptateuchos: Leviticus* 72.

6.294. Compare Lucretius, *De rerum natura* 3.27. The following account of the Resurrection contains more than a few verbal echoes of the raising of Lazarus in Book I.

6.301. Compare Lucretius, *De rerum natura* 4.926.

6.309. Compare *Aeneid* 2.473 and *Georgics* 3.437.

6.306. Nonesuch of a bird: The Phoenix. The use of the Phoenix as a symbol for Christ is very ancient, going back as far as Clement (2nd century CE) in his first Epistle to the Corinthians, 25–6 and Tertullian (3rd century) in his *On the Resurrection* 13. The symbolism was also influential in medieval and Renaissance devotional art.

6.310. For *versicolor* in this position, see *Aeneid* 10.181 and Columella, *De re rustica* 10.256.

6.311. Compare Prudentius, *Psychomachia* 306.

6.319. The Roman province of Cilicia was on the southeast coast of Asia Minor, north of Cyprus, in what is now Turkey.

6.320–1. Compare *Aeneid* 6.160.

6.325–6. Compare *Aeneid* 6.885–6.

6.333. Compare Ovid, *Metamorphoses* 9.9. Compare on 3.145.

6.334. Compare Catullus, *Carmina* 64.350.

6.351–68. This ekphrasis depicts Jonah's three days in the belly of the whale, an event that prefigures for Christians Christ's three days in the tomb (see Matthew 12:40–2 and Luke 11:30–2).

6.359. This line is modeled on *Georgics* 4.486.

6.360. Compare *Aeneid* 8.579 and Lucan, *Bellum civile* 1.635.

6.369–70. Christ appearing to Mary Magdalen as a farmer or gardener (*agricola* in Vida, *hortulanus* in the Vulgate) is a detail mentioned only by John (20:15). It is a motif occurring frequently in devotional art of the period.

6.387. Compare on 3.145.

6.390. Compare *Aeneid* 4.284.

6.392. This line is modeled on Ovid, *Fasti* 2.93.

6.409. Compare Catullus, *Carmina* 68.93.

6.392–409. These lines follow Matthew 28:11–16.

6.409. Compare Catullus, *Carmina* 68.93.

6.418–24. Compare the simile in Claudian, *In Rufinum* 2.460–5.

6.425–36. These lines follow Matthew 16:10–1 and John 20:18.

6.428. Compare Silius Italicus, *Punica* 2.395.

6.436. Compare Lucretius, *De rerum natura* 4.35 and *Georgics* 4.255.

6.437–40. The lines follow Luke 24:36–46 and John 20:19–24.

6.440. Compare Cicero, *Aratea* 51: *mediocre iacit quatiens e corpore lumen*.

6.441. Didymus is the Greek word for twin. The name "Thomas" itself derives from the Aramaic word meaning twin. This account, up to line 484, follows John 20:25.

6.444. Compare Ovid, *Metamorphoses* 4.96.

6.446. Compare *Aeneid* 12.473.

6.453. Compare Paulinus of Nola, *Carmina* 26.175.

6.466. Compare Isaiah 6:5.

6.473. Compare Juvencus, *Evangelia* 3.67 and context.

6.484. Compare Columella, *De re rustica* 10.5, speaking of Vergil.

6.486. Cleophas was one of the two disciples who encountered Christ on the Road to Emmaus. This account, up to line 660, follows Luke 24:13–27. Compare also Mark 16:12–3.

6.491. Compare Ovid, *Epistulae ex Ponto* 4.5.31.

6.492. Compare 6.466.

6.493. *Auribus . . . hausi* is a rearrangement of *Aeneid* 4.359 (*vocemque his auribus hausi*).

6.507. Compare Catullus, *Carmina* 68.23 and 95, from a poem of lamentation clearly on Vida's mind.

6.515–6. Compare *Aeneid* 5.815.

6.521. Compare Matthew 13:10–13:, Mark 4:11–12 and Luke 8:9–10.

6.524–28. Compare Matthew 21:33–46.

6.544. Compare Lucretius, *De rerum natura* 1.542.

6.549–50. Compare *Aeneid* 8.365 and 8.123.

6.558. Compare *Aeneid* 5.503, 11.795 and 6.288.

6.561–595. The appearance to Thomas and the other apostles is narrated in Mark 16:14 and John 20:26–9.

6.566. Compare *Aeneid* 6.899.

6.570. This line is modeled on Lucretius, *De rerum natura* 2.115.

6.574–5. Compare *Aeneid* 4.358–9. Compare 3.519–20, above.

6.584. Others: I.e., Lazarus; see especially above, 1.102, 1.259.

6.588–591. Recalling the famous line of the *Aeneid* 1.203: *Forsan et haec olim meminisse iuvabit.*

6.596–628. These lines follow John 21:1–14.

6.629–660. The commission to the Apostles is found in Matthew 28:16–20, Mark 16:15–18, and Luke 24:44–49.

6.631. Compare *Aeneid* 11.450.

6.633. Compare *Aeneid* 8.533.

6.637. This line is taken from Lucretius, *De rerum natura* 5.1137.

6.639–40. These lines imitate *Aeneid* 4.293–4.

6.646. Compare Lucretius, *De rerum natura* 3.1027.

6.648. Compare *Eclogues* 5.51.

6.657. Compare *Aeneid* 6.432–3, where Vergil descibes Minos, a judge of the Roman underworld.

6.661. The mandate given to Peter, which Vida describes up to line 676, follows John 21:15–23. This fulsome praise of papal power was appropriate, given that two of the descendants of Peter, that is, the Medici popes Leo X and Clement VII, were Vida's patrons.

6.666–7. Compare *Aeneid* 6.851 ff.

6.667–735. Christ's Ascension into heaven is described in Mark 16:19–20 and Luke 24:50–3.

6.703. Here Vida compares Christ's procession to the triumphant march of a Roman general. The Tarpeian Rock is a cliff at the southern peak of the Capitoline Hill in Rome, overlooking the Forum.

6.705. Compare *Georgics* 2.534.

6.727. For *per auras* see note on 1.229, above.

6.730–1. Compare Matthew 28:19–20. The voice heard in 730 is Vida's rendering of the Ascension text *Viri Galilaei, quid admiramini, aspicientes in caelum*, often set as a motet in the Renaissance.

6.740. Compare Psalm 92:3.

6.745. Compare Paulinus of Nola, *Carmina* 20.39. Compare 1.1, above.

6.747. Compare Ovid, *Metamorphoses* 12.39–40.

6.765–6. The doctrine that God dwelt in an eternal present, transcending a merely temporal consciousness of past, present and future, was most famously expounded in Boethius' *Consolation of Philosophy*, Book V.

6.770–1. See Daniel 3:13–30.

6.773. Compare Lucretius, *De rerum natura* 1.3.

6.778. Compare *Aeneid* 7.722.

6.802. Compare *Aeneid* 7.812.

6.809. Compare *Aeneid* 4.210.

6.815. Compare *Aeneid* 8.528.

6.832. Compare *Aeneid* 1.233.

6.844. Compare *Aeneid* 1.256. Compare 1.956 and 3.188, above.

6.846–7. Compare *Aeneid* 8.394–5.

6.847–96. God the Father's speech to God the Son recalls *Aeneid* 6.756–853, where Anchises reveals to his son Aeneas the future career of the Roman Empire.

6.858. Pestilent star: Sirius, the dog-star that heralds and was thought to cause the Dog Days of Summer.

6.860. Bactria was the ancient Greek name of the country between the range of the Hindu Kush and the Amu Darya river; it is roughly equivalent to modern Afghanistan. Ismara was an ancient Ciconian town on the Thracian coast. Bistonia was another Thracian town, on the shores of Lake Bistonis.

6.862. For *virides Britannos* see Ovid, *Amores* 2.16.39. Vida follows the common false etymology of 'a britain' to mean 'an island.'

6.866. Compare Vergil, *Eclogues* 1.66 (of the British).

6.881. The *Christiad* was first published in 1535, almost exactly fifteen centuries after the traditional date of Christ's crucifixion (AD 33), and was dedicated to Clement VII in 1532. Vida envisages a day when poets will turn from pagan themes to writing Christian poetry, following his example.

6.886, 888. The Adda (Latin Abdua, or Addua) is a river in North Italy, a tributary of the Po. It rises in the Alps near the border with Switzerland and flows through Lake Como. The Serio is an Italian river that flows entirely within Lombardy, crossing the provinces of Bergamo and Cremona, the Lombard city where Vida was born. The Po (Eridanus in Latin) is the chief river of North Italy between the Alps and the Apennines.

6.923. Compare *Aeneid* 8.419.

6.924. The Chalybeans, from the vicinity of Pontus and Anatolia in modern Turkey, were an ancient tribe known for their skill in metallurgy.

6.924–5. Compare *Aeneid* 8.452–3.

6.935. Compare Arator, *Historia apostolica* 2.327.

6.938. For *mirabile dictu* in the same position, see, for example, *Aeneid* 4.182.

6.945. The first feast: Passover.

6.948. The Parthians were a tribe who ruled Persia from the mid-fourth century BCE and were the perennial enemies of Rome. The Scythians inhabited the Eurasian steppe in the first millennium BCE. The Thracians were a semi-barbarous people who inhabited the part of the Balkan peninsula that is now Northern Greece. The Phrygians occupied the southern part of Asia Minor, modern-day Turkey and the Garamantes were a Saharan, Berber-speaking people who inhabited parts of modern-day Libya.

6.956–58. Dark cloud . . . moist bodies: I.e., the melancholic humor, "the devil's bath," which takes up residence in moist bodies and helps cause unbelief.

6.975. Ancient prophets: David; see Psalm 19.4–5; Vida is paraphrasing Romans 10:18.

6.976–8. Compare *Aeneid* 7.225–7.

6.979. Lands where Ocean circles the earth: Probably referring to the New World, where the Spanish had begun to convert the native peoples.

6.984–5. Compare *Aeneid* 1.277.

6.985–6. To conclude his epic, Vida evokes one last time the messianism and prophetic authority of Vergil's Fourth Eclogue (ll. 4, 9).

Bibliography

❧❧❧

EDITIONS USED

Marci Hieronymi Vidae Cremonensis Christiados libri sex. Cremona: Ludovicus Brittanicus, 1535.

Marci Hieronymi Vidae Cremonensis Albae episcopi Poemata omnia. Cremona: Joannes Mutius and Bernardinus Locheta, 1550.

OTHER LATIN EDITIONS

Lyons: Gryphius, 1536.

Venice: Melchior Sessa, 1536.

Antwerp: Joannes Steels, 1536. With a *poetae commendatio* by Cornelius Grapheus.

Basel: Balthasar Lasius and Thomas Platter, 1537.

Venice: Melchior Sessa, 1538.

Antwerp: Joannes Steels, 1540.

Basel: Joannes Oporinus, 1540.

Lyon: Sebastian Gryphius, 1541.

Lyon: Sebastian Gryphius, 1547.

Lyon: Sebastian Gryphius, 1548.

Antwerp: Joannes Steels, 1549. (Omitted in Di Cesare's *Vidiana*.)

Nijmegen: Petrus Elzens, 1549. Grapheus' *commendatio*. (Omitted in Di Cesare's *Vidiana*.)

Venice: Petrus Bosellus, 1550.

Antwerp: Joannes Steels, 1553.

Lyons: Sebastian Gryphius, 1554.

Antwerp: Christopher Plantin for Joannes Steels, 1558.

Lyons: Heirs of Sebastian Gryphius, 1559.

Haarlem: Joannes Zurenus, 1562.

Lyons: Antonius Gryphius, 1566.

Antwerp: Christopher Plantin, 1566. (Omitted in Di Cesare's *Vidiana*.)

Antwerp: Philippus Nutius, 1566.

Mantua: Franciscus Osanna, 1567.

Antwerp: Christopher Plantin, 1567.

Cremona: Vincentius Comes, 1567.

Antwerp: Philippus Nutius, 1568.

Pavia: Hieronymus Bartolus, 1569. With a commentary by Bartolomeo Botta.

Venice: Christophorus Zanettus, 1571.

Lyons: Antonius Gryphius, 1578.

Antwerp: Christopher Plantin, 1578.

Cremona: Christophorus Draconius and Thomas Vachellus, 1581.

Lyons: Antonius Gryphius, 1581.

Antwerp: Christopher Plantin, 1585.

Lyons: Antonius Gryphius, 1586.

Brescia: Vincentius Sabbius, 1586.

Antwerp: Martinus Nutius, 1588.

Mantua: Franciscus Osanna, 1588.

Lyons: Antonius Gryphius, 1592.

Lyons: Joannes Pillehotte, 1603.

Geneva: Jacobus Stoer, 1605.

Lyons: Antonius de Harsy, 1606.

Antwerp: Martinus Nutius, 1607.

Lyons: Jacobus Roussin, 1607.

Bautzen: Richterus, 1678. Excerpts from Books II and VI. (Omitted in Di Cesare's *Vidiana*.)

Frankfurt: Joannes Andreae, 1680. Excerpts from Books II and V only.

Oxford: Clarendon Press, 1725. Edited by Edward Owen.

Padua: Josephus Cominus, 1731.

London: Gilliver and Nourse, 1732.

Cambridge: J. Archdeacon; London: J. Fletcher; Oxford: D. Prince, 1768.

Posen: A. Loewe, 1789.

Rome: Linus Contedinius, 1824.

Paris: H. Fournier, 1826 (see below, *French translations*).

Naples: Azzolini et socii, 1833.

Neisse: J. A. Muller, 1849. Edited by August Hübner.

Naples: A. Morano, 1894 (see below, *Italian translations*).

MODERN EDITIONS

An Edition of Vida's The Christiad. Edited by Gertrude Georgina Coyne. Ph.D. dissertation, Cornell University, 1939. With an English translation, introduction and notes.

Marco Girolamo Vida's 'The Christiad': A Latin-English Edition. Edited by Gertrude C. Drake and Clarence A. Forbes. Carbondale, Illinois: Southern Illinois University Press, 1978. A revised version of Coyne's dissertation, but without the introduction or notes.

Luigi Paletto, ed. *M. Gerolamo Vida . . . Crestomazia.* Alba: Edizioni Domenicane, 1961. Selections in Latin accompanied by various Italian translations.

PRINTED TRANSLATIONS

SPANISH

Los Cristiados. Translated by Juan Martín Cordero. Antwerp: Martín Nucio, 1554.

ITALIAN

Della Christiade . . . libro primo. Translated by Alessandro Lami di Federigo. Cremona: Christoforo Draconi, 1573.

La Cristiade. Translated by Tommaso Perrone. Naples: Gennaro Muzio, 1733.

La Cristiade, recanta in ottava rima e in XXIV canti divisa. Translated by Carlo Ercolani. Macerata: Bartolomeo Capitani, stampatore dell'Accademia de' Catenati, 1792.

La Cristiade di Monsignor Vida, recanta in versi liberi da G[iovanni] Z[ucchi]. Carmagnola: Pietro Barbié, 1818.

La Cristiade di Girolamo Vida. Translated by Pietro Bernabò-Silorata. Roma: Antonio Boulzaler, 1828.

La Cristiade. Translated by Domenico Bartolini. Naples: Stamperia Fibreno, 1833.

La Cristiade, poema di M. G. Vida. Translated by Giovanni Chiosi. Cremona: Stampatore Feraboli, 1837. Reprinted 1838.

Della Cristiade, libro 1. Translated by Giuseppe Lazzari. Venice: Andreola, 1840.

Il SS. Natale . . . . Partial translation of Book III by Giuseppe Lazzari. Rovigo: Minelli, 1843.

La spozalizio della Vergine . . . . Partial translation of Book III by Giuseppe Lazzari. Venice: Andreola, 1843.

Della Cristiade, libro 3. Translated by Giuseppe Lazzari. Venice: Andreola, 1846.

La Cristiade. Translated by Giovanni Bono. Genoa, 1859.

La Cristiade: poema latino in sei libri. Translated by Marco Antonio Spoto. Palermo: Giovanni Oliveri, 1888.

Saggio di versione della Cristiade. Book 1 only. Translated by Nicola Romano. Naples: A. Morano, 1890.

La Cristiade. Translated by Nicola Romano. Naples: A. Morano, 1894. With the Latin text.

La Cristiade. Translated by Giuseppe Aloj. Alba: Società San Paolo, 1930.

La Cristiade: il poema di Gesu. Translated by Carlo Ercolani; revised, with a preface and notes by Leopoldo Taruschio. Milan: Sonzogno, 1942.

CROATIAN

Cristiade to' iest Xiuot i diela isukarstoua. Translated by Junije Palmotic (1606–1657). Rome: Mascardus, 1670.

Kerstovka iliti xihot i dyla gospodina nashega Isukerstva. Translated by Junije Palmotic and edited by Igniat Alojzije Brlic. Buda: Gyurian, 1835.

Kristiada: to jest zivot i djela isukrstova. Translated by Junije Palmotic; preface by Andria Torkvato Brlic. Zagreb: Tiskom Narodne-tiskarne L. Gaja, 1852

Djela Gjona Gjora Palmoticá, vol. III, 1–229. Contains Palmotic's Croatian translation of the *Christiad.* Zagreb: Dionicka tiskara, 1890.

ENGLISH

The Christiad: A Poem in Six Books. Translated by John Cranwell. Cambridge: J. Archdeacon; London: J. Fletcher; Oxford: D. Prince, 1768. With the Latin text.

The Christiad, an heroic poem, in six books. Translated by Edward Granan. London: R. Baldwin, 1771.

The Christiad, an heroic poem, in six books. Adapted and abridged from the translation by Granan, possibly by Thomas Moss. Wolverhampton: G. Smart, 1775. "Corrected and Improved from the former Translation; and Rendered Conformable to the Word of God."

GERMAN

Jesus Christus, ein lateinisches Heldengedicht. Translated by Johann David Müller. Hamburg: Hoffmann, 1811.

Anton Büttler. *Über Hieronymus Vida . . . als Dichter.* Contains passages from Books I, IV and V in German translation. Landshut, 1851.

J. G. L. Gerheuser. *Jesu liebliche und geistige Verklärung.* Excerpts from Books I and V in German translation.

FRENCH

La Christiade: poème épique. Translated by Guillaume-Jean-François Souquet de la Tour. Paris: H. Fournier for Colnet, 1826. With the Latin text.

La Christiade: poème épique. Translated by l'Abbé Clément Gérard. Brussels: H. Goemoere, 1868.

(The same.) Aoste: J. B. Mansio, 1876.

ARMENIAN

Vitayi Kristosakan. Translated by Egiay Tóvmacean. Venice: 1832.

PORTUGUESE

Cristiada. Translated by Francisco Inácio de Sequeira. 1876. With the Latin text from the edition of Lyons, 1586. (Omitted in Di Cesare's *Vidiana.*)

STUDIES

Alberson, Hazel Stewart. "Lo Mio Maestro." *Classical Journal* 32 (1937): 193–208.

Bruère, Richard T. "Review Article: Virgil and Vida." *Classical Philology* 61.1 (1966): 21–43. Review article of Di Cesare, *Vida's Christiad*, with important material on Vida's Vergilian sources.

Di Cesare, Mario A. *Vida's Christiad and Vergilian Epic.* New York: Columbia University Press, 1964.

—— *Bibliotheca Vidiana: A Bibliography of Marco Girolamo Vida.* Florence: Sansoni, 1974. An annotated bibliography covering the publishing history of and secondary literature on Vida's works up to 1966. Information on six unpublished Italian translations and one unpublished English translation may be found on p. 244.

Drake, Gertrude C. "Satan's Council in the *Christiad, Paradise Lost,* and *Paradise Regained."* In *Acta Conventus Neo-Latini Turonensis,* ed. Jean-Claude Margolin, 979–89. Paris: Vrin, 1980.

Gregory, Tobias. *From Many Gods to One: Divine Action in Renaissance Epic.* Chicago: University of Chicago Press, 2006.

Haan, Estelle. "'Heaven's purest light': Milton's *Paradise Lost* and Vida." *Comparative Literature Studies* 30:2 (1993): 115–136.

—— "Milton's Latin Poetry and Vida." *Humanistica Lovaniensia* 44 (1995): 282–304.

Holoka, James P. "A Neoplatonic Simile in Vida's *Christiad* (4.10–15)." *Romance Notes* 18 (1977): 243–46.

Kallendorf, Craig. "From Virgil to Vida: The *Poeta Theologus* in Italian Renaissance Commentary." *Journal of the History of Ideas* 56:1 (1995): 41–62.

Lewalski, Barbara Kiefer. *Milton's Brief Epic: the Genre, Meaning, and Art of Paradise Regained.* Providence, Rhode Island: Brown University Press, 1966. Surveys the genre of Biblical epic, including the *Christiad,* and studies Vida's influence on Milton and other writers.

O'Neal, William J. "The Simile in Vida's *Christiad."* In *Actus Conventus Neo-Latini Bononiensis,* ed. Richard J. Schoeck, 558–63. Binghamton: Medieval and Renaissance Texts and Studies, 1985.

Pease, Arthur Stanley, ed. *Publi Vergili Maronis Aeneidos, Liber quartus.* Cambridge, Mass.: Harvard University Press, 1935. Reprint, Darmstadt 1967.

Warner, James C. *The Augustinian Epic, Petrarch to Milton*. Ann Arbor, Michigan: University of Michigan Press, 2005. Contains a chapter on the *Christiad*.

Index

ᚻᚾᚾᚾ

Lowercase roman numerals refer to page numbers in the introduction. Two-part arabic numbers refer to the English translation by book and line number. The letter *n* appended to a book and line citation refers to notes to the translation; notes to the introduction are indicated by page number plus *n* and note number.

Publication of this volume has been made possible by

The Myron and Sheila Gilmore Publication Fund at I Tatti
The Robert Lehman Endowment Fund
The Jean-François Malle Scholarly Programs and Publications Fund
The Andrew W. Mellon Scholarly Publications Fund
The Craig and Barbara Smyth Fund
for Scholarly Programs and Publications
The Lila Wallace–Reader's Digest Endowment Fund
The Malcolm Wiener Fund for Scholarly Programs and Publications